Object-Oriented Design in Java

Using `java.util`

Nicholas J. DeLillo

THOMSON

BROOKS/COLE

Australia • Canada • Mexico • Singapore • Spain • United Kingdom • United States

THOMSON
BROOKS/COLE

Publisher: *Bill Stenquist*
Editor: *Kallie Swanson*
Editorial Assistant: *Aarti Jayaraman*
Technology Project Manager: *Burke Taft*
Executive Marketing Manager: *Tom Ziolkowski*
Marketing Assistant: *Jennifer Gee*
Advertising Project Manager: *Vicky Wan*
Project Manager, Editorial Production: *Kelsey McGee*
Print/Media Buyer: *Jessica Reed*
Permissions Editor: *Sommy Ko*

Production Service: *Matrix Productions, Inc.*
Text Designer: *Lisa Devenish/Devenish Designs*
Copy Editor: *Sally Scott*
Illustrator: *ATLIS Graphics*
Cover Designer: *Denise Davidson/Simple Design*
Cover Image: *Nora Good/Masterfile*
Cover Printing, Printing and Binding: *Webcom*
Compositor: *ATLIS Graphics*

Printed in Canada
1 2 3 4 5 6 7   07 06 05 04 03

For more information about our products,
contact us at:
Thomson Learning Academic Resource Center
1-800-423-0563
For permission to use material from this text,
contact us by: **Phone:** 1-800-730-2214
Fax: 1-800-730-2215
Web: http://www.thomsonrights.com

Library of Congress Control Number: 2003105087

ISBN 0-534-37784-X

Brooks/Cole—Thomson Learning
10 Davis Drive
Belmont, CA 94002
USA

Asia
Thomson Learning
5 Shenton Way #01-01
UIC Building
Singapore 068808

Australia/New Zealand
Thomson Learning
102 Dodds Street
Southbank, Victoria 3006
Australia

Canada
Nelson
1120 Birchmount Road
Toronto, Ontario M1K 5G4
Canada

Europe/Middle East/Africa
Thomson Learning
High Holborn House
50/51 Bedford Row
London WC1R 4LR
United Kingdom

Latin America
Thomson Learning
Seneca, 53
Colonia Polanco
11560 Mexico D.F.
Mexico

Spain/Portugal
Paraninfo
Calle/Magallanes, 25
28015 Madrid, Spain

To the memory of my father-in-law, Dr. Anthony Procaccino, and to my grandchildren Nicholas, Michela, and Giovanna.

CONTENTS

CHAPTER 3   **Search and Sort • 97**

CHAPTER 4   **Hashing: Prelude to the `java.util` Library • 141**

CHAPTER 5   **A General Overview of the `java.util` Library • 175**

CHAPTER 6   **Vectors and Lists • 223**

CHAPTER 7   **Stacks, Queues, and Priority Queues • 266**

CHAPTER 8   **Generic Algorithms and the StringTokenizer Class • 334**

CHAPTER 9   Sets and Maps • 373

CHAPTER 10   Graphs and Networks • 413

APPENDIX   **Assertions and the `assert` Statement • 439**

PREFACE

This text is designed for use in a course in computer science or computer engineering satisfying a number of distinct requirements, including the design, analysis, and implementation of a number of specific data structures and algorithms that are vital in the construction, development, and maintenance of contemporary commercial software. A key element of this text is to provide a source for the study of object-oriented design (OOD) and programming (OOP). These concepts and techniques are integrated with an exposition of those segments of the Java programming language that directly influence the principles of OOD and OOP. In particular, this involves the presentation of Java 2 and the `java.util` library.

OOD involves the presentation of three main concepts: encapsulation, inheritance, and polymorphism. These concepts are introduced in the first two chapters. Each of these is defined and illustrated using easily accessible and fundamental mathematical concepts, and each requires a small amount of mathematical background. Because OOP represents the most popular and highly used contemporary programming paradigm, the knowledge and familiarity of use of the principles of OOP represent important components in the training of any contemporary software designer and programmer, especially as these are implemented in Java—arguably one of the most important and dominant programming languages used in contemporary software design.

Another important requirement is the introduction of the major components of class hierarchies, especially as they appear in the `java.util` library, and particularly as these apply to several of the key issues appearing in commercial data processing. This is accomplished by first introducing traditional concepts such as search, sort, and hashing (the content of Chapters Three and Four). These chapters set the stage for the introduction of predefined classes and generic algorithms appearing in `java.util` and are discussed in detail in the remaining chapters.

As was also the case with my previous text titled *Object-Oriented Design in C++ Using the Standard Template Library,* published in 2002, the current text is not designed for use in a first course in data structures (the designated CS2 course in the ACM Curriculum). Instead, although a number of the topics treated in that course are presented in this text, the primary emphasis of this text is the study of OOD using `java.util`. In many instances, this text discusses topics first introduced in the data structures course, such as linked lists, stacks, queues, and priority queues. In the CS2 course, however, the implementation of each of these data structures in Java generally does not involve any of the classes appearing in the predefined hierarchies of `java.util`. In addition, the CS2 course usually includes a treatment of binary and general n-way trees. Although a discussion of trees is provided in this text, it is done in a cursory manner. This is because trees are used to implement some of the classes and methods defined in `java.util` (such as red-black trees), and because the text assumes the reader has already been exposed to a study of the topics usually studied in the traditional CS2 course (which includes an extensive discussion of trees).

One of the prevailing criticisms regarding the use of the facilities of `java.util` in contemporary software design is that it discourages and deemphasizes the key concepts of OOD, particularly as they apply to inheritance and polymorphism. In several parts of this text, notably in Chapter Four (which discusses hashing using separate chaining), and in Chapter Ten (which discusses the different varieties of graph abstract data types), inheritance and polymorphism emerge as crucial design tools. In this regard, we particularly emphasize the use of linked lists, using the `List` interface and its `LinkedList` implementation class appearing in the `Collection` hierarchy in `java.util`, as they apply to the design of the `Hashtable` class using separate chaining, and in the OOD of a simulator for an elementary version of a local area network.

A new approach to teaching the data structures and algorithms (ACM's CS7) course using Java as the implementation language uses `java.util` as a major component. This is because the use of the predefined classes and facilities of `java.util` implement another important objective of contemporary commercial software design: to present solutions of a number of commonly encountered problems that emphasize correctness, efficiency, reusability, and portability. These are important requirements usually treated in courses in, and in the actual practice of, software engineering. These ideas were highly influential in the design of code encountered throughout this text.

This text follows the same sequence of topics as that of my previous text on C++. As such, the text is unusual in that, at present, no single competing Java book covers all of the topics presented here. While several other texts cover some of the topics mentioned in this work, there is no single unified source covering all of the topics of this text. In the majority of those texts, a key topic is introduced for the first time without any link to a predefined facility seen in `java.util`. Then this topic is revisited using the facilities present in `java.util`, where we now have the additional assurance that these facilities provide the additional guarantee of efficiency and portability. In establishing this association with `java.util`, the following objectives of desirable software engineering practice are attained:

- Programmers no longer have to be concerned with the correctness and efficiency of the code they design—this is no longer a consideration, because the predefined `java.util` facility was designed while paying serious attention to the code's correctness and efficiency.
- These associated `java.util` facilities have been thoroughly tested for correctness and efficiency.
- The code is applicable across all platforms, because `java.util` has also been designed for independence of any specific hardware configuration.
- Students preparing for careers as software development professionals using Java as the implementation language attain two major milestones: They become better acquainted with the theoretical description of the underlying data structures, and they have the ability to write code implementing the methods defined for these structures (with the help of the facilities of `java.util`).

Each chapter begins with a listing of a number of objectives to be satisfied by studying the concepts presented in that chapter. In addition, the primary text of each chapter terminates with a section that summarizes the more central issues discussed in the chapter. This enables students to revisit the appropriate section(s) in the event that they might have overlooked an important idea. The exercises appearing at the end of each chapter attempt to convert students from passive observers to active participants by having them test their problem-solving abilities using the concepts described in the chapter. Furthermore, each chapter presents at least one programming project that extends beyond the usual level of problem-solving capability demanded in the solution of problems commonly seen in the Exercises sections. These projects generally take the form of an extension of the general theory presented in that chapter in some direction that is accessible to interested students, or they provide an alternative form of implementation from that presented in the text. In each case, the exercises and projects have been thoroughly tested for correctness and, in most cases, their formal solutions appear on the accompanying Web site (see *www.brookscole.com.*)

We assume throughout that the reader is familiar with the content of a first course in data structures (the CS2 course). Consequently, the approach taken by this text to such topics takes advantage of this assumed familiarity. In fact, the description of the properties of certain data structures is provided only when needed to enhance the readability of this text.

The book serves in part as a useful self-contained tutorial emphasizing the concepts of OOD and OOP and their implementation in Java using the facilities of `java.util`. On the other hand, this book does not serve as a comprehensive survey of all of the facilities available in `java.util`. Thus, this text is not intended to be encyclopedic in nature; a number of fine treatises cover all of the topics of `java.util`, and the references at the ends of chapters provide a number of such treatments. Most of the concepts introduced in this text are motivated by examples of everyday problems encountered in the contemporary commercial data-processing environment. The solutions of these problems are given in the form of programs, most of which include software tools that invoke the facilities present in `java.util`. The exercises at the end of each chapter often involve variations and generalizations of the concepts presented in that chapter. These exercises range from the most elementary to very challenging extensions of these concepts. In fact, the most challenging exercises are placed in the separate Programming Projects section. As we have already stated, these exercises are designed to draw students into the environment of OOD as active participants rather than as casual spectators.

The following are the topics presented in each chapter:

Chapter One: Classes. In this chapter, a review of the preliminary topics involving the definition, design, and coding of classes appears. The ideas of constructors, data members, and instance methods of classes are defined, along with the description and distinction between a class interface and a class implementing that interface. Each of these concepts is illustrated in some detail by a number of specific and concrete examples. The distinction between `private` and `public` components is presented, together with a discussion as to how the designer of a class might decide which components should be designated as `private` and which are `public`. The idea of data abstraction is stressed throughout this discussion, along with an implementation of an abstract data type (ADT) as an interface and a concrete class. These ideas are all amply illustrated using the specific example of a stack. The use of exceptions and exception handlers are introduced and illustrated, along with the idea of generics and the introduction of the `Object` superclass. Class hierarchies and inheritance are introduced, first with their application to exceptions and later with regard to geometric hierarchies, most of whose detail is postponed until Chapter Two. The idea of `static` data fields and methods is introduced, with a specific application of their use in the applications area of employee payroll processing. Finally, we undertake an abstraction of the complex number system, using many of the concepts introduced in this chapter.

Chapter Two: Inheritance and Polymorphism. This chapter continues the discussion of class hierarchies and inheritance begun in Chapter One, with particular emphasis on illustrating these ideas using simple geometrical hierarchies. The ideas of superclass and subclass are illustrated, along with the introduction of `protected` members of a class, and the distinction among `public`, `protected`, and `private` access modifiers. The idea of `final` classes, methods, and data members is introduced, along with illustrations as to when the use of `final` components is recommended. This is followed by an exposition of the idea of multiple inheritance and Java's limited but effective use of this OOD concept. This is amply illustrated by a number of easily accessible and understood examples. The idea of abstract classes and their use is then introduced, together with illustrations of how their implementation proves to be quite valuable. This chapter ends with discussions of the use of run-time polymorphism and the critical implications of using inheritance and polymorphism in commercial data processing, particularly with the exercise of highly desirable aspects of sound software design and engineering.

Chapter Three: Search and Sort. This chapter contains the first exposure to the idea of an algorithm, as well as a description of some of the more popularly used algorithms employed in searching and sorting. These are applied primarily to linear storage containers, such as one-dimensional arrays and linearly linked lists. Specifically, the ideas of efficiency and its quantification, using big-O, and the idea of a mathematical proof, using Finite Induction, are presented. The concept of recursive programming and the principle of divide and conquer are reviewed. Then these concepts are used to solve classical problems, such as searching using linear (sequential) and binary search, and sorting a finite sequence of values using selection sort, insertion sort, quicksort, and mergesort. These ideas are presented generically, introducing the `Comparable` interface. Other sorting techniques are explained, and some of the details of implementing these other techniques are left as exercises. An extensive and comprehensive treatment of the relative efficiency of many of these search and sort algorithms is presented, using the big-O metric.

Chapter Four: Hashing: Prelude to the `java.util` *Library.* This chapter discusses introductory topics on data storage and retrieval in some depth. This includes the introduction of such topics as hashing, hash functions, hash tables, open addressing and separate chaining, appropriate considerations involving the choice of a hash function, and resolving hash collisions using various forms of probing. In addition, separate chaining is introduced as a means of resolving hash collisions using linearly linked lists. An object-oriented approach to hashing using open addressing with linear probing is discussed in detail, introducing a programmer-defined `hashTable` class whose objects are hash tables employing a hash function using division with remainder.

This chapter also serves as a bridge with the components of `java.util`, in that `java.util` contains a number of components, such as the predefined `Hashtable` class, using many of the ideas on hashing discussed earlier in this chapter. It is important to note that the identity of the actual hash function is kept hidden from the user, yet the hashing techniques used are guaranteed to be as efficient as possible. Finally, these predefined hashing methods are applied to a sequence of integer values and then to a sequence of employee records.

Chapter Five: A General Overview of the `java.util` *Library*. This chapter discusses the Java Collections Framework in detail and introduces the classes and interfaces that comprise the hierarchies of the framework. The `Collection` and `Iterator` interfaces are introduced, and the concrete classes appearing in these hierarchies are identified. The `List`, `Set`, `Map`, `SortedSet`, and `SortedMap` interfaces are defined, along with the `LinkedList`, `HashSet`, `TreeSet`, `HashMap`, and `TreeMap` concrete classes. Each of the methods appearing in these classes is illustrated using very elementary examples; in the case of the `Map` interface, we show how `Map.Entry` provides a connection with `Set` objects. This last connection is said to provide a *view* of the underlying `Map` object. The Legacy Collections classes are discussed, introducing the `HashTable`, `Properties`, `Vector`, `Stack`, and `BitSet` classes. Finally, the `Collections` and `Arrays` classes are introduced, with applications to generic algorithms for searching for and sorting a finite sequence of various objects that are constructed from these classes. This discussion continues in Chapter Eight with a more comprehensive treatment of generic algorithms.

Chapter Six: Vectors and Lists. This chapter presents the basic properties and behavior of two categories of structures defined in the Java Collections Framework. The first of these is the `Vector` class, which is part of Java's Legacy Collections. We observe here that any vector (that is, any `Vector` object) behaves in a manner similar to that for any ordinary one-dimensional array, with one major difference—an ordinary one-dimensional array has a size that is fixed and defined at compile time. Accordingly, any attempt to add extra components beyond the declared capacity for the array throws an exception. In direct contrast to this, a vector has an initial size when defined, and this size is permitted to change dynamically during the course of execution of the method where that vector is defined. An important distinction exists between the current size of a vector and its current capacity, and the programmer is capable of constructing vectors with a specific initial size and capacity. In addition, the instance methods that are defined for `Vector` are *synchronized*, causing execution of any of these to be relatively slow, particularly if invoked from a single processing thread. It is therefore recommended to use another alternative, particularly if the design requirements of the software are time critical. This chapter continues with a discussion of the `List` interface, originally introduced in Chapter Five. Special attention is paid to the `ArrayList` implementation. Important distinctions between `ArrayList` and `LinkedList` objects are made, and recommendations regarding which of the two implementations is most appropriate for certain situations is discussed. The deque ADT is introduced, and several interesting examples of its application in certain situations are discussed. The chapter ends with a survey of a number of useful generic algorithms, such as `binarySearch`, `sort`, `reverse`, `fill`, and `copy` as these apply to `List` objects. A more detailed discussion of these generic algorithms appears in Chapter Eight.

Chapter Seven: Stacks, Queues, and Priority Queues. This chapter begins with a discussion of the stack ADT begun in Chapter One and culminates here by first describing an implementation of this ADT called `Stack`. This is a predefined class appearing in `java.util` and is a subclass of `Vector`. The chapter continues by describing a more efficient implementation of stacks as programmer-defined subclasses of `ArrayList` and `LinkedList`. Then it provides several classical applications of stacks to such problem domains as language design and compilers—such as balanced parentheses, brackets, and braces—as well as evaluates postfix arithmetical expressions and converts an arithmetic expression from its infix form to its equivalent postfix form. This is followed by a description of the queue abstraction, leading to the formal definition of the queue ADT and its programmer-defined implementation in Java. Then we discuss two important applications of queues to the theory of operating systems, particularly with respect to the simulation of a ready queue for processes in a multiprogrammed time-sharing environment. This is followed by a description of the priority queue ADT and its implementation in Java using an OOD involving `ArrayList`. The chapter ends with a detailed description of several applications of priority queues to time-sharing multiprogrammed operating systems.

Chapter Eight: Generic Algorithms and the `StringTokenizer` *Class.* This chapter begins with a discussion of generic algorithms supported by `java.util`. This discussion actually began as early as Chapter Three and is completed in more detailed form here. As a matter of fact, the majority of sections appearing in this chapter are devoted to a detailed discussion of generic algorithms and their application to several different types of data structures defined in the `Collection` hierarchy, primarily their application to objects in the `List` interface. The idea underlying the inclusion of these algorithms, presented as individual methods in `java.util`, is to provide a source for a number of predefined and highly efficient processing tools that are important in a large number of distinct contemporary application domains. Because these generic algorithms are defined for use in familiar situations appearing in the commercial applications area, the professional programmer and software designer would find it valuable to master them. This chapter also includes a more extensive exposition of applications of predefined array-processing algorithms appearing in the `Arrays` utility class. The chapter then introduces `StringTokenizer` class, and it ends by revisiting a number of applications first seen in Chapter Seven, now using `StringTokenizer` as a new alternative.

Chapter Nine: Sets and Maps. This chapter continues a discussion of the `Set` and `Map` interfaces that began in Chapter Five. It begins with a review of the properties of the `Set` interface and its `HashSet` and `TreeSet` implementations. The `Set` interface is then seen to be aptly named, because a number of the usual elementary set-theoretic operations commonly used in mathematical studies of the rudiments of set theory are introduced and implemented in Java. These operations include set membership and inclusion, set union and intersection, as well as set difference and symmetric difference. Each of these is then illustrated using a number of simply understood examples. The `SortedSet` interface is introduced as part of the `Collection` hierarchy, and its instance methods are discussed and illustrated. This is followed by an optional section that describes various forms of trees and their important use as part of the implementation details for the `TreeSet` class. The chapter continues with a more detailed discussion of the `Map` interface and its `HashMap` and `TreeMap` implementations. This is followed by an application of `Map` methods to the theory of prime numbers, in which the Sieve of Eratosthenes is introduced and implemented. A discussion of the `SortedMap` interface follows, and finally an application of `Map` methods to the processing of employee records is given, in which some of the ideas on hashing first described in Chapter Four are revisited in this new context. Then a discussion follows of sorting using nonlinear structures, with particular emphasis on binary search trees, heaps, and heapsort. Again, an OOD is used to produce a highly efficient means of sorting using heaps.

Chapter Ten: Graphs and Networks. The chapter begins with a theoretical discussion of undirected and directed graphs. Then some aspects of an OOD are given for various versions of graph ADTs, and a hierarchy of classes for graphs is defined. These are all implemented in Java, including a discussion and implementation of depth-first and breadth-first traversals of graphs. The idea of a network is introduced, with an implementation in Java of a simulator for the activity of components appearing as part of a local area token ring network.

Also included is a brief appendix on the use of the `assert` statement, a recent (jdx v. 1.4) addition to the language. Here we show several similarities between this and its counterpart in C++.

All of the code presented in this text has been tested for correctness; we used a number of different Java platforms using Java's jdk v. 1.3.1 applying TextPad, Borland's JBuilder v. 3.0 and higher, KAWA from AltaVista, jGrasp from Auburn University, and a number of UNIX-based platforms.

Acknowledgments

This book would not have been possible without the contribution of several groups of very talented people. The first group is the staff at Brooks/Cole, whose help and support were invaluable throughout every stage of production: Bill Stenquist, Kallie Swanson, Kelsey McGee, Tom Ziolkowski, Aarti Jayaraman, and Sommy Ko. The help of production editor Merrill Peterson and copyeditor Sally Scott was also very important.

I also wish to thank the individuals who reviewed the manuscript at various levels of development and provided many constructive comments, corrections, and suggestions: Jack Beidler, University of Scranton; Rani Mikkilineni, Santa Clara University; and Narayan Murthy, Pace University.

Thanks also to my colleagues in the Department of Mathematics and Computer Science and the Department of Electrical and Computer Engineering at Manhattan College, and the School of Computer Science and Information Systems at Pace University, who provided the opportunity to review and class-test this material. In particular, I wish to thank the staff at Manhattan's Computer Center, especially Janice Melino, Bill Staib, Jake Holmquist, and Anthony Spordone, for their help in providing the necessary software support. Special warm thanks go out to my students at Manhattan College and Pace University, both undergraduate and graduate, who often served as test subjects for the contents of this book.

In no small way I wish to thank Drs. Michael Johnson and Donald Miller of Westchester Heart Specialists, Dr. Constantine Plestis, and the staff of the Pacemaker Center at Montefiore Hospital, for their invaluable aid in guiding me through a very difficult and dangerous health episode in the summer of 2002. This book would not have been completed without your help.

Finally, I again wish to thank my wife Rosalie, my children, and grandchildren for their moral support, comfort, and encouragement during the various stages of the writing of this book. This includes the recent addition of my latest granddaughter Giovanna, who, along with Nicholas and Michela, add new meaning and inspiration in my life.

Pelham Manor, New York

CHAPTER 1

Classes

CHAPTER OBJECTIVES:

- To introduce and explain the key aspects of object-oriented design, such as abstraction, encapsulation, and modularity.
- To present and illustrate the definition of classes and objects and their role in the design of contemporary software.
- To define and explain the idea of exceptions and exception handlers and their critical role in the design of software using Java.
- To describe and apply the ideas of generic programming.

1.1 Introduction

Contemporary design of commercial software usually involves the *object-oriented paradigm*. This entails the design of a solution of a software problem in which two fundamental goals are kept in mind:

- Correctness
- Efficiency

A software design is *correct* if it produces the expected solution of the problem for all possible inputs that define the *application domain*, namely, the collection of all input values for which the application (or problem) is defined. In other words, a design is correct if it works properly for all values in its domain of definition. For example, the design of an algorithm for searching for a value in a finite list of values of some specified type is correct if the value sought is retrieved whenever that value actually appears in the list, and an error message such as

VALUE SOUGHT DOES NOT EXIST

is issued whenever that value does not appear in the list.

1

In addition, software solutions must be designed as *efficiently* as possible. This simply means that executing the solution should be a relatively fast process, and it should use only the computer resources that are absolutely necessary for its completion. In many instances, the speed of computation of a solution can be the determining factor between the success and failure of the product. For example, the telemetry and guidance systems used in commercial aircraft should react as quickly as possible to changing weather conditions and to the sudden presence of unexpected obstacles during flight, landing, and takeoff. In summary, the design of correct and efficient solutions to relatively complicated software problems must be a key goal of our efforts. We will see that the proper implementation of the object-oriented paradigm usually satisfies these goals.

The attainment of these goals is not automatic. A great degree of preparation and testing of the design and implementation code must be done. The Java programming language has the advantage of possessing a rich collection of predefined libraries, containing the correct and efficient encoding of many of the algorithms encountered in contemporary data processing. In addition, Java's syntax is similar to that of C and C++, but it avoids some of the inherent problems in these languages such as the use (or misuse) of pointers, the failure to check array boundaries, and the absence of a garbage collection facility.

A major advantage of Java is that it has been designed to be platform independent, which can greatly enhance and simplify the implementation of classes in an object-oriented design (OOD) of a solution of a software problem. Furthermore, Java and its compilation into executable code is supported by any popular Web browser, such as Internet Explorer and NetScape. This places the language in an accessible and convenient position in the modern computing environment.

A main objective of this book is to produce correct and efficient solutions of software problems. This will be achieved by studying a large and varied number of problems whose solutions will be designed with these goals in mind, by using either predefined components appearing in Java packages, or other techniques and concepts lying at the "high end" of the language.

1.2 Principles of Object-Oriented Design

Since the early 1970s research and development of contemporary high-level and general-purpose programming languages have concentrated on two key factors: *simplicity* and *power*. That is, much effort has been given to the development of programming languages whose code is both relatively simple for programmers to write and easily understood by others, and that is sufficiently powerful to satisfy the goals of correctness and efficiency described earlier.

A number of languages proposed over this period have attempted to satisfy these goals and have failed in one or more respects. It is interesting to note that the successful problem-solving methodologies used in meeting these goals have been those implementing the object-oriented paradigm. The Java programming language discussed in this text is an example of one such language.

What are the principal features of OOD? They are

- Abstraction
- Encapsulation
- Modularity

Abstraction

The concept of *abstraction* is an important feature of OOD. The ability of a language to apply the principle of abstraction is the ability to implement a theoretical design concept in specific and precise terms. Generally, the concept may involve a number of separate but cooperating parts. In applying this concept, abstraction enables us to define the distinct parts and formally express their functionality. As an example, let us define a *stack* (of values of some given data type) theoretically as either the empty set or an ordered finite sequence of values of that type, into which additional values of that type can be inserted (pushed) and from which values can be removed (popped). We understand that pushing and popping values from a stack is possible from one end only, known as the *top* of the stack. We can characterize the abstraction of a stack using Figure 1.1.

FIGURE 1.1

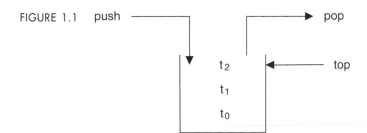

It would also be convenient to be able to test whether the current stack is empty and to retrieve the value at the top of the current stack whenever it is not empty. This represents the complete description of the abstraction of a stack. Once we are satisfied with this definition, the next step is to frame it as an *abstract data type* (ADT). We can define an ADT as a mathematical model of a data structure specifying the type of data stored in the structure, the admissible operations applicable to this data, and the necessary parameters needed for the correct and efficient implementation of these operations. It is important to note that an ADT describes *what* operations are admissible, but it does not necessarily supply any information as to *how* these operations execute.

As an example, an ADT for stacks of values of some given type involves two components:

- an *application domain* consisting of all possible stacks of that type
- a finite collection of *admissible operations* applicable to any member of the application domain.

In the case of stacks, the list of admissible operations is

- a *push* operation, inserting an additional value into the current stack
- a *pop* operation, removing a value from the current stack whenever it is not empty
- an operation (which we will call `isEmpty`) testing whether the current stack is empty
- a *top* operation, retrieving the value at the top of the current stack, whenever it is not empty

This represents the complete characterization of the stack ADT. In Java, this is generally implemented using *classes*. This implementation enables us to define, first, the type of data to be stored in the structure, and also the admissible operations applicable to instances of that class. These instances are called *objects*.

In Java, we can design classes using two major components:

- a *user interface*
- an *implementation class*

This subdivision is particularly useful when describing other aspects of OOD.

Encapsulation

Another quality of OOD is *encapsulation,* or *information hiding.* This principle was first proposed by David Parnas in 1971. Let us view the implementation of the ADT as a class, in the sense just described. Then the idea of encapsulation enforces two major aspects of OOD:

- The class must provide the intended client (user) with *all* of the information required to implement the abstraction, *and nothing more.*
- The class definition must provide the implementation with *all* of the information required to complete the definition of the class, *and nothing more.*

Thus, the user of a class does not know how the class is implemented and cannot write programs that are dependent on that specific implementation. This makes the class easier to maintain, because class designers (implementers) know exactly what code can be changed without affecting any of the users' applications. From another perspective, once the class has been designed and made available for use to clients, the implementers have no way of knowing all of the specific applications of their work performed by clients, except that the necessary functionality has been provided for in the user interface. This simplifies the maintenance of user programs, because programmers have a precise knowledge of what code can or cannot be changed safely.

In the example of the implementation of the stack ADT using Java, the user interface can be described as a listing of the operations available to the user (as `public` methods) and the hiding of a number of the implementation details (as `private` components). The operations described as `public` methods that are available to the user are listed as method declarations, because all the user has to know about these methods is their specific name (such as `push`, `pop`, `is_empty`, and `top`) and the number, order of appearance and the data type of any parameters, and the data type of the return value, if applicable. There is no reason for the user to know how these operations are implemented—that is the concern of the contents of the implementation class.

For example, in the stack ADT, there are two popular implementations that we will discuss later in some detail. These are:

- the *sequential* (or *array*) *implementation*
- the *linked implementation*

Each represents a separate implementation of the admissible operations `push`, `pop`, `isEmpty`, and `top`. The user has no direct exposure to either implementation: The implementation details are of no concern to the user. In fact, a later decision in the design of an implementation of the stack ADT might be to change from the sequential to the linked implementation. In the true spirit of information hiding, this change will have no effect on the user's application.

In this context, we say that the implementation of stacks using classes *encapsulates* the definition of the stack ADT. Hence, encapsulation yields adaptability, because it allows the implementation details of sections of a program to change without affecting other sections of the program's code. The `public` and `private` components of a class definition illustrate how information hiding is applied in the object-oriented paradigm.

Modularity

Contemporary commercial software systems are typically composed of a number of well-organized and well-planned autonomous units, each of which is called a *module*. These modules must be designed in such a way that they will interact with one another correctly, in order to produce the solution for which they were designed. In the context of an object-oriented software system, the design and proper organization of these modules is called *modularity*, which may involve the design of a number of classes whose objects must coordinate properly in order to produce the desired solution. In a number of cases, these classes can be designed in a hierarchical framework in which certain classes may depend upon the existence of other, more general classes. This is implemented in an OOD using the idea of *inheritance*, in which a *base class* (or *parent class*) is defined, with one or more dependent *derived classes* (or *subclasses*) whose objects inherit some of the properties inherent in objects of the base class.

In a hierarchical organization of classes, any object constructed in a derived class is said to satisfy an "is-a" relationship with the corresponding base class. Let us illustrate this idea with an example.

EXAMPLE 1.1   Suppose we look at a group of classes representing a simple hierarchy of two-dimensional geometric figures, organized as in Figure 1.2.

FIGURE 1.2

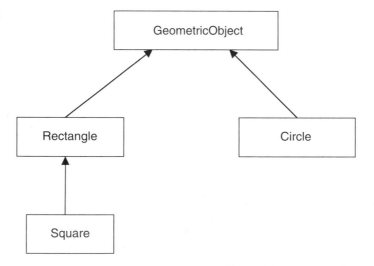

The organizational structure is such that each "box" defines a separate class, with the dependencies as illustrated. Thus, any object constructed from the Rectangle class is also an object of GeometricObject; this dependency is also true of any object constructed from the Circle class. The hierarchy extends one further level: It is possible to construct an object of the Square class, which is a kind of Rectangle, and is in turn a kind of GeometricObject.

Class hierarchies are often very useful in designing solutions for large software problems. This is because the implementation of a hierarchical modular design respects the common functionality of a number of objects from the distinct derived class with the common and more general base class. In addition, the specialized behavior of objects constructed in any of the derived classes is respected.

Using modular design also promotes *reusability* of software. This means that a module designed to solve a specific software problem may also be applicable to the solution of a number of seemingly unrelated software problems. In this case, there is no need to completely recode a second version. Instead, all that needs to be done is to "plug in," or link that module to the modules of the new system. This is certainly possible in Java, where classes designed for the solution of one specific problem may possess a functionality that can be reused to solve others, because that same functionality (in part) applies as well in that second environment.

1.3 **Methods, Classes, and Objects**

Classes undoubtedly represent the central construct of OOD, as implemented in Java. With classes, we can group together associated items of data, together with a number of operations acting on that data. The aggregate consisting of a well-defined set of data, and a finite collection of admissible operations acting on that data, has already been defined as the necessary ingredients of an ADT. It then follows that classes represent an ideal implementation of an ADT.

A *method* in Java is the name used to describe the implementation of an operation applied to a specific set of data values. In the Java environment, methods specify the rules governing the behavior of the data values, and the set of admissible data values are often referred to as the values of the associated *instance variables*. In other high-level programming languages, such as C++ and Ada, methods are usually called *procedures* or *functions*. Methods can accept parameters as arguments, and their behavior is completely determined by the specific instance of the class (that is, the *object*) to which they belong and to the values of any parameters (if such exist) that serve as their arguments.

Every method in Java is specified within the text of some class. In fact, any method definition consists of two parts:

- its *signature,* yielding the name, return data type, and the parameters involved

- its *body,* whose contents describe, in sequence, the actions performed by that method

The syntax for the signature of a method is given by

```
[<methodModifiers>] <returnType> <methodName>
                    ([<formalParameterList>]);
```

where optional parts are enclosed within a pair of matching square brackets ("[" and "]"), and identifiers and keywords are described within a pair of matching angle brackets ("<" and ">").[1]

Method modifiers can take the form of keywords used to restrict the scope of access of members of the underlying class, such as `public` and `private` (and `protected` in certain instances using inheritance, discussed in Chapter 2). Each of the method modifiers just described may be preceded by any one of the following method modifiers, which further restrict the method's applicability: `abstract`, `final`, and `static`. We will discuss these later.

Further, `<returnType>` is either one of Java's *primitive types* (`boolean`, `char`, `byte`, `short`, `int`, `long`, `float`, `double`), indicating that the method returns a value of this type; or it is `void`, indicating that the method is not obliged to return a value; or it is the name of some class, indicating that the return value references a specific object of that class. Also, `<methodName>` is a legal Java identifier naming the method, and `<formalParameterList>` is a finite sequence of pairs `<typeName>` `<parameterName>`, separated by commas, where `<typeName>` is described exactly as `<returnType>`, and where `<parameterName>` is a legal Java identifier. If two or more parameters are appearing in the same `<formalParameterList>`, each must possess a distinct `<parameterName>`.

A specific example of this is

```
public static boolean binSrch(int[] arr, int valueSought);
```

where `<methodModifiers>` is `public static`, `<returnType>` is `boolean`, `<methodName>` is `binSrch`, and `<formalParameterList>` is `int[] arr, int valueSought`. This serves as the signature for the `binSrch` method, performing a binary search on the values of the (sorted) `int`-valued array `arr`, searching for the value currently stored in `valueSought`.

A *class interface* can be defined using the following syntax:

```
[<classModifier>] interface <interfaceName>
{
  <finite sequence of signatures>
}
```

where `interface` is a new Java keyword.

---

[1]In other languages, this is often referred to as a *prototype.*

The sequence `<finite sequence of signatures>` is used to specify the methods of the class without providing any of the implementation details. This is because in Java an interface is not a class but instead specifies a set of requirements for any class whose purpose it is to implement the interface. Example 1.2 illustrates this for `int`-valued stacks.

EXAMPLE 1.2   The following represents a version of the interface for `int`-valued stacks.

```
interface intStack
{
   // Tests whether current stack is empty.
   //  Returns true if so, false if not.
   public boolean isEmpty();

   // Retrieves value at the top of the current stack.
   // Precondition: Current stack is not empty.
   public int top();

   // Push method.  Pushes an int value on the top
   // of the current stack.
   public void push(int value);

   // Pop method.  Removes value at the top of
   // the current stack.
   // Precondition: Current stack is not empty.
   public void pop();

} // Terminates coding of intStack interface.
```

Here are some important observations about interfaces to consider:

1. Methods described in an interface cannot be `static`. This means that every method defined in an interface must attach to some specific object constructed in the class implementing the interface. For example, suppose we have a client program using the class `intArrayStack` implementing the `intStack` interface, and suppose this program contains the constructor

   ```
   intArrayStack iStack = new intArrayStack();
   ```

   If, at some point, we wish to pop `iStack`, we must do so using

   ```
   iStack.pop();
   ```

2. An interface contains only `public` methods. By convention, the keyword `public` can be omitted from the definition of any method defined in an interface—Java will still regard that method as `public`. (For more information, see the works by Gosling, Joy, and Steele [1996],

especially page 99, and Horstmann and Cornell [2001], especially page 252.)

Now that we have justified the purpose and described the interface, how do we produce an implementation of that interface? The syntax for a Java class definition implementing an interface is as follows:

```
[<classModifier>] class <className> implements <interfaceName>
{

  <classBody>


}
```

where `class` and `implements` are new Java keywords, `<className>` is any well-defined identifier naming the class, and where `<classBody>` must contain implementations of each of the methods whose signatures are specified in `<interfaceName>`, together with the description of one or more constructors for the class (if the default constructor is not assumed to be the only constructor involved) and the definition of a number of instance variables or constants.

It is possible for a class to contain a number of *instance variables,* which represent the data associated with the objects constructed from that class. Each such variable must have a designated type, which can be either a *primitive type* (such as `int`, `double`, or `char`, among others), or a *class type* (such as `Node` or `String`) or an array. A single instance variable is declared in Java using the following syntax:

```
[<variableModifier>] <typeName> <variableName> [ = <initialValue>];
```

where `<variableModifier>` can be any one or more of

```
public
private
protected
static
final
```

 A variable is declared as public if any user can access its value; it is declared as protected if only methods of the same class, or any of its subclasses, can access its value (see Chapter 2); it is declared as private if only methods of the same class can access its value. A variable declared as static is used when the variable is associated with the class itself, not with individual objects constructed from that class. We will study examples of classes where the presence of static variables is particularly useful (see Section 1.8 of this chapter). Finally, if an instance variable is declared as final, it must be assigned an initial value that can never change during the course of processing.

<typeName> is either a keyword or an identifier naming the data type of the underlying variable, and <variableName> is an identifier naming the variable. An example of an instance variable definition is

```
private double radius = 1.0;
```

where <variableModifier> is private, <typeName> is double, <variableName> is radius, and <initialValue> is 1.0.

The syntax for a method is almost the same as for its signature, but now we include the *body* of the method. The body of a method is a finite sequence of executable statements (possibly) mixed with a finite sequence of local variable declarations, instance variable declarations, and initializations. The execution of this sequence produces the result for which the method was designed. Thus, the syntax for a method is

```
[<methodModifiers>] <returnType> <methodName> ([<formalParameterList>])
{

    <methodBody>

}
```

A *constructor* is a special kind of method included in the <classBody> of a specific class implementation whose name is <className>, and that creates an object of that class. Also, no <returnType> is defined for a constructor. The process of constructing an object and initializing its instance variables is called *initialization*. The values to be assigned to these instance variables can be passed as parameters to the constructor. We will see this in a number of examples to follow.

As an illustration of these ideas, we continue with the intStack interface as described in Example 1.2. We provide an array implementation described formally as the following:

```
class intArrayStack implements intStack
{

  // Constructor.  Initializes stack as empty.
  intArrayStack(){topValue = -1;}

  // Push operator. Implements push method
  // as described in intStack interface.
  public void push(int value)
  {
   ++topValue;
   Info[topValue] = value;
  }
```

```
// Pop operator.  Implements pop method
// as described in intStack interface.
public void pop(){--topValue;}

// Tests whether current stack is empty.
// Implements isEmpty as described in
// intStack interface.
public boolean isEmpty(){return topValue == -1;}

// Top method. Implements top method as
// described in intStack interface.
// Retrieves value at top of the current stack.
public int top(){return Info[topValue];}

// Instance variables and constants.
final int ArraySize = 10;
private int Info[] = new int[ArraySize];
private int topValue;
} // terminates text of intArrayStack class.
```

A constructor is easy to identify because it always has the same name as <className>, and <classBody> can contain variable and/or constant definitions that are used to clarify the behavior of any object to be constructed from that class. There is one difference between variables and constants defined within the scope of <classBody> and other variables and named constants. Those defined within the scope of <classBody> are not allocated storage until an object of that class is actually constructed (with the notable exception of static variables, as we shall see later in this chapter). In fact, if several variables and/or named constants are declared within the scope of <classBody>, each of these is allocated storage at once and only when an actual object of that class is constructed.

How does the presence of classes aid in the general practice of contemporary software design? The design of a software solution to a problem generally progresses through three fundamental stages. First, the idea is to obtain, in as precise a manner as possible, a clear understanding of the problem to be solved. This is often called the *analysis phase* of software development. The next stage is to identify the key components involved in the proposed solution (the *design phase*.) Finally, the solution is expressed in correct and efficient code (the *programming phase*.) The details of the problem and the attempt to design and encode the proposed solution are often attained through a carefully orchestrated process, consisting of efforts to implement these components in code, producing a solution that is correct and as efficient as possible. In the object-oriented environment, the solution usually requires the presence of a sequence of cooperating classes and objects constructed from these classes.

A Java class defines a *type*—it specifies the behavior of its objects. This behavior includes how these objects are constructed and how they might be manipulated. The main objective in writing effective object-oriented programs is to design classes that capture a simple, fundamental concept relating to the solution of the underlying problem. With this in mind, the question of how these objects are constructed and manipulated must figure heavily in the design.

1.4   An Example of the Use of Constructors for Stacks

We have already defined a constructor as a method appearing in `<class-Body>` whose name is `<className>` and *never specifies a return data type*. A constructor is used to create objects of the class. When invoked in a user program, it allocates storage for each of the object's instance variables and also provides access for each of the methods defined in the class.

If we consider the class `intArrayStack` implementing the `intStack` interface, we note that the constructor is coded as

```
intArrayStack(){topValue = -1;}
```

When this constructor is invoked in a user program, say in the form

```
intArrayStack iStack = new intArrayStack();
```

we can view the allocation of storage as described in Figure 1.3.

FIGURE 1.3   iStack

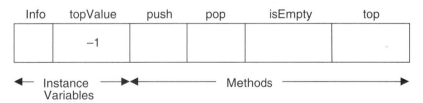

Info	topValue	push	pop	isEmpty	top
	−1				

◄—— Instance ——►◄———————— Methods ————————►
Variables

Here, `Info` is a reference to an array of `int` values, of the form given in Figure 1.4.

The constructor is responsible for the allocation of all of this storage. The implementation of any object in the `intArrayStack` implementation of `intStack` is initialized as in Figure 1.3. The initial value of `-1` for `top-Value` assures that no current value stored in the `Info` array is associated with the current stack. Thus, effectively, `iStack` in its initial form describes

FIGURE 1.4

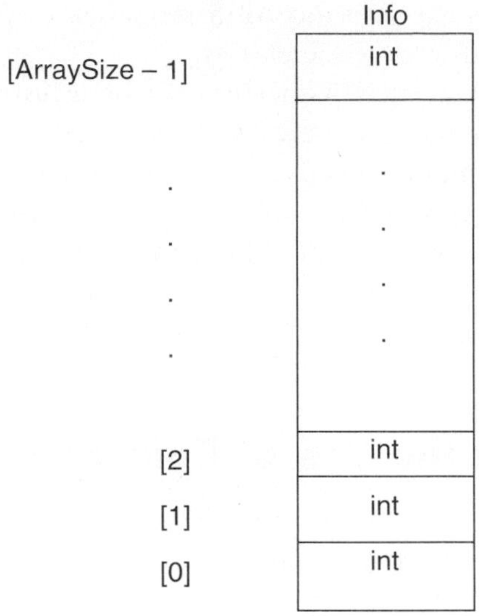

Info

[ArraySize − 1]   int

· · ·   · · ·

[2]   int
[1]   int
[0]   int

an *empty stack*. This form of a constructor is known as a *default constructor*, because its implementation requires no arguments.

Let us analyze the behavior of each of the methods described in int-ArrayStack. For ArraySize with value 10, invoking the constructor using

intArrayStack iStack = new intArrayStack();

allocates storage for the instance variables for iStack, as in Figure 1.5.

FIGURE 1.5

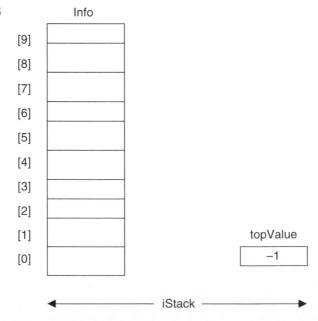

Info

[9]
[8]
[7]
[6]
[5]
[4]
[3]
[2]
[1]
[0]

topValue
−1

← iStack →

This describes iStack as initially empty, because the initial value of topValue is -1.

The code for the push method is given as the following:

```
public void push(int value)
{
 ++topValue;
 Info[topValue] = value;
}
```

This is invoked as

```
iStack.push(value);
```

where value is assumed to store some int value. The result of executing this is to first increment topValue and to then copy the current storage in value into the array location given by Info[topValue].

In a similar manner, the pop method is coded as

```
public void pop()
{
 --topValue;
}
```

which simply increments the array subscript topValue. We invoke this for iStack using

```
iStack.pop();
```

In essence, as a result of doing this, the view of the current stack values as stored inside Info decreases by one number: The view of the stack as implemented by Info begins with Info[0] and ends with Info[topValue] for the newly decremented topValue.

Finally, the retrieval of the value at the top of the current stack is implemented by

```
public int top()
{
 return Info[topValue];
}
```

This does not change the representation of the stack in any way. This is invoked for iStack as

```
iStack.top();
```

and returns the int value in the Info array implementing the stack, whenever iStack is not empty.

The size of the Info array is determined by the declaration

```
final int ArraySize = 10;
```

There is a possible criticism to this: According to the implementation, the stack might contain a maximum number of ArraySize numbers. But what if we attempt to push more values onto iStack beyond the capacity given by ArraySize? The result will be a *run-time error*, because Java very scrupulously checks array subscripts to ensure that no more than the designated number of array subscripts coincide with values on the current stack. Any attempt to exceed this raises a run-time error referred to as an *overflow condition*. In brief, Java will throw an ArrayIndexOutOfBoundsException, which in turn causes an *interrupt* to occur in the course of processing using this array implementation of the stack.

As well, if an attempt is made to pop the current stack when it is empty, or to retrieve the value at the top of the current stack when it is empty, the result is called an *underflow condition;* it generates a run-time error once again by throwing an ArrayIndexOutOfBoundsException.

The programmer can apply two possible alternatives to avoid overflow and/or underflow. The first alternative involves revising the value of ArraySize to a larger value in order to avoid overflow as much as possible. This larger value for ArraySize helps, but it has no effect on underflow. The other alternative is to use *exceptions* and *exception handlers* in order to detect and manage the occurrence of overflow and underflow. We will study the use of exceptions and exception handlers as they apply to the sequential implementation of stacks next.

1.5   A First Look at Exceptions and Exception Handlers

An *exception* is an object used to detect the presence of some abnormal condition or unexpected event occurring in the course of executing a program. For example, if we define

```
public static double ratio(int a, int b)
{
 return (double)a/b;
}
```

and if b is zero, the result is an attempted division by zero. This causes Java to "throw" an exception. In Java, exceptions are "thrown" by code that causes the occurrence of some sort of unexpected event, such as an attempted division by zero, or that processes values in some array so that the value of the array subscript becomes either less than zero or greater than or equal to the array size, or with unexpected input/output (I/O) values. Exceptions can also be thrown by the Java run-time environment, such as running out of memory to allocate to variables in some process.

Exceptions are either predefined or created by the programmer. Java has a number of predefined exceptions, such as

- `ArithmeticException`, thrown in such situations as an attempted division by zero or an attempted evaluation of an even root of a negative number
- `ArrayIndexOutOfBoundsException`, thrown when an array subscript is either less than zero or greater than or equal to the current array size
- `IllegalArgumentException`, thrown when an argument or parameter passed to a method is of the wrong data type
- `IOException`, thrown when an exceptional condition occurs during I/O operations

Exceptions are designed to be *detected* and *handled,* so that the program can resume execution in the presence of an exception instead of shutting down. As a design issue, we should view exceptions as conditions in a program that are expected to occur infrequently, if at all. In general, we should design code with the idea that, if user interaction is involved, the user should be informed (through sufficient probing and documentation) to enter the proper form of data in case the exception is caused by improper input data.

Several factors are involved in processing exceptions:

1. *trying the exception:* The programmer creates a block around the statement sequence whose execution may cause an occurrence of the exception. This block is prefaced with the `try` keyword. The general syntax for a `try` block is

```
try
  {
  < body of try block:
    Code containing statements that may raise exceptions>
  }
```

2. *catching the exception:* Each exception that may occur in the execution of the corresponding `try` block is handled as a new block immediately following this `try` block and preceded by an occurrence of the `catch` keyword. This is followed by the name of the specific exception being caught, followed by an identifier naming a parameter whose type is the name of the exception. The `catch` block contains a code sequence whose execution begins as a result of generating (throwing) the exception in the `try` block. The objective is to apply the result of executing the code in the `catch` block as an alternative to aborting execution of the program.

3. *throwing the exception:* This describes the act of identifying the occurrence of an exception. This must occur within the scope of a `try` block. If the exception is thrown, and if there is no code in the program (in the form of a corresponding `catch` block) for handling the exception,

an interrupt occurs, aborting further execution of the program and resulting in the display of an error message.

Predefined exceptions need not occur within the scope of a `try` block. For example, an `IOException` is thrown as a result of executing the code

```
int value = Integer.parseInt(intIS.readLine());
```

which has been preceded in the text of the user program by

```
BufferedReader intIS = new BufferedReader(
                        new InputStreamReader(System.in));
```

and input has been provided as

21ab

Besides these, programmers can create exception classes and instantiate an exception object of such classes using a `throw` statement, with syntax

```
throw new <exceptionClassName> ([<parameterList>]);
```

where `throw` is a Java keyword, `<exceptionClassName>` is an identifier naming the exception class, and `<parameterList>` is an (optional) list of parameter values passed to the constructor of that exception class.

For example, we can revise the implementation of `intArrayStack` to include a `StackException` class, and then we rewrite the code for the `push` method of `intArrayStack` as follows[2]:

```
public void push(int value) throws StackException
{
 if(topValue != ArraySize - 1)
 {
  ++topValue;
  Info[topValue]= value;
 }
 else
  throw new StackException("push operation aborted - overflow");
} // terminates text of push method
```

Notice that the general syntax of the `throw` statement given here is applied, because `<exceptionClassName>` is `StackException`, and `<parameterList>` has exactly one member: the `String` constant

```
"push operation aborted - overflow"
```

---

[2]The `if` block may be compressed to the single executable statement
```
Info[++topValue] = value;
```

A couple of questions must still be answered regarding exceptions and exception handlers:

1. How do we express the code of a corresponding `catch` statement?
2. In the case of programmer-defined exceptions, how do we design the text of the corresponding exception class?

The syntax for a `catch` block is

```
catch(<exceptionClassName> <identifier>)
{
 < Code for handling the exception of the type named by
    <exceptionClassName> : body of catchBlock>
}
```

EXAMPLE 1.3   The following code represents a simple Java application using exceptions for handling an attempted division by zero. We wish to generate a rational number by interactively inputting `int` values for each numerator and denominator, returning a `double` value representing the value of the quotient whenever possible.

Assume our program contains the code sequence

```
int numerator, denominator;
BufferedReader intIS = new BufferedReader(
                    new InputStreamReader(System.in));
try
{
 System.out.println("Input any integer value for the numerator:");
 numerator = Integer.parseInt(intIS.readLine());
 System.out.println("Input any integer value for the denominator:");
 denominator = Integer.parseInt(intIS.readLine());
 if(denominator == 0)
  throw new IOException("Error:");
  System.out.println("Fraction is " + (double)numerator/denominator);
} // try block
catch(IOException e)
{
 System.out.println(e.getMessage());
 System.out.println("Attempted division by zero");
} // catch block
```

We trace several executions of this code sequence.

Input any integer value for the numerator:
2

Input any integer value for the denominator
9
Fraction is 0.2222222222222222

Here, the `if` clause in the `try` block is ignored. Instead, after providing the input values for `numerator` and `denominator` as described, execution proceeds in the `try` block to

Fraction is 0.2222222222222222

and execution of the `try` block terminates. The `catch` block never executes because entry into the `catch` block requires throwing an `IOException`. This does not occur in this case.

Now consider the following:

Input an integer value for the numerator:
3
Input an integer value for the denominator:
0
Error:
Attempted division by zero

After inputting the value 0 for `denominator`, the `if` clause executes, throwing an `IOException`. At this point, control immediately passes to the corresponding `catch` block, and the statement sequence appearing in `<body of catchBlock>` executes. This produces

Error:
Attempted division by zero

The first line of output results by invoking the predefined `getMessage()` parameter to the `String` constant `"Error:"` and outputting that message.

If we attempt to input a character sequence that does not evaluate to an `int` value, the `parseInt` method defined in `java.io.*` throws an exception that is not caught by the `catch` block defined above, since that exception is not treated as an `IOException`.

Example 1.3 is an example of a more general situation involving `try` blocks and `catch` blocks in Java. The general syntax of a `try-catch` sequence is given by

```
try
{
  < body of tryBlock >
}
catch(< exceptionClassName1 > <identifier1>)
{
  < body of catchBlock1 >
}
```

```
[catch( <exceptionClassName2> <identifier2>)
 {
   < body of catchBlock2 >
 }]



      .
      .
      .


[catch( <exceptionClassNamen> <identifiern>)
 {
   < body of catchBlockn >
 }]
[finally
 {
   < body of finallyBlock >
 }]
```

Any finite number of exceptions can be thrown in the course of executing < body of tryBlock >. Each such exception can be listed and named using < exceptionClassName1 >, . . . , < exceptionClassNamen >, and control of execution passes to the appropriate catch block named by < exceptionClassNamei >, as we described in Example 1.3. In addition, if the sequence also contains a finally block (note that finally is a new Java keyword), then < body of finallyBlock > executes, regardless of whether an exception is thrown when the try block executes.

EXAMPLE 1.4   This code extends that in Example 1.3 to include a finally block and additional code following the try-catch-finally sequence:

```
int numerator, denominator;
BufferedReader intIS = new BufferedReader(
                    new InputStreamReader(System.in));
try{
 System.out.println("Input any integer value for the numerator:");
 numerator = Integer.parseInt(intIS.readLine());
 System.out.println("Input any integer value for the denominator:");
 denominator = Integer.parseInt(intIS.readLine());
 if(denominator == 0)
    throw new IOException("Error:");
 System.out.println("Fraction is " + (double)numerator/denominator);
 } // try block
catch(IOException e)
{
```

```
System.out.println(e.getMessage());
System.out.println("Attempted division by zero.");
} // catch block
finally
{
System.out.println("Executing in finally block.");
} // finally block
System.out.println("Outside of try-catch-finally sequence.");
System.out.println("Terminating execution of program.");
```

We trace several executions of the new code sequence, using the same input values from Example 1.3. The first is

Input any integer value for the numerator:
2
Input any integer value for the denominator:
9
Fraction is 0.222222222222222
Executing in finally block.
Outside of try-catch-finally sequence.
Terminating execution of program.

The second run yields

Input any integer value for the numerator:
3
Input any integer value for the denominator:
0
Error:
Attempted division by zero.
Executing in finally block.
Outside of try-catch-finally sequence.
Terminating execution of program.

Summarizing, we have answered the first question concerning the matter of exceptions; we have therefore treated in some detail the syntax and semantics of `catch` blocks. To respond in some depth to the question of designing our own exception classes, however, we require some knowledge of class hierarchies and inheritance, and how these are implemented in Java. That is the content of the next section.

1.6 A First Look at Class Hierarchies and Inheritance

A key concept of OOD is that of *class hierarchies*. Figure 1.2, shown earlier, illustrates a simple geometric hierarchy of two-dimensional objects: squares, rectangles, and circles, all of which derive from a single class called Geo-metricObject. Referring again to Figure 1.2, we can say that it illustrates an organizational structure of classes, where each upward link displays an "is a" relation occurring between classes in the hierarchy. For example, any object constructed from the Square class is a special kind of rectangle. Furthermore, any rectangle and any circle is a geometric object, but no rectangle is a circle or vice versa. As we will see, particularly in Chapter 2, hierarchies are useful tools in the design of software, because they group together certain classes of objects sharing a common functionality, and they extend the behavior of certain objects to more specialized cases.

Our purpose in discussing class hierarchies here is to show how they apply to the design of exception classes by the programmer. We begin this discussion with the observation that Java organizes a number of predefined classes in a hierarchy, with the Object class at the root. That is, every other Java class, whether predefined or designed by the programmer, is in a hierarchical structure with Object as the root class. We can also state this by saying that every class is a descendant of the Object class. With regard to exceptions, Java supports the hierarchy of predefined classes seen in Figure 1.6.

FIGURE 1.6

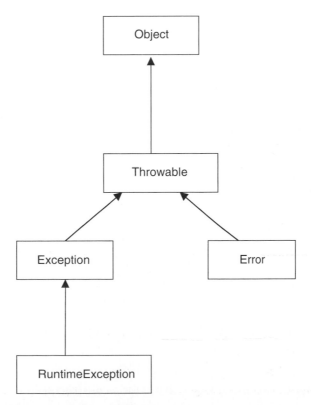

The objects appearing in the `Throwable` class (for more detail, see Gosling, Joy, and Steele [1996]) represent any objects that can be thrown and caught. Specifically, any object constructed in `Exception` "is an" object that can be thrown and caught. In turn, any object constructed in `RuntimeException` "is an" exception—an object in `Exception`. In particular, `Throwable` contains a constructor whose signature is

```
public Throwable(String message);
```

which initializes a newly constructed `Throwable` object by saving a reference to the message string passed as the value of the parameter. This constructor can be inherited by any subclass of `Throwable`. For example, using Figure 1.6, each of `Exception`, `RuntimeException`, and any subclass in this hierarchy and designed by the programmer will inherit this constructor.

How is this constructor inherited in a class hierarchy, as shown in Figure 1.7?

FIGURE 1.7

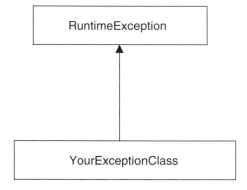

Here we understand that `YourExceptionClass` names an exception class that is defined by the programmer and whose immediate superclass is `RuntimeException`. Using inheritance, every method defined in `RuntimeException` is automatically a method of `YourExceptionClass` unless overridden in `YourExceptionClass` by providing a new definition of that method within the scope of `YourExceptionClass`.

A subclass, such as `YourExceptionClass`, might have its own specific constructors. The immediate superclass from which it was derived (`RuntimeException` in this case) also has its own collection of constructors. A possible action of `YourExceptionClass` in such a hierarchical relationship is to invoke a constructor coming from `RuntimeException`. Java uses the keyword `super` to call any method defined in a superclass. For example, the body of a constructor for `YourExceptionClass` is

```
super(str);
```

The result of executing this is to invoke a constructor in `RuntimeException`.

It is important to observe that the call to the constructor in `Runtime-`
`Exception` as part of the text of `YourExceptionClass` is not

```
RuntimeException(str);
```

Instead, this call takes the form

```
super(str);
```

Important Observations

1. The invoking of `super` must be the *first* statement in a constructor of
   `YourExceptionClass`. You cannot invoke `super` in a later instruction
   in the body of this constructor.
2. If you do not include a constructor for `YourExceptionClass`, Java will
   automatically include a call to the default constructor of the superclass
   whenever an object of `YourExceptionClass` is constructed.

We will not go into any further detail here on inheritance and class hierarchies. Instead, Chapter 2 gives more detail on the general principles of
inheritance and polymorphism as these apply in OOD.

To indicate that `YourExceptionClass` is a subclass of `RuntimeExcep-`
`tion`, the syntax for `YourExceptionClass` must be given by

```
class YourExceptionClass extends RuntimeException
{
  < body of YourExceptionClass >
}
```

where `< body of YourExceptionClass >` contains the complete coding
of any methods appearing in that class that are not inherited from `Run-`
`timeException`, or any overridden methods described in `RuntimeExcep-`
`tion`.

EXAMPLE 1.5   This example revises the coding of the `intStack` interface and the implementation class `intArrayStack` to include exceptions involving overflow
and underflow. We include the coding of `StackException`, a programmer-
defined class for constructing these exceptions.

The revision of `intStack` is given as

```
interface intStack
{
 // Tests whether current stack is empty.
 // Returns true if so, false if not.
 public boolean isEmpty();

 // Retrieves value at the top of the current stack.
 // Precondition: Current stack is not empty.
 public int top() throws StackException;
```

```
// Push method.  Pushes an int value on the top
// of the current stack.
public void push(int value) throws StackException;

// Pop method.  Removes value at the top of the
// current stack.
// Precondition: Current stack is not empty.
public void pop() throws StackException;
} // terminates coding of intStack interface.
```

The coding of the `StackException` class is

```
class StackException extends RuntimeException
{
// Constructor.
public StackException(String str)
{
 super(str);
} // terminates text of constructor.
} // terminates text of StackException class.
```

Note that `StackException` contains no instance variables and only a single `public` method—a constructor, inherited from `RuntimeException`. As the revision for the implementation class `intArrayStack` will show, the value of the `String` parameter passed to `super` will differentiate between overflow and underflow. The revision of `intArrayStack` is

Class implementation

```
class intArrayStack implements intStack
{
// Constructor.  Initializes stack as empty.
public intArrayStack(){topValue = -1;}
// Push operator. Includes text for overflow.
public void push(int value) throws StackException
{
 if(topValue < ArraySize - 1) // Current stack is not full.
                              // Legitimate push operation.
  Info[++topValue] = value;
 else  // Current stack is full. Signal overflow.
  throw new StackException("Error: Overflow.");
}
// Pop operator. Includes text for handling underflow.
public void pop() throws StackException
{
 if(!isEmpty()) // Current stack is not empty.
                // Legitimate pop operation.
    --topValue;
```

```
  else // Current stack is empty. Signal underflow.
    throw new StackException("Error: Underflow.");
}
// Tests whether current stack is empty.
public boolean isEmpty(){return topValue == -1;}
// Retrieves value at top of the curent stack.
// Includes text for handling underflow.
public int top() throws StackException
{
  if(!isEmpty()) // Current stack is not empty.
                 // Legitimate retrieval operation.
    return Info[topValue];
  else // Current stack is empty. Signal underflow.
    throw new StackException("Error: Underflow.");
}

final int ArraySize = 10;
private int Info[] = new int[ArraySize];
private int topValue;
} // terminates text of intArrayStack class.
```

You should write a driver for this. See the exercises at the end of this chapter.

1.7 **Generic Programming**
Generic Classes

Starting with Section 1.2, we began the design of and produced an implementation for the ADT of int-valued stacks, using classes. But what about stacks whose contents are not int-valued, such as character- or real-valued stacks? Our earlier design of the intArrayStack, although quite correct and efficient, does not apply. In fact, although the design of the underlying code turns out to be nearly identical to that given for int-valued stacks, it will have to be rewritten for each distinct data type for values to be stored on the stack. This is repetitive and tedious, because we are faced with the prospect of supplying an implementation whose only change is to replace each occurrence of int with an occurrence of the name of the new data type.

Java supports another, more sensible alternative. Rather than naming a specific data type, such as int, we can design a "generic" form of the implementation using Object as the data type of the values to be stored on the stack. The class definition using this generic form is called a *generic class*.

The same subdivision described in Section 1.3—a subdivision into an interface and an implementation class—applies in this context, except that each occurrence of the same specific data type (such as `int`) is replaced with an occurrence of `Object`. Besides this, there are some other relatively simple modifications in syntax, which we will explain while describing the syntax of this generic form.

We begin by noting that any value of any class type, predefined or otherwise, can be stored in any variable of type `Object`. In particular, any `String` value is an object. Thus, a perfectly legal declaration and initialization in Java is given by

```
Object objValue = "Rosalie";
```

On the other hand, any value from a primitive numeric type (such as `int`, `double`, or `char`) or a `boolean` value is not regarded as an object. Thus, each of the following assignments produces a compile-time error:

```
objValue = -6;
objValue = true;
```

For such primitive values, we require the use of the appropriate *wrapper class* (`Integer` for `int`, `Double` for `double`, `Character` for `char`, `Boolean` for `Boolean`, and so on). Each "primitive" value must first be "wrapped" in the appropriate object and then passed as a value to `objValue`, as in

```
Integer intValue = new Integer(-6);
Boolean boolValue = new Boolean(true);
```

Then each of the following assignments are valid:

```
objValue = intValue;
objValue = boolValue;
```

How do these ideas apply to a generic form of an interface for the stack ADT? Suppose we recode the interface given in Example 1.5, replacing each appropriate occurrence of `int` with an occurrence of `Object`:

EXAMPLE 1.6
```
interface Stack
{
 // Tests whether current stack is empty.
 // Returns true if so, false if not.
 public boolean isEmpty();

 // Retrieves value at the top of the current stack.
 // Precondition: Current stack is not empty.
 public Object top() throws StackException;
```

```
// Push method.  Pushes an Object value on the top
// of the current stack.
public void push(Object value) throws StackException;

// Pop method.  Removes value at the top of the
// current stack.
// Precondition: Current stack is not empty.
public void pop() throws StackException;
} // terminates coding of Stack interface.
```

The coding of the StackException class is identical to that given earlier in Example 1.5. This is because no mention is made of the specific type of data stored on the stack. The generic implementation of stacks using arrays can then be described by

```
class objArrayStack implements Stack
{
// Constructor.  Initializes stack as empty.
public objArrayStack(){topValue = -1;}
// Push operator. Includes text for overflow.
public void push(Object value) throws StackException
 {
  if(topValue < ArraySize - 1) // Current stack is not full.
                            // Legitimate push operation.
   Info[++topValue] = value;
  else  // Current stack is full. Signal overflow.
   throw new StackException("Error: Overflow.");
 }
// Pop operator. Includes text for handling underflow.
public void pop() throws StackException
 {
  if(!isEmpty()) // Current stack is not empty.
              // Legitimate pop operation.
     --topValue;
  else // Current stack is empty. Signal underflow.
   throw new StackException("Error: Underflow.");
 }
// Tests whether current stack is empty.
public boolean isEmpty(){return topValue == -1;}
// Retrieves value at top of the current stack.
// Includes text for handling underflow.
public Object top() throws StackException
 {
```

```
      if(!isEmpty()) // Current stack is not empty.
                     // Legitimate retrieval operation.
       return Info[topValue];
      else // Current stack is empty. Signal underflow.
       throw new StackException("Error: Underflow.");
   }


  final int ArraySize = 10;
  private Object Info[] = new Object[ArraySize];
  private int topValue;
} // terminates text of objArrayStack class.
```

The key advantage in using generic class definitions is that we no longer have to write a separate class definition for stacks storing values of type char, or for stacks storing real values (such as float or double), or for stacks of values defined by the user. All that needs to be done is to instantiate the data type of the values to be stored in the stack(s) required in the user's code. For example, if a user method requires two separate Integer-valued stacks called iStack1 and iStack2, and one Character-valued stack called cStack, all that needs to be done in the text of the user method is to first establish a linkage with objArrayStack, using

```
objArrayStack iStack1 = new objArrayStack();
objArrayStack iStack2 = new objArrayStack();
objArrayStack cStack = new objArrayStack();
```

Thus, the constructor of objArrayStack is invoked three times: for two instances of Integer-valued stacks and for a single instance of a Character-valued stack. The push method again checks for overflow, using the same form of StackException as that already defined for the intArrayStack class:

```
public void push(Object value) throws StackException
{
  if(topValue < ArraySize - 1) // Current stack is not full.
                               // Legitimate push operation.
   Info[++topValue] = value;
  else  // Current stack is full. Signal overflow.
   throw new StackException("Error: Overflow.");
}
```

Similarly, the generic version of pop checks whether the underflow condition exists. Its code is shown here:

```
public void pop() throws StackException
{
  if(!isEmpty()) // Current stack is not empty.
             // Legitimate pop operation.
```

```
       --topValue;
  else // Current stack is empty. Signal underflow.
    throw new StackException("Error: Underflow.");
}
```

   The testing as to whether the current stack object is empty clearly does not depend on the type of values stored on the stack. Consequently, the same code executes regardless of the data type of the stack values. In fact, the only code that depends on the type of values stored on the stack is the push method described earlier, and the top method, which again returns the value stored at the top of the current stack (if the current stack is not empty) and whose code is shown here:

```
public Object top() throws StackException
{
  if(!isEmpty())  // Current stack is not empty.
                  // Legitimate retrieval operation.
    return Info[topValue];
  else // Current stack is empty. Signal underflow.
    throw new StackException("Error: Underflow.");
}
```

   In summary, we conclude that generic classes provide a higher level of abstraction and reuse, because they can be defined when the same class structure is applicable on different types in exactly the same way. All that is needed is for the user to specify the data type of the values to be stored on the stack.

Generic Methods

Java allows for a second type of generic abstraction, used when the same algorithm is applicable to different types of parameters. This form of abstraction and reuse is commonly known as *generic methods* and is applicable to static methods. To illustrate this, we recognize one of the most frequently used algorithms involved in interchanging (or swapping) the values stored in two variables. The swap is accomplished by invoking the method

```
public static void swapValues(Object[] a, int i, int j)
{
  Object tempHolder = a[i];
  a[i] = a[j];
  a[j] = tempHolder;
}
```

where a is an array, a[i] and a[j] are variables holding the values to be swapped, and tempHolder is an auxiliary variable of the same data type as that of `a[i]` and `a[j]`. Note that we have not specified any type, because this method will work regardless of the type. For example, if we wish to swap the values of two `int` variables, the operable form of the swap function would be coded as

```
public static void swapValues(int[] a, int i, int j)
{
 int tempHolder = a[i];
 a[i] = a[j];
 a[j] = tempHolder;
}
```

The method for swapping two `char` values is

```
public static void swapValues(char[] a, int i, int j)
{
 char tempHolder = a[i];
 a[i] = a[j];
 a[j] = tempHolder;
}
```

A similar `static` method exists for each distinct data type. Without generics, a separate method is required for each different data type. Because Java permits overloading of method names, the same identifier (`swapValues` in this case) can be used for different versions of the swapping method, so long as these different versions are distinguished by different type names in their respective formal parameter lists.

In place of this, Java allows use of the generic form of `swapValues` just described, provided that any primitive values to be swapped are placed in their appropriate wrapper objects. Thus, for example, if we wish to swap the `int` values `val0` and `val1`, we first wrap each in an `Integer` object, as in

```
Integer intVal0 = new Integer(val0);
Integer intVal1 = new Integer(val1);
```

and then assign those `Integer` values in the `Object`-valued array `a`, as in

```
a[0] = intVal0;
a[1] = intVal1;
```

and then invoking

```
swapValues(a,0,1);
```

to effect the swap.

If we then wish to swap the `char` values `cval0` and `cval1`, we would first create the `Character` objects `charVal0` and `charVal1`, defined by

```
Character charVal0 = new Character(cval0);
Character charVal1 = new Character(cval1);
```

and then execute

```
a[0] = charVal0;
a[1] = charVal1;
```

and finally invoke

```
swapValues(a,0,1);
```

In summary, generic methods allow for the creation of an entire category of specific methods, one for each distinct instance of the data type serving as a specific substitute for Object.

1.8   static **Fields and Methods**

We have already discussed the idea of instance variables and, we mentioned the existence of static variables in Section 1.3. static variables are also called *static fields* or *class variables*. Any such variable is independent of any of the objects constructed for that class. In other words, the storage allocated for a class variable is not viewed as a data value of that class. Instead, it stands apart from any of the specific objects constructed for that class, while each object has its own separate copy of all instance variables for that class. Java allows only one class variable per class. In addition, any static method defined in an implementation is not allowed to appear in a class interface.

For example, suppose we wish to maintain a running count of the number of objects constructed from a given class. We wish to maintain that count, initialized at zero, in some int-valued variable associated with that class. We also wish to be capable of viewing the current value stored in that class variable. With these ideas in mind, we consider Example 1.7.

EXAMPLE 1.7   We begin with the design of an interface for the class named staticClass:

```
interface staticClass
{
 public void print();
} // terminates text of staticClass
```

Thus, any object constructed from an implementation of staticClass can invoke the instance method print(). The implementation class for staticClass is

```
class staticClassImplementation implements staticClass
{
 // Constructor.
 public staticClassImplementation()
 {
```

```
        ++val1;
        ++val2;
        ++objectCount;
      } // closes constructor
     public void print()
     {
      System.out.println("Class val1 = " + val1);
      System.out.println("Class val2 = " + val2);
     } // closes print
     public static int objectCount()
     {
      return objectCount;
     }
     private int val1 = 0;
     private int val2 = val1 + 1;
     private static int objectCount = 0;
    } // terminates text of staticClassImplementation
```

Note that `staticClassImplementation` contains two methods, `print()` and `objectCount()`, yet the only member of the `staticClass` interface is `print()`. This is due to the <u>Java regulation that the only signatures described in a class interface must be non-static.</u>

Let us examine the result of executing the user program

```
public static void main(String [] args)
{
 staticClassImplementation cls1 = new staticClassImplementation();
 staticClassImplementation cls2 = new staticClassImplementation();
 cls1.print();
 cls2.print();
 System.out.print("The number of objects constructed is: ");
 System.out.println(staticClassImplementation.objectCount());
} // Terminates main method
```

Two objects are constructed, and an "external" storage location for `objectCount` is allocated, as described in Figure 1.8.

The results as pictured are those occurring after executing the user function described earlier. Note that with each occurrence of the construction of an object of this class, the initial value of `val1` increments to 1, and that of `val2` becomes 2. Because `objectCount` is a class variable, however, its initial value of 0 increments by one each time a new object of the class is constructed. We should also note that `print()` can output only the current values stored in `val1` and `val2`, because `objectCount` is not part of either of the objects `cls1` or `cls2`. Thus, in order to output the current value of `objectCount`, we designed a `static` method `objectCount()`,

FIGURE 1.8   cls1

val1	val2	print()
1	2	

cls2

val1	val2	print()
1	2	

objectCount

2

which returns the current value of objectCount. In order to output this value, we cannot attach objectCount() to any specific object constructed from that class; instead, we apply

```
System.out.println(staticClassImplementation.objectCount());
```

This is the way static methods have to be invoked when such methods are defined within the text of a class definition. Tho output obtained by executing the driver is

```
Class val1 = 1
Class val2 = 2
Class val1 = 1
Class val2 = 2
The number of objects constructed is: 2
```

It is important to note that a static method is invoked in any user program by

```
<className>.<methodName>([<actualParameterList>]);
```

where <className> names the class within whose context the static method named by <methodName> is found, and <actualParameterList> is a list (possibly empty) of actual parameters. For example, we invoked the static method objectCount() for output using

```
staticClassImplementation.objectCount();
```

As was the case for static class variables, the reference to any static method of a class appears outside the allocated memory for any specific object constructed from that class.

EXAMPLE 1.8   This example illustrates the design, behavior, and the advantage of using static methods and variables to solve a business-oriented problem. We wish to design a class based on the following observations: Each object constructed from the class represents the salary data and behavior of a single employee. Each employee is issued a specific base salary, with the possible addition of a salary bonus that may differ from one employee to the next. The firm also has a policy of awarding, when applicable, an additional common bonus to every employee. Our design of the class takes all of these factors into consideration, and its user interface can be coded as

```
interface Employee
{
 public void computeBonus(double base);
 public double computeSalary();
} // terminates text of Employee interface
```

The implementation class for Employee is called EmployeeImplementation, and it is coded as

```
class EmployeeImplementation implements Employee
{
 // Constructor.  Computes base salary for each employee.
 public EmployeeImplementation(double base)
 {
  baseSalary = base;
 }


 // Computes individual bonus based on a specific percentage
 // of base salary.
 public void computeBonus(double perCent)
 {
  personalBonus = baseSalary * perCent;
 }


 // Static method adjusting the amount of general bonus
 public static void adjustGeneralBonus(double amount)
 {
  generalBonus = amount;
 }



 // Computes salary for each employee, including all bonuses.
 public double computeSalary()
 {
  return baseSalary + personalBonus + generalBonus;
 }
```

```
                    // Data fields
                    private double baseSalary;
                    private double personalBonus;
                    private static double generalBonus = 225;
                } // completes text of EmployeeImplementation
```

Suppose the main method is the following:

```
public static void main(String [] args)
{
 // Construct two EmployeeImplementation objects, establishing
 // base salary for each:
 EmployeeImplementation emp1 = new EmployeeImplementation(4000);
 EmployeeImplementation emp2 = new EmployeeImplementation(6000);

 // Computes personal bonus for each:
 emp1.computeBonus(0.10);
 emp2.computeBonus(0.25);

 // Output salary for each employee before general bonus adjustment.
 System.out.println("Before general bonus adjustment:");
 System.out.println("Employee 1 earns $" + emp1.computeSalary());
 System.out.println("Employee 2 earns $" + emp2.computeSalary());

 // Invoke static method adjustGeneralBonus
 EmployeeImplementation.adjustGeneralBonus(500);

 // Now output salary after general salary adjustment.
 System.out.println("After general bonus adjustment:");
 System.out.println("Employee 1 earns $" + emp1.computeSalary());
 System.out.println("Employee 2 earns $" + emp2.computeSalary());
} // terminates text of main method
```

Figure 1.9 illustrates the initial values and allocated storage for emp1 and emp2, together with that for the class variable generalBonus.

We now trace execution of the main method:

1. When emp1.computeBonus(0.10) executes, the personalBonus field of emp1 gets the value 400.
2. When emp2.computeBonus(0.25) executes, the personalBonus field of emp2 gets the value 1500.
3. When emp1.computeSalary() executes the first time, the value 4625 is returned.
4. When emp2.computeSalary() executes the first time, the value 7725 is returned.

FIGURE 1.9   emp1

emp2

generalBonus

5.   Then the `static` method `EmployeeImplementation.adjustGeneral-Bonus(500)` executes, changing the initial value of `generalBonus` from 225 to 500. This means that each employee will get an additional general bonus of $500 instead of the previous $225. When these changes are reflected in the general salary, they are displayed in the last two lines of execution.

6.   When `emp1.computeSalary()` executes a second time, the value 4900 is returned.

7.   When `emp2.computeSalary()` executes a second time, the value 8000 is returned.

Finally, the output of the main method is

```
Before general bonus adjustment:
Employee1 earns #4625.0
Employee2 earns $7725.0
After general bonus adjustment:
Employee1 earns $4900.0
Employee2 earns $8000.0
```

We can summarize the behavior of the two forms of methods described in this chapter. An instance method has three attributes:

* It can access the `private` members of the class where it is defined
* It lies in the scope of that class

- It must be invoked by an object of that class—that is, it uses the qualified reference (as in `emp1.computeSalary()`) applied to a specific object of that class

If we are instead dealing with a `static` method of a class, that method has only the first two attributes and replaces the qualified reference of an object constructed from that class by the class name (as in `EmployeeImplementation.adjustGeneralBonus(500)`).

1.9 **An Abstraction for Complex Numbers**

An important numeric type used in many mathematical and engineering applications is the *complex numbers*. A typical complex number has the form

`<realPart> + <imaginaryPart> i`

where `<realPart>` and `<imaginaryPart>` are real numbers, and where `i` is the symbol used to denote the square root of `-1`. Here the "+" symbol performs no arithmetic operation—it simply acts as a *separator* between the real and imaginary parts of the complex number.

In defining the complex number ADT, the admissible operations are

- *addition* of any two complex numbers, defined as

    $(a_1 + b_1 i) + (a_2 + b_2 i) = (a_1 + a_2) + (b_1 + b_2)i$

- *subtraction* of any two complex numbers, defined as

    $(a_1 + b_1 i) - (a_2 + b_2 i) = (a_1 - a_2) + (b_1 - b_2)I$

- *equality* of two complex numbers, defined as

    $(a_1 + b_1 i) == (a_2 + b_2 i)$ if and only if $(a_1 == a_2)$ && $(b_1 == b_2)$

- an *assignment operator* = , which permits the copying of an already-existing complex value into a declared complex variable
- an *output function,* which outputs the real and imaginary parts of any specific object of that class.[3]

Our design involves an implementation of this ADT using an interface called `Complex` and an implementation class called `ComplexNumber`, any of whose objects represents a single complex number with two instance variables, `realPart` and `imaginaryPart`, each of type `double`. The `ComplexNumber` class also contains a constructor and an implementation of each of the admissible operations just described.

---

[3]These operations can be extended to include a *multiplication operator* * and a *division operator* / with the latter defined for any complex denominator having either a nonzero real part or a nonzero imaginary part, or both. We leave this extension as an exercise.

The constructor involves two `double` parameters and is given by

```
public ComplexNumber(double re, double imag)
{
 realPart = re;
 imaginaryPart = imag;
}
```

Here, `realPart` and `imaginaryPart` are referred to as *implicit parameters,* because they refer to data fields of the object currently under construction. Thus, any `ComplexNumber` object will be constructed with two `double` members, in the order `realPart` and `imaginaryPart`. If the user wishes to construct a `ComplexNumber` object z1 with `4.1` as the value of `realPart` and `-3.8` as the value of `imaginaryPart`, the user will invoke the constructor in the form

```
ComplexNumber z1 = new ComplexNumber(4.1,-3.8);
```

This constructs the `ComplexNumber` object z1 as described in Figure 1.10.

FIGURE 1.10

Java initializes any `double` value by default as `0.0` if the user fails to supply a value. In the case of the constructor for `ComplexNumber`, however, a compile error occurs if the user invokes this constructor using

```
ComplexNumber z2 = new ComplexNumber();
```

assuming that `realPart` and `imaginaryPart` will be assigned `0.0`. In order for this to work, the programmer must explicitly code the default constructor

```
public ComplexNumber(){}
```

as an additional constructor.

Another useful form of a constructor is known as the *copy constructor.* We illustrate this form for the case of the `ComplexNumber` class, assuming that a `ComplexNumber` object z1 already exists. A copy constructor will construct a completely new `ComplexNumber` object containing the same values for `realPart` and `imaginaryPart` as z1; it is invoked using

```
ComplexNumber z3 = new ComplexNumber(z1);
```

The code for the copy constructor is given by

```
public ComplexNumber(ComplexNumber z)
{
```

```
realPart = z.realPart;
imaginaryPart = z.imaginaryPart;
}
```

Here we distinguish between the parameters `realPart` and `z.real-Part` and between `imaginaryPart` and `z.imaginaryPart`. The parameter `realPart` is an example of an implicit parameter because it refers to the object of type `ComplexNumber` under construction, whereas `z.realPart` is an *explicit parameter* because it is a field of the parameter enclosed between parentheses. The same is true of the pair `imaginaryPart` and `z.imaginaryPart`.

Is it possible to apply the `clone()` method defined in `Object` in place of a copy constructor? This might be in the form

```
ComplexNumber z4 = z3.clone();
```

The answer to this question is "no," because the `clone()` method is a `pro-tected`[4] method of `Object`. This implies that this code, even if we cast as

```
ComplexNumber z4 = (ComplexNumber)z3.clone();
```

results in a compile-time error.

There are other alternatives. We note that this is a keyword referring to the object under construction. Thus, for example, the first version of the constructor for `ComplexNumber` could also have been given as

```
public ComplexNumber(double re, double imag)
{
this.realPart = re;
this.imaginaryPart = imag;
}
```

and an alternative form for the copy constructor could be expressed as

```
public ComplexNumber(ComplexNumber z)
{
this.realPart = z.realPart;
this.imaginaryPart = z.imaginaryPart
}
```

An interesting observation about `this` is that it can be used in another way in a constructor. If, for example, a constructor for a class has a first statement involving `this` followed by a parameter list, as in

```
public classA(int i1, int i2)
{
this("classA is",i1,i2);
}
```

---

[4]We will discuss the `protected` access type in detail in Section 2.3.

then this version calls another constructor named classA of the same class (whose name is classA), all of whose components are declared explicitly, such as

```
public classA(String str, int i1, int i2)
{
name = new String(str);
first = i1;
second = i2;
}
```

and where the definition of classA includes the data field (instance variable) declarations

```
private String name;
private int first;
private int second;
```

In this sense, we say that the first version of the constructor is *defined recursively* from the second version.

What about the code for the admissible operations for the complex ADT? For addition, we have

```
public ComplexNumber sum(ComplexNumber z)
{
 ComplexNumber result = new ComplexNumber();
 result.realPart = realPart + z.realPart;
 result.imaginaryPart = imaginaryPart + z.imaginaryPart;
 return result;
}
```

This is applied as z2.sum(z1) for already existing ComplexNumber objects z1, z2. For subtraction, we have

```
public ComplexNumber difference(ComplexNumber z)
  {
   ComplexNumber result = new ComplexNumber();
   result.realPart = realPart - z.realPart;
   result.imaginaryPart = imaginaryPart - z.imaginaryPart;
   return result;
  }
```

This is applied as z1.difference (z2); in order to compute z1 - z2.

The assignment operation is coded as

```
 public ComplexNumber assign(ComplexNumber z)
 {
// ComplexNumber result = new ComplexNumber();
  realPart = z.realPart;
  imaginaryPart = z.imaginaryPart;
```

```
    return this;
}
```

This assumes that each of `z1` and `z2` are already-constructed `ComplexNumber` objects. If we then apply `z2.assign(z1);`, a copy of each of the `realPart` and `imaginaryPart` values of `z1` will be copied into the respective `realPart` and `imaginaryPart` data fields of `z2`.

Testing equality of two `ComplexNumber` values is done using

```
public boolean isEqual(ComplexNumber z)
{
    return ((realPart == z.realPart)
            && (imaginaryPart == z.imaginaryPart));
}
```

and is applied as `z2.isEqual(z1)`. Finally, the code for `printValue()` is

```
public void printValue()
{
    System.out.println(realPart + " + " + imaginaryPart + " i ");
}
```

1.10 Suggested Improvements in the Design of the `Complex` Interface

Our initial design of the `ComplexNumber` class in Section 1.9, although correct and efficient, raises a number of questions. First, we have already commented on the fact that the methods defined for addition, subtraction, and testing equality show one parameter, yet each is viewed mathematically as a *binary function*. Thus, in order for these to be applied as an instance method of `ComplexNumber`, each had to be applied to a single `ComplexNumber` argument as the object being acted upon, with the second argument appearing as a parameter. For example, the sum of the `ComplexNumber` objects `z1` and `z2` has to be expressed either as `z1.sum(z2)` or `z2.sum(z1)` instead of the more legible alternative `sum(z1,z2)`.

The question, then, is whether it is possible for a binary function to be expressed as a method of a class and to display both of its arguments as parameters. In the strict sense of pure instance methods, the answer to this question is "no"; however, Java has a facility that allows for a compromise. Java uses `static` methods for this. To illustrate, the `static` method computing the sum of two `ComplexNumber` parameters can be coded as

```
public static ComplexNumber sum(ComplexNumber arg1, ComplexNumber arg2)
{
ComplexNumber result = new ComplexNumber();
result.realPart = arg1.realPart + arg2.realPart;
```

```
  result.imaginaryPart = arg1.imaginaryPart + arg2.imaginaryPart;
  return result;
}
```

The coding for the method computing the difference of the `ComplexNumber` values can be given by

```
public static ComplexNumber difference(ComplexNumber arg1,
           ComplexNumber arg2)
{
 ComplexNumber result = new ComplexNumber();
 result.realPart = arg1.realPart - arg2.realPart;
 result.imaginaryPart = arg1.imaginaryPart - arg2.imaginaryPart;
 return result;
}
```

For assignment, we can use

```
public static ComplexNumber assign(ComplexNumber z)
{
 ComplexNumber result = new ComplexNumber();
 result.realPart = z.realPart;
 result.imaginaryPart = z.imaginaryPart;
 return result;
}
```

Similarly, the `boolean`-valued method can be rewritten as a binary `static` method, using

```
public static boolean isEqual(ComplexNumber arg1, ComplexNumber arg2)
{
 return ((arg1.realPart == arg2.realPart) &&
      (arg1.imaginaryPart == arg2.imaginaryPart));
}
```

The complete coding of the `ComplexNumber` implementation class can then be given by

```
class ComplexNumber
{
 // Default constructor coded explicitly.
 public ComplexNumber() { }

// Constructor.
 public ComplexNumber(double re, double imag)
 {
  realPart = re;
  imaginaryPart = imag;
 }
```

```
// Copy constructor.
public ComplexNumber(ComplexNumber z)
{
 realPart = z.realPart;
 imaginaryPart = z.imaginaryPart;
}


// Sum of two ComplexNumber values.
public static ComplexNumber sum(ComplexNumber arg1, ComplexNumber arg2)
{
 ComplexNumber result = new ComplexNumber();
 result.realPart = arg1.realPart + arg2.realPart;
 result.imaginaryPart = arg1.imaginaryPart + arg2.imaginaryPart;
 return result;
}


// Difference of two ComplexNumber values.
public static ComplexNumber difference(ComplexNumber arg1,
                ComplexNumber arg2)
{
 ComplexNumber result = new ComplexNumber();
 result.realPart = arg1.realPart - arg2.realPart;
 result.imaginaryPart = arg1.imaginaryPart - arg2.imaginaryPart;
 return result;
}


// Assignment of a ComplexNumber value.
public static ComplexNumber assign(ComplexNumber z)
{
 ComplexNumber result - new ComplexNumber();
 result.realPart = z.realPart;
 result.imaginaryPart = z.imaginaryPart;
 return result;
}


// Testing equality for two ComplexNumber values.
public static boolean isEqual(ComplexNumber arg1, ComplexNumber arg2)
{
 return ((arg1.realPart == arg2.realPart) &&
      (arg1.imaginaryPart == arg2.imaginaryPart));
}


// Output function.
```

```
public void printValue()
{
 System.out.println(realPart + " + " + imaginaryPart + " i ");
}
// Data fields.
private double realPart;
private double imaginaryPart;
}
```

1.11 **Chapter Summary**

Object-oriented software is designed for correctness and efficiency. The most important aspects of object-oriented design (OOD) involve three principles:

- *abstraction*, in which abstract data types (ADTs) are created to aid in the formulation of the solution to the underlying software problem
- *encapsulation* (or *information hiding*), in which the user is shielded from the implementation details of the solution and is granted access only to those components that he or she must apply and nothing more
- *modularity*, in which the problem decomposes into smaller and autonomous units, each of which contributes to the solution and cooperates to accomplish that solution. Modular systems promote *software reuse*, in which a module designed to contribute to the solution of one problem might also aid in the solution of others

The Java language, especially with its support of the methods of OOD, is especially suited to promoting the solution of software problems, applying these design principles.

Classes are generally designed with two major components: the *user interface* and the *implementation part*. Ideally, the user should have access only to the methods described in the user interface. Consequently, the design of that component should be as user friendly as possible. The typical user interface contains a listing of the available instance methods, and the implementation part contains the formal coding of a number of versions of the constructor as well as that for the instance methods described in the user interface and any data fields (instance variables) necessary in describing objects to be constructed from that class.

This chapter concentrated on the design of three examples: the implementation of the stack ADT, the complex number system, and a payroll problem. The stack ADT was eventually implemented as a generic class, using exceptions and exception handlers. The implementation allows for the construction of stack objects that store values of *any* type, simply by instantiating the specific type of the values to be stored on the stack. In the array implementation, an *overflow* condition can occur, in which the `Info` array holding the stack values may be full and an attempt is made to push a new value onto the stack. Besides this, and independent of the implementation, an *underflow* condition is possible in which we attempt either to pop or to retrieve the value at the top of the current stack when that stack is empty.

The design of the class `ComplexNumber` includes some of the more elementary properties of the arithmetic of the complex number system, useful in many application areas. We presented two alternative designs: The first involved defining a number of "pure" instance methods that are non-static, for addition, subtraction, assigning a `ComplexNumber` value to a `ComplexNumber` variable, and a comparison for equality of two complex numbers, with each such complex number viewed as a separate object of the `ComplexNumber` class. Although this design embraced all of the desirable design principles we described earlier, we noted that it was somewhat unnatural because each of these operations are generally described as *binary functions,* requiring two arguments. The second design of the `ComplexNumber` class provides an alternative that expresses each of these operations with two arguments and involves the idea of `static` instance methods of a class. These operations have an implementation that is somewhat closer to their formal mathematical description.

The payroll example shows how it is useful to define `static` data fields as well as `static` methods of a class. There exist a number of special situations in the object-oriented design of solutions to software problems in which the use of such data fields and methods are often indispensable. Data fields (instance variables) declared as `static` have the property that they are stored separately from any of the objects constructed from that class but whose contents are shared by all such objects.

The idea of object-oriented solutions to software problems can include the construction of a *class hierarchy,* with `Object` as the ultimate superclass and with a number of predefined or programmer-defined subclasses. In such situations, objects constructed in any one of the associated subclasses of some hierarchy are said to exhibit an "is a" relationship with any of its superclasses. This idea will be studied in greater detail in Chapter 2.

EXERCISES

1. Design and write code for a driver for the `intStack` interface and the `intArrayStack` implementation class as described in Example 1.5.

2. Using Exercise 1, now replace the programmer-defined `StackException` class by the predefined `ArrayIndexOutOfBoundsException` class.

3. Write the formal code for the static methods difference and isEqual as described in Section 1.10, and then design a driver for this revised version of the ComplexNumber class.

4. Find the exact form of the output that results from executing

```
import java.io.*;


class Rectangle
{
// Constructor
public Rectangle(double lt, double wd)
{
 this.length = lt; this.width = wd;
}
// Perimeter method.
public void perimeter()
{
 System.out.println("Perimeter = " + 2*(length + width));
}
// Area method.
public void area()
{
 System.out.println("Area = " + length * width);
}
// data fields
private double length;
private double width;
} // terminates coding of Rectangle class.

public class ex14
{
 public static void main(String [] args)
 {
  Rectangle rect = new Rectangle(4,6);
  rect.perimeter();
  rect.area();
 } // terminates coding of main method
} // terminates coding of ex14
```

5. Describe the result of executing the following:

```
import java.io.*;

class Rectangle
{
```

```
 public Rectangle(double lt, double wd)
 {
  this("",lt,wd);
 }
 public Rectangle(String st, double lt, double wd)
 {
  name = st;
  length = lt;
  width = wd;
 }
 public double perimeter()
 {
  return 2*length + 2*width;
 }
 private String name;
 private double length, width;
}
public class ex15
{
 public static void main(String [] args)
 {
  Rectangle namedRect = new Rectangle("named",5,6);
  Rectangle unnamedRect = new Rectangle(4,3);
  System.out.println("namedRect perimeter = " + namedRect.perimeter());
  System.out.println("unnamedRect perimeter = " +
                     unnamedRect.perimeter());
 }
}
```

6. Given the following class definition,

```
class counter
{
// Constructor.
public counter()
{
 this.data = 0;
}
// print() method
public void print()
{
 System.out.println(data);
}
// resetData as an internal non-static method
public void resetData(int val)
```

```
    {
     this.data = val;
    }
    // Data field
    private int data;
} // closes text of counter class.
```

a. What is accomplished by constructing an object from this class and then invoking `resetData` for that object?

b. Write a driver for this class, applying `resetData` to the object constructed, using a value of `12`.

7. Suppose we define an ADT for *three-dimensional vectors* with `double`-valued components whose list of admissible operations is defined as follows:

a. *vector addition*, defined as $\langle x_1, y_1, z_1 \rangle + \langle x_2, y_2, z_2 \rangle = \langle x_1 + x_2, y_1 + y_2, z_1 + z_2 \rangle$

b. *vector subtraction*, defined as $\langle x_1, y_1, z_1 \rangle - \langle x_2, y_2, z_2 \rangle = \langle x_1 - x_2, y_1 - y_2, z_1 - z_2 \rangle$

c. *vector cross product*, defined as $\langle x_1, y_1, z_1 \rangle * \langle x_2, y_2, z_2 \rangle = \langle y_1 z_2 - y_2 z_1, x_2 z_1 - x_1 z_2, x_1 y_2 - x_2 y_1 \rangle$

d. *vector assignment*, defined as `w = u`, where `w` is a three-dimensional vector variable and `u` is a three-dimensional vector whose components are copied into the corresponding components of `w`.

e. *vector dot product*, defined as $\langle x_1, y_1, z_1 \rangle * \langle x_2, y_2, z_2 \rangle + x_1 x_2 + y_1 y_2 + z_1 z_2$

f. an *output method*, which prints the values of the three components of any three-dimensional vector.

   Implement this as a class in Java, using instance methods for vector sum, difference, assignment, output, cross product, and dot product.

8. Write a driver for the generic method `swapValues` in which three swaps are attempted: one for `int` values, a second instance for `char` values, and a third instance for `double` values.

9. Extend the definition of the `ComplexNumber` class to include methods implementing multiplication and division. Multiplication is defined by

   `(a + bi)*(c + di) = (ac - bd) + (ad + bc)I`

   and division is defined by

   `(a + bi)/(c + di) = (a + bi)*(c + di)`$^{-1}$

   where `(c + di)`$^{-1}$ is defined as $\dfrac{c}{c^2 + d^2} - \dfrac{d}{c^2 + d^2} i$

   (Here we assume that at least one of `c` and `d` is non-zero).

10. Find the exact form of the output for

```
public static void main(String [] args)
  {
   intPair value1 = new intPair();
```

```
value1.initialize(3);
System.out.print("Originally value1 is the pair: ");
value1.print();
System.out.println("Apply the method increment() to value1:");
value1.increment();
System.out.print("value1 now is the pair: ");
value1.print();
} // closes main method
```

and where `intPair` is defined by the following:

```
class intPair
{
 public void initialize(int b)
  {
   this. second = b;
   this.first = b + 1;
  }

 public intPair increment()
 {
  first++;
  second++;
  return this;
 }

 public intPair retrieve()
 {
  return this;
 }

 public void print()
 {
  System.out.println(first + "," + second);
 }

 // Data fields
 int first, second;
} // terminates text of class intPair
```

11. a. Write an equivalent version of the `intPair` class for `char` values.

b. Can `intPair` be rewritten as a generic class? Explain why, or why not.

12. A *quaternion* is defined as an expression of the form

$a = a_0 + a_1i + a_2j + a_3k$, where a_0, a_1, a_2, a_3 are real numbers.

The *sum* of any two quaternions $a = a_0 + a_1i + a_2j + a_3k$ and $b = b_0 + b_1i + b_2j + b_3k$ is defined as $a + b = (a_0 + b_0) + (a_1 + b_1)i + (a_2 + b_2)j + (a_3 + b_3)k$, and the *difference* is defined as $a - b = (a_0 - b_0) + (a_1 - b_1)i + (a_2 - b_2)j + (a_3 - b_3)k$. Furthermore, their *product* obeys the condition $i^2 = j^2 = k^2 = -1$ and $ij = -ji = k$, $jk = -kj = i$, $ki = -ik = j$; thus,

$$a * b = (a_0b_0 - a_1b_1 - a_2b_2 - a_3b_3) + (a_0b_1 + a_1b_0 + a_2b_3 - a_3b_2)i + (a_0b_2 + a_2b_0 + a_3b_1 - a_1b_3)j + (a_0b_3 + a_3b_0 + a_1b_2 - a_2b_1)k$$

and where we define *equality* for two quaternions by

$a == b$ if and only if $(a_0 == b_0)$ && $(a_1 == b_1)$ && $(a_2 == b_2)$ && $(a_3 == b_3)$.

Design a class for quaternions using three constructors: a default constructor (coded explicitly), one passing four parameters, and a copy constructor. In addition, design methods for addition, subtraction, multiplication, equality, and an output method.

13.   Suppose we have the following class definition:

```
class intClass
{
// Constructor
public intClass(int val)
{
  intValue = val;
}

// Output method.
public void print()
{
  System.out.println("Value of class = " + intValue);
}

// Static method
public static int intCount()
{
  return intCount;
}

// Data fields
private int intValue;
public static int intCount = 0;
} // terminates text of intClass.
```

Find the exact form of the output obtained by executing

```
public static void main(String [] args)
 {
  intClass obj1 = new intClass(5);
  intClass.intCount++;
  intClass obj2 = new intClass(25);
  intClass.intCount++;
  obj1.print();
  obj2.print();
  System.out.print("Current value of intCount = ");
  System.out.println(intClass.intCount);
}
```

14. Look at the following variation of Exercise 6:

```
class counter
{
 // Constructor
 public counter()
 {
  data = 0;
 }

 // Output method.
 public void print()
 {
  System.out.println(data);
 }

 // Static method
 public static void resetData(int val)
 {
  data = val;
 }
 // Data fields
  private static int data;
}
```

and main method

```
public static void main (String [] args)
 {
  counter obj = new counter();
  System.out.print("obj has value = ");
  obj.print();
  counter.resetData(5);
  System.out.print("obj now has value = ");
```

```
    obj.print();
}
```

a. Find the exact form of the output for this program.

b. What happens if we change the data field declaration to

```
private int data;
```

PROGRAMMING PROJECTS

1. Design a class template `rational` implementing the ADT for *rational numbers*. That is, the ADT should define a *constructor* that defines a `rational` object that in turn takes the form of a quotient *a/b* whose numerator is any integer and whose denominator is any integer > 0. Besides, there should be defined an *assignment operator* = that assigns the value of an already-existing `rational` object to another. As well, the usual binary arithmetical operations should be defined for `rational` objects, according to the definitions

   a/b + c/d = (ad + bc)/bd;
   a/b = c/d = (ad − bc)/bd;
   *(a/b) * (c/d) = (ac)/(bd);*
   (a/b) / (c/d) = (ad)/(bc).

   Your code should also define *relational operators* == and < for `rational` objects, according to the definitions

   a/b = c/d if and only if ad = bc;
   a/b < c/d if and only if ad < bc.

   Your coding of this class should take the necessary precautions about zero denominators, and it should reduce any `rational` value to its lowest terms. In the latter case, for example, the `rational` value *15/12* should be reduced to *5/4*. In addition, your code should take all of the necessary precautions regarding the encapsulation of code and information hiding. The class should include an output function that outputs any `rational` value in the form *a/b*, where b is not zero.

   Finally, your code should include a *driver program* that uses all of these facilities.

2. (This project is for those with some prior knowledge of linearly linked lists.) Implement the stack ADT as a class template with the same fundamental set of `public` member functions as those defined for the implementation of stacks as described earlier in this chapter. Thus, a `stack` object for some instantiation of the type parameter `T` is constructed as an initially empty linked list of nodes whose data components will contain specific values of the instantiated type. In addition, when the stack is not empty, the initial node will be viewed as the top of the stack: Therefore, the push operation

will insert a new node at the front of the current linked list, and a pop operation will be implemented (whenever possible) as the removal of that initial node. The test as to whether the current stack is empty will be that of determining whether the current list is null, and the operation that retrieves the top of the current stack, whenever it is nonempty, is implemented as the return of the initial data value of the corresponding node.

Test this version of a stack using the test for balanced parentheses, brackets, and braces for an input character string.

REFERENCES

Gosling, James, Bill Joy, and Guy Steele. 1996. *The Java Language Specification.* Reading, Mass: Addison-Wesley.

Horstmann, Cay S., and Gary Cornell. 2001. *Core Java.* Vol. 1, *Fundamentals.* Englewood Cliffs, NJ: Prentice-Hall.

Parnas, D. L. 1971. "Information Distribution Aspects of Design Methodology." *Proceedings of the IFIP Congress,* Ljubljana, Yugoslavia. pp. 339–44.

CHAPTER 2

Inheritance and Polymorphism

CHAPTER OBJECTIVES

- To introduce the concept of inheritance and class hierarchies and their value in object-oriented design.
- To study the relationship between superclasses and subclasses and the objects constructed from each.
- To distinguish between simple and multiple inheritance and the value of each in problem solving.
- To define the concept of abstract classes and their importance in creating class hierarchies and the run-time selection (polymorphism) of methods defined for objects constructed in such hierarchies.

2.1 Introduction

We have seen that object-oriented design (OOD) models real-world situations with software simulations, using classes and objects. One important aspect of OOD, alluded to in Chapter 1, is its ability to take advantage of relationships between classes, where objects of certain classes share a common set of characteristics. More specifically, an object-oriented design may be applied to display a *hierarchical organization* among classes, in which newly created classes can be derived from existing classes by inheriting characteristics of these existing classes and yet can display certain unique characteristics of their own. Such a design paradigm is known as *inheritance;* Java supports two general classifications of this concept: *simple inheritance* and *multiple inheritance.*

The relationship existing among classes designed using inheritance is commonly referred to as an "is a" relationship. This relationship specifies that one abstraction (realized as a *subclass*) is a particular instance of another (a *parent class*). In Example 1.1, we illustrated this concept by noting that any Square object is a special kind of Rectangle object that, in turn, is a special kind of `GeometricObject`. Similarly, a `Circle` object is another special kind of `GeometricObject`.

Another useful attribute connected with class hierarchies is *polymorphism,* which can be defined as the ability of an entity to assume a number of different forms. In an object-oriented design, we can view polymorphism as the property of a message to be interpreted in a number of different ways, depending on the class in the hierarchy of which the current object is a member. For example, if, in the class hierarchy of Example 1.1, we are currently referencing an object of the `Rectangle` class and we wish to compute its perimeter, the value returned by that object would be computed using the formula `2*length + 2*width`, where the respective values of `length` and `width` would be given as values of the data fields of the class definition of `Rectangle`. If, on the other hand, an object of the `Circle` class is currently being referenced and we wish to compute its perimeter, the value returned would be `PI*diameter`, where the value of `diameter` would be stored in a data field of that object. Our design of the hierarchy of geometrical shapes of Example 1.1 presumes that a `public` method called `perimeter` is defined in each of the classes. This clearly overloads the `perimeter` method because it assumes different forms, depending on which class of the hierarchy was used to construct the object.

As we will see, Java supports a *dynamic* form of polymorphism by permitting a run-time selection of methods associated with the object currently being referenced. In the case of the geometrical hierarchy of Example 1.1, we will observe that the perimeter value returned will depend on the current class of the geometric object chosen during execution of any program in which this hierarchy appears.

We will begin this chapter by investigating ideas associated with class hierarchies and inheritance. We will then turn to a study of how polymorphism is implemented in such hierarchies.

2.2   **Inheritance: Superclasses and Subclasses**

Inheritance is the mechanism of defining new classes by using existing classes as a basis. These new classes are called *subclasses* or *derived classes;* the existing classes are called *superclasses,* or *parent classes,* or *base classes.* Inheritance promotes code reuse, because each subclass inherits the code existing in the parent class unless recoded (overridden) in the subclass. It is generally true that any derived class is developed from one (or possibly more than one) parent class either by adding extra code not appearing in the parent class or by altering code (overloading) existing in the parent class.

We can illustrate this using the geometric hierarchy defined in Example 1.1. If we look at the accompanying *inheritance diagram* given in Figure

1.2, we see that the superclass is identified as `GeometricObject`. We offer no separate interface code here; instead, we simply describe the superclass `GeometricObject` by the following:

```
class GeometricObject
{
 // Perimeter method.
 public double perimeter(){return 0;}
}
```

This class has no `private` components, and it defines a single method `perimeter()`. Using this definition of `GeometricObject`, it is possible for any user method to apply the default constructor for this class to construct an object `obj` and then compute `obj.perimeter()`, returning a value of `0`. This is not a good design for the superclass of this hierarchy, because the description of `GeometricObject` is too general to admit the construction of meaningful objects—after all, what do we mean by a "geometric object"? Is it a circle, or a rectangle, or a square, or perhaps some other figure we have not as yet considered but that may well be included in this hierarchy. Our intention here is to use `GeometricObject` as a *hub* (or *root*) for the subclasses in this hierarchy, where each subclass admits the construction of well-defined and useful geometric objects (such as circles, rectangles, and squares).

Our design shows that `Circle` and `Rectangle` are direct descendants of `GeometricObject`. How do we express this in syntax? In general, to declare that a specific class is a subclass of a given superclass, we require the following syntax:

```
class <className> extends <superclassName>
{
  <body of className>
}
```

where `<className>` is an identifier naming the new class; `<superclass-Name>` is an identifier naming the superclass, which may be predefined or already coded by the programmer; and extends is a Java keyword. `<body of className>` contains all of the instance methods, data fields, and (possibly) `static` methods defining the derived class named by `<className>`. This idea was discussed briefly in Section 1.6 as it applies to programmer-defined exception classes.

In our example of the geometric hierarchy of Example 1.1, we can define

```
class Circle extends GeometricObject
{
 // Explicit constructor.
 public Circle(double d)
```

```
  {
   this.diameter = d;
  }
  // Perimeter method -- overrides inherited perimeter method.
  public double perimeter(){ return PI * diameter; }

  // local data fields
  private double diameter;
  final double PI = 3.14159;
} // completes coding of Circle subclass.¹
```

Similarly, we code `Rectangle` as

```
class Rectangle extends GeometricObject
{
 // Explicit constructor.
 public Rectangle(double lt, double wd)
  {
   this.length = lt;
   this.width = wd;
  }
 // Perimeter method -- overrides inherited perimeter method
 // from GeometricObject superclass.
 public double perimeter(){ return 2*length + 2*width; }

 // local data fields.
 private double length, width;
} // terminates coding of Rectangle subclass.
```

Note that the code for `GeometricObject` contains no explicit form of a constructor. This is because we do not intend to ever have any need to construct a specific object from `GeometricObject`, for the reasons we gave earlier. However, this is not to detract from the possibility of constructing a "default" object from `GeometricObject`. All we need to do is write

```
GeometricObject obj = new GeometricObject();
```

however meaningless this may be. We would judge this to be an example of a poor design, because no such objects should be possible. In Section 2.6, we will improve this design by introducing the concept of *abstract classes and methods,* which, for one thing, will not permit the construction of such meaningless objects as `obj` and still preserve `GeometricObject` as the "hub" of the same geometric hierarchy.

---

[1]The `Math` class contains the predefined constant `PI` that yields the closest approximation to π. This implies that it is not necessary for the programmer to define `PI` as we have done. Instead, we need only rewrite `PI*diameter` as `Math.PI*diameter`.

How do we code `Square`? Observe that `Square` is not a direct descendant of `GeometricObject`, but rather is a direct descendant of `Rectangle`, implementing the idea that any square "is a" kind of rectangle. In fact, we can view any square as a rectangle whose length and width have the same value. To implement this, we override the constructor for `Rectangle`, using `super` as described in Section 1.6, using the special case of the `Rectangle` constructor with equal length and width. The formal coding for `Square` is then given as

```
class Square extends Rectangle
{
// Constructor.
 public Square(double side)
 {
  // Invoking Rectangle constructor.
  super(side,side);
 }
// local data field
 double side;
} // Terminates coding of Square subclass.
```

Is it possible to override this form and instead consider the alternative design for `Square` given by

```
class Square extends Rectangle
{
// Constructor
 public Square(double x)
 {
  side = x;
 }
// Data member
 private double side;
}
```

The answer is "no": the semantics for Java expect a design for `Square` that inherits properties handed down from `Rectangle`, so this design must enforce the "is a" relationship. Hence, any attempt of a user program to construct a `Square` object using

```
public Square(double x)
{
 side = x;
}
```

will generate a compile-time error. Similarly, the attempt to compute the perimeter of a `Square` object using

```
public double perimeter
{
 return 4*side;
}
```

will also fail.

2.3 `public`, `private`, **and** `protected` Access Modifiers

Instance methods of a class are usually defined as `public`, and data fields are ordinarily defined as `private`. These are examples of *access modifiers*, because they describe the mode of access available for these classes and fields. If, for example, we designate a method as `public`, we allow for this method to be inherited by any subclasses of the given class. Because data fields are generally not inherited, they are designated as `private` and are thus inaccessible to any such subclass. As an example, note that the `perimeter()` method is inherited by `Square` from `Rectangle`, while the `length` and `width` fields are inaccessible to any `Square` object. That is, if we attempt to apply either `length` or `width` to any `Square` object, the result does not compile.

EXAMPLE 2.1 Suppose we modify the definition of the `Rectangle` class in the geometrical hierarchy just described to include the additional method `diagonal()`, which produces the length of the diagonal of any `Rectangle` object (see Figure 2.1). The revised version of `Rectangle` then takes the following form:

```
class Rectangle extends GeometricObject
{
```

FIGURE 2.1

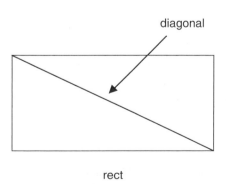

rect

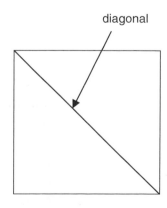

sq

```
// Explicit constructor.
public Rectangle(double lt, double wd)
{
 this.length = lt;
 this.width = wd;
}
// Perimeter method -- overrides inherited perimeter method
// from GeometricObject superclass.
public double perimeter(){ return 2*length + 2*width; }
// Diagonal function.  Inherited by Square subclass of Rectangle.
public double diagonal(){return Math.sqrt(length*length + width*width);}

// local data fields.
private double length, width;
} // terminates coding of Rectangle subclass.
```

The code for the `Square` subclass remains the same. Now execute the main method

```
public static void main(String [] args)
 {
  Circle circ = new Circle(5);
  Rectangle rect = new Rectangle(4,6);
  Square sq = new Square(9);
  System.out.println("Diameter of circ = " + circ.perimeter());
  System.out.println("Diameter of rect = " + rect.perimeter());
  System.out.println("Diameter of sq = " + sq.perimeter());
  System.out.println("Diagonal of rect = " + rect.diagonal());
  System.out.println("Diagonal of sq = " + sq.diagonal());
 } // terminates code of main method
```

The output is

Perimeter of circ = 15.70795
Perimeter of rect = 20.0
Perimeter of sq = 36.0
Diagonal of rect = 7.211102550927978
Diagonal of sq = 12.727922061357855

In fact, Java supports four different access modes for data fields and methods of a class. They are listed here, without any specific order of importance:

- package access
- public access
- private access
- protected access

A *package* in Java is a collection of classes that are connected by some common functionality. These classes may interact with one another, and classes contained in a package may be imported by other classes using the `import` statement whose syntax is given by

```
import java.<packageName>;
```

where `<packageName>` is an identifier naming the package.

Some of the major predefined packages that we might encounter are

- `lang`—for basic language applications
- `util`—for additional useful utilities
- `io`—for input/output facilities
- `text`—for specialized formatting
- `awt`—for graphics and graphical user interfacing
- `awt.event`—for handling events from the keyboard, mouse, and so on
- `applet`—or creating Java programs that run on the Web
- `net`—for networking

Suppose we wish to place a number of classes of our own design into a single named package. We must do two things in this situation:

1. Add a `package` statement at the top of each class to be included in the package.
2. Place the package in an appropriately named location in your computer's file system.

For example, suppose we wish to create a package called `myPackage`, whose contents will consist of three classes named `Class1`, `Class2`, and `Class3`. The `package` statement at the top of each class would be

```
package myPackage;
```

Note that `package` is a new keyword. Thus, the typical syntax of the class defined as `Class1` is

```
package myPackage;
      .

      .

      .

class Class1
{
 <body of Class1>
}
```

Because `myPackage` is a package of our own design, it does not come precompiled in any typical Java development environment (such as jdk version 1.3.1) that you might be using. We must therefore first create the `myPackage` package before the `import` statement

```
import myPackage;
```

will be effective.

If `myPackage` contains several classes, the `import` statement will take the form

```
import myPackage.*;
```

in order to access all of the `public` components of all of the classes of the package. We have already used this form for the predefined `java.io` package as

```
import java.io.*;
```

If, alternatively, the facilities required from the package are all members of a single class `myClass` of `myPackage`, we can still import the package using the "wild card" version above, or use

```
import myPackage.myClass;
```

instead.

The package access mode is the default mode, used when no access modifier is stated. In such a situation, package access permits any data field or method to be accessed by any method in any class contained in the same package. We will discuss packages briefly in Chapter 3.

If a data field or method is designated explicitly using the keyword `public`, such fields or methods can be exported outside the package where they were defined. Thus, any such fields or methods are accessible to any method invoking them. In an inheritance hierarchy, any `public` methods or fields of a superclass are accessible to any class invoking the hierarchy. On the other hand, `private` fields and methods of a class are accessible only to other components of that same class. The `private` protection mode is the preferred access mode for most data fields. In the event that such data is made available for use outside the class where the field is defined, a useful device is to return the data using a `public` instance method defined in that class.

Besides these access modes, Java supports a form of access between `public` and `private`, known as protected access, where `protected` is a new keyword. The `protected` access modifier can be applied equally to instance methods and data fields of a class. Note that access to a `protected` member from within the same package is exactly the same as package access. Thus, using `protected` as an access mode to a component method or a data field of a class contained in a package affects the accessibility of that component from other classes in the same package.

However, access to a `protected` component from classes outside the package containing the class where that component is defined is permitted only when the accessing class is a subclass of the class with the `protected` component. Thus, it is possible to extend the class definitions to include possible `protected` components.

Example 2.2 shows how `protected` members of a superclass are instrumental in the design of a simple geometric hierarchy.

EXAMPLE 2.2   We design a class hierarchy with a superclass called Vertex whose objects are two-dimensional vertices, that is, two-dimensional points in the plane. The constructor for this class requires two double parameters, representing the respective values of the x- and y-coordinates of the point. Vertex also contains a single overloaded output method that returns the values of these coordinates, in order. The syntax for the definition of Vertex is given by the following:

```
class Vertex
{
 // Constructor.
 public Vertex(double x, double y)
 {
  this.xCoord = x;
  this.yCoord = y;
 } // ends constructor code

 // overloaded output function.
 public void output()
 {
  System.out.println("(" + xCoord + "," + yCoord + ")");
 }

 // Data members.
 protected double xCoord, yCoord;
} // terminates text of Vertex superclass.
```

The double-valued data fields xCoord, yCoord are declared as protected, so that their values can be inherited in any of the subclasses to follow. In fact, the hierarchy continues with the definition of the Ellipse subclass. We use the fact that any ellipse is completely characterized by its vertex (the *center* of the ellipse) and by the lengths of its horizontal and vertical axes. The lengths represent the respective horizontal and vertical distances from the center to the periphery of the ellipse.[2] The Ellipse class also contains an overloaded output method yielding the coordinates of the center, and determining whether the major axis (the longer axis) is vertical or horizontal, and similarly for the minor axis (the shorter axis). The class also contains a method for computing the area of an ellipse, using the formula π * (length of horizontal axis) * (length of vertical axis). Ellipse can then be coded as

```
class Ellipse extends Vertex
{
```

[2]We assume the ellipse is not tilted: Its axes are horizontal and vertical, as opposed to those ellipses with nonhorizontal and nonvertical axes.

```
// Constructor.  First two parameters are the coordinates
// of the vertex, and the last two are the respective
// lengths of the axes in the x-direction and y-direction.
public Ellipse(double x, double y, double h, double v)
{
 super(x,y);
 horizAxis = h;
 vertAxis = v;
}

// overloaded output function.  Determines whether the major
// (minor) axis is horizontal (vertical).
public void output()
{
 System.out.print("Ellipse has vertex = (" + xCoord + ",");
 System.out.println(+ yCoord + ")");
 if(horizAxis > vertAxis)
 {
  System.out.print("Major axis is horizontal of length = ");
  System.out.println(horizAxis);
  System.out.print("Minor axis is vertical of length = ");
  System.out.println(vertAxis);
 }
 else
 {
  System.out.println("Major axis is vertical of length = " + vertAxis);
  System.out.println("Minor axis is horizontal of length = ");
  System.out.println(horizAxis);
 }
} // terminates text of output function.

// Computes area of ellipse.
public double area()
{
 return Math.PI * horizAxis * vertAxis;
}

// Protected data members.
protected double horizAxis, vertAxis;
} // terminates code for Ellipse class.
```

It is important for us to note here that, in the coding of the constructor for the `Ellipse` class, we invoke

```
super(x,y);
```

This provides the values of the respective x- and y-coordinates of the vertex. These were inherited from Vertex, because the data fields declared in Vertex were declared as protected, not private. Also, in that same constructor code, the invoking of super appears first, according to important observation (1) stated in Section 1.6 regarding the invocation of super. Finally, we note that the double-valued data fields horizAxis and vertAxis were also declared as protected, because our design calls for a subclass Circle of Ellipse using these components. Simply put, we intend to exploit the idea that any Circle object "is a" special kind of Ellipse object whose major and minor axes are equal in length and are jointly called the radius. Using these ideas, we can then code the Circle subclass as

```java
class Circle extends Ellipse
{
 // Constructor.  Views circle "as an" ellipse with equal
 // vertical and horizontal axes.
 public Circle(double x, double y, double r)
 {
  super(x,y,r,r);
  radius = horizAxis;
 }

 // Overloaded output function.
 public void output()
 {
  System.out.println("Center = (" + xCoord + "," + yCoord + ")");
  System.out.println("Radius = " + radius);
 }

 // Overloaded area function.
 public double area()
 {
  return Math.PI * radius * radius;
 }

 // Data field
 private double radius;
} // terminates coding of Circle subclass.
```

Again, the code for the constructor for Circle begins with the call

```java
super(x,y,r,r);
```

because the values of the respective x- and y-coordinates were passed from Ellipse (which inherited these from Vertex), while the values of the last two parameters (which are equal) were inherited directly from Ellipse.

An exercise at the end of this chapter (see Exercise 2) explores the possibility of omitting the code for the `area()` method appearing in `Circle`, instead of letting that method be inherited directly from `Ellipse`.

The hierarchy diagram for these classes is given in Figure 2.2.

FIGURE 2.2

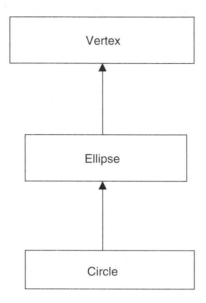

The design of `Circle` represents a variant of the design of `Circle` seen in Section 2.2. In the current design, we characterize any circle by defining its center (or vertex) and its radius. A driver for this hierarchy is given by the following:

```
public static void main(String [] args)
  {
  Vertex vert = new Vertex(0,-3);
  vert.output();
  Ellipse eObject1 = new Ellipse(4,2,6,4);
  eObject1.output();
  System.out.println("Area of first ellipse = " + eObject1.area());
  Ellipse eObject2 = new Ellipse(2,1,5,9);
  eObject2.output();
  System.out.println("Area of second ellipse = " + eObject2.area());
  Circle circ = new Circle(2,-1,6);
  circ.output();
  System.out.println("Area of circle = " + circ.area());
  } // terminates text of main method.
} // terminates text of class Example22.
```

The output resulting from executing this is

```
(0.0,-3.0)
Ellipse has vertex = (4.0,2.0)
Major axis is horizontal of length = 6.0
Minor axis is vertical of length = 4.0
Area of first ellipse = 75.39822368615503
Ellipse has vertex = (2.0,1.0)
Major axis is vertical of length = 9.0
Minor axis is horizontal of length = 5.0
Area of second ellipse = 141.3716694115407
Center = (2.0,1.0)
Radius = 6.0
Area of circle = 113.09733552923255
```

2.4 The Use of `final` Classes and Methods

Occasions might arise in designing a class hierarchy when we wish to prevent a class from having any subclasses. Java has a mechanism for designing such classes: Simply define the class as `final`. For example, if we consider the geometric hierarchy of Example 1.1 and now define the `Rectangle` class as

```
final class Rectangle extends GeometricObject
{
 // Explicit constructor.
 public Rectangle(double lt, double wd)
 {
  this.length = lt;
  this.width = wd;
 }
 // Perimeter method -- overrides inherited perimeter method
 // from GeometricObject superclass.
 public double perimeter(){ return 2*length + 2*width; }

 // local data fields.
 private double length, width;
} // terminates coding of Rectangle subclass.
```

and then we attempt to encode the `Square` class as

```
class Square extends Rectangle
{
 // Constructor.
 public Square(double side)
```

```
{
 // Invoking Rectangle constructor.
 super(side,side);
}
// local data field
double side;
} // Terminates coding of Square subclass.
```

a compile-time error results. Such classes are called *final classes.*

It is also possible to declare a particular method in a Java class as `final`, even though the class in which that method appears is not a final class. All that has to be done is to include the `final` modifier in the method's code. As an example, we can rewrite the formal code for the area method in the `Ellipse` class of Example 2.2 as

```
public final double area()
{
 return Math.PI * horizAxis * vertAxis;
}
```

If we then attempt to encode the `Circle` subclass as before, including the `area()` method for `Circle`, a compile-time error results. If, on the other hand, that code is omitted, `Circle` inherits the `area()` method directly from `Ellipse`, and the area of any `Circle` object is computed as a special kind of `Ellipse` object.

Any method declared as `private` and all methods declared in a final class are implicitly `final` methods, because it is impossible to override such methods. It is not necessary to include the `final` modifier for each method declared in a final class, because Java views such methods as `final` anyway.

The purpose of defining a method as `final` is to prevent any subclasses of the class in which that method appears from overriding it. Also, a constructor cannot be declared `final`, because a constructor is not inherited by any subclass in the strict sense. (Try to inherit a constructor by default.)

2.5 Multiple Inheritance

Each of the situations discussed so far in this chapter involves a form of inheritance in which each subclass is derived from a single parent class. This form of inheritance is known as *simple inheritance.* The property permitting a subclass to be derived from two or more distinct parent classes is known as *multiple inheritance.* In Java, multiple inheritance is permitted for interfaces but not for actual classes. This is because the methods described in an interface never have bodies, but actual classes (some of which are used to implement interfaces) always have bodies. Therefore, if Java were to permit multiple inheritance in this wider sense, two or more classes might have a method with the same name but radically different bodies, causing confusion in the subclass as to which version of the method to employ. This potential source of confusion would not exist in interfaces, because none of the methods included therein have bodies.

Many software designers favor this limited version of multiple inheritance and refer to this as the *mix-in technology.* Using this paradigm, it is possible to define a number of classes that are never intended for the construction of objects of their own but instead are primarily designed to add functionality to existing classes. In the Java environment, this materializes in the form of a number of parent classes, and the subclasses derived from these parent classes inherit a substantially richer level of functionality. In fact, we can use multiple inheritance in this sense to define subclasses that combine the functionality offered by any number of parent classes, and the subclass also has the capability of adding more functionality (in the form of additional methods) of its own.

Example 2.3 provides a simple illustration of this idea.

EXAMPLE 2.3   Suppose we have a multiple inheritance hierarchy as described in Figure 2.3.

FIGURE 2.3

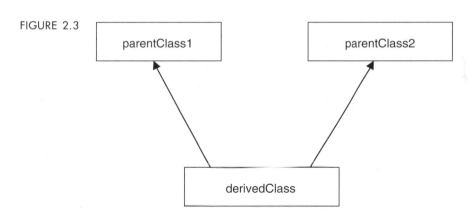

Suppose `parentClass1` defines an interface that inputs and outputs `int` values into an object constructed in `derivedClass`, and `parentClass2` does the same except for `char` values. The interfaces `parentClass1` and `parentClass2` can then be coded as follows:

```
interface parentClass1
{
// Input an int value into an object.
public void setintValue(int value);
// Retrieve an int value from object.
```

```
       public int getintValue();
      } // terminates coding of interface parentClass1

      interface parentClass2
      {
       // Input a char value into an object.
       public void setcharValue(char value);
       // Retrieve a char value from object.
       public char getcharValue();
      } // terminates coding of interface parentClass2

      // Derived class implementing parentClass1, parentClass2
      class derivedClass implements parentClass1, parentClass2
      {
       // Methods appearing in parentClass1
       public void setintValue(int value)
       {
        intValue = value;
       }

       public int getintValue()
       {
        return intValue;
       }

       // Methods appearing in parentClass2
       public void setcharValue(char value)
       {
        charValue = value;
       }

       public char getcharValue()
       {
        return charValue;
       }

       private int intValue;
       private char charValue;
      }   // terminates coding of derivedClass.
```

Suppose we design and execute the main method given by

```
public static void main(String [] args)
 {
  derivedClass obj = new derivedClass();
```

```
obj.setintValue(5);
obj.setcharValue('T');
System.out.println(obj.getintValue() + "," + obj.getcharValue());
} // terminates coding of main method
```

The resulting output is

5,T

Note that the bodies of the methods whose signatures appear in each of the interfaces are filled in within the text of the subclass derived from and implementing these interfaces.

2.6 Abstract Classes

In referring to the geometric hierarchy of Section 2.2, we commented that the design was not satisfactory primarily because it is possible to construct concrete objects from the GeometricObject class. Recall that the reason for including GeometricObject in our design was that it serves as a *root* (or *hub*) for the remaining subclass in the hierarchy: Rectangle, Square, and Circle. In principle, because there are no concrete examples of pure "geometric objects," we should be able to mimic this by not allowing the construction of any specific objects in GeometricObject.

In general, in many inheritance hierarchies, as we move up the hierarchy from subclass to parent class the more general and more abstract the classes become. It may well be the case (as is true for the geometric hierarchy described earlier) that the root class becomes so general that it serves as a basis for all the other classes and it has no meaningful objects of its own. Any methods described in this base class must then be treated abstractly, with the understanding that they will be overridden in those subclasses of the hierarchy that construct meaningful and concrete objects. In such a situation, Java allows for the construction of *abstract classes,* and any method appearing in such a class is regarded as an *abstract method*. These abstract methods will be overridden in subclasses in the hierarchy. In fact, we can view any abstract method as one whose implementation is deferred until it is overridden by a specific version in a subclass. For this reason, such methods are also called *deferred methods.*

The syntax for the definition of an abstract class is

```
abstract class <className>
{
    <classBody>
}
```

where abstract is a new keyword, <className> is as before, and <classBody> can contain abstract methods and instance variables. An abstract class whose <classBody> consists of nothing but abstract methods has the same behavior as an interface.

An abstract method has the syntax

```
public abstract <returnType> <methodName>([<formalParameterList>]);
```

or

```
abstract public <returnType> <methodName>([<formalParameterList>]);
```

Thus, if it exists at all, <formalParameterList>, contained within enclosing parentheses, is followed immediately by a semicolon and has no body. An example of an abstract method is given by

```
public abstract double area();
```

Abstract methods can appear only within the text of an abstract class. An example of an abstract class definition is given by

```
abstract class GeometricObject
{
 public abstract double area();
 public abstract double perimeter();
}
```

As is the case with interfaces, it is not possible to construct an object from an abstract class. In addition, a subclass of an abstract class must provide an implementation of each of the abstract methods defined in the abstract superclass, unless the subclass is also an abstract class. Ultimately, the inheritance hierarchy terminates with a sequence of subclasses that are *concrete* (that is, contain no abstract methods).

This is exactly what we were looking for in our geometric hierarchy, because declaring GeometricObject as abstract prohibits the construction of meaningless objects from that class. As well, the remaining subclasses in that hierarchy (Circle, Rectangle, Square) are all concrete and contain implementations of the abstract methods described in GeometricObject. Example 2.4 illustrates these ideas.

EXAMPLE 2.4 The following hierarchy represents an improvement in the design described in Example 2.1. Unlike the original design, GeometricObject contains abstract methods for computing both the area and the perimeter of any concrete object in the hierarchy. The text for GeometricObject is now

```
abstract class GeometricObject
{
 // Abstract methods for computing the area and perimeter
 // of any concrete geometric object in the hierarchy.
 public abstract double area();
 public abstract double perimeter();
} // terminates definition of GeometricObject class.
```

The text of each of the subclasses in the hierarchy is given as

```
// Rectangle class as a concrete subclass of GeometricObject
class Rectangle extends GeometricObject
{
 // Constructor
 public Rectangle(double lt, double wd)
 {
  this.length = lt;
  this.width = wd;
 }

 // Perimeter method.
 public double perimeter()
 {
  return 2*length + 2*width;
 }

 // Area method.
 public double area()
 {
  return length * width;
 }

 // Data fields.
 private double length, width;

} // terminates definition of Rectangle subclass.

// Square class as a (concrete) subclass of Rectangle
class Square extends Rectangle
{
 // Constructor.
 public Square(double side)
 {
  super(side,side);
 }

 // Data field
 double side;
} // terminates definition of Square subclass.

// Circle class as a concrete subclass of GeometricObject.
class Circle extends GeometricObject
{
```

```
                  // Constructor.
                  public Circle(double rad)
                  {
                   radius = rad;
                  }

                  // Perimeter method.
                  public double perimeter()
                  {
                   return 2 * Math.PI * radius;
                  }

                  // Area method.
                  public double area()
                  {
                   return Math.PI * radius * radius;
                  }

                  // Data field.
                  private double radius;
                  } // terminates definition of Circle subclass.
```

A class should be declared as abstract only if our design is intended to create subclasses of that class to complete its implementation. This was our intent when we redesigned the geometric hierarchy in this section. Another example of a possible redesign of a hierarchy is that for the hierarchy involving the Vertex superclass, with subclasses Ellipse and Circle, of Example 2.2.

EXAMPLE 2.5 In our earlier design of the geometric hierarchy in Example 2.2, Vertex was a concrete class containing a constructor and an overloaded version of an output method that outputs the coordinates of any Vertex object. In fact, this class did nothing more than produce a pair of coordinates for the center of any Ellipse or Circle object. Thus, constructing specific objects of the Vertex class contributes nothing of any value to the hierarchy. The sole purpose of this class is to establish a hub for the hierarchy. Consequently, in the presence of abstract classes and methods, it would be more sensible to redefine Vertex as an abstract class, using it as a hub for the current sequence of classes in the hierarchy and for other classes we might wish to adjoin as additional classes in the hierarchy. We will do so for a version of Rectangle, in which the four vertices of any Rectangle object are input. The new hierarchy diagram is pictured in Figure 2.4.

FIGURE 2.4

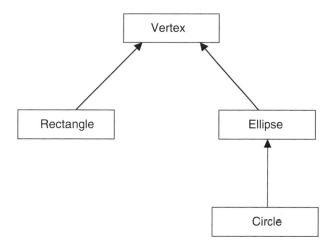

The formal coding details of `Vertex` are given by

```
abstract class Vertex
{
 abstract public void output();
}
```

Note that this version of `Vertex` does not contain any `protected` data fields defining the coordinates of any `Vertex` object. This will instead appear in the `Ellipse` and `Rectangle` subclasses whose formal code is

```
// Subclass Ellipse.
class Ellipse extends Vertex
{
 // Constructor.  First two parameters are the coordinates
 // of the vertex, and the last two are the respective
 // lengths of the axes in the x-direction and y-direction.
 public Ellipse(double x, double y, double h, double v)
 {
  xCoord = x;
  yCoord = y;
  horizAxis = h;
  vertAxis = v;
 }

 // overloaded output function.  Determines whether the major
 // (minor) axis is horizontal (vertical).
 public void output()
 {
  System.out.print("Ellipse has vertex = (" + xCoord + ",");
  System.out.println(+ yCoord + ")");
  if(horizAxis > vertAxis)
```

```
 {
  System.out.println("Major axis is horizontal of length = " + horizAxis);
  System.out.println("Minor axis is vertical of length = " + vertAxis);
 }
 else
 {
  System.out.println("Major axis is vertical of length = " + vertAxis);
  System.out.println("Minor axis is horizontal of length = " + horizAxis);
 }
} // terminates text of output function.


// Computes area of ellipse.
public double area()
{
 return Math.PI * horizAxis * vertAxis;
}


// Protected data members.
 protected double xCoord, yCoord, horizAxis, vertAxis;
} // terminates code for Ellipse class
```

The definition of `Circle` as a subclass of `Ellipse` is essentially that of Example 2.2, except that the constructor uses the fact that the coordinates of the center of any `Circle` object is derived directly from `Ellipse`, because `Vertex` has no data fields.

The `Rectangle` class has a `private` data field section defining the respective x- and y-coordinates of the four vertices of any `Rectangle` object. We have omitted the possibility of checking whether the user has input the vertices of the rectangle properly, leaving the details as an exercise. This implementation depends on the order of initialization of the parameters representing the coordinates of the vertices, and it assumes that these have been input in order in a clockwise (or counterclockwise) fashion and that the objects constructed from this class are rectangles with two vertical and two horizontal edges. The coding for `Rectangle` is then given as

```
// Rectangle class as a subclass of Vertex.
class Rectangle extends Vertex
{
 // Constructor.  Constructs Rectangle object, given four sets
 // of coordinates for its vertices.
 public Rectangle(double x1, double y1, double x2, double y2,
                  double x3, double y3, double x4, double y4)
 {
  xCoord1 = x1; yCoord1 = y1;
  xCoord2 = x2; yCoord2 = y2;
```

```
 xCoord3 = x3; yCoord3 = y3;
 xCoord4 = x4; yCoord4 = y4;
} // terminates coding of constructor for Rectangle.

// Overloaded output method.
public void output()
{
 System.out.println("Coordinates of vertices for rectangle are:");
 System.out.println("First vertex = (" + xCoord1 + "," + yCoord1 + ")");
 System.out.println("Second vertex = (" + xCoord2 + "," + yCoord2 + ")");
 System.out.println("Third vertex = (" + xCoord3 + "," + yCoord3 + ")");
 System.out.println("Fourth vertex = (" + xCoord4 + "," + yCoord4 + ")");
} // terminates text for output method.

// Overloaded area method.
public double area()
{
 return Math.abs((xCoord2 - xCoord1)*(yCoord3 - yCoord2));
}

// Data fields.  Defined here as private, but if design calls for
// a Square subclass of Rectangle, these will be redefined as protected.
private double xCoord1, yCoord1, xCoord2, yCoord2, xCoord3, yCoord3,
 xCoord4, yCoord4;
} // Terminates code for Rectangle class.
```

You should write a driver for this revised hierarchy and also explore the possibility of adjoining a Square subclass of Rectangle whose objects are those rectangles with all sides of equal length. This again uses the "is-a" relationship.

2.7 **Polymorphism**

We can define *polymorphism* as an entity's ability to assume a number of different forms. In the context of OOD, this can be viewed as the ability of the value of an object variable (that is, a variable capable of referencing objects in a class) to take on different forms. In other words, polymorphism is a means of providing different meanings to a message by localizing the response to the type of data being processed. For example, we consider the instruction in a program to compute the area of some two-dimensional geometric object. A different response occurs if the values involved are objects constructed from Square or Rectangle or from Ellipse or Circle. Thus, we have overloaded the area() method so that we can apply `obj.area()` to objects coming from any one of `Square`, `Rectangle`, `Ellipse`, or `Circle`. Another example of an overloaded method whose value depends on the type of object constructed is the function `output()` described in Example 2.2.

Generic classes and methods provide another form of polymorphism, depending on the value(s) assigned to specify `Object`. The decision as to the specific form assumed by the operation is decided upon at *compile time*, that is, as the underlying code is compiled. This form of polymorphism is commonly called *static binding* (or *compile-time polymorphism*).

Besides this, Java offers another form of polymorphism known as *runtime polymorphism* (or *dynamic binding*). This version permits the choice of an appropriate instance method from among those appearing in a superclass of some hierarchy and those with the same name in a subclass *during program execution*. In order to accomplish this, Java supplies the operator `instanceof`, which is also a keyword, and with syntax

```
<instanceVariable> instanceof <className>
```

where `<instanceVariable>` is an identifier assuming the role of an instance variable of some concrete class or of some generic class (such as `Object` or `Comparable`), and where `<className>` is an identifier naming some class of objects. This expression assumes a `boolean` value.

For example, suppose we declare an array of values of type `Object`, such as

```
Object objArr[] = new Object[3];
```

An array such as `objArr` is called a *generic array*, because its components might involve different kinds of objects. That is, `objArr[0]` might be a `String` value, while `objArr[1]` might be of type `Double`, and `objArr[2]` might be a `Rectangle` object. We can then use `instanceof` to determine the type of object stored in that component, and we can then process that component accordingly. This can apply in the form of a conditional beginning with the clause

```
if(objArr[index] instanceof <className>)
   <process according to methods described in class <className>>;
else
   <take alternative action>;
```

The alternative action can take the form of throwing some appropriate exception or some other appropriate alternative. Example 2.6 illustrates these ideas.

EXAMPLE 2.6   We define two classes, `baseClass` and `derivedClass`, with the latter defined as a subclass of the former. Each of these classes constructs objects with a single `char`-valued data field, and each contains a method `getValue()` (`derivedClass` inherits this method from `baseClass`) permit-

ting the retrieval of the char value stored in each object. The code for the
two classes is given as

```
class baseClass
{
 // Constructor.
 public baseClass(char ch)
 {
  chValue = ch;
 }
 // Retrieves data value.
 public char getValue()
 {
  return chValue;
 }
 // Data field.
 protected char chValue;
} // terminates coding of baseClass.


// Subclass derivedClass.
class derivedClass extends baseClass
{
 // Constructor
 public derivedClass(char ch)
 {
  super(ch);
 }
} // terminates coding of derivedClass
```

The reason for declaring the char-valued data field chValue as protected in baseClass is to allow any constructed object of derivedClass
to inherit that value.

Now suppose the main method is coded as

```
public static void main(String [] args)
 {
  // Declare generic array.
  Object objArr[] = new Object[2];
  // Instantiate generic array components.
  objArr[0] = new baseClass('b');
  objArr[1] = new derivedClass('d');
  // Execute for-loop
  for(int index = 0; index <= 1; ++index)
   if(objArr[index] instanceof derivedClass)
   {
```

```
   derivedClass obj = (derivedClass)objArr[index];
   System.out.print("Outputting value " + obj.getValue());
   System.out.println(" inside derivedClass");
  }
 else if(objArr[index] instanceof baseClass)
 {
  baseClass obj = (baseClass)objArr[index];
  System.out.print("Outputting value " + obj.getValue());
  System.out.println(" inside baseClass");
 }
 else
 {
 System.out.println("Current object is neither in baseClass");
 System.out.println("nor in derivedClass");
 }
} // terminates main method
```

Executing this code produces the output

Outputting value b inside baseClass
Outputting value d inside derivedClass

This example illustrates run-time polymorphism, because the decision as to which of the two classes applies to the appropriate `objArr` component occurs during execution of the `for`-loop and at no earlier point during computation. It is important to design the conditional so that the `derivedClass` situation appears as the `if`-clause, and that of `baseClass` appears as the alternative. If these are switched, the output states that each of b and d are values in `baseClass`. Compare this with the output obtained from executing the code appearing in Exercise 9 at the end of this chapter. The distinction lies in the observation that a *compile-time* decision occurs in the latter case.

EXAMPLE 2.7   The following implements run-time polymorphism on the geometric hierarchy described in Example 2.4. The main method accomplishing this is

```
public static void main(String [] args)
 {
  Rectangle newRect = new Rectangle(7.0,2.0);
  Square newSq = new Square(4.0);
  Circle newCirc = new Circle(5.0);
  Object arr[] = new Object[3];
  arr[0] = newRect;
  arr[1] = newSq;
  arr[2] = newCirc;
  for(int index = 0;index < arr.length;++index)
```

```
if(arr[index] instanceof Square)
{
 System.out.println("Component " + index + " is a member of Square");
 System.out.println("Its area is " + newSq.area());
 System.out.println("and its perimeter is " + newSq.perimeter());
}
else if(arr[index] instanceof Rectangle)
{
 System.out.println("Component " + index + " is a member of
                     Rectangle");
 System.out.println("Its area is " + newRect.area());
 System.out.println("and its perimeter is " + newRect.perimeter());
}
else if(arr[index] instanceof Circle)
{
 System.out.println("Component " + index + " is a member of Circle");
 System.out.println("Its area is " + newCirc.area());
 System.out.println("and its perimeter is " + newCirc.perimeter());
}// terminates if-clause and for-loop
} // terminates text of main method
```

The output obtained from executing this is

```
Component 0 is a member of Rectangle
Its area is 14.0
and its perimeter is 18.0
Component 1 is a member of Square
Its area is 16.0
and its perimeter is 16.0
Component 2 is a member of Circle
Its area is 78.53981633974483
and its perimeter is 31.41592653589793
```

2.8   Implications of Inheritance and Polymorphism for Software Engineering

Inheritance is a design paradigm promoting *code reuse*, which is highly desirable from the standpoint of efficiency. In fact, most software problems emerging in the contemporary commercial environment are solvable by observing that the problem domain consists of a number of subproblems whose solution generally involves the design of class hierarchies. Each such hierarchy begins with a superclass and a number of subclasses, each of which contributes to the solution of the original problem and for which an "is-a" relationship exists with the superclass. This is certainly the case with the geometric hierarchies studied in this chapter. In each case, the respective classes `GeometricObject` and `Vertex` were designed optimally as abstract classes, with a number of concrete subclasses.

A sensible decomposition of a simple inheritance hierarchy also promotes the inclusion of new subclasses into the original hierarchy without causing a major revision of the existing code. We can demonstrate this using the geometric hierarchy described in Example 2.4, where we now consider appending a new subclass of `Rectangle` called `RightTriangle`. The hierarchical diagram associated with this new design is described in Figure 2.5.

FIGURE 2.5

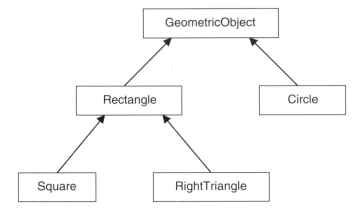

A key observation underlying this new design is that we can consider any right triangle as half a rectangle, with the diagonal of the associated rectangle also serving as the hypotenuse of the triangle, as in Figure 2.6.

FIGURE 2.6

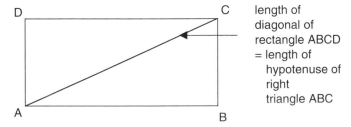

The new design requires that we add another method called `diagonal()` to the list of existing methods for `Rectangle`, with code given by

```
public double diagonal()
```

```
{
 return Math.sqrt(length*length + width*width);
}
```

as described in Example 2.1. Any `Square` object automatically inherits this method—consequently, there is no need to include it explicitly among the list of methods available in `Square`. In fact, we can view the coding of the `Square` class as

```
class Square extends Rectangle
{
 // Constructor.
 public Square(double side)
 {
  super(side,side);
 }
 // Data field.
 Double side;
}
```

Each of the perimeter, area, and diagonal methods is inherited from the `Rectangle` superclass. The coding of the new `RightTriangle` class is given by

```
class RightTriangle extends Rectangle
{
 // Constructor
 public RightTriangle(double lt, double wd)
 {
  super(lt,wd);
 }
 // Perimeter method
 public double perimeter()
 {
  return length + width + Math.sqrt(length*length + width*width);
 }
 // Area method.  Uses the fact that the area of any right triangle
 // is half of the area of its associated rectangle.
 public double area()
 {
  return super.area()/2;
 }
 // Returns length of hypotenuse.
 public double hypotenuse()
 {
  return Math.sqrt(length*length + width*width);
```

```
 }
 // Data fields inherited from Rectangle.
} // closes text of RightTriangle class.
```

In order for the data fields `length`, `width` to be inherited from Rectangle, they must be declared in `Rectangle` as `protected`.

In the case of multiple inheritance as a problem-solving tool, the relationship between a subclass and several distinct parent classes causes a number of conceptual complications. First, the "is-a" relationship is unclear, because no single parental attribute exists between parent and base classes. Second, in principle, when an object is constructed in a subclass that is inherited from several parents, the object is the summation (or absorption) of objects that are constructible from each of the parents. Such an object can be viewed as a form from each of its parent classes. The behavior of this object has to be carefully controlled—otherwise, the original design plan becomes cloudy at best. All of this notwithstanding, a carefully controlled environment involving multiple inheritance becomes an important design paradigm promoting code reuse, and it often represents an extremely powerful and useful alternative to simple inheritance.

The idea of run-time polymorphism represents another extremely useful and efficient design paradigm. When programs involving hierarchies involve polymorphism, the text of the user program assumes an appearance that is relatively easy to follow. This simplification also creates simpler venues for testing, debugging, and maintaining code. When designing and writing code using polymorphism, the design of the underlying classes remains general and close to the theoretical concepts being implemented, and it also permits the user's code invoking this design to become more specific, using instances of the application domain. This results in a software design that is easier to maintain and that has relatively few bugs.

2.9 **Chapter Summary**

This chapter concentrated on two major tools of OOD: inheritance and polymorphism. Inheritance is the facility enabling a new class to be derived from already existing classes, in which we designate the existing class as the *superclass* (or *parent class,* or *base class*) and the newly defined class as the *subclass* (or *derived class*). In defining the subclass, the methods and (possibly) the data fields of the superclass are present as methods and data fields of the subclass, unless overridden by a new definition of the method or the presence of new data fields in the subclass. Accordingly, we say that an "is-a" relation exists for any object constructed in the subclass having the corresponding superclass as its parent.

A subclass can be designed from a single existing base class using the syntax

```
class <className> extends (superclassName>
{
 <body of className>
}
```

This establishes a state of *simple inheritance* between the subclass named by <className> and the superclass named by <superclassName>.

A public member of a class, whether in the form of a method or a data field, is accessible throughout its scope, including any user methods. A private member is accessible only to methods defined in its own class. A protected member is a compromise between public and private members: Such a member is accessible to other methods within its class and to any class immediately derived from that class.

We can designate a class as final if our intention is to prohibit the design of any potential subclass derived from that class. This is accomplished by inserting the final keyword in the class definition, as in

```
final class Rectangle extends GeometricObject
{
 <body of Rectangle>
}
```

We can also designate a method of a class as final, although the class in which that method appears might not be a final class. The programmer simply inserts final in that method's code, as in

```
public final double area()
{
 return Math.PI * horizAxis * vertAxis;
}
```

Any method or data field appearing in the body of a final class is automatically designated as final.

Multiple inheritance allows for the possibility of a class to be a subclass of two or more distinct parent classes. Java supports a somewhat limited form of multiple inheritance, applying the concept to interfaces. For example, if we have the sequence of interfaces

```
interface parent1
{
 <text of parent1>
}

interface parent2
{
```

```
 <text of parent2>
}



       .

       .

       .


interface parentn
{
 <text of parentn>
}
```

then the subclass `derivedClass` derived from `parent1, parent2, . . . ,`
`parentn` involves the syntax

```
class derivedClass implements parent1, parent2, . . . , parentn
{
 <body of derivedClass>
}
```

Any subclass derived by simple inheritance can have its own specific
constructors, each of which invokes a constructor defined in its parent
class. The syntax for such a constructor uses `super`, as illustrated in the
geometric hierarchy of Example 1.1 by

```
class Square extends Rectangle
{
 // Constructor.
 public Square(double side)
 {
  super(side,side);
 }
 // Local data field.
 double side;
}
```

We can regard a subclass as an implementation of a subtype of a data
type implemented by the parent class. In view of this, it is possible to assign the value of any object constructed in a subclass to an object of the
parent class, but not conversely.

Java permits the definition of `abstract` classes and methods as useful
design tools. The purpose of defining a class to be `abstract` is to allow it
to serve as a "hub" class, from which concrete classes can be derived as subclasses. This also permits a sensible construction of class hierarchies, as was
done in the two cases described in this chapter: the hierarchy containing
the `abstract` version of `GeometricObject` and that for the `abstract` version of `Vertex`.

Any methods appearing in an `abstract` class are designated as `abstract` methods. An `abstract` class and an `abstract` method in some class include the `abstract` keyword, as in

```
abstract class GeometricObject
{
 // Abstract methods for computing the area and the perimeter
 // of any concrete geometric object in the hierarchy.
 public abstract double area();
 public abstract double perimeter();
}
```

Note that an `abstract` method has no body and is designed with the intention that a subclass will contain a concrete version of this method.

Java also supports the run-time selection of objects of varying types to be processed, whether these objects appear in subclasses or a parent class of some class hierarchy. This is usually done using generic containers such as `Object`-valued arrays whose components are then instantiated and selected for processing using the predefined `instanceof` method. This process is commonly defined as *run-time polymorphism*, and it represents a major tool in contemporary commercial software design.

Inheritance is an important tool for software engineering, because it promotes code reuse. Furthermore, it allows for an organized way of separating more general forms of modules into simpler and more specific forms, using the idea that a parent class is a hub for a number of more specific subclasses that solve a number of subproblems generated by this decomposition. Facilities permitting the implementation of encapsulation, inheritance, and polymorphism are critical in contemporary OOD.

EXERCISES

1. What will happen if we rewrite the `Square` class in the geometrical hierarchy described in Section 2.2 by

```
 class Square extends Rectangle
 {
 // Constructor.
 public Square(double side)
 {
  // Invoking Rectangle constructor.
  super(side,side);
 }

 // Perimeter method for Square using perimeter method
 // inherited from Rectangle.
```

```
      public double perimeter()
      {
       return super.perimeter();
      }
      // local data field
      double side;
    } // Terminates coding of Square subclass.
```

2. In the geometric hierarchy described in Section 2.2, omit the code of the `area()` method in `Circle`, and use the same driver to test whether the resulting coding of the hierarchy still produces the area of a `Circle` object.

3. In the geometric hierarchy described in Example 2.2 in Section 2.3, rewrite the `area()` method of `Ellipse` as `final`, omit the coding of `area()` in `Circle`, and then show that the area of any `Circle` object is correctly computed as the area of that same object, now viewed "as a kind of" `Ellipse` object.

4. Show that a compile-time error results in the `GeometricObject` hierarchy when we erase the specific constructor for `Square` and we then attempt to construct `Square` objects using the constructor defined in `Rectangle`. This illustrates the fact that constructors of a class are not inherited by any of its subclasses.

5. Here is another example of multiple inheritance as implemented in Java. This version not only uses `parentClass1`, `parentClass2`, but `derivedClass` also provides additional functionality. Trace the code and give the exact form of the output:

```
interface parentClass1
{
 public void setintValue(int value);
 public int getintValue();
} // terminates coding of interface parentClass1

interface parentClass2
{
 public void setcharValue(char value);
 public char getcharValue();
} // terminates coding of interface parentClass2

class derivedClass implements parentClass1, parentClass2
{
 // Methods appearing in parentClass1
 public void setintValue(int value)
 {
  intValue = value;
 }
```

```java
public int getintValue()
{
 return intValue;
}

// Methods appearing in parentClass2
public void setcharValue(char value)
{
 charValue = value;
}

public char getcharValue()
{
 return charValue;
}

// Methods defined in derivedClass
public void setdblValue(double value)
{
 dblValue = value;
}

public double getdblValue()
{
 return dblValue;
}

private int intValue;
private char charValue;
private double dblValue;
}  // terminates coding of derivedClass.

// Driver method
public static void main(String [] args)
{
  derivedClass obj = new derivedClass();
  obj.setintValue(5);
  obj.setcharValue('T');
  obj.setdblValue(7.664);
  System.out.print(obj.getintValue() + "," + obj.getcharValue());
  System.out.println( "," + obj.getdblValue());
} // terminates coding of main method
```

6. Repeat Exercise 5, but now consider a third interface parentClass3 whose functionality is exactly the same as each of parentClass1, parentClass2, except for double values. In addition, derivedClass no longer has any methods except those implemented from the three interfaces. Show that the driver given in Exercise 5 produces the same output.

7. Show that the following code represents an improvement of the design of Example 2.2, using abstract classes and methods. Show that this version produces the same output as that of Example 2.2, except that no possible objects are constructed from Vertex.

```
abstract class Vertex
{
 // Abstract overloaded output method.
 abstract public void output();


 // Data members.
 protected double xCoord, yCoord;
} // terminates text of Vertex superclass.


// Subclass Ellipse.
class Ellipse extends Vertex
{
 // Constructor.  First two parameters are the coordinates
 // of the vertex, and the last two are the respective
 // lengths of the axes in the x-direction and y-direction.
 public Ellipse(double x, double y, double h, double v)
 {
  xCoord = x;
  yCoord = y;
  horizAxis = h;
  vertAxis = v;
 }


 // overloaded output function.  Determines whether the major
 // (minor) axis is horizontal (vertical).
 public void output()
 {
  System.out.print("Ellipse has vertex = (" + xCoord + ",");
  System.out.println(+ yCoord + ")");
  if(horizAxis > vertAxis)
  {
   System.out.println("Major axis is horizontal of length = " + horizAxis);
   System.out.println("Minor axis is vertical of length = " + vertAxis);
  }
```

```
  else
  {
   System.out.println("Major axis is vertical of length = " + vertAxis);
   System.out.println("Minor axis is horizontal of length = " + horizAxis);
  }
 } // terminates text of output function.

 // Computes area of ellipse.
 public double area()
 {
  return Math.PI * horizAxis * vertAxis;
 }

 // Protected data members.
 protected double horizAxis, vertAxis;
} // terminates code for Ellipse class

// Circle class as a subclass of Ellipse.
class Circle extends Ellipse
{
 // Constructor.  Views circle "as an" ellipse with equal
 // vertical and horizontal axes.
 public Circle(double x, double y, double r)
 {
  super(x,y,r,r);
  radius = horizAxis;
 }

 // Overloaded output function.
 public void output()
 {
  System.out.println("Center = (" + xCoord + "," + yCoord + ")");
  System.out.println("Radius = " + radius);
 }

 // Overloaded area function.
 public double area()
 {
  return Math.PI * radius * radius;
 }

 // Data field
 private double radius;
} // terminates coding of Circle subclass.
```

8. Extend the hierarchy described in Example 2.5 to include a `Square` subclass of `Rectangle`.

9. Suppose `baseClass` and `derivedClass` are coded exactly as in Example 2.6. Show that the execution of the main method

```java
public static void main(String [] args)
  {
    Object objArr[] = new Object[2];
    // Instantiate generic array components.
    objArr[0] = new baseClass('b');
    objArr[1] = new derivedClass('d');
    if(objArr[0] instanceof baseClass)
    {
        baseClass obj = (baseClass)objArr[0];
        System.out.print("Outputting value " + obj.getValue());
        System.out.println(" inside baseClass");
    }
    if(objArr[1] instanceof derivedClass)
    {
     derivedClass obj = (derivedClass)objArr[1];
     System.out.print("Outputting value " + obj.getValue());
     System.out.println(" inside derivedClass");
    }
  }
```

produces the same output as the main method of Example 2.6.

10. Extend the hierarchy described in Example 2.4 in several ways:
    a. Introduce a new subclass of `Rectangle` called `RightTriangle`.
    b. Include a method in `Rectangle` called `diagonal()`, returning a `double` value, which is the length of the diagonal of any `Rectangle` object. This method is inherited by `Square` and `RightTriangle`.
    c. The diagonal method is renamed as `hypotenuse()` in `RightTriangle`.
    d. The data fields of `Rectangle` are now declared as `protected` and are inherited by `RightTriangle`.

11. Use the hierarchy developed in Exercise 10 and apply

```java
public static void main(String [] args)
  {
    // Create four-component generic array.
    Object objArr[] = new Object[4];
    // Create Square, Rectangle, Circle, RightTriangle objects
    Rectangle newRect = new Rectangle(7.0,2.0);
    Square newSq = new Square(4.0);
    Circle newCirc = new Circle(5.0);
    RightTriangle newRtTri = new RightTriangle(3.0,4.0);
```

```
  // Instantiate objArr components
  objArr[0] = newRect;
  objArr[1] = newSq;
  objArr[2] = newCirc;
  objArr[3] = newRtTri;

  // Polymorphic selection.
  for(int index = 0; index < objArr.length; ++index)
   if(objArr[index] instanceof Square)
   {
    System.out.println("Component " + index + " is a member of Square");
    System.out.println("Its area is " + newSq.area());
    System.out.println("Its perimeter is " + newSq.perimeter());
    System.out.println("and its diagonal length is " + newSq.diagonal());
   }
   else if(objArr[index] instanceof RightTriangle)
   {
   System.out.println("Component " + index + " is a RightTriangle object");
   System.out.println("Its area is " + newRtTri.area());
   System.out.println("Its perimeter is " + newRtTri.perimeter());
   System.out.println("and its hypotenuse is " + newRtTri.hypotenuse());
   }
   else if(objArr[index] instanceof Rectangle)
   {
    System.out.println("Component " + index + " is a member of Rectangle");
    System.out.println("Its area is " + newRect.area());
    System.out.println("Its perimeter is " + newRect.perimeter());
    System.out.println("and its diagonal length is " + newRect.diagonal());
   }
   else if(objArr[index] instanceof Circle)
   {
   System.out.println("Component " + index + " is a member of Circle");
   System.out.println("Its area is " + newCirc.area());
   System.out.println("and its perimeter is " + newCirc.perimeter());
   }
 // teminates conditional and for-loop
}
```

12. Create a "pair hierarchy" with abstract superclass discPair coded as

```
abstract class discPair
{
 abstract public void print();
}
```

and with subclasses `intPair` and `charPair` coded as in Exercises 10 and 11 of Chapter 1. Then define a run-time polymorphism operation that selects an object from each of `intPair` and `charPair`, using the concrete version of `print()` for each subclass.

PROGRAMMING PROJECT

Define the following hierarchy of employees for a large firm:

a. `Employee` names a base class containing the following data common to all employees:
1. social security number (as a 9-character string)
2. date of initial employment (using the format `mm/dd/yy`)
3. status (choose between the `char` values
     `'a'` for administrator: (chief executive, other executives, department heads);
     `'b'` for assembly line worker;
     `'c'` for clerical staff

b. `FullTimeEmployee` names a subclass of `Employee`, every object of which contains the additional fields:
1. weekly gross pay (based on a standard 40-hour work week)
2. overtime wages (based on the number of weekly hours over 40)
3. deductions (for employee credit union, health insurance)
     Each of these should be in a `double` format.

c. `PartTimeEmployee` names a second derived class of `Employee`, every object of which contains the additional fields:
1. number of hours worked this week (`int` value; total must be less than 40)
2. hourly rate of pay (as a `double` value)

Design and code a driver program that first creates a list of employees interactively and then outputs the records just created in that list.

CHAPTER 3

Search and Sort

CHAPTER OBJECTIVES

- To study methods for searching through and sorting a finite sequence of values stored in an array, for a specific value, using a variety of algorithms designed for that purpose.
- To define and develop efficient algorithms for searching and sorting, using the techniques of object-oriented design.
- To quantify the concept of efficiency of algorithms, using formal mathematics.
- To introduce the Principle of Finite Induction and recursive design and programming, and to demonstrate their importance in testing the efficiency and correctness of algorithms.

3.1 Introduction

Two of the most important problems encountered in commercial data processing are, undoubtedly, those of sorting a sequence of values and searching for a value from a given finite collection of values stored in some fixed data structure. One objective of this chapter is to define and develop efficient algorithms for search and sort, using object-oriented design (OOD). The ideas presented here begin a sequence leading to a discussion and thorough examination of the facilities for this purpose that appear in the predefined Java library `java.util`, whose presentation and detailed discussion appears throughout the remainder of this text.

We begin by defining the concept of algorithm, and then we examine the design and refinement of algorithms. The design process begins with a somewhat naïve first description, and, through a sequence of refinements, culminates in a "final" version that can be translated into formal code in a seamless manner. An important consideration we will always keep in mind is the efficiency of the underlying algorithm and the study of formal mathematical techniques providing a quantification of efficiency.

3.2   **The Concept of an Algorithm**

We can define an algorithm as a carefully constructed finite sequence of instructions that, when executed in the order of their appearance, constitutes the solution of a specific programming problem. Once we have formulated an algorithm, the path to a solution of the problem involves testing whether the sequence of instructions succeeds in arriving at that solution. Our emphasis in this text involves describing an algorithm as a finite sequence of well-formulated instructions, for the purpose just described. But what constitutes a "well-formulated" instruction? This chapter will emphasize what constitutes well-formulated instructions as they apply to solving sorting and searching problems.

Several key factors underlie the design of well-formulated algorithms:

- *There must be a clear and unambiguous description of the input data required for the solution.* This also implies that the problem presented for solution must be stated in a clear and unambiguous form so that the input data, when presented in this environment, permits the algorithm to complete its execution in a finite number of steps. Moreover, this execution must yield an anticipated output, at which point the computation terminates successfully.

- *Each instruction must be clearly and unambiguously stated, without any chance of misinterpretation.* A well-formulated instruction eliminates the possibility that there exist more than one possible consequence of its execution. That is, a well-formulated instruction must be deterministic. As an example, attempting to formulate instructions in some spoken language such as English or French generally leads to ambiguities. This is because such languages are, by their very nature, filled with terms having several alternative interpretations.

- *The algorithm must be correct.* As described in Chapter 1, the algorithm must yield the anticipated output as the value(s) solving the stated problem for the given input value(s). In certain cases, the proof of correctness may be quite formal and rigorous. Such proofs may use such formal mathematical tools as the Principle of Finite Induction, seen later in Section 3.5.

- *The algorithm must produce a computation that terminates in a finite number of steps.* We must safeguard against a design that, for example, might result in an infinite loop of an infinite chain of invocations of some method. However, it is not necessary that we predict the exact number of computational steps involved. Instead, the only requirement is that we determine an upper bound beyond which no further computational steps can occur. This determination will rely on concepts studied later in this chapter, when we study methods of quantifying efficiency of algorithms.

- *The output and purpose of the algorithm must be clearly specified in advance.* There should be no doubt as to the intended purpose of the algorithm. Often, certain unanticipated side effects arise, even from carefully formulated code. These side effects can be subtle in nature and can arise in subtle ways. They often appear as run-time bugs, requiring a carefully planned strategy of code examination and testing to track down their origin. We will not go into any great detail describing such strategies in this text; this is properly the concern of software engineering. It is a commonly accepted fact that even the most carefully defined and well-formulated algorithms contain a number of occurrences of run-time bugs. Our objective, then, is to minimize the number of such occurrences and to purge the resulting code of as many of these as possible.

3.3   **Design with Classes and Objects**

A number of powerful tools exist for designing algorithms involving classes and objects. If the problem to be solved can be cast in an environment whose application domain can be modeled using classes and objects, several questions arise:

- Which classes and objects are required in the design of the solution?
- Does the most suitable solution require predefined methods and classes, such as those present in `java.util`?
- Does the solution require the facilities of classes of our own design?
- Which facilities of classes of our own design should be made `public`?
- If several classes are involved in the solution, do these classes form a hierarchy involving a well-defined superclass and several well-defined subclasses, or do they involve multiple inheritance?

In the traditional design process, the algorithm first appears in a relatively crude form, and it then evolves gradually by a sequence of refinements into a form that closely resembles the final coded version. In previous chapters, we have emphasized solving problems using classes and objects. Now we will show that many of these problems are solvable using certain predefined Java libraries. One advantage gained from using these predefined tools is that a large burden of the design of these solutions is lifted from our shoulders, because we can now rely on the fact that these tools represent reusable methods that have already been thoroughly tested for efficiency. The only question is, How suitable are these facilities to the solution of the specific problem at hand?

Our approach in this chapter will be that of studying techniques for searching and sorting values stored in an array, using a variety of traditional algorithms designed for that purpose. In later chapters we will study a number of facilities that are predefined in Java for sorting a sequence of values and for searching a finite sequence for a specific value. In so doing, we hope to acquire a deeper appreciation for these predefined libraries and their facilities as a valuable collection of tools for the software designer who is using Java as the implementation language for solving such problems.

Before we begin this study, we introduce some of the more important and fundamental mathematical concepts used to place this design in a more formal and rigorous setting. Consequently, the next several sections will introduce the idea of complexity measures and their application to algorithms for searching and sorting; the Principle of Finite Induction is an important component in the analysis of algorithms to follow.

3.4 **Efficiency Issues: Preliminary Discussion**

We have emphasized the importance of efficient software solutions to problems from the very beginning of this text. Up to this point, however, our idea of efficiency has been intuitive, and little more. In order to add more precision to this idea, we begin by posing the following question:

> Is it possible to quantify efficiency in some way, in the form of some common and easily understandable metric, in order to compare the efficiency of a number of algorithms serving as alternative solutions to some specific software problem?

One way to measure efficiency is by the amount of processing time, in the form of the number of processing steps, required to complete the algorithm's execution. As we will see, efficiency is directly related to the time required to process the data stored in some container. In this context, we use the current size n of the sequence as an argument and define a (time) complexity function t(n) for an algorithm as the (maximum) number of processing steps required for the algorithm to terminate execution.

More precisely, suppose f(n) is a function with nonnegative integer values, defined for all nonnegative integers n. We say that an algorithm has *order of complexity* f(n) if

t(n) $\leq$ C * f(n) for n $\geq$ K

for suitable choices of the positive constants C and K, and we use the terminology that the algorithm is $O(f(n))$.

We now list some of the more important orders of complexity associated with algorithms we will treat in this text.

- An important and fundamental search algorithm is known as *sequential* (or *linear*) *search*. We will show that the processing time required to complete execution of this search algorithm is proportional to the number n of values in the sequence. Because this form of search involves at most n comparisons, and because each comparison is regarded as a separate processing step, we conclude that sequential search is an algorithm of order $O(n)$. We say that this algorithm processes its data in *linear time*.

- Another important search algorithm is called *binary search*. We will show that this algorithm is of order $O(\log_2 n)$. We can characterize this as an algorithm that processes its data in *logarithmic time*.[1]

- Several of the popular sorting algorithms (such as selection sort and insertion sort) have complexity $O(n^2)$. We say that such algorithms process their data in *quadratic time*.

- Some versions of sorting algorithms, such as quicksort and (internal) mergesort have complexity that, on average, are of order $O(n \log n)$.

- Certain algorithms do not depend on the number of elements appearing in the sequence. That is, for such algorithms, there are constants C and K such that $t(n) \leq C$ for $n \geq K$. We say that such algorithms execute in *constant time*, and we denote this order of complexity by $O(1)$.

In analyzing the time complexity algorithms, much stress is placed on what is called *worst-case complexity* and *average-case complexity*. This entails finding upper bounds for the number of computations involved in executing the algorithm for the worst possible case and the average situation, respectively. For instance, in executing quicksort, the worst possible case occurs when the sequence of values to be sorted appear in the reverse order of size. Similarly, in the average case, quicksort involves placing a "pivot" value in its proper position in the sequence by splitting the sequence into two parts, each of which has roughly the same number of elements. Quicksort is $O(n \log n)$ in the average case, and is $O(n^2)$ in its worst case.

---

[1]We will drop the subscript with the understanding that, unless we specify otherwise, any reference to $\log$ will be a reference to $\log_2$.

3.5 **The Principle of Finite Induction**

We state the following mathematical result known as *The Principle of Finite Induction:*

> **Principle of Finite Induction:** Let P(n) be a Boolean-valued statement whose value depends on the value of the nonnegative integer argument n. If P(0) is true (that is, P is true for the case n = 0), and if, for each value of k, k ≥ 0, P(k+1) is true whenever P(k) is true, then P(n) is true for every choice of a nonnegative integer n.

An important step described in the statement of the principle is

for each k, P(k+1) is true whenever P(k) is true.

This is called the *inductive step,* and it provides the means of moving to the next highest level of P, knowing that P is true at the current level. The way to use Finite Induction in mathematical proofs is to prove, separately and independently, that P(0) is true for the proposed P(n). Once this is established, the inductive step will verify P(1); applying the inductive step once again, we obtain the truth of P(2), and so on.

EXAMPLE 3.1 Finite Induction is useful in verifying certain inequalities for nonnegative integers. Some of these inequalities also prove to be invaluable for comparing the efficiency of certain key algorithms. One such inequality states that $n < 2^n$ for all choices of a nonnegative integer n. Suppose we denote this statement by P(n). We first show that P(0) is true. This is done by replacing each occurrence of n in P(n) by 0, yielding $0 < 2^0$, which is certainly true. We next assume P(k) is true for some choice of a nonnegative integer k: thus, we assume $k < 2^k$ for this k. If we add 1 to both sides of this inequality, we get $k + 1 < 2^k + 1$. But we can show (by a separate argument using Finite Induction) that $2^k + 1 \leq 2 * 2^k = 2^{k+1}$ for every nonnegative integer k. This yields $k + 1 < 2^{k+1}$, establishing the truth of P(k+1). By Finite Induction, it follows that $n < 2^n$ for all nonnegative integers n.

3.6 **Comparing Algorithms: Using "Big O" Notation**

We have already observed that a number of questions arise in a natural way when analyzing the efficiency of algorithms:

- How can we measure efficiency?
- What factors enter into the decision as to which of a number of candidates represents the most efficient and desired version of an algorithm for solving a specific software problem?

The choice of the most efficient algorithm from a list of possible candidates is an important factor in solving a software problem. The detailed study of the comparison of algorithms for efficiency is at the heart of the discipline in computer science known as *algorithm analysis*.

Two measures are commonly used for efficiency of algorithms: *space efficiency* and *time efficiency*. Space efficiency is concerned primarily with the amount of storage required to implement the underlying algorithm in hardware. It is generally understood that algorithm A is more space efficient that algorithm B if A requires less storage to solve the underlying problem than B. On the other hand, time efficiency involves counting the number of processing steps required to solve the problem. We say that algorithm A is more time efficient than algorithm B if A requires fewer computational steps than B to solve the problem.

Before proceeding any further, it is important for us to observe that correctness should never be sacrificed for either time or space efficiency. If a proposed algorithm is being considered over other candidates because it is more time or space efficient, but it does not perform satisfactorily in all cases, then there should be no doubt as to the decision: Choose the candidate that is correct in all cases.

EXAMPLE 3.2   **The Factorial Function**

Define the factorial function for all nonnegative integers n by

$$
factorial(n) = \begin{cases} 1, \text{if n } = 0; \\ n * (n-1) * (n-2) * \ldots * 3 * 2 * 1, \text{ if } n \geq 1. \end{cases}
$$

Thus, `factorial(0) = factorial(1) = 1`, `factorial(2) = 2 * 1 = 2`, `factorial(3) = 3 * 2 * 1 = 6`, `factorial(4) = 4 * 3 * 2 * 1 = 24`, and so on. We can observe that the rate of growth of the values returned by `factorial` is very rapid. In fact, we can use "big O" to find an upper bound on its growth. We will show that `factorial(n)` is $O(n^n)$. To see this, note that for n > 0,

$$
factorial(n) = n * (n-1) * (n-2) * \ldots * 3 * 2 * 1 \\
\leq \underbrace{n * n * n * \ldots * n}_{n} = n^n.
$$

`factorial(n)` is more commonly denoted by `n!`.

3.7 More on Generics: The `Object` Class and the `Comparable` Interface

This section extends the ideas on generics begun in Section 1.7 and is indispensable for our presentation of the implementation of search and sort strategies in Java. It is a self-contained presentation of some of the basic properties defined in the `Object` class and the `Comparable` interface that are needed to complete our discussion of the generic versions of these implementations. As a result, the student who is already familiar with the ideas presented here can skip this section without any loss of continuity with respect to the results discussed in the remaining sections of this chapter.

Every class in Java descends from the `Object` class, described as `java.lang.Object`. If no inheritance relationship is specified when a class is defined by the programmer, we assume the superclass of that class is `Object`. All of the classes we describe in this text are (implicitly) subclasses of `Object`.

We should be familiar with the `equals()` method that is predefined in `Object`, because it is useful in a variety of circumstances. It is certainly useful in implementing generic versions of search and sort strategies in Java, as we will soon see. The prototype (signature) for `equals()` is given by

```
public boolean equals(Object obj);
```

The `equals()` method tests whether two objects from the same class are equal, returning `true` if so and `false` if not. The syntax for this method is

```
object1.equals(object2);
```

where we assume the arguments `object1` and `object2` are objects defined in the same class.

The default implementation of `equals()` in `Object` is

```
public boolean equals(Object obj)
{
  return(this == obj);
}
```

Thus, using the `equals()` method is equivalent to applying the `==` operator to members of the `Object` class.

Generic methods requiring the comparison of two objects constructed from a specific class can be written using the method `compareTo()`, which is the only method appearing in the interface `java.lang.Comparable`. This interface can be viewed as a superclass of any of the number wrapper classes defined in Section 1.7; it is described graphically by the inheritance diagram pictured in Figure 3.1.

The `compareTo` method is used as follows: Suppose `myObject` and `yourObject` are objects of the same class for which a comparison operator `<` is defined. Then

```
myObject.compareTo(yourObject)
```

FIGURE 3.1

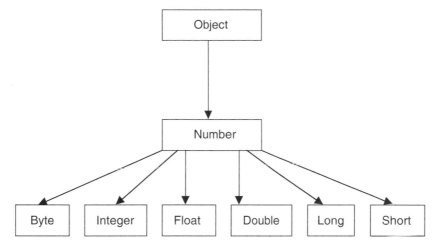

returns an integer value according to the definition

$$\texttt{myObject.compareTo(yourObject)} \text{ is } \begin{bmatrix} < 0, \text{ if } \texttt{myObject} < \texttt{yourObject} \\ = 0, \text{ if } \texttt{myObject} = \texttt{yourObject} \\ > 0, \text{ if } \texttt{myObject} > \texttt{yourObject} \end{bmatrix}$$

We will use `compareTo` in a variety of situations. The most notable will be in implementing the binary search algorithm in Section 3.11 and in the generic implementation of each of the sort strategies discussed later in this chapter.

3.8 Search Algorithms for Arrays: Linear (Sequential) Search

Our objective in this section and the next is to present and analyze search strategies for values stored in an array. In doing so, we should seek search strategies that are relatively easy to implement and that are as efficient as possible. The analysis of the efficiency of the search algorithm under consideration will be somewhat rigorous and will involve some basic mathematical concepts.

An *array* is a form of linear container, since we can view the values currently stored in an array as being arranged in some linear path. However, we should be aware of other forms of linear containers: The properties of vectors, linked lists, and others will be studied later in the text.

We begin with an analysis of linear (sequential) search as it applies to an array. Assume T is some given data type, and then assume that there exists a finite sequence of values of type T in which the search is to be conducted. Our version of linear search will retrieve the first occurrence of the value we seek in the array, returning `true` if such a value occurs in the array; otherwise, `false` is returned. Informally, we can state the linear search algorithm as

> *Begin by probing the initial value of the sequence. If the value we seek appears there, stop the search and report success; otherwise, continue the search by examining the next value in the sequence. This process eventually terminates either by finding the value sought at some component of the array (in which case* `true` *is returned), or by exhausting all of the array's components without finding that value (in which case* `false` *is returned), indicating an unsuccessful search.*

Our final version of the algorithm expresses linear search as a generic method returning a `boolean` value, and a for-loop ranging over the subscripts of the array containing the sequence. The code for this is given by the following:

```
public static boolean linsrch(Object[] arr,Object valueSought)
 {
  // Implements linear search algorithm.
  // Precondition: array components have been assigned values
  // with no specific ordering.
  // Postcondition: "true" is returned whenever the first occurrence
  // of the value sought (if it exists) is found, and "false" if the
  //  value sought does not appear in the array.
  for(int index = 0; index < arr.length; ++index)
   // Invariant: the values in arr up to and including position
   // index - 1 have already been inspected, if index > 0.
   if(valueSought.equals(arr[index])) return true;
  // ends for-loop
  return false;
 } // terminates text of linsrch generic method
```

We can make several observations about this implementation. First, note that we use the fact that, for any array `arr`, Java provides an attribute `length`—namely, the number of distinct components of `arr`. Also, note that the method uses a for-loop with the comment

```
// Invariant: the values in arr up to and including position
// index - 1 have already been inspected, if index > 0.
```

This is an example of a *loop invariant,* which is an assertion that

1. in some sense captures the essence of the computation performed in the loop
2. is true when the control of execution enters the loop for the first time
3. is true each time that control of execution reenters the loop body

In the case of the invariant stated for `linsrch`, we can observe that initially the invariant is satisfied vacuously, because no component of the array has been examined on initial entry into the loop. If the need exists to reenter the loop at some later time, this is because the value sought has not as yet been found.

How can we output the number of probes required to decide whether there is an array component containing the value sought? We can accomplish this by initializing a conformant `int`-valued array `probes` in the caller, as follows:

```
int probes[] = {0};
```

We can then pass a third parameter to `linsrch` as an `int`-valued array `arrValue`, and then restructure the `for`-loop of `linsrch` as

```
for(int index = 0; index < arr.length; ++index)
  {
  ++arrValue[0];
  if(valueSought.equals(arr[index])) return true;
  } // ends for-loop
```

We would then invoke `linsrch` in the caller as

```
linsrch(objArray,objValue,probes);
```

where `objArray` identifies the array in which the linear search is to be conducted, and `objValue` identifies the value sought in `objArray`. We leave the coding details of this form to the student as an exercise.

We will study other implementations of linear search in later chapters, as it applies to other forms of linear containers.

3.9 **Analysis of Linear Search**

Suppose we have a sequence of n values of some fixed data type. We wish to determine the *average* number of comparisons (that is, processing steps) necessary to decide whether a specific value is a member of the sequence. For linear search, the value sought might be the initial member of the sequence (in which case only one comparison is necessary), or the next (in which two comparisons are required), and so on. If we assume that examining each position of the sequence occurs with the same probability, the average number of comparisons involved is

$$\frac{1 + 2 + 3 + \ldots + n}{n}$$

A well-known mathematical result is

$$1 + 2 + 3 + \ldots + n = \frac{n * (n+1)}{2}$$

for any positive integer n. This last result can be verified using Finite Induction and is left as an exercise. Because

$$\frac{1 + 2 + 3 + \ldots + n}{n} = \frac{n + 1}{2}$$

the average number of comparisons required to perform a linear search is

$$\frac{n + 1}{2}$$

The *worst possible case* for linear search occurs when either the value sought is the last value in the sequence or the value sought does not appear at all. In either case, exactly n comparisons are required. In fact, even if we apply linear search only to sequences that are already sorted in order of increasing size, then on average n/2 comparisons are required to arrive at a conclusion. Thus, on average and in the worst possible case, linear search is O(n).

3.10 Review of Recursive Programming

This section is devoted to recursive programming, an important problem-solving tool with many key ramifications. The concepts discussed in this section will be used extensively in the remainder of the text. This section also represents a self-contained exposition of recursive methods in software design and programming. As a consequence, the student who is already familiar with the subject can effectively skip this discussion without any loss of continuity.

Problem-solving methods exist that invoke themselves from their own scope. This paradigm is known as *recursive design* and *recursive programming,* and the resulting functions are called *recursive functions.* In a very natural way, stacks are used in implementing recursion. We illustrate this with an example.

EXAMPLE 3.3 **The Factorial Function, Recursive Form**
In Section 3.6 we defined the *factorial function* as

$$\text{factorial(n)} = \begin{cases} 1, & \text{if } n = 0; \\ n * (n-1) * (n-2) * \ldots * 3 * 2 * 1, & \text{if } n \geq 1. \end{cases}$$

A simple way to compute the values of factorial is to use loops; that is, we give an *iterative* implementation of factorial as

```java
public static int factorial(int value)
  {
  // Iterative form computing the values of the
  // factorial function.
```

```
if(value == 0) return 1;
else
{
 int prod = 1;
 for(int index = 1; index <= value; ++index)
 // Invariant: prod = 1 * 2 * ... * (index - 1) for
 // 1 < index <= value.
 prod *= index;
 return prod;
} // terminates else-clause
} // terminates code for factorial method
```

Iterative

We can also design a recursive version of `factorial` using the observation that for all nonnegative integers n, we have

$$factorial(n) = \begin{cases} 1, & \text{if } n = 0; \\ n * factorial(n-1), & \text{if } n > 0 \end{cases}$$

Here we note that `factorial(0)` = 1, `factorial(1)` = 1 * `factorial(0)` = 1, `factorial(2)` = 2 * `factorial(1)` = 2, `factorial(3)` = 3 * `factorial(2)` = 6, and so on. Java allows us to capture this recursive version in formal code as

```
public static int factorial(int value)
 {
  // Recursive form computing the values of the
  // factorial function.
  if(value == 0) return 1;
  else
  return value * factorial(value - 1);
} // terminates code for factorial method
```

Recursive

Suppose we invoke `factorial(4)`. Tracing execution of the recursive version, the initial call to `factorial` involves assigning the value 4 to the formal parameter `value`. If we now trace execution of the body of `factorial` for `value` equal to 4, we note that

```
4 * factorial(3)
```

must be computed. Because the value of `factorial(3)` is not computed as yet, control of execution pushes 4 onto an initially empty run-time stack, followed by the attempt to compute the value of `factorial(3)`. This is accomplished by reentering the body of `factorial` with the new formal parameter value 3. As this executes, the value of

```
3 * factorial(2)
```

must be found. Again, because the value of `factorial(2)` is not computed as yet, 3 is pushed onto the run-time stack and the body of `factorial` is reentered with 2 as the new value of the formal parameter. In a similar manner, the value of

```
2 * factorial(1)
```

must be determined. Because the value of `factorial(1)` has not as yet been computed, 2 is pushed onto the stack and the body of `factorial` is reentered with parameter value 1. The same outcome occurs, leading to the execution of

```
1 * factorial(0)
```

pushing 1 onto the run-time stack and then invoking `factorial(0)`. At this point, the run-time stack is as in Figure 3.2.

FIGURE 3.2

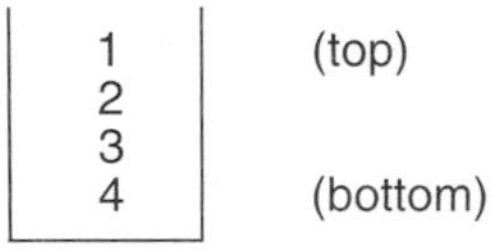

```
1     (top)
2
3
4     (bottom)
```

When `factorial(0)` executes, the `if`-clause returns a value of 1 to the caller, which is

```
1 * factorial(0)
```

inside of the text of `factorial(1)`. The value of 1 * `factorial(0)` = 1 is returned to the text of `factorial(2)`, and 1 is popped from the stack. In turn, the value of 2 * `factorial(1)` = 2 is returned to the text of `factorial(3)`, and 2 is popped from the stack. Similarly, 3 is popped from the stack, and 3 * `factorial(2)` = 6 is returned to the text of `factorial(4)`, the original call. This prompts a popping of 4 from the stack, rendering the stack empty, and returns the value of 4 * `factorial(3)` = 24 to the caller.

The successive calls to `factorial` generated by executing the `else`-clause when executing `factorial(4)`, `factorial(3)`, `factorial(2)`, and `factorial(1)` continues until the call to `factorial(0)` occurs. This last call provides the necessary "escape" that prevents the occurrence of an infinite sequence of calls to `factorial`, and it also prompts a popping of the run-time stack until it becomes empty, signaling the end of the computation.

Summarizing, it is possible to develop recursive algorithms to solve specific programming problems, if we can establish each of the following criteria:

- The original problem is decomposable into several "smaller" versions of the same problem.
- Each subsequent call to the algorithm diminishes the value(s) for which the problem is originally defined.

- There must exist an instance of the problem whose solution is specific and does not involve another call to the algorithm (the "escape").
- The escape is realized after a finite sequence of calls to the algorithm.

There are a number of exercises at the end of this chapter whose solution is obtained by recursive methods. In addition, we will study a number of problems later in this chapter whose solution requires the application of recursive design and programming.

3.11 **Binary Search**

In this section, we consider a new search strategy called *binary search,* whose algorithm can be designed either iteratively or recursively. Binary search executes differently from linear search, and it assumes a precondition that is not required in linear search: The values in the sequence to be searched are assumed to be sorted in order of increasing size, counting any possible repetitions. This strategy mimics the kind of search we would perform when we seek a student's record in some file, where these records are assumed to be sorted in lexicographic order according to surname. We first look at the "middle record." If that is the one we seek, we stop the search successfully; if not, we compare the record we have located to the one we seek. If the record we seek appears before this middle record, we resume the search for the record in the "upper half" consisting of the records of students whose surnames occur before that contained in the current middle record. If the record we seek appears after this middle record, however, we resume the search in the "lower half" consisting of the records whose surnames appear after that of the current middle record. Eventually, we either locate the record we seek or determine that the record does not appear in the current file.

Binary search is an example of a design strategy known as *divide and conquer,* because we break down the problem of searching for a specific student record into the problem of searching for that record (if not located initially) in a file whose size is half of the original file, and then half of that file, and so on, until we arrive at a conclusion either by locating the record sought or by discovering that the record sought does not appear in the file.

Intuitively, this strategy is more efficient than that for linear search, because we are discarding entire sections of the file each time we determine a new "middle record" when we do not find the record we seek. Although we use the example of seeking a student record in an alphabetical file, there is no reason why this cannot be generalized to the problem of searching for a value of type T in a sorted finite sequence of values of that type.

Here is a pseudocode version of the algorithm, first using iterative methods:

// Initialize the sequence, presumed stored in an array.
int low = 0, high = ARRAY_SIZE − 1;
while(there are more components to search and the value sought has not as yet been found)
{
* // Compute the current middle index.*
* int mid = (low + high)/2;*
* if(a[mid] == value) // If we find the value we seek in the mid position of the array.*
*   return "true" to signal a successful search;*
* else // Value sought has not as yet been found.*
*   if(value < a[mid]) // Value we seek is smaller than that found in the*
*   // mid position of the array.*
*   high = mid − 1; // Resume search in "upper half."*
*   else // Value we seek is larger than that found in the*
*   // mid position of the array.*
*   low = mid + 1; // Resume search in "lower half."*
} // terminates while-loop
// Processing resumes here only in the case of an unsuccessful search.
return "false" to signal an unsuccessful search;

The formal coding of this algorithm follows, given in the form of a generic method; it is nearly a literal copy of the pseudocode. This version also counts the number of iterations (probes) needed to arrive at a conclusion as to whether the binary search was successful or not.

```
public static boolean binsrch(Comparable[] arr, Comparable valueSought,
                          int[] prb)
// Binary search method, iterative form.
// Precondition: the components of arr are sorted
// in order of increasing size.
// Postcondition: "true" is returned if valueSought is found
// among the components of arr; otherwise, "false" is returned.
{
 int low = 0;
 int high = arr.length - 1;
 while(low <= high)
 {
  // Invariant: valueSought has not as yet been found
  // and low <= high.
  ++prb[0];
```

```
  int mid = (low + high)/2;
  // valueSought has been found.  Indicate success.
  if(valueSought.equals(arr[mid])) return true;
  else if(valueSought.compareTo(arr[mid]) < 0)
   // valueSought  arr[mid]
   high = mid - 1;
  else // valueSought > arr[mid]
   low = mid + 1;
 } // terminates text of while-loop
 // If processing resumes here, this signals unsuccessful search.
 return false;
} // terminates text of iterative form of binsrch method.
```

The syntax for the initial call to this iterative version of binsrch takes the form

```
binsrch(arrayName,valueSought,loopIterations);
```

The recursive version of the algorithm makes very few changes. For example, the while-loop in the iterative version is replaced by successive calls to binsrch from within its text for updated values of some of the parameters. The values of these parameters change, based on the continuation of the search, either in the "upper half" or "lower half" of the remaining array segment, whichever is appropriate. Its final code is given by the following:

```
public static boolean binsrch(Comparable [] arr, int first, int last,
                    Comparable valueSought, int [] arrayValue)
 {
  // Binary search method, recursive form.
  // Precondition: the components of arr are sorted
  //  in order of increasing size.
  // Postcondition: "true" is returned if valueSought is found
  //  among the components of arr; otherwise, "false" is returned.
  ++arrayValue[0];
  int low = first, high = last, mid = (low + high)/2;
  if(low > high) return false; // Return unsuccessful search.
  else if(valueSought.equals(arr[mid])) // Return successful search.
   return true;
  else if(valueSought.compareTo(arr[mid]) < 0)
   // valueSought < arr[mid]
   return binsrch(arr,low,mid-1,valueSought,arrayValue);
  else // valueSought > arr[mid]
   return binsrch(arr,mid+1,high,valueSought,arrayValue);
 } // terminates text of recursive version of binsrch
```

Here, the syntax for the initial call to the recursive version of `binsrch` assumes the form

`binsrch(arrayName,0,arrayName.length-1,valueSought,recursiveCalls);`

where `recursiveCalls` counts the number of recursive calls necessary for `binsrch` to complete its execution.

3.12 Analysis of Binary Search

Regardless of whether we choose the iterative or recursive form of binary search, the analysis of the underlying algorithm is essentially the same. Assume that the sequence involved in the search has already been sorted in order of increasing size. The algorithm begins execution by inspecting the middle value of the array where the sequence is stored and then "halving" the sequence (if necessary) until we find the value sought, if it occurs in the array.

The worst possible case occurs if we arrive at a subset of the original sequence containing exactly one value. The search thus ends successfully if the value sought matches that value and otherwise ends unsuccessfully. Thus, the worst possible case involves m "halving" operations, where

$$\frac{n}{2^{m-1}} = 1$$

and where n is the size of the original sequence. This yields $2^{m-1} = n$ and $m - 1 = \log n$. This in turn implies that, in the worst possible case, binary search is of order $O(\log n)$.

For sequences with relatively small numbers of values, there is hardly any difference in the processing speed of linear and binary search. As the size of the sequence gets increasingly larger, however, it becomes apparent that binary search is more efficient than linear search.

3.13 Sorting Algorithms: Selection and Insertion Sort

The specific problem we wish to solve can be stated as

Given a fixed finite list of values, we wish to rearrange these values (if necessary) in order of increasing size.

A combinatorial and straightforward way to solve this problem would be to store the list in some data structure, usually a one-dimensional array, and then apply some sorting algorithm on that structure. One possibility uses *selection sort*. This begins by scanning the entire list (of size n) to find the smallest value. Once that value is found, it is swapped with the value currently occupying the initial position in the list. The processing continues by finding the smallest value in the remaining list, beginning with the value immediately following the initial value, then swapping this value with that currently occupying the second position, and so on, until only one (unsorted) value remains. This last value remains exactly where it is, and the entire list is sorted.

The formal code for selection sort is given in the text of selSort, coded in generic form using the Comparable interface. In addition, the code of selSort contains a counter for the number of swaps required to sort the entire sequence.

```java
public static void selSort(Comparable [] arr, int[] swaps)
 {
  int smallest; // Holds subscript of smallest remaining array value
  for(int index1 = 0; index1 < arr.length - 1; ++index1)
  {
   // Invariant: components of arr in positions index1
   // to arr.length  - 1 remain unsorted.

   // Initialize the value of smallest as the first remaining
   // array value.
   smallest = index1;
   // Then find subscript of the smallest remaining array value
   for(int index2 = index1 + 1; index2 <= arr.length - 1; ++index2)
    if(arr[index2].compareTo(arr[smallest]) < 0)
      smallest = index2;
   // terminates text of inner for-loop
   // Swap array values, if necessary
   if(arr[index1].compareTo(arr[smallest]) > 0)
   {
      ++swaps[0];  // Increase count for swaps.
    swapValues(arr,index1,smallest);
   } // terminates if
  } // terminates text of outer for-loop
 } // terminates text of selSort
```

This method is invoked using the syntax

```
selSort(arrayName,swapCounter);
```

The number of swaps required to sort the array is done by assigning an initial value of 0 to the one-component int-valued array named by *swapCounter* and then passing that array as the second parameter.

Insertion sort obtains the same result by a markedly different computation. Unlike selection sort, the complete list of n values in the array are not immediately visible to the algorithm. In fact, the values are revealed one at a time during the execution of each new cycle of an outer loop, with an inner loop sorting the values that are already visible. Thus, insertion sort proceeds as follows: Trivially sort the first value, then the first two, then the first three, and so on, until the entire sequence is visible, at which time the resulting sort produces the desired sorting of the entire array.

Accordingly, we can describe the underlying algorithm as follows: Assume the initial segment of values in positions 0, 1, 2, . . . , q-1 of the sequence are already sorted among themselves, where $1 \leq q < n$. We use temp as a temporary storage location to hold the next value in the sequence until its value is compared to the values contained in the current initial segment. The inner loop in the following implementation code is used to make room for the new value by shifting down one position all the values in the current initial segment that are larger than the new value. This enables the new value to be placed in its proper position in the revised initial segment. Similar to selection sort, the version of insertion sort is coded as a generic method, with a counter on the number of interchanges required to determine the proper position of each new value in the sequence.

```
public static void inSort(Comparable[] arr, int[] interchanges)
 {
  // Performs insertion sort on array arr.
  // Postcondition: the array arr will have components
  // sorted in order of increasing size.
  for(int index1 = 1; index1 <= arr.length - 1; ++index1)
  // Invariant: Values in initial segment from position 0
  // up to index1 - 1 are sorted among themselves.
  {
   Comparable temp = arr[index1];
   // Create temp to hold reference to the next value to be
   // sorted in the new initial segment.
   int index2 = index1;
   while(index2 != 0 && (arr[index2 - 1].compareTo(temp) > 0))
   {
    // Move larger values in current initial segment down one
    // position in order to make room for the new value.
    ++interchanges[0];
    arr[index2] = arr[index2 - 1];
    --index2;
   } // terminates inner while-loop
   // Now place new value in its proper position
   arr[index2] = temp;
  } // terminates for-loop
 } // terminates inSort
```

3.14 **Analyzing Selection and Insertion Sort**

Recall from the previous section that the selection sort algorithm presupposes that the entire sequence to be sorted is visible initially. Also, recall that the sorting operation begins by singling out the smallest value in the entire sequence and placing it in the initial position. The operation continues by determining the next smallest value and placing it in the next available position in the sequence, and so on, until the entire sequence is exhausted. The result is the sorted version of the original sequence in order of increasing size.

We now show that selection sort is an $O(n^2)$ algorithm. To see this, we note that the implementation uses a pair of nested `for`-loops. The first cycle of the outer loop finds the smallest value in the sequence and places that value in the initial position. This involves comparing `n - 1` members of the sequence and is accomplished by executing the inner loop. The next cycle of the outer loop looks for the next smallest value to place in the second position, requiring `n - 2` comparisons by the inner loop, and so on. This continues until the inner loop makes a single comparison of the remaining two (unsorted) values. Thus, the total number of comparisons required to sort the entire sequence is

$$(n-1) + (n-2) + . . . + 3 + 2 + 1 = \frac{n*(n-1)}{2}$$

This implies that selection sort is an $O(n^2)$ algorithm.

In analyzing insertion sort, we note that, at the completion of the initial cycle of the outer `for`-loop, the first two values of the sequence are sorted among themselves; after the completion of the next cycle, the first three values are sorted among themselves, and so on until the completion of the last cycle. At that point, the entire sequence is sorted. The inner `while`-loop executes as many times as is necessary to adjust positions in the new initial segment in order to place the next new value in its proper location. Thus, in the worst case, one shift is required for the first loop cycle, two for the next, three for the next, until the last, which requires a shift of `n - 1` positions to make room for the new (and last) value. Thus, in the worst possible case, the total number of shifts amounts to

$$(n-1) + (n-2) + . . . + 3 + 2 + 1 = \frac{n*(n-1)}{2}$$

Consequently, in the worst possible case, insertion sort is an $O(n^2)$ algorithm.

The best possible case for insertion sort occurs when the input sequence is already sorted in order of increasing size, thus requiring no shifts at all in the resulting execution of insertion sort. This can be illustrated by executing `inSort` for the case of n values in reverse order for the worst possible case, and for the case of n values already sorted in order of increasing size for the best possible case.

If we were to consider all possible representations of an input sequence of n values, we would conclude that, on average, the number of shifts required in the inner `while`-loop would cause insertion sort to be proportional to n^2. Therefore, on average, insertion sort is $O(n^2)$.

3.15   Quicksort and Recursive Algorithms

Selection and insertion sort have been shown to be $O(n^2)$ algorithms. However, a number of sort algorithms are defined for one-dimensional arrays as well as for other data structures that are more efficient. In this section, we describe an $O(n \log n)$ sort algorithm called *quicksort,* which uses such design strategies as recursive programming and divide and conquer. Quicksort was first designed in 1962 by C. A. R. Hoare (see the References section at the end of this chapter). In fact, quicksort is $O(n \log n)$ in almost all cases. To get some idea as to the relative processing speed of selection and insertion sort to quicksort, we consult Table 3.1.

The asterisks at certain positions in the table indicate that the number is too large to be listed. Using Table 3.1 for the case n = 32, we note that n^2 = 1024 and n log n = 160. From these observations, we can conclude that in sorting 32 values, selection sort and insertion sort require approximately 1024 processing steps, whereas quicksort, or, for that matter, any other $O(n \log n)$ sort algorithm, requires only about 160 steps. Thus, the efficiency of an $O(n \log n)$ sort algorithm over one that is generally $O(n^2)$ is evident. In fact, this difference becomes even more striking as the number of values to be sorted gets progressively larger.

We can illustrate how quicksort works by using the analogy stated earlier for selection and insertion sort. We begin quicksort by choosing any one

TABLE 3.1   **Growth Rates for Certain Selected Functions**

n	log n	n log n	n^2	n!	n^n
1	0	0	1	1	1
2	1	2	4	2	4
4	2	8	16	24	256
8	3	24	64	256	1677216
16	4	64	256	40320	*
32	5	160	1024	*	*
64	6	384	4096	*	*

of the values of the sequence at random and referring to that value as the *pivot*. We then compare the pivot to each of the other values in the sequence: Any value less than or equal to the pivot is placed to the left of the pivot in no particular order, and every value greater than the pivot is placed to its right. Once this is done, we then choose a pivot from each of these smaller sequences and continue as before. The process continues until we arrive at sequences whose size is no greater than one. When we reach this stage, the sorting of the original sequence is completed.

How do we design the quicksort algorithm? After choosing the pivot from the original sequence, we partition the sequence as we have described and then apply the same strategy to the *initial segment* (the sequence whose members are those that are not greater than the pivot) and to the *final segment* (those whose values are greater than the pivot). We can then give a preliminary pseudocode description of quicksort as

Choose a pivot from among the sequence members;
Partition the sequence by placing individual members either into
 an initial or final segment relative to the value of the current pivot;
Apply quicksort to the initial segment;
Apply quicksort to the final segment;

The pivot is placed in its proper position each time the segments are partitioned.

This is an example of a recursive algorithm, because quicksort calls itself (twice) from its own text. As already described in Section 3.10, the key to using recursion is that each subsequent invocation of the algorithm is for a smaller collection of values, with an eventual escape from the recursion. For quicksort, the escape is realized when no more than one value is on each side of the pivot. In this case, divide and conquer is implemented through a sequence of calls to quicksort, ending with the escape condition just described. Applying these ideas, a final refinement of the quicksort algorithm can be given as

```
void quicksort(arrayType arr,int first,int last)
{
 int pos;
 if(first < last)
 {
  Partition arr using the pivot by placing the pivot in position pos;
  quicksort(arr,first,pos − 1);
  quicksort(arr,pos + 1,last);
 }
}
```

The key problem that must be solved is the implementation of the partition algorithm. In order to accomplish this, we must be able to interchange values of the sequence. The proper position for the pivot is determined by ensuring that any value of the sequence greater than the pivot is moved to the right of the pivot, and any value less than or equal to the pivot is moved to its left. We can do this systematically by beginning with the initial member of the segment and moving forward until we locate a member whose value is larger than the pivot. The forward movement eventually stops at some position referenced by the current value of the index i (see the final coding of the placePivot method that follows). We then interchange the values of i and index1 (the loop index) and continue by resuming the forward movement from the current position of the loop index, looking for the next value greater than the pivot, and so on, until all of the components of the current array segment have been examined relative to the pivot, which we will take as the leftmost component. As a result of this processing, the proper position of the pivot is determined by the value of i when the loop completes its execution. Interchanging the array value at that position with the pivot results in the proper positioning of the pivot.

The placePivot method, coded next, summarizes this description, returning the proper position of the pivot.

```
public static int placePivot(Comparable [] arr, int first, int last)
 // Precondition: the pivot will be chosen as the first value
 // of the current array segment.
 // Postcondition: Returns the subscript of the pivot of arr.
 // When the method completes execution, this will be the subscript i
 // such that arr[first],...,arr[i-1] constitutes the initial
 // segment, and arr[i+1],...,arr[last] constitutes the final segment.
 {
  Comparable pivot = arr[first]; // Pivot is chosen as the first
                                 // value of array segment.
  int i = first;
  for(int index1 = first + 1;index1 <= last;++index1)
   // Invariant: arr[first+1],...,arr[i] < pivot
   // and arr[i+1],...,arr[index1-1] >= pivot.
   if(arr[index1].compareTo(pivot) <= 0)
   {
    ++i;
    swapValues(arr,index1,i);
   } // end if
  // terminates for-loop
  // Place pivot in its proper location and reveal its position.
```

```
// This location is the current value of i.
swapValues(arr,first,i);
return i;
} // terminates text of placePivot
```

The next method is the implementation of quicksort, using `placePivot` as the implementation of the partition algorithm. The last parameter keeps track of the number of recursive calls to `quickSort`.

```
public static void quickSort(Comparable [] arr,int first,int last, int[]
  count)
{
  int pivotLocation;
  if(first < last)
  {
    // Induce partition of current array segment
    pivotLocation = placePivot(arr,first,last);
    // Increase count of number of calls to quickSort.
    ++count[0];
    // quicksort the initial segment.
    quickSort(arr,first,pivotLocation-1,count);
    // quicksort the final segment.
    quickSort(arr,pivotLocation+1,last,count);
  } // terminates if-clause
} // terminates text of quickSort
```

Note that the signature of `quickSort` is not identical with those of `sel-Sort` or `inSort`. In a sense, the version of `quickSort` we have described allows for more generality. By choosing the initial values of `first` and `last`, we can apply `quickSort` to a smaller segment of the entire array. If, on the other hand, we wish to apply a version of `quicksort` similar to that given for `selSort` and `inSort`, all we need do is use the following version, called `qSort`:

```
public static void qSort(Comparable[] arr,int[] count)
  // Implements quicksort with the same parameter list
  // as setSort and inSort.
  {
    // Invoke the specific version of quickSort from 0 to
    // arr.length - 1.
    quickSort(arr,0,arr.length - 1,count);
  }
```

EXAMPLE 3.4   **Tracing** `placePivot`

We illustrate the action of `placePivot` on an `int`-valued array `arr` with nine components. Suppose `arr` appears initially as in Figure 3.3a.

FIGURE 3.3a

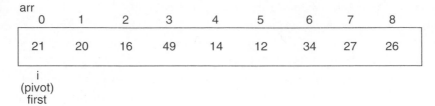

arr

0	1	2	3	4	5	6	7	8
21	20	16	49	14	12	34	27	26

i
(pivot)
first

The processing begins at index1 = 1, incrementing the value of i until the value of arr[index1] is larger than the current pivot value of 21. This value is found at component 3, as illustrated in Figure 3.3b.

FIGURE 3.3b

arr

0	1	2	3	4	5	6	7	8
21	20	16	49	14	12	34	27	26

first   i

At this point, the value of i does not increment, but instead the value of index1 increments to 4. We note that arr[index1] = arr[4] = 14, less than the pivot value of 21. Consequently, the value of i increments to 3, and the values of arr[3] and arr[4] are interchanged, yielding the result pictured in Figure 3.3c.

FIGURE 3.3c

arr

0	1	2	3	4	5	6	7	8
21	20	16	14	49	12	34	27	26

first   i

The value of index1 then increments to 5, and arr[index1] = arr[5] = 12 is compared to the pivot. Because the condition of the if-clause is true, the value of i increments to 4 and arr[index1] and arr[i] interchange values, as described in Figure 3.3d.

FIGURE 3.3d

arr

0	1	2	3	4	5	6	7	8
21	20	16	14	12	49	34	27	26

first   i

Nothing changes by the processing of this cycle—in fact, looking ahead to the execution of the remaining cycles, each subsequent value of arr[index1] is greater than the current pivot. Hence, after exhausting the for-loop, the array appears as in Figure 3.3e.

FIGURE 3.3e

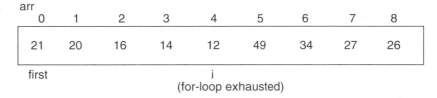

```
arr
    0      1      2      3      4      5      6      7      8
  ┌────────────────────────────────────────────────────────────┐
  │  21     20     16     14     12     49     34     27     26  │
  └────────────────────────────────────────────────────────────┘
   first                              i
                              (for-loop exhausted)
```

At this point, `swapValues(arr,first,i)` executes, producing the partition as shown in Figure 3.3f.

FIGURE 3.3f

```
arr
    0      1      2      3      4      5      6      7      8
  ┌────────────────────────────────────────────────────────────┐
  │  12     20     16     14     21     49     34     27     26  │
  └────────────────────────────────────────────────────────────┘
   first                       i
```

The current value of `i` (equal to 4 in this case) is returned as the proper location of the pivot value.

Quicksort is not *stable;* that is, there is no guarantee that equal values in the original (unsorted) sequence will retain their relative positions in the final sorted result. On the other hand, from the very nature of their descriptions, selection and insertion sorts are stable.

3.16 **Analysis of Quicksort**

Let `C(n)` be the number of comparisons performed by quicksort when applied to a sequence of n values. Then

$$C(0) = C(1) = 0 \qquad \text{Eq. 3.1}$$

because no comparisons are necessary either for an empty sequence or for a sequence with exactly one value. In any other case, quicksort compares the pivot with every other value in the sequence once. Thus, quicksort involves exactly n - 1 comparisons for sequences of length n ≥ 2. Suppose the two segments created by the partition have the respective lengths k and n - 1 - k. Then the number of recursive calls that count the number of comparisons required to properly place the pivots involved are given by `C(k)` and `C(n-1-k)`, and

$$C(n) = n - 1 + C(k) + C(n - 1 - k) \qquad \text{Eq. 3.2}$$

Equation 3.2 is an example of a *recurrence relation,* because it equates a value of C to values of C for smaller arguments. In fact, this equation shows that the value of `C(n)` depends on the choice of k.

We first consider the worst case, occurring when the partition fails to split the sequence. This happens when the members of the sequence are close to, or actually are, in order of increasing or decreasing size. In the most extreme case, one of the segments contains all of the values and the other segment is empty. Setting `k = 0` in Equaton 3.2 and using Equation 3.1 produces

```
  C(n)   = n - 1 + C(n-1)
C(n-1) = n - 2 + C(n-2)
C(n-2) = n - 3 + C(n-3)
```

$$\cdot$$
$$\cdot$$
$$\cdot$$

```
  C(3) = 2 + C(2)
  C(2) = 1 + C(1) = 1
```

Thus

```
C(n) = (n-1) + (n-2) + (n-3) + . . . + 3 + 2 + 1
```

$$= \frac{n*(n-1)}{2}$$

This affirms that, in the worst case, quicksort is $O(n^2)$.

In the average case, we observe that any value in the sequence can be chosen as the pivot. Let `p` denote the index of the proper position for the pivot. Setting `k = p-1` in Equation 3.2, we get

$$C(n) = n - 1 + C(p - 1) + C(n - p) \qquad \text{Eq. 3.3}$$

for `p = 1,2, . . . ,n`. If we add these n instances of Equation 3.3 and solve for `C(n)`, we obtain

$$C(n) = n - 1 + \frac{2}{n} [C(0) + C(1) + . . . + C(n-1)]$$

If we replace n by `n-1` in the last equation, we get

$$C(n-1) = n - 2 + \frac{2}{n-1}[C(0) + C(1) + . . . + C(n-2)]$$

Then

```
nC(n) - (n-1)C(n-1) = 2(n-1) + 2C(n-1)
```

which in turn yields

$$\frac{C(n)}{n+1} = \frac{C(n-1)}{n} + \frac{4}{n+1} - \frac{2}{n}$$

This reduces to

$$\frac{C(n)}{n+1} = \frac{4}{n+1} + 2\left[1 + \frac{1}{2} + . . . + \frac{1}{n}\right]$$

Finally, multiplying this last equation by n+1, we get

$$C(n) = 4 + 2(n+1) \left[1 + \frac{1}{2} + . . . + \frac{1}{n} \right]$$

where the sum $1 + \frac{1}{2} + . . . + \frac{1}{n}$ estimates the area under the graph of $f(x) = \frac{1}{x}$ from 1 to n, which is log n. This shows that, in the average case, quicksort is of order O(n log n).

3.17 **Mergesort**

Mergesort is another recursive sorting algorithm employing divide and conquer. The divide-and-conquer strategy applied in mergesort differs from that described for quicksort. In quicksort, the sequence is rearranged so that, when the initial and final segments are sorted around the pivot, the entire sequence is sorted. In contrast, mergesort breaks down the original sequence into two parts, each of which is sorted, and then these two parts are combined into a single sorted sequence. Thus, quicksort first calls for a decomposition of the original sequence and then sorts each part. Mergesort, on the other hand, first sorts each segment and then merges the results into a single sorted entity. In addition, mergesort is more "even-tempered" than quicksort and will be shown to be of order O(n log n) for all situations, although it is slightly less efficient in the same average cases than quicksort.

Here is a preliminary version of the mergesort algorithm:

if(first < last)
{
Find index of the midpoint mid of the segment;
Apply mergesort to the segment referenced from first to mid;
Apply mergesort to the segment referenced from mid + 1 to last;
Merge the sorted segments;
}

EXAMPLE 3.5   **Tracing Mergesort**
We illustrate mergesort using the same int-valued array used in Example 3.4. Thus, we begin with

a

0	1	2	3	4	5	6	7	8
21	20	16	49	14	12	34	27	26

This is broken up into the two halves shown in Figures 3.4a1 and 3.4a2.

FIGURE 3.4a1

FIGURE 3.4a2

The first half, illustrated in Figure 3.4a1, is decomposed as in Figure 3.4b:

FIGURE 3.4b

In turn, each of the segments shown in Figure 3.4b decomposes further as

A further decomposition of the two-member array segment produces

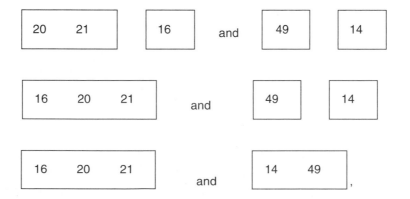

The following sequence of sorts and merges are performed:

and then the version shown in Figure 3.4c1.

FIGURE 3.4c1

| 14 | 16 | 20 | 21 | 49 |

Similarly, Figure 3.4a2 is decomposed and merged into Figure 3.4c2.

FIGURE 3.4c2

| 12 | 26 | 27 | 34 |

Finally, the sorted halves shown in Figures 3.4c1 and 3.4c2 are sorted and merged into Figure 3.4d.

FIGURE 3.4d

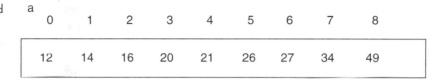

a

0	1	2	3	4	5	6	7	8
12	14	16	20	21	26	27	34	49

How do we implement the merge operation? We define a second array called `temp` to hold the merged halves at each stage of the decomposition. According to the mode of application of recursion in this case, sorting does not begin until after the halving process produces single-value sequences. Merging and sorting begins with these sequences and continues until the process is applied to all of the members of `temp`, completing the sorting phase of the algorithm. After this completes, the members of `temp` are copied back into the original array, terminating execution.

The merging operation is implemented as a `void` generic method called `merge` and requires five parameters: a reference `a` to the original array, a reference to `temp`, `first` = index of the initial value of the current array segment, `last` = index of the final value of the current array segment, and `mid` = index of the midpoint of the current array segment. Accordingly, `merge` is coded as the following:

```
public static void merge(Comparable [] a, Comparable [] temp,
                 int first, int mid, int last)
// Method which merges two sorted array segments
// into a single sorted array segment.
{
  // Precondition: a[first],...,a[mid] and
  // a[mid + 1],...,a[last] are already sorted.
  int first1 = first; // Beginning index of the first array segment
  int last1 = mid; // Last index of first array segment
  int first2 = mid + 1; // Beginning index of the second array
```

```
                              // segment.
    int last2 = last; // Last index of the second array segment.
    int index = first1; // Index of next usable component of temp array.

    // While both segments are not empty,
    // copy the smaller value into temp.
    while((first1 <= last1) && (first2 <= last2))
    // Invariant: temp[first1],...,temp[index - 1] is sorted,
    // and temp[first2],...,temp[index - 1] is sorted.
    {
     if(a[first1].compareTo(a[first2]) < 0)
      temp[index] = a[first1++];
     else
      temp[index] = a[first2++];
     ++index;
    } // terminates text of while-loop

    // At this point, at least one of the array segments
    // has been copied completely into temp.
    // Fill in the empty components of the leftover segment.

    // Fill in the remaining components of the first segment,
    // if necessary.
    while(first1 <= last1)
    // Invariant: temp[first1],...,temp[index - 1] is already
    // sorted.
    {
     temp[index] = a[first1++];
     ++index;
    }
    // Fill in the remaining components of the second segment,
    // if necessary.
    while(first2 <= last2)
    // Invariant: temp[first2],...,temp[index - 1] is already
    // sorted.
    {
     temp[index] = a[first2++];
     ++index;
    }

    // Copy the current contents of temp back into a.
    for(int index1 = first;index1 <= last;++index1)
```

```
    a[index1] = temp[index1];
} // terminates text of merge method.
```

The recursive code for mergesort follows. It contains an additional int-valued single-component array parameter count, which keeps track of the number of recursive calls to the mergeSort method.

```
public static void mergeSort(Comparable [] a, Comparable [] temp,
                              int first, int last, int [] count)
// Postcondition: a[first],...,a[last] is sorted in order
// of increasing size.
{
 int mid;  // Middle index.
 if(first < last)
 {
  // Determine the middle index of the current array segment.
  mid = (first + last)/2;
  // Increment the count on the number of recursive calls
  // to mergeSort
  ++count[0];
  // Mergesort first segment.
  mergeSort(a,temp,first,mid,count);
  // Mergesort second segment.
  mergeSort(a,temp,mid + 1,last,count);
  // Merge the two sorted segments:
  merge(a,temp,first,mid,last);
 } // terminates text of if-clause.
} // terminates text of mergeSort.
```

We can also design a version of mergesort called mSort, containing only three parameters: a reference to the original array, a reference to the temporary array, and an int-valued count parameter described earlier. Its implementation is

```
public static void mSort(Comparable [] a, Comparable [] temp,
                          int [] count)
 {
  mergeSort(a,temp,0,a.length - 1,count);
 } // terminates text of mSort
```

The syntax for the original call to mSort from the text of the caller can then be given by

```
mSort(arrayName,temporaryArrayName,counterArray);
```

where *arrayName* and *temporaryArrayName* identify the original array to be sorted and the temporary array, respectively. The identifier *counterArray* names the single-component `int`-valued array, initialized in the caller with value zero, keeping track of the number of recursive calls to `mSort`.

3.18 Analysis of Mergesort

Each call to `merge` for the segments `a[first]`, . . . ,`a[mid]` and `a[mid+1]`, . . . , `a[last]` involves a total of `k = last - first + 1` values and requires a maximum of `k + 1` comparisons.

For example, suppose we trace the merging of the segments

16	20	21	and	14	49

from Example 3.5, with `k = 5`. The following comparisons can be made:

1. Because `16 > 14`, copy 14 from `a[mid + 1]`, . . . ,`a[last]` into `temp[0]`.
2. Because `16 < 49`, copy 16 from `a[first]`, . . . ,`a[mid]` into `temp[1]`.
3. Because `20 < 49`, copy 20 from `a[first]`, . . . ,`a[mid]` into `temp[2]`.
4. Because `21 < 49`, copy 21 from `a[first]`, . . . ,`a[mid]` into `temp[3]`.

At this point, `a[first]`, . . . ,`a[mid]` is exhausted. Copy the remaining value `a[last] = 49` into `temp[4]`. This results in

temp

0	1	2	3	4
14	16	20	21	49

and requires four comparisons.

Each call to `mSort` involves two further calls to itself and halves the current segment. The next set of recursive calls halves each of these segments to form four segments of the original sequence, and so on, until nothing remains but segments consisting of single values. If n is the size of the original segment, there are `(int)(1 + log n)` calls to `mergeSort`.

The first call to `mergeSort` calls `merge` once, and `merge` merges all the members of the sequence, using a maximum of `n - 1` comparisons. This call results in two subsequent calls to `mergeSort`, and hence two more calls to `merge`, each of which involves `(n/2) - 1` comparisons. If we generalize, at any level j of the recursion, there are 2^j calls to merge, each of which requires $(n/2^j) - 1$ comparisons. Consequently, there are $n - 2^j = 2^j((n/2^j) - 1)$ comparisons. Because there are (int)(1 + log n) calls to mergeSort, we conclude that mergesort is of order O(n log n) in any case.

Mergesort is judged to be slightly slower than quicksort because mergesort involves the additional overhead of copying the sorted values into temp and then finally copying the completed temp back into a. This could involve substantial extra processing time for "larger" sequences.

3.19 **Chapter Summary**

An *algorithm* is a formal description of the steps involved in the solution of a specific programming problem. The initial version of the algorithm is usually stated in informal terms, containing a general yet accurate description of the steps involved in solving the problem in pseudocode. After a sequence of successive refinements, the final result is very close to the implementation in formal code.

In any object-oriented design of the solution, we must give serious attention to each of the following factors:

1. the classes and objects needed to contribute to the solution
2. the specific behavior of the classes and objects just chosen and used for the solution
3. if several classes are used, the contribution of each, and the relationship among them in arriving at the final solution
4. the interface existing between these classes and users

Important considerations in the ultimate choice of the solution is the algorithm's efficiency and correctness. In earlier chapters, we discussed the correctness of a proposed solution in either formal or informal terms. Informal methods for testing involve a clearly stated set of pre- and postconditions that accompany member functions of some class or the formal coding of some algorithm. An example of formal tests for correctness involve loop invariants, applying such mathematical results as the Principle of Finite Induction.

A key criterion used in choosing the most appropriate version of an algorithm is its efficiency. A metric used for measuring the relative efficiency of algorithms is big-O. More precisely, we use O(f(n)), where f(n) gives a quantitative estimate of the number of computations involved in completing the execution of the algorithm. When O(f(n)) produces the smallest values, the underlying algorithm is then judged to be in its most efficient form. Correctness should never be sacrificed for the sake of some streamlined alternative, however. We must assume that each candidate has been thoroughly tested for correctness and efficiency before it is incorporated as part of the solution of the original problem.

This chapter was primarily devoted to solving problems in searching and sorting as these apply to arrays. In later chapters, we will revisit these as they apply to other containers for data, such as those predefined in the class templates available in the Standard Template Library. In each case, we can consider these solutions as *reusable software tools,* which are stored permanently and invoked when necessary. The quality of reusability is enhanced by the flexibility of application to sequences of values from any well-defined data type T, because such solutions are presented in the form of generic methods and classes.

We also studied the use of *recursive algorithms* and their implementation. These were used in binary search, as well as quicksort and mergesort, and represent important and concise applications of the problem-solving paradigm known as *divide and conquer.* Using recursive methods usually involves the additional overhead of extra internal bookkeeping, however, because the processor must keep track of the current value assigned to each parameter in the current call to the recursive method. This is particularly critical when the original call to the method requires a considerable number of subsequent recursive calls. In defense of this methodology, the coding of a recursive algorithm is usually easily legible and in many cases represents the only viable alternative. In summary, using recursive methods generally enhances the efficiency of the entire design of the solution. This became particularly evident when we analyzed quicksort and mergesort and compared these to selection and insertion sort.

Finally, we may note that Java has a predefined util library that can be invoked from any user program. This library has many useful facilities that will be discussed in this text, starting with Chapter 4. Among these are two predefined methods for searching and sorting the values in any array; these appear as methods in the Arrays class in util. The user program can establish a linkage with this class using either

```
import java.util.*;
```

or

```
import java.util.Arrays;
```

The Arrays class contains a binarySearch method whose signature is

```
static int binarySearch(Object [] a,Object key);
```

This method searches the array for a specific object using the binary search algorithm. Because binarySearch is given in generic form, the array components must represent instances of the Comparable interface and must appear sorted in order of increasing size. The key parameter names the value to be searched for in the array. The int value returned is the subscript of the array `a` where `key` is located, if it appears in the array. Otherwise the negative value - `index` - 1 is returned, where `index` refers to the position in `a` where `key` may be inserted to maintain the ordering of the array values.

For example, this can be implemented as

```
Arrays.binarySearch(intArray,valueSought);
```

where `intArray` is an `Integer`-valued array, and `valueSought` is some `Integer`-valued expression holding the value to be sought in `intArray`.

In addition, `Arrays` contains a `sort` method with signature

```
static void sort(Object [] a);
```

This method sorts the components of `a` in order of ascending size and requires a precondition that these components must be objects that appear in the `Comparable` interface. We will study each of these methods and others in detail in Chapter 8. As an example, if `intArray` is defined as just described,

```
Arrays.sort(intArray);
```

will produce a sorted version of `intArray` whose `Integer`-valued components will be sorted in order of ascending size. For an easily readable account of the predefined `sort` method, see David Wagstaff's 2001 article, listed in the References section.

EXERCISES

1. Write a driver for `linsrch`. Include a variable `probes` that counts the number of probes required for `linsrch` to locate the first occurrence (if it exists) for the value sought in the sequence.

2. Using the Principle of Finite Induction, show, for any positive integer `n`,

    $$1 + 2 + 3 + . . . + n = \frac{n*(n+1)}{2}$$

3. a. Design a version of linear search that returns the subscript of the first occurrence of the value sought in the sequence (if such an occurrence exists), and otherwise returns the value -1.

    b. Design a version of linear search that counts all occurrences of the value sought in the sequence and returns the number of such occurrences.

4. Design a version of binary search that returns an `int` value: the array subscript where an instance of the value sought is found (if such a value exists). Otherwise, the value returned is -1.

5. Design a version of binary search in which we also pass a lower and upper index of the array segment in which the search is to be conducted.

6. Design a version of selection sort in which, instead of sorting the entire array as the only possible alternative, we pass two `int`-valued parameters: the subscripts of the beginning and end, respectively, of the array segment to be sorted.

7. Redo Exercise 6, using insertion sort.

8. Apply `inSort` to the sequence of integers

10 9 8 7 6 5 4 3 2 1

and conclude that exactly $45 = \dfrac{10*9}{2}$ interchanges are necessary to complete the sort. Similarly, apply `inSort` to the sequence

1 2 3 4 5 6 7 8 9 10

and conclude that 0 interchanges are necessary.

9. Show that an alternative form of `placePivot` is given by

```
 public static int placePivot(Comparable [] arr,int first,int last)
// Precondition: the pivot will be chosen as the last value
// of the current array segment.
// Postcondition:  Returns the subscript of the pivot of arr.
// When the method completes execution, this will be the subscript i
// such that arr[first],...,arr[i-1] constitutes the initial segment
// and arr[i+1],...,arr[last] constitutes the final segment.
{
 Comparable pivot = arr[last]; // Pivot is chosen as the last
                               // value of the array segment.
 int i = last;
 for(int index1 = last - 1;index1 >= first;--index1)
 // Invariant: arr[first],...,arr[i] < pivot
 // and arr[i+1],...,arr[index1-1] >= pivot.

  if(arr[index1].compareTo(pivot) >= 0)
  {
   −i;
   swapValues(arr,index1,i);
  } // ends if
 // terminates for-loop
 // Place pivot in its proper location, and reveal its position.
 swapValues(arr,last,i);
 return i;
} // terminates text of placePivot.
```

10. Test the code of `selSort`, `inSort`, `qSort`, and `mSort` on the same ten-component `int`-valued, then `char`-valued, and then `double`-valued array. Compare the number of swaps needed by `selSort` to complete the sort with the number of shifts needed for inSort, and then again with the number of recursive calls to each of qSort and mSort.

11. Is mergesort an example of a stable sort algorithm? Give reasons to support your answer.

12. Design an algorithm that searches a finite sequence of values of a common type for the largest value contained in that sequence. Then design an algorithm that searches the same sequence and retrieves the largest and smallest values contained in that sequence.

13. Design and implement an algorithm that conducts a linear search on a finite sequence of values of a common type, already sorted in order of increasing size. Discuss the benefits of performing a linear search on sequences with this property.

14. Rewrite the algorithms for selection sort and insertion sort, conducting the sort on the "high end" of the sequence—that is, the new version for each should include a loop invariant

```
// Invariant:  the values in the array from position p to
//  position last - 1 are sorted among themselves.
```

15. Write code for a recursive version of the *power function* defined for two int-valued parameters u,v, with $u \neq 0$, $v \geq 0$ as

$$power(u,v) = \begin{cases} 1, & \text{if } v = 0; \\ u * power(u,v-1), & \text{if } v > 0 \end{cases}$$

Thus, for any such u, v, power(u,v) = u^v.

16. The *Ackermann function* is defined as ACK(m,n) for any two nonnegative integers m,n according to the equations

a. ACK(0,n) = n + 1
b. ACK(m,0) = ACK(m-1,1), if m > 0
c. ACK(m,n) = ACK(m-1,ACK(m,n-1)), if m > 0 and n > 0

a. Compute ACK(0,4), ACK(2,0), ACK(1,2), and ACK(2,2) by hand.
b. Write code for a recursive version of a method that computes the values of ACK. Include a counter that keeps track of the number of recursive calls to this method.

17. The *Fibonacci function* FIB is defined for all positive integers n by

$$FIB(n) = \begin{cases} 1, & \text{if } n = 1,2; \\ FIB(n-1) + FIB(n-2), & \text{if } n > 2. \end{cases}$$

a. Compute the values of FIB(1), FIB(2), FIB(3), FIB(4), FIB(5) by hand.
b. Design an algorithm and write code for a recursive method computing the values of FIB. Also include a counter: an int-valued parameter that keeps track of the number of recursive calls to FIB.

18. Show that the following alternative also computes the values of the Fibonacci function:

```
public static int fastFib(int a, int b int n)
{
  if(n == 0) return b;
  else if(n == 1) return a;
  else return fastFib(a+b,a,n-1);
}
```

What should be the values of a,b in the text of the caller? Use a counter and compare the number of recursive calls to fastFib to those of FIB from Problem 17 of these exercises.

19. Use the Principle of Finite Induction to prove each of the following, valid for any positive integer n:

a. $1^2 + 2^2 + 3^2 + \ldots + n^2 = \dfrac{n*(n+1)*(2n + 1)}{6}$

b. $1 + 3 + 5 + \ldots + (2n - 1) = n^2$

c. $1 + \dfrac{1}{2} + \dfrac{1}{2^2} + \ldots + \dfrac{1}{2^n} = 2 * \left[1 - \dfrac{1}{2^{n+1}} \right]$

d. $\dfrac{1}{1*2} + \dfrac{1}{2*3} + \ldots + \dfrac{1}{n*(n+1)} = \dfrac{n}{n+1}$

20. Use the Principle of Finite Induction to show that $2^n \le n^n$ for all $n > 1$.

21. Design and implement a recursive method called writeBackwards, defined for character strings of any finite length by

writeBackwards(str) = characters of str written backwards.

For example, if str = "Hello, there!" then writeBackwards(str) = "!ereht ,olleH".

22. Use the code for writeBackwards from Exercise 21 to design and implement a boolean-valued method called palinTest, having a character string of finite length as its only parameter. The functionality of palinTest decides whether the current argument is a *palindrome,* namely, a character string that is the same whether read from left to right or from right to left.

PROGRAMMING PROJECTS

1. Let a,b be positive integers, with $a > b$. Define gcd(a,b) = *greatest common divisor* of a,b = largest positive integer dividing both a,b. Show each of the following:

a. If b is not a divisor of a, then gcd(a,b) = gcd(b,a%b);

b. Using (a), show

$$gcd(a,b) = \begin{cases} b, & \text{if } a\%b = 0 \\ gcd(b,a\%b), & \text{if otherwise} \end{cases}$$

Then use this recursive version of gcd(a,b) to design code computing gcd.

c.   There is an algorithm for finding gcd(a,b) for any positive a,b called the *Euclidean algorithm:* Assuming a >= b, divide a by b, obtaining

```
a = b*q + r
```

If r = 0, then b = gcd(a,b); otherwise continue. It then follows that gcd(a,b) = gcd(b,r). Now divide b by r to obtain

```
b = r*q₁ + r₁
```

Note also that r_1 < r. Now divide r by r_1, and so on, repeating this process until r_{n+1} = 0 for some n. This must certainly occur, because the remainders are decreasing. Then r_n = gcd(a,b). Using a loop and the Euclidean algorithm, write code for an iterative version of an implementation for gcd.

d.   Maintain counters in each of the iterative and recursive versions of gcd(a,b) and design drivers for each, comparing the count of loop cycles in the iterative version to the number of function calls for the recursive version.

2.   The following represents an "improvement" on insertion sort, called *Shell sort.* (See the article by D. L. Shell in the References Section). The algorithm sorts separate components of the original array, using components that are spaced k units apart from one another, for a finite sequence of diminishing values of k. The value of k is called an *increment.* After k array segments are sorted (using insertion sort), a new and smaller value of k is chosen, and the array is partitioned once again into a new set of segments. Each of the larger segments is sorted, and the process continues with a yet smaller value of k, culminating in the last phase where k = 1; at this point the resulting array is completely sorted. Initially, a finite sequence of diminishing increments is input, with the last value 1.

For example, if the original int-valued array arr contains the values, in sequence, given by

```
8   15   24   6   -3   12   0   5
```

and the sequence of increments is

```
5   3   1
```

then the first iteration (k = 5) produces the sorted segments

```
arr[0], arr[5]
arr[1], arr[6]
arr[2], arr[7]
arr[3]
arr[4]
```

The second iteration (k = 3) produces the sorting of

```
arr[0], arr[3], arr[6]
arr[1], arr[4], arr[7]
arr[2], arr[5]
```

The final iteration (k = 1) produces the sorting of the entire array.

a. Show that Shell sort can be implemented by

```java
public static void shellSort(Comparable [] arr,int [] increments,
                             int incrementSize, int [] count)
{
  // Performs shellSort on arr.
  // "increments" is an int-valued array containing the
  // diminishing increments of the sort.
  for(int index = 0; index < incrementSize; ++index)
  {
   // Invariant: increments[index] is the current size of the
   //  increment.
   int incSize = increments[index];
   for(int i = 0; i < arr.length;++i)
   {
    // Insert arr[i] in its proper position
    Comparable value = arr[i];
    int i2 = i - incSize;
    while(i2 >= 0 && value.compareTo(arr[i2]) < 0)
     {
       ++count[0];
       arr[i2 + incSize] = arr[i2];
       i2 -= incSize;
     }
    arr[i2 + incSize] = value;

   } // terminates innermost for-loop


   // The following code segment outputs the result of each pass.
   // Serves as a trace to the steps involved in shellSort.

   System.out.println("After cycle number " + index + 1 + ":");
   for(int i3 = 0; i3 <= arr.length - 1; ++i3)
    System.out.print(arr[i3] + "  ");

   System.out.println();
 } // terminates text of outermost for-loop
} // terminates text of shellSort method
```

by tracing this code by hand on the array component of `arr` just given, and then by writing a driver for this function.

b. Compare the number of processing steps involved between Shell sort and insertion sort, using loop counters for each.

3. The `Comparator` interface is predefined in Java. Objects that are constructed from `Comparator` represent objects that encapsulate a binary ordering. `Comparator` defines a single method called `compare`, and the interface for `Comparator` is described as

```
public interface Comparator
{
  int compare(Object obj1, Object obj2);
}
```

The `compare` method compares its two arguments and returns either a negative integer, zero, or a positive integer, according to whether the first argument is less than, equal to, or greater than the second. This represents a generalization of the `Comparable` interface, because `compare` can be coded by the programmer as any well-defined method returning an `int` value. For example, we can define

```
static class Comparing implements Comparator
{
  public int compare(Object obj1, Object obj2)
  {
    Comparable c1 = (Comparable)obj1;
    Comparable c2 = (Comparable)obj2;
    int compValue = c1.compareTo(c2);
    return compValue;
  } // terminates text of compare method
} // terminates text of Comparing class
```

Use this (as well as other candidates for the recoding of `compare`) to implement each of binary search, selection sort, insertion sort, quicksort, and mergesort, in order to sort any finite sequence of values according to the binary ordering you explicitly define for `compare`. In each case, you will require an additional parameter for the `Comparing` type, such as, for example

```
public static void selSort(Comparable [] arr, int [] swaps,
                           Comparing comp);
```

You will have to adjust the code to accommodate `compare` as the replacement for `compareTo`. Use the version of `Comparing` just supplied, and then redefine `Comparing` for sorting and performing a binary search for finite sequences of values to be rearranged in order of decreasing size. A variation of this appears later, in Section 12 of Chapter Seven, Application 2.

REFERENCES

Hoare, C. A. R. 1962. Quicksort. *Computer Journal* 5:10–12.

Knuth, Donald E. 1973. *The Art of Computer Programming, Volume 3: Sorting and Searching.* Reading, MA: Addison-Wesley.

Shell, D. L. 1959. A High Speed Sorting Procedure. *Communications of the ACM* 2 (July):30–32.

Wagstaff, David. 2001. Sorting Made Easy. *C/C++ Users Journal Java Solutions, Supplement.* (December):10–12.

CHAPTER 4

Hashing: Prelude to the `java.util` Library

CHAPTER OBJECTIVES

- To define the concept of hashing.
- To justify hashing as an important tool in contemporary data processing.
- To examine various forms of hashing and some of the drawbacks inherent in each form.
- To present a specific design of a hashing method using objects and classes.
- To introduce the facilities of the `java.util` library, particularly with respect to predefined facilities designed for hashing.

4.1 Introduction

In Chapter 3, we studied search algorithms for data stored in one-dimensional arrays. In each case, the search was conducted using a *key*, which was either the value sought or was part of an aggregate containing other related values, such as the data usually given in student or employee records. This chapter is devoted to the study of efficient methods of data storage and retrieval using the idea of hashing and its implementation in various forms.

In addition, we will begin a discussion of some of the facilities available in the `java.util` library and how these can be used to implement some of these hash strategies. In so doing, we can view this chapter as, in part, an introduction to the predefined structures, algorithms, and methods that implement those algorithms that are available in the Java environment.

4.2 Hashing as an Efficient Method of Data Storage and Retrieval

Let us consider the problem of storing employee records maintained in a one-dimensional array. Suppose the employee's social security number is

141

used as both a search key and an array subscript. Because the values of a social security number can be viewed as an integer ranging from a lowest possible value of 0 (formally represented by 000000000) and a highest possible value of 999999999, the array would have to contain as many components as there are distinct possible social security numbers—10^9 in all!

More precisely, suppose we design employee records using

```
class employeeRecord
{
 String surname;
 String name;
 char mi; // Middle initial.
 String dob; // Date of birth, using ddmmyy format.
    .
    .
    .

 // Other pertinent employee information.
    .
    .
    .

} // Terminates definition of employeeRecord.
```

We can then define the array of employee records (assuming an integer type large enough[1] to handle the range 0 . . . 999999999 as `employeeRecord employees = new employeeRecord[1000000000];` See Figure 4.1.

Although there is no difficulty in finding any specific employee record, there is clearly a serious problem in maintaining an array of this size. Allocating storage for this array is clearly inefficient because only a very small number of components will contain pertinent employee information. For example, suppose the firm employs 300 workers. All but 300 components of the array will be void, yet this excessive storage will still be allocated. Arrays of this kind are generally characterized as *sparse.*

To provide a more efficient means of storing and retrieving such data, we first define the idea of an *address calculator.* This is a function whose argument is a key and whose value is an address in a data structure containing the actual data. If the data structure is an array, the address calculator uses the array subscripts as access values. The process of converting the

---

[1]Java supports a predefined `BigInteger` type. The "big integer" values are realized as objects of the `BigInteger` class in the `java.math` package. Such values have no limits on size and precision, and we use `add`, `subtract`, `multiply`, and `divide` methods to perform the usual arithmetic operations. For more on the `BigInteger` type, see the work of Chan, Lee, and Kramer in the References section.

FIGURE 4.1

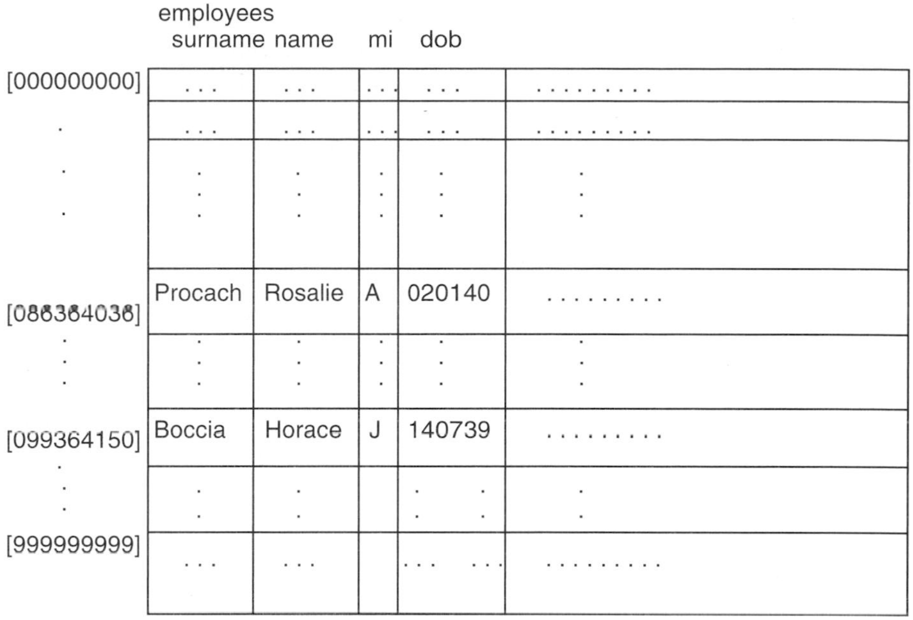

employees

	surname	name	mi	dob	
[000000000]	. . .	. . .	. .	. . .	. . . .
	. . .	. . .	. .	. . .	. . . .
	.	.	.	.	.
	.	.	.	.	.
	.	.	.	.	.
[088364038]	Procach	Rosalie	A	020140	. . . .
	.	.	.	.	.
	.	.	.	.	.
	.	.	.	.	.
[099364150]	Boccia	Horace	J	140739	. . . .
	.	.	.	.	.
	.	.	.	.	.
[999999999]	. . .	. . .		. . . . . .	. . . .

search key into an access value is called *hashing*, and the function that performs the conversion is called a *hash function*. The data structure that holds the actual data is generally called the *hash table*.

How does hashing influence the efficiency of data retrieval? In Chapter 3, we described two strategies for searching for and retrieving data: linear (sequential) search and binary search. We also showed that for an array of size n, linear search is of order O(n) and binary search is of order O(log n). For sufficiently large values of n, we observed that binary search is substantially more time efficient than linear search (see Table 3.1). In each case, the efficiency of the search strategy depends on the choice of n, the size of the underlying hash table.

Is it possible to improve on this? Specifically, does hashing establish a level of efficiency better than O(log n)? If we reexamine the example of maintaining employee records, hashing on the key of employee social security number yields the exact location (using array subscripts) of the data we seek—provided that the individual with that social security number is an employee of the firm. In effect, the search for employee data using the employee's social security number as the search key is of order O(1)—that is, it is a search strategy that completes execution in constant time, no matter where the data we seek appears in the array. The only drawback to this, so far, is that the array serving as the hash table is too large and sparse, if the hash function simply produces the array subscript of the actual social security number.

Can we effect a compromise? That is, can we diminish the size of the hash table to make it more manageable in size and at the same time maintain a level of efficiency of O(1)? As an example, we continue with the problem of maintaining employee records, using the social security number as the key. Suppose we define the following hash function H:

H(*social security number*) = *sum of its digits.*

Then the hash table becomes an array of employee records with subscripts ranging from 0 = H(000000000) to 81 = H(999999999). In particular, H(086364036) = 36 and H(099364150) = 37. Referring to Figure 4.2, all

FIGURE 4.2

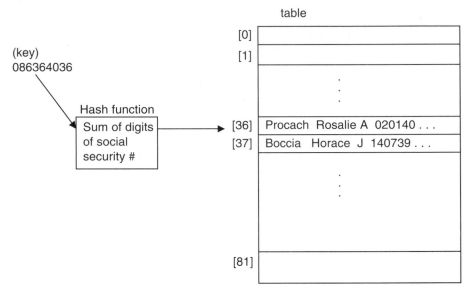

of the pertinent information about `Rosalie A. Procach` appears in the hash table at position 36, and that of `Horace J. Boccia` appears in position 37.

A number of potential problems arise with many hashing operations. To illustrate one with the hash function just described, suppose another employee has the social security number 066606661. Then H(066606661) = 37, a position already occupied by `Horace J. Boccia`. This results in a *hash collision*, because at least two candidates are vying for the same location in the hash table. A hash function for which hash collisions are impossible is called *perfect*. An example of a perfect hash function is

H(*social security number*) = *social security number, omitting leading zeros.*

This uses the observation that no two individuals share the same social security number. In this case, the price of perfection is too costly, for the reasons given earlier.

We must therefore face the reality of choosing hash functions that are practical, efficient, and appropriate for our needs. Several factors should influence our decision in choosing a suitable hash function:

- It should produce values lying in the subscript range of the resulting hash table.
- It should be easily and efficiently computable.
- It should avoid as many hash collisions as possible.

Given the reality that any choice of a reasonable hash function is prone to producing a certain number of hash collisions, we must decide on a course to follow when a collision does occur.

4.3 **Choosing an Appropriate Hash Function**

The efficient storage and easy and timely retrieval of large volumes of data are important considerations in the design of a large segment of commercial software. Inevitably, the design requires the use of hash functions. In this section, we will explore some of the more commonly used hash functions and the course to follow in the event of a hash collision.

We stated earlier that one of the criteria to consider in choosing a hash function is its *ease of computation*. We should anticipate applying the hash function frequently, because the associated software will generally involve a large number of searches in the hash table either for data currently stored there or for locations that are currently unoccupied where the newly acquired data can be stored. Consequently, computing values of the hash function should be done as simply and as efficiently as possible.

Another factor to consider is the ability of the hash function to produce values that are *widely distributed throughout its complete range*. Thus, the hash function should avoid a frequent repetition of a relatively small number of specific values and neglecting the rest of the possible values. Choosing a hash function with this ability or property will have the favorable side effect of avoiding the occurrence of a large number of possible hash collisions. For example, suppose we choose a hash function H for the employee example obtained by extracting its first three digits, omitting any leading zeros.[2] Then H(099364150) = 99 and H(237488710) = 237; if we assume that the hash table is in the form of any array, it will have 1000 components ranging from a subscript of 0 to a subscript of 999. This hash function has the undesirable side effect of producing an unequal distribution of hash values, however, because relatively few individuals have social security numbers whose first three digits are close to 0 or close to 1000. This results in a *clustering* of values in a small segment in the hash table.

[2]If the social security number begins with at least three zeros, this number hashes to zero.

Any one of a number of different methods can be applied in choosing an appropriate hash function. Many of these choices are treated in greater detail in Knuth's book on computer programming. (See the References section at the end of this chapter).

Method 1: The Middle Square Technique

This method takes the square of the key and then extracts a small number of consecutive digits (usually three) from the middle digits of the result. For example, using three consecutive digits on the social security numbers, the possible hash results range from 0 = 000 through 999. As an illustration, $(099364150)^2$ = 9873234305222500, omitting any leading zeros. If we then extract the seventh through ninth digits, the hash value is 430. Experimental evidence shows that a fairly even distribution of values throughout the complete range of subscripts in the hash table occurs when this technique is applied. As a downside, the process of squaring a key as large as a social security number, even when omitting any leading zeros, and then dividing the result by an appropriate power of ten to extract the desired digits requires computing with integer values that are generally beyond the range supported by any of the usual predefined integer types. A `BigInteger` type would have to be used to accommodate the values produced by this computation.

Method 2: Random Number Generators

This method defines the hash function as a *random number generator* whose values would have to be restricted to the subscript range of the hash table. Such random number generators usually begin by passing an `int`-valued parameter (the *seed*) and then computing a finite sequence of random integers lying in the subscript range of the hash table. In Java, a predefined method (appearing in `Math`) called `random()`, which generates a random number between 0.0 and 1.0, as well as a class called `Random` in the `java.util` library, constructs random numbers. In either case, the number of random values to be generated is then set by the programmer. The rationale for generating more than one random number is to provide several alternative hash table subscripts in the event of a hash collision. In fact, using such a random number generator in the context of hashing involves presenting the search key as the initial seed.

Method 3: Folding

This method uses the digits of the key in some arithmetical combination, with a result falling in the numerical range of the hash table subscripts. Method 1, the Middle Square Technique, is a special case of folding. In fact, we earlier discussed another form of folding using social security numbers, taking the sum of the digits.

Another version is called *shift folding*, in which a social security number is broken down into smaller groups and then added. For instance, 099364150 is first decomposed as 99, 364, 150 (omitting any leading zeros) and then added as 99 + 364 + 150 = 613. If the keys are not BigInteger values, such as character strings, a conversion of each char value in the string, in the order of appearance, into its equivalent ASCII (or UNICODE) code number would precede any folding operation. As an example, suppose the key is the character string "money". The equivalent ASCII code for this string is 109111110101121, which is then folded as 109 + 111 + 110 + 101 + 121 = 552.

Projection is another form of folding in which certain digits of the key are removed before the key is mapped to a subscript of the hash table. To illustrate this, suppose serial numbers of products handled by a firm are to be hashed, where these numbers might begin or end with a certain fixed group of digits (or characters). For example, suppose the serial numbers of all items stored in a warehouse are nine-digit integers beginning with 011, with each of the remaining six digits ranging over the integers from 0 through 9. An efficient projection map would ignore the first three digits and hash the remaining six by some specific method. One such possibility adds the remaining six digits, as in H(011236809) = 28 and H(011364150) = 19. The hash values would then lie in the range from 0 through 54. Not all of these values are equally likely to occur, however.

Method 4: Division with Remainder

In this case, the hash value is the remainder obtained when the key is divided by some suitably chosen positive integer maxSize, as in

```
H(key) = key % maxSize
```

The hash values lie in the range from 0 through maxSize - 1. It is not difficult to code this hash function; if maxSize is chosen to be a suitable prime number, the number of possible hash collisions is minimized. For example, suppose maxSize = 2011, and suppose we use the example of folding the last six digits of the serial numbers described earlier. Then H(011236809) = 1522, because 236809 = 2011 * 17 + 1522, and H(011225909) = 677, since 225909 = 2011 * 112 + 677. These values lie in the subscript range from 0 through 2010.

4.4 **Strategies for Resolving Hash Collisions**

Despite the efficiency of some of the proposed hash functions, there remains the inevitable reality that hash collisions might still occur. In response, we consider several alternative strategies to pursue in the event of a hash collision. We classify these into two major categories: *open addressing* and *separate chaining.* (Separate chaining is discussed in the next section.)

Strategies for Open Addressing

When a hash collision occurs in an open addressing scheme, we look for some unoccupied position in the hash table. This implies that the number of records capable of being stored in the hash table cannot exceed the size of the table. Descriptions of some of the more frequently used open addressing strategies—linear probing, quadratic probing, and double hashing—follow.

Linear Probing

A simple open addressing strategy is *linear probing,* which can best be described by an example. Suppose `key` hashes to `k` for some specific value of `key`, and suppose that the component of the hash table at position `k` is already occupied. Thus, we have a hash collision. If we assume the hash table (declared as `hTable`) has subscripts in the range of `0` through `hTable.length`, we then probe the next component in the hash table, located at position `(k + 1)%hTable.length`. If this location is empty, the data will be inserted there; if not, we continue the linear search for the first available unoccupied slot. The hash function in this case takes the form

```
H(key) = key%hTable.length
```

The effect of combining linear probing with searching the hash table using modular arithmetic is that, if all table positions from `k` through `hTable.length - 1` are currently occupied, we "wrap around" to position `0` and test whether it is occupied, and so on, until an available slot is found. Figure 4.3 illustrates the use of linear probing in a hash table of `int` values with `hTable.length = 11` for the sequence `23, 36, 89, 12, 134`.

FIGURE 4.3a   hTable

	23									
0	1	2	3	4	5	6	7	8	9	10

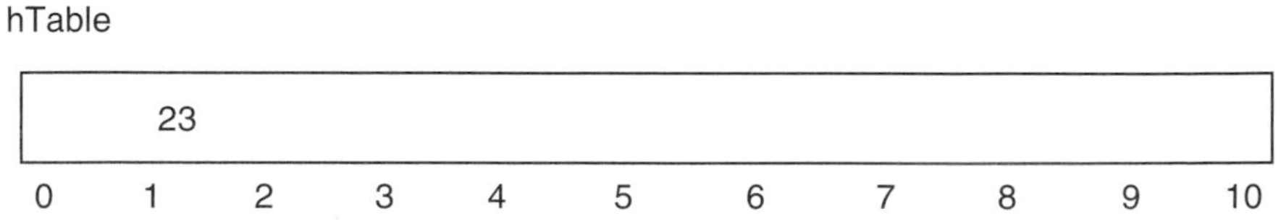

FIGURE 4.3b   hTable

	23		36							
0	1	2	3	4	5	6	7	8	9	10

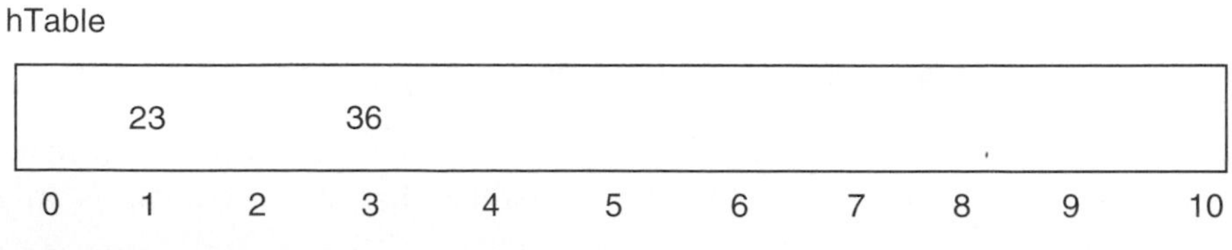

FIGURE 4.3c   hTable

	23	89	36							
0	1	2	3	4	5	6	7	8	9	10

FIGURE 4.3d   hTable

	23	89	36	12						
0	1	2	3	4	5	6	7	8	9	10

FIGURE 4.3e   hTable

	23	89	36	12	134					
0	1	2	3	4	5	6	7	8	9	10

Linear probing is prone to *primary clustering*, which is a tendency for a large number of keys to hash to a relatively small group of locations close to one another. When this happens, searching for a location in which to insert a new value will be unsuccessful for a large number of probes if the search is currently going on in a large cluster. This diminishes the efficiency of linear probing. In fact, the efficiency diminishes dramatically as the set of values to be hashed increases, because there is a tendency for smaller clusters spread throughout the hash table to collect into increasingly larger clusters.

Quadratic Probing

Quadratic probing is an alternative to linear probing that eliminates (to some extent) the type of clustering associated with linear probing. As an example of how quadratic probing works, suppose we once again apply the hash function `H(key) = key%hTable.length`, and suppose `H(key) = k`. In this case, if the location with subscript k is occupied, we probe position `(k + 1²)%hTable.length = (k + 1)%hTable.length`. If this position is occupied, we next probe position `(k + 2²)%hTable.length = (k + 4)%hTable.length`, then position `(k + 3²)%hTable.length`, and so on, until an unoccupied location is found.

Quadratic probing has its own set of subtle setbacks. For example, if `hTable.length = 16` and `H(key) = 5`, then any further probing in the event of an initial collision will inspect only positions `6`, `9`, `14`, and no others. This phenomenon is called *secondary clustering* and severely limits the effectiveness of quadratic probing, especially if these table positions are already occupied. Figure 4.4 illustrates quadratic probing for the same hash table and input sequence already used in linear probing.

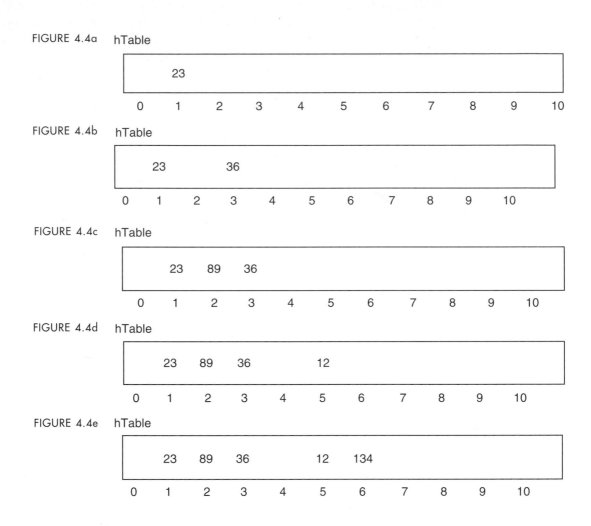

FIGURE 4.4a   hTable

FIGURE 4.4b   hTable

FIGURE 4.4c   hTable

FIGURE 4.4d   hTable

FIGURE 4.4e   hTable

One way to avoid secondary clustering is to generate more than one table subscript at a time by applying several hash functions to the key when a collision occurs. This technique is called *rehashing* and proceeds as follows: If a collision occurs on a specific key with the first hash function, apply the second hash function, and so on, until an unoccupied location is found in the table. If the sequence does not produce a suitable location, we attempt linear or quadratic probing from the value produced from the first hash function until an unoccupied location is found. If this does not work for the first hash function, proceed to the second and repeat the entire sequence, and so on. The worst possible case arising from this would be if none of the hash functions using any of the probing strategies results in the successful placement of the data in the table. At that point, we can simply declare that the table is full and abort the operation. This strategy clearly depends on the sequence of hash functions chosen and the tendency of each of these to produce primary and secondary clustering. We will say no more about this here. Instead, we will discuss one rehashing method (called *double hashing*) that has proven successful in a large number of specific situations.

The strategies for resolving collisions discussed so far are characterized as *circular hashing methods,* because the course of probing leads to a "wrapping around" to the initial locations of the hash table if we continue to the end of the table before locating an unoccupied position.

Double Hashing

In *double hashing,* we define a primary hash function H_1 and a secondary hash function H_2. These work in combination by using H_1(key) to provide the initial probe into the hash table and then using H_2(key) to give an interval length in the probe sequence, if necessary. H_2 is chosen so as to always give a value relatively prime to the value of hTable.length.

For example, suppose hTable.length = 17, so that hTable has components 0, 1, . . . , 16. In addition, suppose we define H_1(key) = key%hTable.length = key%17, and H_2(key) = 11 - (key%11). If key = 39, then H_1(key) = 5; if hTable[5] is unoccupied, then the data is placed there. On the other hand, if a collision results, then the probe sequence with increment given by H_2(key) = H_2(39) = 11 - (39%11) = 5. The probe sequence is then given by 5, 10, 15, 3, 8, 13, 1, 5, 11, 16, 4, 9, 14, 2, 7, 12, 0. Note that each component of hTable may be probed at some point, owing to the fact that hTable.length = 17 and 11 are relatively prime. Because each location of hTable is probed at some point, clustering is avoided.

Figure 4.5 illustrates the application of double hashing on the same input sequence as that used earlier for linear and quadratic probing, but now using H_1(key) key % 11 and H_2(key) = 7 - (key % 7). Note that the probe sequence is 1, 6, 0, 5, 10, 4, 9, 3, 8, 2, 7, if key = 23.

FIGURE 4.5a   hTable

	23									
0	1	2	3	4	5	6	7	8	9	10

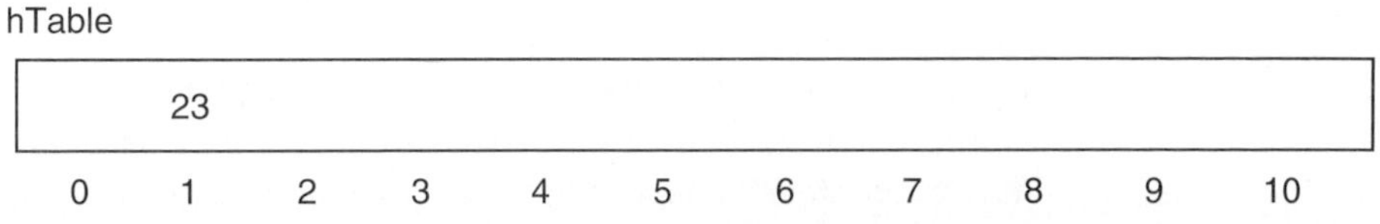

FIGURE 4.5b   hTable

	23		36							
0	1	2	3	4	5	6	7	8	9	10

FIGURE 4.5c   hTable

	23		36		89					
0	1	2	3	4	5	6	7	8	9	10

FIGURE 4.5d   hTable

	23		36		89		12			
0	1	2	3	4	5	6	7	8	9	10

FIGURE 4.5e   hTable

	23	134	36		89		12			
0	1	2	3	4	5	6	7	8	9	10

4.5   Resolving Hash Collisions Using Buckets and Linked Lists

In the previous section, we discussed the problem of hash collisions, based on the principle of *open addressing:* Only one data record is permitted to occupy any position in the hash table. But what if hash collisions could be avoided by somehow permitting more than one data record to be stored at the same position in the hash table? There are two possible ways to implement this: *bucket hashing* and *separate chaining.*

Bucket Hashing

Here we visualize the hash table as being capable of maintaining an array of records (called a *bucket*) at each location. The buckets will have a common size, fixed in advance. Thus, the hashing operation can be captured in pseudocode as

Compute `H(key) = k;`
Let `hTable[k]` = *kth bucket. Search the components*
`hTable[k][0], . . . , hTable[k][bucketSize - 1]` *of* `hTable[k]`
for an unoccupied component;

if(no unoccupied component is available) abort the operation;
else place data in `hTable[k][j]`, *where* `j` = *subscript of next available*
unoccupied component in `hTable[k]`;

It is important in the implementation of this design to define buckets whose common size is not too small (to avoid collisions when a bucket becomes full) and not too large (to avoid wasting storage). The search for the next available unoccupied component in a bucket is done sequentially, beginning with component `hTable[k][0]`, if linear search is used, or the search can be conducted using binary search.

We illustrate bucket hashing using Figure 4.6 with `bucketSize = 4` for the same hash function and input sequence treated earlier.

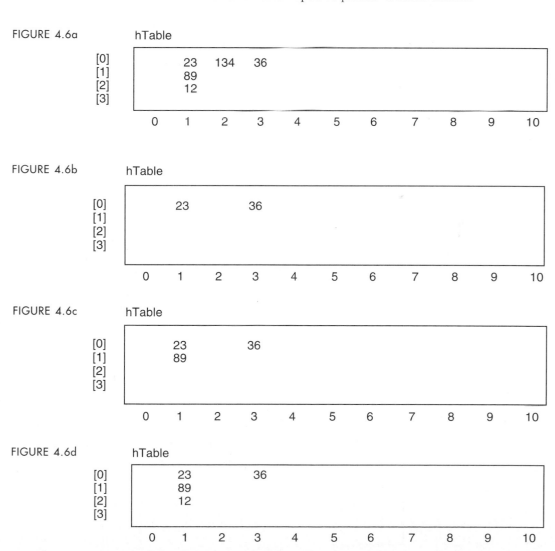

FIGURE 4.6a

FIGURE 4.6b

FIGURE 4.6c

FIGURE 4.6d

FIGURE 4.6e

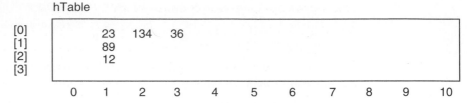

Bucket hashing is a viable candidate for a paradigm that avoids as many hash collisions as possible, but it has limitations in efficiency and represents an alternative that is no better than separate chaining. To see how efficiency is compromised, note that `H(key) = k` implies that an unoccupied location in `hTable[k]` is sought. Because `hTable[k]` is itself an array, we must search that bucket (using linear or binary search) for an unoccupied location in case we wish to deposit a new data record in the hash table. Therefore, bucket hashing eventually becomes an operation that is either `O(n)` or `O(log n)`.

FIGURE 4.7

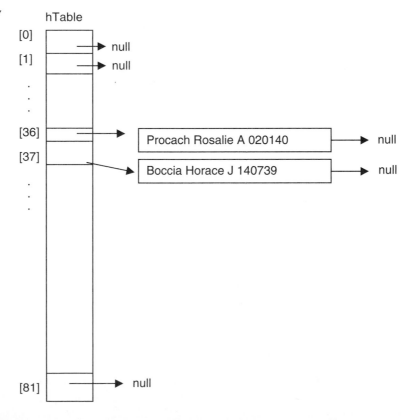

Linked Implementations: Separate Chaining

Separate chaining involves a design in which the hash table is an array of references to linearly linked lists. This approach avoids the threat of hash collisions entirely, unlike the situation with buckets. In this case, if a new data record hashes to a value in hTable that is already occupied, the new record is inserted in the same linked list given by that table location. For example, suppose we revisit the example of employee records discussed earlier. After the records of Rosalie A. Procach and Horace J. Boccia have been inserted, hTable looks like Figure 4.7.

Suppose an employee named Bart W. Jones with birthday 11/10/53 and with social security number 066666610 joins the firm. Note that Jones' social security number also hashes to 37. Instead of experiencing a hash collision, this record is inserted into hTable in location 37, as shown in Figure 4.8.

FIGURE 4.8

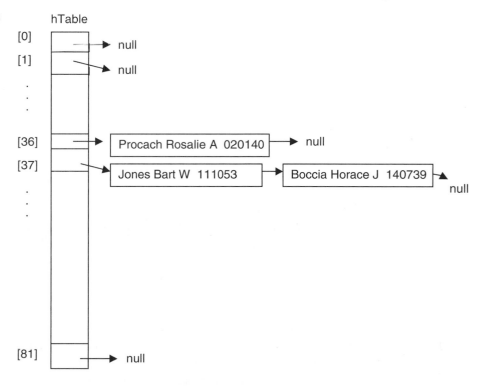

Accordingly, each component of hTable is a reference to a *chain* (linearly linked list) of records hashing to the same value. In this way, the only limitations we face are those imposed by the hardware involving the amount of storage allocated for creating new nodes. Searching for a specific record involves, first, hashing to the proper location in hTable, and then performing a sequential search through the list (if not empty) for the desired record. Inserting, removing, and retrieving records then become familiar list operations.

Suppose we apply separate chaining to the eleven-component array `hTable`. Its components now are references to linked lists whose nodes contain `info` components that hash according to `H(key) = key % hTable.length = key % 11`. If we again use the same input sequence as before, the result obtained is as shown in Figure 4.9.

FIGURE 4.9

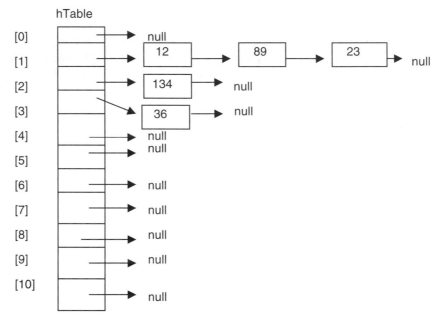

4.6 Implementations of Hashing Using Generic Classes in Java

Our primary objective is to place hashing in an application domain using classes and objects. This implies that we can define an abstract data type (ADT) having its foundation in the hashing process. In order to accomplish this task, we anticipate the design of a class called `hashTable`, whose objects will be specific hash tables with certain operations that are important to hashing, ultimately becoming the associated instance methods for this class.

Several preliminary observations about hashing influence this design.

1. In describing the user interface, we observe that the user need not be aware of the specific choice of the hash function.
2. The user has no need to know which strategy for resolving hash collisions is adopted (whether it be linear or quadratic probing, double hashing, buckets, or separate chaining).

3.   The only operations available to the user should be:
   a.   a *constructor,* which creates a new `hashTable` object, with a key value coming from a type associated with the remaining data to be installed in the table
   b.   an *insertion operator,* in which the user provides the specific data to be installed in the table
   c.   an operator *retrieving* a specific data item stored in the table
   d.   a *removal operator,* permitting the removal of data that are no longer needed from the table.

Our design includes one of a generic type characterizing the structure of any record to be processed in the hash table. Our initial design views any such record as consisting of two major components:

1.   a *key* field, specifying the data type of the keys used in the hashing operation
2.   a *data* field, containing the pertinent data found in each value to be stored in the table

Thus, any such item assumes the form pictured in Figure 4.10.

FIGURE 4.10

keyField	*dataField*

All of the examples we have described so far in this chapter can be viewed as `hashTable` objects whose *keyField* is instantiated as `int`. Consequently, the hash function defined in the proposed `hashTable` class will be an `int`-valued function of a single `int` variable. This hash function will return a value lying in the range `0 . . MaxSize - 1`, where `MaxSize` will be some convenient positive integer whose value represents the size of the proposed table.

We begin by formally defining the structure `keyedStructure` of data records to be hashed. This design will include a `boolean` field `emptyVal` whose initial value is `true` and remains `true` for that component of `hashTable` until an insertion is performed at that location. After the insertion, `emptyVal` is assigned `false`. This also simplifies the removal operation, because all that is required to decide whether a component in the hash table is empty is whether the current value of its `emptyVal` field is `true` (regardless of the contents of that component's *dataField* value). In the case of removal, all that needs to be done is to change the component's `emptyVal` value from `false` to `true`. A subsequent insertion at that location will perform two operations: copy over the previous value of the current `dataVal` value with the new value, and change the current value of that component's `emptyVal` field from `true` to `false`. With these modifications, our code for `keyedStructure` is given as

```
class keyedStructure
{
 int keyVal;
 Object dataVal;
 boolean emptyVal;
}
```

We also define the size of the hash table array using

```
final int MaxSize = some convenient positive integer;
```

We now turn to the design of `hashTable`. In doing so, we must make some preliminary decisions as to whether we will use an open addressing strategy, or if we wish to implement buckets or separate chaining. In the case of open addressing, we must decide whether to resolve hash collisions, should they occur, by linear or quadratic probing or by double hashing. We will choose an open addressing scheme using linear probing as a collision resolution strategy.

The `public` portion of `hashTable` lists methods for a parameterless constructor and for those implementing insertion, retrieval, and removal. We begin the coding of the implementation details with the coding of the constructor. The object constructed will contain an array called `hTable`, each of whose components will have an `emptyVal` field initialized as `true`, to simulate an empty array. The formal code is given by

```
// Constructor. Constructs hash table of the specified size
// with all empty components.
// Postcondition: the emptyVal field of each component
// of the hash table is initialized as true, indicating
// each such component is empty.
public hashTable()
{
 for(int index = 0; index < MaxSize; ++index)
 hTable[index].emptyVal = true;
} // terminates text of constructor.
```

The insertion operation implements open addressing with linear probing. It is coded as a `void` method with a single `keyedStructure` parameter.

```
// Insertion operation. Implements open addressing with
// linear probing.
// Postcondition: value is copied into hTable at position
// given by H(value).emptyVal of the next available location
// determined by linear probing.
```

```
void insert(keyedStructure value)
{
 int position;
 position = H(value.keyVal);
 while(!hTable[position].emptyVal) // Linear probing enforced
  position = (position + 1)%MaxSize;
 hTable[position].dataVal = value.dataVal;
 hTable[position].emptyVal = false;
} // terminates text of insert method.
```

The retrieval operation uses a `boolean`-valued variable called `continueSearch` that is assigned `true` initially and that remains `true` until the value sought (the value stored in the `dataVal` field of the first parameter) is found (if ever). The second parameter is assigned `true` upon exiting the method just when the search is successful, and `false` otherwise. The second parameter is defined as a single-component array to take advantage of the parameter pass by reference.

```
// Retrieval operation.
// Postcondition: value of second parameter becomes true
// if value sought appearing as first parameter is found
// in hash table; otherwise, false.
boolean retrieve(keyedStructure value)
{
 int position, initialPosition;
 boolean continueSearch = true;
 initialPosition = H(value.keyVal);
 position = initialPosition;
 do
 {
  // If value sought is located at position, or position
  // is empty, terminate the search.
  if(hTable[position].dataVal.equals(value.dataVal)
     || hTable[position].emptyVal)
    continueSearch = false;
  else // continue search
   position = (position + 1)%MaxSize;
} while(position != initialPosition && continueSearch);
 return hTable[position].dataVal.equals(value.dataVal);
 // Return value indicates whether the dataVal field
 // of valueSought is found in hTable.
} // terminates text of retrieve method.
```

The design of the removal operation reflects the philosophy about determining whether a component of the hash table is judged empty. The method returns `true` in the case of a successful removal, and otherwise returns `false`.

```
// Removal operation. This version maintains the value of the
// dataVal component until copied over. Effectively, that dataVal
// component has been removed because the value of its emptyVal
// field is changed from false to true in the case of a successful
// removal.
// Postcondition: returns true in the case of a successful removal,
// otherwise returns false.
boolean remove(keyedStructure value)
{
 int position, initialPosition;
 initialPosition = H(value.keyVal);
 position = initialPosition;
 do
 {
 // If value is found in hash table
 if(hTable[position].dataVal.equals(value.dataVal))
 {
  // Empty hash table at that position and announce
  // successful removal.
  hTable[position].emptyVal = true;
  return true;
 }
 else // Otherwise, resume search
  position = (position + 1)%MaxSize;
 } while(position != initialPosition);
 return false; // Report unsuccessful search.
} // terminates text of remove method.
```

The code for the definition of the hash function is `private`, conforming to our design plan. We also decide that this version will always involve keyed structures whose `keyVal` field has `int` values. Thus, we have

```
// Coding of hash function. Uses division with remainder.
private int H(int value)
{
 return value % MaxSize;
}
```

Finally, because the user requires no knowledge of the internal structure of the actual array implementing the hashing operation, we define `hTable`—as a `private` component of `hashTable`—as

```
private keyedStructure[] = new keyedStructure[MaxSize];
```

We can test hashTable using the input values described earlier, using the program described in Example 4.1.

EXAMPLE 4.1   The following represents a driver for hashTable, where we hash the five int values 23, 36, 89, 12, 134.

```
public static void main(String [] args)
 {
 // Construct hashTable object.
 hashTable intTable = new hashTable();

 // Create Integer wrappers for the sequence 23, 36, 89, 12, 134.
 int intArray[] = {23,36,89,12,134}; // Conformant array.
 Integer IntegerArray[] = new Integer[intArray.length];
 for(int index = 0; index < IntegerArray.length; ++index)
 IntegerArray[index] = new Integer(intArray[index]);

 // Declare five keyedStructure objects.
 keyedStructure intStruct0 = new keyedStructure();
 intStruct0.keyVal = 23;
 intStruct0.dataVal = IntegerArray[0];
 intStruct0.emptyVal = true;

 keyedStructure intStruct1 = new keyedStructure();
 intStruct1.keyVal = 36;
 intStruct1.dataVal = IntegerArray[1];
 intStruct1.emptyVal = true;

 keyedStructure intStruct2 = new keyedStructure();
 intStruct2.keyVal = 89;
 intStruct2.dataVal = IntegerArray[2];
 intStruct2.emptyVal = true;

 keyedStructure intStruct3 = new keyedStructure();
 intStruct3.keyVal = 12;
 intStruct3.dataVal = IntegerArray[3];
 intStruct3.emptyVal = true;

 keyedStructure intStruct4 = new keyedStructure();
 intStruct4.keyVal = 134;
 intStruct4.dataVal = IntegerArray[4];
 intStruct4.emptyVal = true;

 // Now insert these five keyedStructure objects into intTable.
```

```
intTable.insert(intStruct0);
intTable.insert(intStruct1);
intTable.insert(intStruct2);
intTable.insert(intStruct3);
intTable.insert(intStruct4);

// Test for keyedStructure values appearing in intTable
if(intTable.retrieve(intStruct0))
 System.out.println(intStruct0.keyVal + " is in intTable");
else
 System.out.println(intStruct0.keyVal + " is not in intTable");

if(intTable.retrieve(intStruct1))
 System.out.println(intStruct1.keyVal + " is in intTable");
else
 System.out.println(intStruct1.keyVal + " is not in intTable");

if(intTable.retrieve(intStruct2))
 System.out.println(intStruct2.keyVal + " is in intTable");
else
 System.out.println(intStruct2.keyVal + " is not in intTable");

if(intTable.retrieve(intStruct3))
 System.out.println(intStruct3.keyVal + " is in intTable");
else
 System.out.println(intStruct3.keyVal + " is not in intTable");

if(intTable.retrieve(intStruct4))
 System.out.println(intStruct4.keyVal + " is in intTable");
else
 System.out.println(intStruct4.keyVal + " is not in intTable");

} // terminates text of main method
```

The output is given by

```
23 is in intTable
36 is in intTable
89 is in intTable
12 is in intTable
134 is in intTable
```

The fact that linear probing was applied appears in the code of three methods: `insert`, `retrieve`, and `remove`. For example, `insert` contains the code segment

```
while(!hTable[position].emptyVal)
  position = (position + 1)%MaxSize;
```

If we decide to apply quadratic probing instead, this would be changed to

```
int increment = 1;
while(!hTable[position].emptyVal)
{
 position = (H(value.keyVal) + increment*increment)%MaxSize;
 ++increment;
}
```

Similar changes must be made in `retrieve` and `remove`. We leave these coding details as an exercise. (See Exercise 6 at the end of this chapter.)

Suppose we decide to implement separate chaining in our design of `hashTable`. As stated earlier, this would involve viewing each component of `hTable` as a reference to a (possibly empty) linked list of nodes, each of whose `info` components is capable of storing a value of type `Object` (for the *dataField* component), however `Object` is instantiated. Thus, `hashTable` has to be recoded so that each of its objects will have components that reference linearly linked lists of nodes, where each node contains an `info` component whose value is of the type of the instantiated *dataField*.

The question before us now is whether we choose to design and code a generic class for linearly linked lists by hand or instead use some predefined version in Java, should it exist. This is the bridge to `java.util` that we described in the introduction to this chapter.

4.7 **Hashing in** `java.util`

We begin this section by describing an interface of `java.util` that is closely associated with hash tables. This interface is called `Enumeration` and provides facilities for *traversing,* that is, moving through and processing finite sequences of objects. `Enumeration` defines two non-`static` methods for traversing a finite sequence of objects.[3] These are

- `hasMoreElements()`
- `nextElement()`

The `hasMoreElements()` method returns a `boolean` value. This value is `true` when the associated object has more values to be processed, and otherwise returns `false`. The `nextElement()` method returns the next

---

[3]An `Enumeration` object is sometimes called an *iterator.*

value in the sequence to be processed and must not be invoked if `has-MoreElements()` returns `false`.

Java provides the predefined class `Hashtable`, which is part of a hierarchy of classes in `java.util`. The hierarchy can be expressed as illustrated in Figure 4.11.

FIGURE 4.11

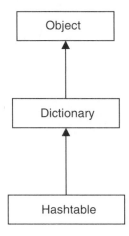

Thus, a number of the methods appearing in `Hashtable` are inherited from `Dictionary`. `Dictionary` is an abstract class that provides a collection of methods for processing pairs whose general syntax takes the form

keyValue, dataValue

keyValue is understood to be a non-`null` object used to find the associated pair in the dictionary, and *dataValue* is the non-`null` object corresponding to *keyValue*. `Dictionary` is aptly named, because the use of the pair *keyValue,dataValue* mimics the appearance in the typical dictionary: When we look up a term in an ordinary dictionary, the word (or words) used represents the *keyValue*, and the corresponding *dataValue* represents the entry's explanation (or definition) found in the dictionary.

As an example, a *keyValue, dataValue* pair could be an employee social security number (as the *keyValue*), and his or her employee record as the corresponding *dataValue*. The `Dictionary` object in this case (appearing in some subclass, as `Dictionary` is abstract) would take the form of an employee database, keyed on the social security number of the employee.

The `Dictionary` class also provides methods for finding the member sought in the dictionary and for inserting new members, updating current members, and removing current members. The `abstract` methods defined in `Dictionary` are

- `elements()`, which retrieves a list of all of the members present in the current dictionary

- `get()`, which retrieves the member associated with this key
- `isEmpty()`, which tests whether the current dictionary contains any members
- `put()`, which adds a *keyValue, dataValue* pair to the current dictionary
- `remove()`, which removes a *keyValue, dataValue* pair from the current dictionary
- `size()`, which retrieves the number of members currently in the dictionary

The objects constructed from the `Hashtable` class implement hash tables. Each object consists of an array of *hash buckets,* and each hash bucket contains zero or more *hash table entries.* Each entry takes the form of a *key-Value, dataValue* pair, neither of which is `null`. When an entry is added to a specific hash table, *keyValue* is used to hash to one of the buckets of the table, and the corresponding entry is stored in that bucket. It is possible to store more than one entry in a single bucket (as was the case earlier with `Horace J. Boccia` and `Bart W. Jones`). Although a hash collision results, the solution does not necessarily involve any probing to find another position in the hash table for the second (or subsequent) entry.

During the process of locating an entry in the hash table, *keyValue* is used to hash to the bucket where the entry has been inserted. If that bucket currently has more than one entry, *dataValue* is compared with the *dataValue* of each entry (using the `equals()` method from `Object`) to determine the entry sought. The search strategy implemented is linear search. Hashing using `Hashtable` is *dynamic:* As more values are inserted into the hash table, the size of each of the buckets increases. As a result, we recognize that a highly desirable property of a `Hashtable` object is that entries are evenly distributed among all of the buckets.

The implementation of `Hashtable` produces *extensible* objects: As these objects fill, they grow in size to contain all of the entries. When a hash table fills, it grows dynamically and automatically. As a result of this growth, each of its current entries must be rehashed using the new table size. It therefore follows that this growth operation, while kept hidden from the user, can be costly with respect to time efficiency.

In response, Java provides a version of a constructor for `Hashtable` involving a *load factor.* The load factor is defined as the ratio of the number of entries in the current hash table divided by its current size. When the current load factor of the table exceeds the load factor specified in the constructor, the table grows. The syntax for this version of the constructor is given by

`Hashtable(initialCapacity, loadFactor)`

where *initialCapacity* is a positive integer indicating the number of items of storage allocated to the hash table, and *loadFactor* is a positive decimal less than `1.0` specifying the load factor.

For example, a load factor of `0.6` means that when the table reaches `60` percent full, it automatically grows to its next size. A low load factor (close to zero) means that the table grows when it contains relatively few entries, allowing for the potential of a small number of hash collisions. On the other hand, a load factor close to one implies that the table grows when it is quite full, thereby increasing the number of occurrences of hash collisions but also avoiding the overhead of a relatively large number of growing and rehashing operations.

A larger hash table size means that more memory is required to support hashing. On the other hand, a small load factor implies that relatively few of the buckets in the hash table are being used. As a consequence, the hash table is inefficient with respect to storage allocation.

The `Hashtable` class provides two other constructors:

`Hashtable()`

and

`Hashtable(`*initialCapacity*`)`

The first of these constructs an empty hash table with a default initial capacity of `101` buckets and a default load factor of `0.75`. The second constructs an empty hash table with an initial capacity specified by *initialCapacity* and a default load factor of `0.75`.

The following is a summary of some of the more important `public` methods available in `Hashtable` (besides those described earlier from `Dictionary`):

- `clear()`—This is a `void` method, which removes all keys and entries from the current hash table.
- `contains(`*dataValue*`)`—This is a `boolean`-valued method, returning `true` if the current hash table contains *dataValue*, and `false` if not (this can also be invoked as `containsValue(`*dataValue*`)`.
- `containsKey(`*keyValue*`)`—This is a `boolean`-valued method, returning `true` when the hash table contains *keyValue*, and `false` when the hash table does not contain *keyValue*.

In the case of the last two methods, if the parameter is `null`, a `NullPointerException` is thrown.

We can illustrate these ideas for the hash table `IntegerTable` applied to hashing the `int`-valued sequence `23, 36, 89, 12, 134`.

EXAMPLE 4.2   The following main method uses `java.util.Hashtable` to construct an `Integer`-valued hash table `IntegerTable` and then hashes the `int`-valued sequence 23, 36, 89, 12, 134. Note that, before inserting these values into `IntegerTable`, we must first convert each of these `int` values to its appropriate `Integer` wrapper value. After this is done, each value is inserted using the `put()` method whose arguments are an appropriate pair *keyValue, dataValue*. In this case, each member of the pair *keyValue, dataValue* is identical.

```java
public static void main(String [] args)
 {
 // Construction of Hashtable object called IntegerTable
 // using the default constructor.
 Hashtable IntegerTable = new Hashtable();
 // Conformant array of int values
 int intArr[] = {23,36,89,12,134};
 // Installation of associated Integer-valued wrappers
 // in IntegerTable.
 for(int index = 0; index < intArr.length; ++index)
  IntegerTable.put(new Integer(intArr[index]),
                   new Integer(intArr[index]));
 // Test whether current IntegerTable is empty.
 if(IntegerTable.isEmpty())
  System.out.println("IntegerTable is empty");
 else
  System.out.println("IntegerTable is not empty");
 // Output contents of the current IntegerTable
 System.out.println("Contents of IntegerTable:");
 for(Enumeration e = IntegerTable.elements(); e.hasMoreElements();)
  System.out.print(e.nextElement() + " ");
 System.out.println();
 // Empty the current IntegerTable:
 IntegerTable.clear();
 // Test whether current IntegerTable is empty.
 if(IntegerTable.isEmpty())
  System.out.println("IntegerTable is empty");
 else
  System.out.println("IntegerTable is not empty");
 // Output contents of the current IntegerTable
 System.out.println("Contents of IntegerTable:");
 for(Enumeration e = IntegerTable.elements(); e.hasMoreElements();)
  System.out.print(e.nextElement() + " ");
 System.out.println();
 } // terminates text of main method.
```

The output is

```
IntegerTable is not empty
Contents of IntegerTable:
36   134   12   89   23
IntegerTable is empty
Contents of IntegerTable:
```

A number of subtle computations have occurred. First, note that although the input sequence is given by 23, 36, 89, 12, 134, the output sequence rearranges these values as 36, 134, 12, 89, 23. This is because `IntegerTable` is a container that does not necessarily preserve the sequential order of appearance of the input sequence. Later in the text, when we study `Vector` objects (Chapter 6), the underlying iterator outputs the same sequential order as that appearing among the values of the input sequence.

Another method inherited from `Dictionary` not used in the previous example is the `remove` method; this removes the entry in the hash table whose value is the *keyValue* supplied by the parameter. That is, `remove` is applied using the syntax

```
HashtableObject.remove(keyValue);
```

which removes the pair *keyValue, dataValue* from the current *HashtableObject*, if this pair appears in the current *HashtableObject*, and otherwise does not change the sequence of values stored there.

Second, note the effect of `clear()`: After it is applied, and output is requested for the current version of `IntegerTable`, the output returned is

```
IntegerTable is empty
Contents of IntegerTable:
```

and no further output. Thus, there are no `Integer` values to be output.

Note also that `isEmpty()` inherited from `Dictionary` has been applied to `IntegerTable` to test whether it is currently empty.

Although this was not part of the current method, if we included the code

```
Integer val = new Integer(23);
if(IntegerTable.containsKey(val))
  System.out.println(val + " is in IntegerTable");
else
  System.out.println(val + " is not in IntegerTable");
```

the result would begin with the construction of an `Integer` object `val` whose data value is 23. Then `containsKey(val)` is applied to `IntegerTable` to test whether `val` matches a current entry of `IntegerTable`. Because that match occurs, the message

```
23 is in IntegerTable
```

is output.

We end this section by returning to the problem of storing employee records, as was discussed at the beginning of this chapter. However, we will now use the facilities of `java.util.Hashtable` to complete the task. Example 4.3 creates a class `Employee`, in which the employee's name, social security number, and date of birth will be stored as a data item (identified as an instance of `Employee`) in a `Hashtable` object called `employeeRecord`. The search key we choose is that of the employee's social security number. After inserting three such items into `employeeRecord`, we output the current contents of the hash table, using our overloaded version of `toString()`, coded as a `public` method of the `Employee` class. When this is done, we search for a record with key `"099364150"` in `employeeRecord` and then return the result of the search.

EXAMPLE 4.3   The `Employee` class is defined as

```
class Employee
  {
   private String employeeName;
   private String socsecNumber;
   private String dob;

   // Constructor
   Employee(String name, String ssNo, String date)
   {
   employeeName = name;
   socsecNumber = ssNo;
   dob = date;
   } // closes text of constructor

   public String toString()
   }
           return(employeeName + " " + " " + socsecNumber + " "
                  + dob);
   } // closes text of toString
   } // closes text of Employee
```

The main method is coded as

```
public static void main(String [] args)
{
 // Create an employee record using social security number as key,
 // and Employee data as dataValue.
 Hashtable employeeRecord = new Hashtable();

 // Input 3 employee records into employeeRecord
```

```
employeeRecord.put("099364150",
   new Employee("Horace J Boccia","099364150","140739"));
employeeRecord.put("086364036",
   new Employee("Rosalie A Procach","086364036","020140"));
employeeRecord.put("066666610",
   new Employee("Bart W Jones","066666610","101153"));
for(Enumeration e = employeeRecord.elements(); e.hasMoreElements();)
  System.out.println(e.nextElement());

// Search for employee record with key "099364150"
if(employeeRecord.containsKey("099364150"))
 System.out.println("Record with key 099364150 is in employeeRecord");
else
 System.out.println("Record with key 099364150 not in employeeRecord");
}
```

If we run this program, the output is

Rosalie A Procach 086364036 020140
Bart W Jones 066666610 101153
Horace J Boccia 099364150 140739
Record with key 099364150 is in employeeRecord

4.8 Chapter Summary

The main objective of hashing is to provide a search paradigm that is reasonably efficient from the standpoint of the amount of memory required to store the data items to be accessed, and whose time complexity is as close to $O(1)$ as possible. To attain this objective, we studied a number of diverse hashing methods: middle squares, random number generators, folding, and division with remainder. Thus, the choice of a suitable form of a hash function is an important factor in our design.

Another important function is whether to apply open addressing, buckets, or separate chaining. In each of these, there exists the possibility of several different data items yielding the same value when the hash function is applied. This is called a *hash collision*. Accordingly, our design must consider a suitable strategy to follow in the case of an occurrence of a hash collision. Popular among these are linear and quadratic probing and rehashing in the form of applying several cooperating hash functions when using either open addressing or buckets.

The technique of separate chaining resolved hash collisions by adding new nodes to a linearly linked list of nodes, in which the *info* component of each contains the pertinent data to be stored in the table. The hash table consists of a sequence of references to nodes in the linked lists, any one of which refers to the list of nodes whose *info* components have the same key value when acted on by the underlying hash function. This method resolves the problem of hash collisions, but the downside is that generally more processing time is required to maintain and update a hash table using linked lists.

We also presented an implementation of hash tables called `hashTable`, involving objects whose data components are presented in generic form. This implementation uses a hash function employing division with remainder, with open addressing and linear probing. In addition, we suggested techniques implementing other forms of resolving hash collisions using our design as a prototype.

This chapter terminated with a discussion of one of the facilities that is predefined in the `java.util` library—the `Hashtable` class, which is a subclass of the abstract `Dictionary` class. The `Hashtable` class enables us to construct concrete objects, each of which is a hash table whose data component involves two parts: a *keyValue* and *dataValue.* Inserting values into any `Hashtable` object involves the insertion of both the key and the actual data. In addition, removing a value from a `Hashtable` object involves the removal of both the key value and the data value.

The `Enumeration` class is closely associated with the `Hashtable` class, containing objects (sometimes called *iterators*) that have the functionality of traversing a finite sequence of values contained in any `Hashtable` object. We used iterators to output the current set of data values stored in any `Hashtable` object. We will see other uses of iterators later in Chapters 5, 6, 8, 9, and 10.

In brief, hashing provides an effective bridge between the basic concepts of OOD treated in the first two chapters, together with efficient searching and sorting paradigms. The implementation of many of these ideas are predefined and appear in the `java.util` library.

EXERCISES

1. Suppose we have a hash table in the form of the `int`-valued array `arr` given by

arr

Apply the hash function

H(*search_key*) = *search_key* % 7

to the sequence $9,1,2,8,16$
a.   using linear probing
b.   using quadratic probing
c.   using double hashing, using the secondary hash function

$H_2(search\_key) = 5 - (search\_key \% 5)$

2.   Suppose we have a hash table in the form of an `int`-valued array `arr`, whose storage is represented as

Apply the hash function $H(search\_key) = search\_key \% 9$ to the int-valued sequence $9,1,2,18,27$
a.   using linear probing
b.   using quadratic probing
c.   using double hashing, using the secondary hash function

$H_2(search\_key) = 7 - (search\_key \% 7)$

3.   a.   Suppose the hash table `arr` of Exercise 1 is now defined to store references to `int`-valued nodes of linked lists. Using the hash function `H` as just defined and separate chaining, and the input sequence $9,1,2,8,16$, describe the result of applying the hash operation to that input sequence.

   b.   Redo (a), but now assume the array `arr` of Exercise 2 is defined to store references to `int`-valued nodes of linked lists. Using the input sequence $9,1,2,18,27$, describe the result of applying the hash operation `H` given in Exercise 2 to this sequence.

4.   Use the same input sequence and hash function as defined in Exercise 1, but now assume each component of `arr` is defined as an `int`-valued bucket of size four.

5.   Suppose we rewrite the implementation code for the `keyedStructure` class to include a constructor, as follows:

```
class keyedStructure
  {
  // Constructor
  public keyedStructure(int kVal, Object dVal, boolean eVal)
   {
    keyVal = kVal;
    dataVal = dVal;
    emptyVal = eVal;
```

```
        } // terminates code for constructor
        int keyVal;
        Object dataVal;
        boolean emptyVal;
      }
```

How would this affect the coding of the main method described in Example 4.1?

6. Complete the coding details for the implementation of hashTable in Section 4.6, now using quadratic probing as the strategy for resolving hash collisions.

7. Expand the program described in Example 4.2 to include tests as to whether 200 and 201, as the respective data values of Integer objects, appear in IntegerTable using the instance methods contains and containsValue.

8. The remove() method inherited by Hashtable from Dictionary requires a single parameter *dataValue*. When applied to a Hashtable object, the result produces a hash table from which the pair *keyValue, dataValue* has been removed. Apply this to the program described in Example 4.2 to remove the Integer object wrapping the int value 23.

9. Continue with Exercise 8, now using the size() method, showing that the size of IntegerTable has decreased by one after the application of remove().

10. Given the following program:

```
public static void main(String [] args)
 {
   // Constructor specifying size and load factor for IntegerTable.
   // Initial size = 5, load factor = 0.25.
   Hashtable IntegerTable = new Hashtable(5,0.25f);
   // Define 5 int values in conformant array intArr:
   int intArr[] = {23,36,89,12,134};

   // Insert each of these in IntegerTable, using Integer wrappers:
   for(int index = 0; index < intArr.length; ++index)
      IntegerTable.put(new Integer(intArr[index]),
       new Integer(intArr[index]));
   // Output current size of IntegerTable.
   System.out.println("Current size on IntegerTable is "
                     + IntegerTable.size());
 // Now define a second conformant array of int values:
 int newintArr[] = {19,89,-109,49,77,209};

 // Insert each of these in IntegerTable, using Integer wrappers:
 for(int index = 0; index < newintArr.length; ++index)
  IntegerTable.put(new Integer(newintArr[index]),
```

```
                            new Integer(newintArr[index]));
// Output new size of IntegerTable.
  System.out.println("Current size on IntegerTable is "
                      + IntegerTable.size());
```

```
} // terminates text of main method
```

      a. Give the exact form of the output derived from this program.

      b. Explain why the new value of size is 10 instead of 11.

      c. Determine if `rehash()` is invoked during execution of this program.

11. Apply the `remove` method to the `employeeRecord` hash table defined in Example 4.3. Show the contents of `employeeRecord` before the removal—there should be three employee records stored there. Then remove the employee record whose key value is the social security number represented by the `String` value `"099364150"`. After this is done, display the contents of `employeeRecord`.

PROGRAMMING PROJECT

Design and implement the `hashTable` class using separate chaining. To do this, there is no need to design an accompanying `list` class implementing linked lists. All that needs to be done is to rewrite the instance methods of `hashTable` using linked lists, applying the revision of `keyedStructure` given as

```
class keyedStructure
 {
 // Constructor
 public keyedStructure(int kVal, Object dVal)
 {
  keyVal = kVal;
  dataVal = dVal;
 } // terminates code for constructor
 int keyVal;
 Object dataVal;
}
```

REFERENCES

Chan, Patrick, Rosanna Lee, and Douglas Kramer. 1998. *The Java Class Libraries, Second Edition, Volume 1.* Reading, MA: Addison-Wesley, 99–133.

Knuth, Donald E. 1973. *The Art of Computer Programming, Volume 3: Sorting and Searching.* Reading, MA: Addison-Wesley.

A General Overview of the `java.util` Library

CHAPTER OBJECTIVES

- To study the recent additions offered by Java 2 in the `Collection` Application Programming Interface (the `Collection` API), and its integration with the rest of the Java programming language.
- To study the relationship between the `Collection` API and `java.util`.
- To introduce the ADTs present in the `Collection` and `Map` hierarchies and their implementation.
- To present some of the utility methods of the `Collections` and `Arrays` interfaces.
- To provide a first look at the structures of Java's Legacy Collections.

5.1 Introduction

In 1998, the release of the Java 2 platform was announced. Until that time, the number of predefined classes that comprised the Java Application Programming Interface (known as the Java API) was relatively small. We can view the API for Java (or, for that matter, for any other programming language) as a built-in collection of software tools provided by the language for easier and more efficient problem solving. Prior to the release of Java 2, this collection consisted of a small number of generic classes and interfaces among whose number are some that we have already discussed, such as `Enumeration` and `Hashtable`. Others in this original collection that we will discuss later in this book are `Vector` (in Chapter 6) and `Stack` (in Chapter 7).

The design plan for Java 2 included an expansion of this set of fundamental classes, but not in a way that mimics the inclusion of the Standard Template Library (or simply STL) that is now part of the standard API for C++. (For a discussion of STL, see my earlier book on C++, listed in the References section at the end of this chapter.) The STL was judged to be too complex, but the use of generic algorithms pioneered by STL was considered to be a highly desirable addition to the new Java 2 platform. In response, the designers of Java 2 included an interface called `java.util.Collection,` which, as the name suggests, is part of `java.util.`

It turns out that `java.util.Collection` is but one of many predefined interfaces provided by the Java 2 platform. As we will see, this `Collection` interface,[1] as well as others in the Java 2 platform, makes heavy use of the distinction between interface and implementation, as well as inheritance. This chapter, at least in part, will be devoted to the study of the organization of the `Collection` interface and its interaction with the rest of the Java language.

5.2 The Java Collections Framework

We can think of a *collection* as a finite group of objects viewed as a single conceptual unit. In addition, the objects that comprise any collection are assumed to be stored and organized so as to provide efficient access to these objects.

The `java.util` package contains interfaces and classes that provide a general framework for collections, called the *Java Collections Framework.*[2] This framework is a unified set of collection interfaces, combined with efficient implementations of these interfaces. The implementations take the form of *reusable data structures,* which are combined with the implementation of algorithms performing useful and efficient computations on these structures.

The design of the Java Collections Framework aims at achieving the following goals:

- **reduces programming effort**—The Collections Framework accomplishes this by providing pertinent predefined data structures. In doing so, it allows the programmer to concentrate on the more important parts of the application. In other words, the programmer no longer has to be concerned with the lower-level programming details of the implementation of the associated instance methods.
- **enhances program efficiency**—The Collections Framework accomplishes this by providing efficient implementations of useful data structures (such as stacks, hash tables, lists, and dynamic arrays) and algorithms (such as those used for sorting and searching). In addition,

---

[1]Unless specified otherwise, we will refer to `java.util.Collection` as `Collection`, and Java 2 simply as Java.

[2]The collections framework for C++ is the Standard Template Library (STL).

because the implementations of a single interface can be interchanged, the most convenient implementation can be chosen by the programmer.

- **promotes software reuse**—Data structures that conform to the standard collection interfaces in the Collections Framework are reusable, as are the group of algorithms that operate on objects implementing these interfaces.

These goals represent an extremely important and valuable list of benefits for designing commercial software. Any designer, programmer, or engineer of commercial software places a high value on the principles of minimizing programming effort and enhancing efficiency and reuse when designing, evaluating, and testing commercial software for correctness.

5.3 The `Collection` and `Iterator` Interfaces

The interface serving as the root for collections is the `Collection` interface. Closely associated with `Collection` is the `Iterator` interface, whose objects return values from a collection in some specific sequential order. The order in which these values are returned depends on the specific class implementing `Collection`.

A key purpose of `Collection` is to process collections of objects in a general setting. In actual practice, `Collection` will be implemented using classes whose objects will be special kinds of collections (such as an implementation of linked lists described as a concrete class). Thus, the methods described in `Collection` capture the basic operations that would be expected to apply to finite collections of objects. The code for the `Collection` interface takes the following form:

```
public interface Collection
{
 // Returns the number of objects in the current collection.
 int size();

 // Returns true if the current collection is empty; otherwise
 // returns false.
 boolean isEmpty();

 // Returns true if the collection contains at least one object
 // whose value is obj; otherwise, returns false.
 boolean contains(Object obj);

 // Adds the object described by the parameter to the collection.
 // The value returned is true if the object added changes the
```

```
// contents of the collection.
boolean add(Object obj);

// Removes an object whose value is given by the parameter from
// the current collection.  Returns true if an actual removal
// occurs; otherwise, returns false.
boolean remove(Object obj);

// Returns an iterator that can be used to traverse all of
// the values of the current collection.
Iterator iterator();

// Returns true if the current Collection object contains all of
// the objects in the Collection object defined by the parameter.
boolean containsAll(Collection otherCollection);

// Adds all of the objects appearing in the collection described by
// the parameter to the current collection.  Returns true if the
// current collection was changed as a result of this call.
boolean addAll(Collection otherCollection);

// Removes all objects in the collection described by the parameter
// from the current collection. Returns true if the current collection
// was changed as a result of this call.
boolean removeAll(Collection otherCollection);

// Removes all objects from the current collection that are not equal
// to one of the objects in the collection described by the parameter.
// Returns true if the collection changed as a result of this call.
boolean retainAll(Collection otherCollection);

// Removes all objects from the current collection.
void clear();

// Returns an array of the objects in the current collection.
Object[] toArray();
}
```

Before proceeding any further, it is important for us to note a subtle but important use of the `toArray()` method just described. While it is true that `toArray()` is applicable to any `Collection` object `collObj` using any implementation of `Collection`, we should observe that `collObj.to Array()` returns an array of type `Object[]`. Although `collObj` contains values of a specific type, say, `Integer`, applying a cast such as

```
Integer[] intValues = (Integer[])collObj.toArray();
```

produces a compile-time error. In order to properly cast `intValues` as an array receiving the `Integer` values of `collObj`, we must apply a variation of `toArray()`, as follows. Assign an (anonymous) array of length zero of the desired type, such as

```
Integer[] intValues = (Integer[])collObj.toArray(new Integer[0]);
```

and `intValues` will then receive, in some sequential order defined by the specific implementation, the members of `collObj`.

Now that we have defined the `Collection` interface, it is important to have the ability to traverse and, in some way, process the objects stored in a specific collection. This action is supported in Java by defining an `Iterator` interface. Note that one of the instance methods described in `Collection` defines an `Iterator` object applicable to that collection. This is done for the reason described earlier—to have an object with the functionality of traversing and processing the objects stored in the `Collection` object constructed. Just as was true for `Collection`, `Iterator` is one of the interfaces appearing in `java.util`.

`Iterator` objects have a behavior that is similar to, but not identical with, `Enumeration` objects. The distinction can be described by the following observations:

1. An iterator allows for the *removal* of objects from the current collection to which the iterator applies; `Enumeration` objects do not possess this functionality.
2. The remaining instance methods described in `Iterator` perform similar operations as their `Enumeration` counterpart, but are named differently:

    `next()` is used instead of `nextElement()`
    `hasNext()` is used instead of `hasMoreElements()`

The formal description of the `Iterator` interface is given by

```
public interface Iterator
{
 // Returns true if there is another object in the collection.
 boolean hasNext();

 // Returns the next object to process.  Throws a
 // NoSuchElementException if the end of the collection has
 // been reached.
 Object next();

 // Removes and returns the last object traversed.
 // Precondition: this method must be applied immediately after
```

```
// traversing an object.  An IllegalStateException exception is
// thrown if the underlying collection is modified in any other way
// while the iteration operation is in progress.
Object remove();
}
```

Here is an example of a programmer-defined method that removes all strings of a given length from any finite collection of strings:

```
public void removeStrings(Collection collObject, int specifiedLength)
{
 for(Iterator iter = collObject.iterator(); iter.hasNext();)
 {
  String str = (String)iter.next();
  if(str.length() == specifiedLength) iter.remove();
 }
}
```

The cast is included to guarantee that the result of the traversal is a `String` object. We use the `iterator()` method to obtain an `Iterator` object `iter` that traverses the objects stored in `collObject` one at a time. This traversal proceeds as long as `hasNext()` returns `true`, indicating that there are more members of `collObject` to process. Each time we cycle through the `for`-loop, we obtain the next member of `collObject` using the `next()` method. If any string in `collObject` has the length specified by the value of `specifiedLength`, we invoke the `remove()` method to remove that string from `collObject`. It is important to note that the `removeStrings` method is to be treated as *generic*—any class that implements `Collection` or a subclass of any implementation of `Collection` that uses `String` objects can now invoke `removeStrings` to remove strings of a specified length appearing in any given finite collection of `String` values.

The behavior of iterators in Java is different from their counterpart in other programming languages, such as iterators defined in STL in C++. In STL, iterators behave like array subscripts. For example, for an iterator defined in STL, we can access the value currently referenced by the iterator in a manner similar to accessing the value stored in the array `arr` at position `index` simply by using `arr[index]`. As well, the current position of `index` can be changed by using either an autoincrement operator `++index` or an autodecrement operator `--index` wherever applicable, without necessarily having to access the value stored in `arr` at the new position of `index`. This is *not* the case in Java—here, the only way to access a value in a collection is to invoke `next()`, which automatically performs a lookup of the value stored at the new position.

In light of this behavior, we should view the position of any iterator `iter` as follows: When `iter.next()` executes, `iter` "jumps over" the next value and returns a reference to the value it has just passed, as in Figure 5.1.

FIGURE 5.1   collObject

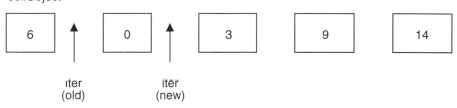

If `iter`'s current position is `iter(old)`, and `iter.next()` executes, then the value 0 is returned and the new position of `iter` is indicated by `iter(new)`. This behavior also extends to the proper use of the `remove` method. When `iter.remove()` executes, the value removed from the underlying collection is that accessed by the last call to `iter.next()`. Thus, in order to properly remove a value from a collection, the iterator must first pass over the value using `next` and then remove the value using `remove`. Referring once again to Figure 5.1, the `Integer` value 0 will be removed by executing the sequence

```
iter.next();
iter.remove();
```

In fact, Java will not permit a call to `remove` without being immediately preceded by a call to `next`. Thus, for example, if we wish to remove the first two consecutive values from a collection, we must invoke

```
Iterator iter = collObject.iterator();
for(int count = 0; count < 2; ++count)
{
 iter.next();
 iter.remove();
}
```

5.4   A First Look at Concrete Collection Classes: The `List` Interface and the `LinkedList` Implementation

Let us consider an implementation of the `Collection` interface. The implementation is the predefined concrete class `LinkedList`, and we appeal to our intuition and our background in data structures about the concept of linked lists and their functionality. We will study the formal connection between linked lists and `Collection` in greater detail in Chapter 6 as an implementation of the `List` interface, but these details are not needed here. Instead, all we need here is to observe that, in Java, `List` extends `Collection` to define collections whose objects appear in a specific order. That is, each object in a list appears in a specific position. We can refer to the hierarchical diagram provided in Figure 5.2 to describe the hierarchy involving `Collection`, `List`, and `LinkedList`.

FIGURE 5.2

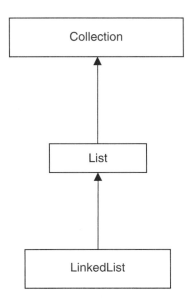

In particular, in this section we will discuss only those methods inherited by `LinkedList` from `Collection`. In Chapter 6 we will study a number of methods described in `List` and implemented in `LinkedList`. In particular, the `add` method in `Collection` is implemented in `LinkedList`, adjoining the `Object`-valued parameter argument to the *end* of the current `LinkedList` object, and the (parameterless) constructor `LinkedList()` constructs an initially `LinkedList` object of size zero.

EXAMPLE 5.1   The following code sequence

```
LinkedList strings = new LinkedList();
strings.add("Nicholas");
strings.add("Anthony");
strings.add("Rocco");
strings.add("Patty");
strings.add("Vivian");
```

```
strings.add("Marie");
strings.add("Rosalie");
```

constructs a linked list of `String` values described in Figure 5.3.

FIGURE 5.3   strings

Nicholas	Anthony	Rocco	Patty	Vivian	Marie	Rosalie

The following program constructs this linked list and then invokes the method `removeStrings` to systematically scan each member of `strings` and remove those whose length is five.

```
public static void main(String [] args)
{
 // Construct strings as a LinkedList object.
 LinkedList strings = new LinkedList();
 // Add seven String values to strings.
 strings.add("Nicholas");
 strings.add("Anthony");
 strings.add("Rocco");
 strings.add("Patty");
 strings.add("Vivian");
 strings.add("Marie");
 strings.add("Rosalie");
 // Display the current contents of strings:
 System.out.println("The original strings collection is:");
 output(strings);
 // Now remove all members of strings of length five.
 removeStrings(strings,5);
 // Display the contents of strings after invoking removeStrings:
 System.out.println("After removing all strings of length 5 from");
 System.out.println("the original collection, the revised collection");
 System.out.println("is given by:");
 output(strings);
} // terminates text of main method
```

The `output` method is coded as

```
public static void output(Collection collObject)
{
 for(Iterator iter = collObject.iterator();iter.hasNext();)
  System.out.println(iter.next());
}
```

When the program executes, the output is

```
The original strings collection is:
Nicholas
Anthony
Rocco
Patty
Vivian
Marie
Rosalie
After removing all strings of length 5 from
the original collection, the revised collection
is given by:
Nicholas
Anthony
Vivian
Rosalie
```

Each of the methods `removeStrings` and `output` use an `Iterator` object called `iter`. When implemented by `LinkedList`, `iter` assumes a form in which the members of the `LinkedList` object (`strings`, in this case) are traversed in the order of their insertion using the `add` method. This is the reason for the specific form of the output sequence we observed, for example, when we executed the program described in Example 5.1. Besides this, `List` also provides iterators with a richer functionality than those appearing in `LinkedList`. These are defined in the `ListIterator` interface—these iterators can traverse a list either forward or backward, or they can modify any member of a list during a traversal, or they can retrieve the current position of the iterator. The hierarchical relationship between `Iterator` and `ListIterator` is described in Figure 5.4.

FIGURE 5.4

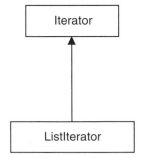

Further details on the topic of lists will be given in Chapter 6, where we investigate linked lists as fundamental containers for data storage.

How can we process collections of integers? If we choose to involve `Collection`, we have to represent each integer in any `Collection` object as an `Integer` value. Besides, it will be convenient to represent any such collection as a `LinkedList` object. As an example, if we choose to design the linked list of integers named `intList` and represented as in Figure 5.5, we can apply the code segment

FIGURE 5.5   intList

2	3	4	7	8	1

```
LinkedList intList = new LinkedList();
int intArr[] = {2,3,4,7,8};
for(int index = 0; index < intArr.length; ++index)
 intList.add(new Integer(intArr[index]));
```

If we then wish to output the current contents of `intList`, we can apply

```
horizOutput(intList);
```

where we assume `horizOutput` is coded as

```
public static void horizOutput(Collection collObject)
{
 for(Iterator iter = collObject.iterator(); iter.hasNext();)
  System.out.print(iter.next() + "  ");
 System.out.println();
}
```

Now suppose we use `compare` to test whether a specific `Integer`-valued collection contains a specific `Integer` value. Suppose, in particular, we wish to test whether `intList` contains 7. We would "wrap" 7 and represent it as `Integer(7)`, and we would apply the code sequence

```
Integer seven = new Integer(7);
if(intList.contains(seven))
 System.out.println("intList contains 7");
else
 System.out.println("intList does not contain 7");
```

Suppose we also construct an object such as the one shown in Figure 5.6

FIGURE 5.6   newIntList

1	−1	7	1

and we apply

`intList.add(newIntList);`

the result of invoking this method is given by the object shown in Figure 5.7.

FIGURE 5.7   intList

2	3	4	7	8	1	1	−1	7	1

Instead, suppose `intList` is as shown in Figure 5.5 and `newIntList` is as shown in Figure 5.6, and we invoke

`NewIntList.addAll(intList);`

the result is shown in Figure 5.8.

FIGURE 5.8   newIntList

1	−1	7	1	2	3	4	7	8	1

Again, suppose `intList` is as shown in Figure 5.5 and `newIntList` is as shown in Figure 5.6. Then the code segment

```
if(intList.containsAll(newIntList))
  System.out.println("intList contains every member of newIntList");
else
  System.out.println("intList does not contain every member of newIntList");
```

outputs the message

intList does not contain every member of newIntList

This is because not every member of `newIntList`, as shown in Figure 5.6, is a member of `intList`, as shown in Figure 5.5. Furthermore, suppose we execute

`intList.removeAll(newIntList);`

The result of this execution is shown in Figure 5.9.

FIGURE 5.9   intList

2	3	4	8

This is because every member of intList appearing in newIntList is removed from intList.

Suppose we apply

intList.retainAll(newIntList);

with intList shown in Figure 5.5 and newIntList shown in Figure 5.6. The result is shown in Figure 5.10.

FIGURE 5.10   intList

7	1

This is because intList.retainAll(newIntList) removes all members of intList that are not members of newIntList. Finally, if we apply

intList.clear();

the result is as shown in Figure 5.11, because clear() applied to any Collection object removes every member currently stored in that object.

FIGURE 5.11   intList

The methods containsAll, addAll, removeAll, retainAll, and clear are classified as *bulk operations,* because each performs an operation on a collection in a single execution, without causing the programmer to iterate contains, add, or remove operations on single members. Therefore, the bulk operations are more efficient than iterating their single-member counterparts.

5.5 The Set Interface and the HashSet Implementation

Lists and arrays are examples of collections that allow the programmer to specify the order of appearance of its members. If we wish to construct a collection where the emphasis is on efficiency of the search operation, however, lists and arrays might not be the best available choice. This is because such collections involve iterators that effect a traversal of its members in order, usually in order of appearance, until a match is found (if such a match exists). As we discovered in Chapter 3 for arrays, the efficiency of the underlying search algorithm depends directly on the size of the collection. If order of appearance of its members is not a major consideration, we can consider collections that permit more efficient forms of search. This was described in part in Chapter 4, where we discussed hashing. The downside is that these collections provide no control for the programmer for the order of appearance of its members.

We have seen that hash tables are perhaps the most efficient choice of a data structure used for searching. In fact, hash tables can be used to implement *sets*. We define a *set* as a special kind of collection, in that a set does not allow for the storage of duplicate members. Java supports the `Set` interface, viewed as a subclass of `Collection`. In fact, `Set` contains no new methods—that is, `Set` contains no methods except those inherited from `Collection`, with the additional restriction that duplicate values are not permitted.

Because `Set` is a subclass of `Object`, any two `Set` objects can be compared using `equals`, even if their implementations differ. Intuitively, two `Set` objects are judged equal if they contain exactly the same values.

The formal description of the `Set` interface is as follows:

```
public interface Set
{
// Returns the number of elements in the current set.
int size();

// Returns true if the current set is empty; otherwise
// returns false.
boolean isEmpty();

// Returns true if the set contains one object
// whose value is obj; otherwise, returns false.
boolean contains(Object obj);

// Adds the object described by the parameter to the set.
// The value returned is true if the object added changes the
// contents of the set.
boolean add(Object obj);

// Removes an object whose value is given by the parameter from
// the current set.  Returns true if an actual removal occurs;
// otherwise, returns false.
boolean remove(Object obj);

// Returns an iterator that can be used to traverse all of
// the values of the current set.
```

```
Iterator iterator();

// Returns true if the current Set object contains all of
// the objects in the Collection object defined by the parameter.
boolean containsAll(Collection otherCollection);

// Adds all of the objects appearing in the collection described by
// the parameter to the current set.  Returns true if the current
// set was changed as a result of this call.
boolean addAll(Collection otherCollection);

// Removes all objects in the collection described by the parameter
// from the current set.  Returns true if the current set was
// changed as a result of this call.
boolean removeAll(Collection otherCollection);

// Removes all objects from the current set that are not equal
// to one of the objects in the collection described by the parameter.
// Returns true if the set was changed as a result of this call.
boolean retainAll(Collection otherCollection);

// Removes all objects from the current set.
void clear();

// Returns an array of the objects in the current set.
Object [] toArray();
}
```

What concrete predefined classes implement the Set interface? The HashSet class implements the Set interface (and, by inheritance, implements the Collection interface) using a hash table. Modifying any Set object, or testing whether it contains a specific value, are $O(1)$ operations—the processing time required to execute any of these is independent of the number of objects currently contained in the set. In addition, HashSet has four different constructors:

1. public HashSet()—constructs a HashSet object with a default initial capacity and load factor[3]
2. public HashSet(int initialCapacity)—constructs a HashSet object with an initial capacity provided by the value of the parameter and with a default load factor

---

[3]Recall the definitions of initial capacity and load factor and their respective default values from Section 4.7.

3. public HashSet(int initialCapacity, float loadFactor)—constructs a HashSet object with an initial capacity provided by the value of the first parameter and a load factor provided by the value of the second parameter

4. public HashSet(Collection otherCollection)—constructs a new HashSet object whose initial values are those currently stored in otherCollection (note otherCollection need not be a HashTable object; for instance, it can be a LinkedList object). The initial capacity of the HashSet object under construction is that of otherCollection, and the load factor of this HashSet object is the default

It is important to observe that, similar to the behavior of hash tables described in Chapter 4, there is no guarantee about the specific order of appearance of the values stored in any HashTable object. Thus, an iterator defined on a HashTable object does not necessarily traverse the values stored in that hash table in the order in which those values were added to the table. As well, Java supports an output function in which the values currently stored in the hash table are output, enclosed between a matching pair of left and right square brackets and separated by commas.

EXAMPLE 5.2   This is an example of a program that scans a collection of Integer values, looking for duplicates, placing these duplicates in a Set object called duplicateIntegers, and placing the remaining values in a Set called uniqueIntegers. After this is completed, the contents of duplicateIntegers and uniqueIntegers are output. The code is given by

```
public static void main(String [] args)
{
  Set uniqueIntegers = new HashSet();
  Set duplicateIntegers = new HashSet();

  int intArr[] = {2,3,4,7,8,1,1,-1,7,1}; // conformant array
  // Corresponding array of Integer values.
  Integer intValues[] = new Integer[intArr.length];
  // Copy int value from intArr into Integer value in intValues
  for(int index = 0; index < intArr.length; ++index)
   intValues[index] = new Integer(intArr[index]);
  // Form duplicate and unique hash sets.
  for(int index = 0; index < intValues.length; ++index)
   if(!uniqueIntegers.add(intValues[index]))
    duplicateIntegers.add(intValues[index]);
  // Destructive set difference.
  uniqueIntegers.removeAll(duplicateIntegers);
```

```
    // Output results.
    System.out.println("Unique integers: " + uniqueIntegers);
    System.out.println("Duplicate integers: " + duplicateIntegers);
} // terminates main method
```

The output is given by

Unique integers: [8, 4, 3, 2, -1]
Duplicate integers: [7, 1]

It is appropriate to make an observation about programming style at this point. The code described in Example 5.2 refers to the collection by its interface type name (Set) rather than by its implementation type name (HashSet, in this case), as in

```
Set uniqueIntegers = new HashSet();
```

and

```
Set duplicateIntegers = new HashSet();
```

This is a highly recommended programming and design practice, because it enables the programmer to change implementation simply by changing the name of the implementation type provided by the constructor. For example, in Section 5.6 we will see that there is another predefined implementation of the Set interface called TreeSet, which sorts the members of the structure as well as avoids the appearance of duplicate values. All that needs to be done is to change the code of the constructors above to

```
Set uniqueIntegers = new TreeSet();
```

and

```
Set duplicateIntegers = new TreeSet();
```

As a matter of fact, we could just as well declare uniqueIntegers and duplicateIntegers as Collection objects with an appropriate type name for the implementation type, such as

```
Collection uniqueIntegers = new HashSet();
```

and

```
Collection duplicateIntegers = new HashSet();
```

These observations apply to the implementations of List described in the previous section. For example, we could have defined the constructor of Example 5.1 using the interface type (List) and the implementation type (LinkedList) as the implementation type, as in

```
List strings = new LinkedList();
```

or, for that matter

```
Collection strings = new LinkedList();
```

Again, the reason for this, as we will observe later, is that the `List` interface may also be implemented by the `ArrayList` class. Such "mixed" forms for constructors allow for more flexibility.

5.6   The `SortedSet` Interface and the `TreeSet` Implementation

The `TreeSet` class also implements the `Set` interface. The distinction between a `HashSet` object and a `TreeSet` object is that the latter produces a sorted collection.

How is the sorting determined? There is a predefined subclass of the `Set` interface called `SortedSet`. In Java2, `SortedSet` is an interface designed to arrange the members of any set in sorted order. This order can be predefined (the *default*)—for example, for the `Integer` class, the default is "less than." A second possibility is any ordering explicitly defined by the programmer—the programmer defines a `Comparator` object used to order the members of the set in place of the default.

What is `Comparator`? The `java.util` package contains a `Comparator` interface containing the single method whose signature is

```
public int compare(Object obj1, Object obj2);
```

This is used to provide an ordering similar to `compareTo`, used in Chapter 3 and applicable to `Comparable` objects. In brief, if `obj1`, `obj2` are objects of the same concrete class,

- `compare(obj1,obj2)` < 0 means `obj1` is "less than" `obj2`
- `compare(obj1,obj2)` = 0 means `obj1`, `obj2` are "equal"
- `compare(obj1,obj2)` > 0 means `obj1` is "greater than" `obj2`

In all of the applications in this text, we will use the default ordering. We should note that the default ordering between any two non-`null` `String` values is the usual lexicographic ("dictionary") ordering.

The `SortedSet` interface extends `Set` by including several extra methods and is coded as follows:

```
public interface SortedSet extends Set
{
  // Returns the Comparator used by the sorted set, or
  // returns null if the default ordering is used.
  public Comparator comparator();

  // Returns the first (smallest) object in the current sorted set.
  public Object first();
```

```
// Returns the last (largest) object in the current sorted set.
public Object last();

// Returns a representation of the sorted set that contains all of the
// members of the current sorted set that are at the same time greater
// than or equal to the value of the first parameter and less than
// the value of the second parameter.
public SortedSet subSet(Object minValue, Object maxValue);

// Returns a representation of the sorted set that contains all of the
// members of the current sorted set that are less than the value
// of the parameter.
public SortedSet headSet(Object maxValue);

// Returns a representation of the sorted set that contains all of the
// members of the current sorted set that are greater than or equal to
// the value of the parameter.
public SortedSet tailSet(Object minValue);
}
```

The TreeSet class is a concrete class implementing SortedSet. Thus we have the hierarchical diagram shown in Figure 5.12.

FIGURE 5.12

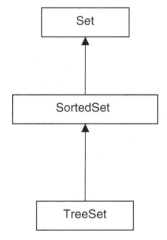

The TreeSet includes no new instance methods but does define four constructors.

1. public TreeSet()—This version constructs a TreeSet object that is sorted according to the default "less than" order of the member type.

2. `public TreeSet(Collection otherCollection)`—This version constructs a copy of the parameter using the default ordering and removing any duplicate members of the parameter.
3. `public TreeSet(Comparator compValue)`—This version constructs a `TreeSet` object that is sorted according to the order defined by `comp-Value`.
4. `public TreeSet(SortedSet setValue)`—This version constructs a `TreeSet` object whose initial contents are those of `setValue` and is sorted according to the same order as that used in `setValue`.

EXAMPLE 5.3   The following is an example of a program that displays the difference between the representation of a collection of `Integer` values as a `HashSet` object and as a `TreeSet` object. Note that the same output operation defined earlier for `HashSet` objects applies as well to `TreeSet` objects.

```
public static void main(String [] args)
{
  Set hashedIntegers = new HashSet();
  Set treesetIntegers = new TreeSet();

  int intArr[] = {2,3,4,7,8,1,1,-1,7,1}; // Conformant array
  // Corresponding array of Integer values.
  Integer intValues [] = new Integer[intArr.length];
  // Copy int values into Integer values in intValues
  for(int index = 0; index < intArr.length; ++index)
   intValues[index] = new Integer(intArr[index]);
  // Form sets hashedIntegers and treesetIntegers
  for(int index = 0; index < intValues.length; ++index)
  {
   hashedIntegers.add(intValues[index]);
   treesetIntegers.add(intValues[index]);
  }

  // Output results
  System.out.println("Contents of hashedIntegers: " + hashedIntegers);
  System.out.println("Contents of treesetIntegers: " +
                     treesetIntegers);
} // terminates text of main method
```

The output obtained from running this program is

Contents of hashedIntegers: [-1, 8, 7, 4, 3, 2, 1]
Contents of treesetIntegers: [-1, 1, 2, 3, 4, 7, 8]

Note that neither `hashedIntegers` nor `treesetIntegers` contain any duplicate values, and `treesetIntegers` returns a sorted version of the `Set` object.

5.7 The `Map` and `SortedMap` Interfaces and Their Implementations

In Section 5.5, we noted that a fundamental feature of sets is their efficient implementation of search. We also observed that `HashSet` and `TreeSet` represent two implementations of the `Set` interface, with additional features of hashing (for `HashSet`) and a sorting of the members (for `TreeSet`). These implementations work very well, provided that an *exact copy* of the object sought in a particular set is provided. But what if the storage of the exact copy is not known in every specific detail? This is particularly true in the case of employee records for a large firm or for inventory records for merchandise stored in a warehouse of some large department store or mail order house. The exact form and order of appearance of the data items stored in a record are generally not known in the detail required for a `Set` implementation to perform an efficient search.

It is usually the case that, for such complex items of storage, a relatively few pieces of data are known to the user, but not all. That is, the user is generally aware of some of the items of information required for a lookup, but not all. In such situations, Java supplies a `Map` interface for this purpose, because any implementation of `Map` constructs objects storing a *pair* of data items, of the form

keyValue, dataValue

in a way that is similar to the storage of values in `Hashtable` objects described in Section 4.7. Thus, *dataValue* can be retrieved in any `Map` object (if it appears at all), so long as the user provides the proper search key in the form of a *keyValue*. For example, in the case of employee records, a popular choice for *keyValue* is the employee's social security number; in the case of merchandise inventory, a popular choice for *keyValue* is the store identification number for this item.

The `java.util` library supplies three general purpose implementations of the `Map` interface: `HashMap`, `WeakHashMap`, and `TreeMap`. A `HashMap` or `WeakHashMap`[4] object stores its *keyValue, dataValue* pairs by applying a hash function to the value stored in *keyValue*, whereas a `TreeMap` object is formed by organizing the *keyValue* components of the elements stored in the object in a sorted order (using a *search tree*). The hash function (for `HashMap`) and the comparison operator (for `TreeMap`) is applied only to the *keyValue* part of the data item—not to the complete pair *keyValue, dataValue*.

Which of these implementations represents the best choice? Hashing is slightly faster in processing speed; however, if the processing of data

---

[4]Because the properties of `WeakHashMap` are similar to those of `HashMap` and are used only infrequently in actual practice, we will not discuss `WeakHashMap` any further in this text.

required traversing all of the items stored in the object in sorted order, the better choice is to store these data items in a `TreeMap` object.

The `Map` interface is coded as follows:

```
public interface Map
{
 // Puts the associated pair provided by the values of the two
 // parameters into the Map object.  If the keyValue is already
 // present in the Map object, the new object replaces the old one
 // associated with the previous version of keyValue.  This method
 // returns the old keyValue, or null if keyValue was not
 // present previously.
 // Precondition: the value of the second parameter cannot be
 // null.
 Object put(Object keyValue, Object dataValue);

 // Retrieves the dataValue associated with the value of the
 // parameter.  Returns null if keyValue is not part of an object
 // found in the Map object.
 Object get(Object keyValue);

 // Removes any Map object associated with the value of the
 // parameter.  The value returned is that of dataValue if present,
 // or null if no member of the current Map object exists with the
 // current keyValue.
 Object remove(Object keyValue);

 // Returns true if the current Map object contains a member with
 // the current keyValue.
 boolean containsKey(Object keyValue);

 // Returns true if dataValue appears as part of a current Map object;
 // returns false otherwise.
 boolean containsValue(Object dataValue);

 // Returns the size of the current Map object.
 int size();

 // Returns true if the current Map object contains no members.
 boolean isEmpty();

 // Bulk operation.  Puts all of the members of the parameter
 // into the current Map object.
 void putAll(Map otherMap);
```

```
// Bulk operation.  Removes all members of the current Map object.
void clear();


// Method permitting the current Map object to be viewed as a
// collection.  Returns a Set object whose members are the
// key values of the current map.
Set keySet();


// Method permitting the current Map object to be viewed as a
// collection.  Returns a Collection object whose members are
// the data values of the current map.
Collection values();


// Returns a Set whose members are Map.Entry objects: the
// keyValue, dataValue pairs in the current Map object.
// Note that Map.Entry is a nested interface containing three
// methods designed to manipulate the members of the current
// entrySet object.
Set entrySet();


// Nested interface for entrySet members.
public interface Entry
{
 // Returns the keyValue for the current entry.
 Object getKey();

 // Returns the dataValue for the current entry.
 Object getValue();

 // Changes the dataValue in the associated Map object to a
 // new dataValue, and returns the old dataValue.
 Object setValue(Object dataValue);
} // terminates text of Entry interface
} // terminates text of Map interface
```

The `SortedMap` interface extends the `Map` interface by requiring that its objects store members whose `keyValue` components are sorted in ascending order, either by the default ordering or according to a `Comparator` object defined when the `SortedMap` object is constructed. Because `SortedMap` defines an interface, we will see later that `TreeMap` is a concrete class implementing `SortedMap`, and one of the constructors for `TreeMap` objects requires the use of a single `Comparator` parameter. Clearly, this will affect the order of appearance of the members of any `SortedMap` objects constructed in this way. In addition, `SortedMap` contains a number of instance methods that rely on the fact that the underlying objects are sorted. Specifically, the syntax for `SortedMap` is

```
public interface SortedMap extends Map
{
// Returns the Comparator object used as the basis of sorting
// the current Map object.  If the default ordering is used,
// the return value is null.
Comparator comparator();

// Returns the lowest (first) keyValue of any member
// of the current SortedMap object.
Object firstKey();

// Returns the highest (last) keyValue of any member
// of the current SortedMap object.
Object lastKey();

// Returns a view of a portion of the current SortedMap object
// whose keyValue components have values greater than or equal to
// the value of the first parameter, and less than the value
// of the second parameter.
SortedMap subMap(Object minKey,Object maxKey);

// Returns a view of the portion of the current SortedMap object
// whose keyValue is less than the value of the parameter.
SortedMap headMap(Object maxKey);

// Returns a view of the portion of the current SortedMap object
// whose values are greater than or equal to the value of the
// parameter.
SortedMap tailMap(Object minKey);
}
```

We can thus describe two hierarchies: one whose hub is the `Collection` interface, and the other whose hub is the `Map` interface. This is because `Collection` and any of its subclasses store single objects, whereas `Map` and any of its subclasses store pairs of the form *keyValue, dataValue*. Figure 5.13 illustrates the `Collection` hierarchy, and Figure 5.14 illustrates the `Map` hierarchy.

Because `Map`, `SortedMap`, `HashMap`, `WeakHashMap`, and `TreeMap` are either interfaces involving pairs of the form *keyValue, dataValue* or are implementations of these interfaces, there are no direct relationships between

FIGURE 5.13

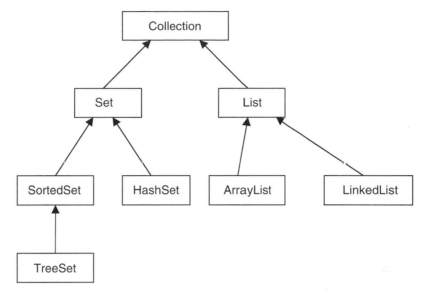

FIGURE 5.14

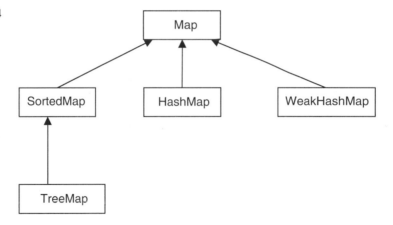

these and the Collection hierarchy. However, Java provides a way to "view" members of the Map hierarchy as individual collections. This is done using the instance methods of Map defined as keySet(), values(), and entrySet(). Each of these returns either a Set object or a Collection object, which can be processed by appropriate Collection methods. Besides, entrySet() provides a Set version of the Map object that can be processed using getKey(), getValue(), or setValue().

Note also that there is no provision for iterators in the description of instance methods for either Map or SortedMap. This is because iterators emerge when a "view" of a Map or SortedMap object is provided, as a Set or a Collection.

As stated earlier, `HashMap` implements `Map` using a hash table. A carefully designed `HashMap` implementation will result in `put`, `get`, `remove`, or `contains` operations for a `keyValue` or `dataValue` that are `O(1)`. This results in an extremely efficient way to associate a `keyValue` with a `dataValue`—in fact, for such reasons, `HashMap` is a popular application among commercial software designers.

The `HashMap` class defines four constructors.

1. `HashMap()`—This constructs a new `HashMap` object with a default initial capacity and load factor.
2. `HashMap(int initialCapacity)`—This constructs a new `HashMap` object with an initial capacity given by the value of the parameter and a default load factor.
3. `HashMap(int initialCapacity, float loadFactor)`—This constructs a new `HashMap` object with an initial capacity given by the value of the first parameter and a load factor given by the value of the second parameter.
4. `HashMap(Map mapObject)`—This constructs a new `HashMap` object whose members are exactly those of `mapObject`. The initial capacity is that of `mapObject`, and it uses the default load factor.

The `TreeMap` class implements the `SortedMap` interface, with the `keyValue` components of any object sorted according to the comparison operator used to define `TreeSet`. That is, the *keyValue*, *dataValue* pairs stored in any `TreeMap` object are sorted in exactly the same order as for the *keyValue* components in the associated `TreeSet` object. The `TreeMap` implementation is a popular choice if the sorted order of *keyMap*, *dataMap* pairs is an essential component of the design of a solution to a specific programming problem.

The `TreeMap` class defines four constructors.

1. `TreeMap()`—This constructs a `TreeMap` object that is sorted according to the default order of the `keyValue` components.
2. `TreeMap(Comparator comparator)`—This constructs a `TreeMap` object that is sorted according to the `Comparator` object defined by the parameter.
3. `TreeMap(Map mapObject)`—This constructs a `TreeMap` object whose initial values are the values stored in `mapObject`, sorted in the order defined by the default.
4. `TreeMap(SortedMap mapObject)`—This constructs a `TreeMap` object whose initial values are sorted in exactly the same way as the sorting that already exists for the parameter.

Example 5.4 describes a program applying the Map interface to produce a frequency table for a collection of String values input by the user. This version implements the Map interface using HashMap.[5]

EXAMPLE 5.4

```
// Sample program illustrating the use of the Map interface and
// the HashMap implementation, to count the frequency of
// occurrence of String values in an array of String values.

public static void main(String [] args)
 {
  // Construct array of input strings as a conformant array.
  String arr[] = {"I","think","therefore","I","am"};

  // Construct Map object whose members are pairs with keyValue
  // component is the String value, and whose dataValue component
  // is its frequency of occurrence in the text.
  Map stringFrequency = new HashMap();

  // Initialize frequency of occurrence of each member of arr
  // from conformant array.
  for(int index = 0; index < arr.length; ++index)
  {
   Integer intFreq = (Integer)stringFrequency.get(arr[index]);
   if(intFreq == null)
    intFreq = new Integer(1);
   else
   {
    int value = intFreq.intValue();
    intFreq = new Integer(value + 1);
   }
   stringFrequency.put(arr[index],intFreq);
  } // terminates text of for-loop
  System.out.println("The input sentence contains " +
       stringFrequency.size());
  System.out.println("distinct words.");
  System.out.println(stringFrequency);
 } // terminates text of main method
```

[5]This is based on a program described in Campione, Walrath, and Huml, p. 489. See the References section at the end of this chapter.

The output derived from running this program is

The input sequence contains 4
Distinct words.
{I = 2, therefore = 1, am = 1, think = 1}

The `for`-loop produces the following computations, in order of presentation: First,

```
Integer intFreq = (Integer)stringFrequency.get(arr[index]);
```

retrieves the current *dataValue* of `arr[index]` and casts this as an `Integer` value called `intFreq`. If the current *keyValue* stored in `arr[index]` has not been previously scanned, `intFreq` is assigned `null`. This value is changed to the `Integer` wrapper holding 1 as its data value, signaling the successful processing of the first occurrence of the `String` value stored in `arr[index]`. Otherwise, the `String` value stored in `arr[index]` has been previously scanned; the conditional then increments its value by one. The only `String` values stored in the `HashMap` object are those in the input string. The `HashMap` implementation places these *keyValue*, *dataValue* pairs in a hash table according to the hash method used, whose definition is kept hidden. This is evident from the output provided by executing

```
System.out.println(stringFrequency);
```

Compare this to the result of executing the version obtained when `Map` is implemented by `TreeMap`. The only change required is in implementing the constructor of the `Map` object as

```
Map stringFrequency = new TreeMap();
```

The processing described earlier using the `HashMap` implementation is virtually the same as that for `TreeMap`, except that now the `put` method described in the `for`-loop as

```
stringFrequency.put(arr[index],intFreq);
```

inserts the *keyValue*, *dataValue* pairs in the default order for `String` values, with

```
System.out.println(stringFrequency);
```

producing output

{I = 2, am = 1, therefore = 1, think = 1}

EXAMPLE 5.5   Suppose we continue our discussion of the instance methods of the `Map` interface by illustrating the application of each of `keySet()`, `values()`, `remove()`, and `entrySet()` on `stringFrequency`, implemented as a `HashMap` object whose contents are currently those described in Example 5.4. That is, suppose the text of the main method is exactly the same as that in Example 5.4, up to and including the `for`-loop. We replace the output methods following the `for`-loop with the following code segment:

```
// Output contents of the keyValues stored in stringFrequency.
System.out.println("stringFrequency.keySet() =");
System.out.println(stringFrequency.keySet());

// Now output the dataValue components stored in stringFrequency.
System.out.println("stringFrequency.values() =");
System.out.println(stringFrequency.values());

// Now apply remove to remove the keyValue "I" from the
// current version of stringFrequency.
System.out.println("Removing \"I\" from stringFrequency:");
stringFrequency.remove("I");

// Return a Set object whose members are the keyValue, dataValue
// pairs in the current version of stringFrequency.
System.out.println("stringFrequency.entrySet() =");
System.out.println(stringFrequency.entrySet());
```

When this code segment executes, the output sequence is

```
stringFrequency.keySet() =
[ I, therefore, am, think]
stringFrequency.values() =
[ 2, 1, 1, 1]
Removing "I" from stringFrequency:
stringFrequency.entrySet() =
[ therefore = 1, am = 1, think = 1]
```

As indicated in Figure 5.14, `Map` is not part of the `Collection` hierarchy, and no instance method described in the `Map` interface defines an iterator traversing over values stored in a `Map` object, as is found in the `Collection` interface. Consequently, it appears that iterators cannot be defined over `Map` objects. In response, there are instance methods defined in `Map` that permit `Map` objects to be "viewed" as `Collection` objects in several distinct ways:

1. The `Map` interface provides a `keySet()` method that returns a `Set` object whose members are just the *keyValue* components of the current members of the `Map` object.
2. The `Map` interface also provides a `value()` method that returns a `Collection` object whose members are just the *dataValue* components of the current members of the `Map` object.
3. The `Map` interface also provides an `entrySet()` method that returns a `Set` object whose members are the *keyValue*, *dataValue* pairs maintained in the current `Map` object. The return value is a set whose members are `Map.Entry` objects, where `Map.Entry` is a nested interface

containing the three methods `getKey`, `getValue`, and `setValue` described earlier.

Specifically, the `keySet()` method returns an object of a class that implements the `Set` interface. The identity of this class is kept hidden from the user—all the user needs to know is that this class contains methods for operating on the original `Map` object. This class is called a *view* of the original `Map` object.

Because the `Map` interface provides these three `Collection` views, we can define iterators for them because iterators are definable over any `Collection` objects.

EXAMPLE 5.6   Here is a sample program illustrating the use of the `Map` interface and the `HashMap` implementation, showing a `Collection` view of the `HashMap` object called `stringFrequency`. The `Set` object constructed by invoking `stringFrequency.keySet()` is acted on by an `Iterator` object called `iter`, used for computing the *keyValue* components of the members stored in `stringFrequency`. The main method is exactly the same as that for Example 5.4, up to and including the text of the `for`-loop. After this, the current method iterates over the *keyValue* components of `stringFrequency`. The actual code is given by

```
for(Iterator iter =
        stringFrequency.keySet().iterator();iter.hasNext();)
  System.out.println(iter.next());
```

The output derived from this loop is

```
I
therefore
am
think
```

EXAMPLE 5.7   How can we iterate over *keyValue*, *dataValue* pairs? Here we use the nested interface `Entry` and its `getKey()` and `getValue()` methods to the `Set` object returned by applying `stringFrequency.entrySet()`. Because a `Set` object is returned as a result of this invocation, an iterator can be defined over the members of this object, traversing its values.

Again, assume `stringFrequency` is defined as above. The following code segment traverses the values of `stringFrequency.entrySet()`, using `getKey()` and `getValue()`:

```
for(Iterator iter =
        stringFrequency.entrySet().iterator();iter.hasNext();)
{
 Map.Entry entry = (Map.Entry)iter.next();
```

```
System.out.println(entry.getKey() + "," + entry.getValue());
}
```

The output resulting from this is

```
I,2
therefore,1
am,1
think,1
```

EXAMPLE 5.8   We can use `Map` objects and `entrySet()` methods to solve a number of interesting and useful data-processing problems. As an example, suppose we have two collections of strings, and suppose we wish to know whether these collections have the same values occurring with the same frequency. That is, these two collections are to be judged equal if the only possible difference between them is the order of appearance of their respective members.

One possible way to solve this problem is to construct two `Map` objects, implemented using `HashMap`, whose *keyValue* components are the strings and whose corresponding *dataValue* components are the positive integers counting their respective frequency of occurrence. The algorithm would then construct the `entrySet()` value for each and then check whether the respective `entrySet()` values are equal. If equal, the two collections of strings are identical up to their order of appearance, and unequal if otherwise.

Assume the `Map` objects are called `stringFrequency` and `newstringFrequency`. We would then have to test whether `stringFrequency` and `newstringFrequency` have identical `entrySet(()` values, using

```
if(stringFrequency.entrySet().equals(newstringFrequency.entrySet()))
 System.out.println("stringFrequency = newstringFrequency");
else
 System.out.println("stringFrequency not = newstringFrequency");
```

For example, if `stringFrequency` is the `HashMap` object whose key values are formed using the conformant array declaration

```
String arr[] = {"I","think","what","I","think","and","I","am","what",
        "I","think"};
```

and suppose `newstringFrequency` is the `HashMap` object with key values formed using the conformant array declaration

```
String newarr[] =
{"I","think","what","I","think","and","I","am","what",
          "I","am"};
```

Then `stringFrequency.entrySet()` is `[I=4,and=1,am=1,what=2, think=3]` and `NewstringFrequency.entrySet()` is `[I=4,and=1,am=2, what=2,think=2]`.

Finally, this code segment outputs

```
StringFrequency not = newstringFrequency
```

This result could be obtained using a combination of the methods `key-Set()` and `values()` on each of `stringFrequency` and `newstringFrequency`.

5.8 Legacy Collections

Before the Java 2 platform was released in 1998, Java supported a small number of collection classes. This original group of classes is commonly called the collection of *legacy classes*. Specifically, the legacy classes are

- the `Hashtable` class, discussed in Section 4.7
- the `Properties` class
- the `Vector` class, to be discussed in Chapter 6
- the `Stack` class, a subclass of `Vector`, and discussed in Chapter 7
- the `BitSet` class

An object constructed from the `Properties` class has the same basic structure of a `Map` object—its *keyValues* and *dataValues* are strings, and it is a subclass of `Hashtable`. Standard `Hashtable` methods are used for processing `Properties` objects, and such objects are generally used to define the environment of the underlying Java system. Because this class is used primarily for these reasons, we do not have any further need to discuss its functionality in this text.

The `BitSet` class constructs objects that represent finite sequences of *bits*. Any such object can grow dynamically and can then be viewed as an array of bits (0 representing `false`, and 1 representing `true`). Each bit is therefore viewed as a component of this array. In fact, any `BitSet` object is initialized with all of its components `false`.

Two constructors are defined for `BitSet`:

`public BitSet(int size)`—This version constructs a `BitSet` object with sufficient initial storage to explicitly represent bits index from 0 to size − 1, with all bits initialized to `false`.

`public BitSet()`—This version constructs a `BitSet` object with a default amount of initial storage, with all bits initialized to `false`.

Three instance methods process individual bits, each of which throws an `IndexOutOfBoundsException` exception if the index value is negative:

`public void set(int index)`—This method sets the bit specified by the parameter to `true`.

public clear(int index)—This method sets the bit specified by the parameter to false.

public boolean get(int index)—This method retrieves the value of the bit specified by the parameter.

The next group of methods modifies the current BitSet object by applying bitwise logical operations using the bits from another BitSet object, as described by the parameter:

public void and(BitSet otherObject)—This method performs the "and" operation between the current BitSet object and otherObject, and it changes the value of the current BitSet object to this result.

public void andNot(BitSet otherObject)—This method clears (renders false) all bits in the current BitSet object that are set (rendered true) in otherObject. The resulting BitSet object will have bit values that are true only if it is originally true and if its corresponding value in otherObject is false.

public void or(BitSet otherObject)—This method performs the logical "or" operation on the current BitSet object and otherObject and changes the value of the current BitSet object to the result.

public void xor(BitSet otherObject)—This method performs the logical "exclusive or" operation between the current BitSet object and otherObject. The value of the current BitSet object is changed to this result.

In addition, BitSet contains the methods

public int size()—This method returns the number of bits actually allocated for the current BitSet object. If the programmer explicitly sets a bit index (using the set method described earlier) to a value greater than or equal to the current number of bits, the bit size of this object increases.

public int length()—This method returns the index of the highest bit plus one.

public boolean equals(Object otherObject)—This method returns true if all of the bit values appearing in otherObject match those of the current BitSet object.

Example 5.9 gives an illustration of an efficient application of the use of BitSet objects.

EXAMPLE 5.9   Suppose there are two squadrons of bombers, called squadron1 and squadron2. In addition, suppose there are fifteen targets to be bombed by both squadrons—the same targets are to be bombed by both squadrons. We label the targets with consecutive integers from 0 through 14. Each of the targets is represented by an individual bit in a `BitString` object of size 15.

We assume that a bit value of 0 (representing `false`) describes the situation that the target represented by that bit has not as yet been bombed, and a bit value of 1 (representing `true`) describes the situation that the target represented by that bit has been bombed. Several different possibilities exist:

- both squadrons bomb the same target
- one squadron bombs a target, and the other squadron either misses that target or overlooks that target
- both squadrons fail to bomb a target

If a target is bombed that has not, as yet, been bombed by the other squadron, the bit value of that target is changed from `false` to `true`. If a squadron bombs a target that has already been bombed by the other squadron, there is no change in the bit value corresponding to that target.

We wish to design a program that defines three `BitSet` variables: `squadron1`, `squadron2`, and `combined`. The first two record the number of targets hit by each of the respective squadrons, and the last records the combined number of hits.

We begin by naming a constant defining the number of targets:

```
final int numberOfTargets = 15;
```

and the `BitSet` objects

```
BitSet squadron1 = new BitSet(numberOfTargets);
BitSet squadron2 = new BitSet(numberOfTargets);
BitSet combined = new BitSet(numberOfTargets);
```

Let us assume `squadron1` has hit targets 0, 3, 7, 8, 12:

```
squadron1.set(0);
squadron1.set(3);
squadron1.set(7);
squadron1.set(8);
squadron1.set(12);
```

and `squadron2` has hit targets 1, 2, 7, 8, 11, 14:

```
squadron2.set(1);
squadron2.set(2);
squadron2.set(7);
squadron2.set(8);
squadron2.set(11);
squadron2.set(14);
```

We also introduce counter variables, each initialized at 0 counting the number of hits for each squadron and also for the combined number of hits. By our description, no target hit by both squadrons is counted twice. Thus, we have

```
int count1 = 0, count2 = 0, combinedCount = 0;
```

Now echo the number of hits for each squadron:

```
for(int index = 0; index < numberOfTargets; ++index)
  if(squadron1.get(index))
  {
   System.out.println("squadron1 has hit " + squadron1.get(index));
   count1++;
  }


  for(int index = 0; index < numberOfTargets; ++index)
  if(squadron2.get(index))
  {
   System.out.println("squadron2 has hit " + squadron2.get(index));
   count2++;
  }
```

Now compute the combined targets and their count:

```
combined.or(squadron1);
combined.or(squadron2);

for(int index = 0; index < numberOfTargets; ++index)
  if(combined.get(index))
    combinedCount++;

System.out.println("The combined number of targets hit are: " +
                   combinedCount);
```

The output generated by executing this collection of code sequences is

```
squadron1 has hit 0
squadron1 has hit 3
squadron1 has hit 7
squadron1 has hit 8
squadron1 has hit 12
squadron2 has hit 1
squadron2 has hit 2
squadron2 has hit 7
squadron2 has hit 8
squadron2 has hit 11
squadron2 has hit 14
squadron1 hit 5 targets
squadron2 hit 6 targets
The combined number of targets hit are: 9
```

Using this design over other alternatives has a number of advantages. First, individual bits are used for each designated target rather than, say, a single `char` value for each. Each `char` value is itself a bitstring—consequently, `BitSet` objects make more efficient use of space. Also, processing a single bit rather than a bitstring for each corresponding `char` value is more time efficient. In fact, the computer is processing individual bits in the `BitSet` object, which is what digital computers are supposed to do.

5.9 Algorithms and the `Collections` and `Arrays` Classes

The `Collections` class, predefined in Java, contains a wide range of static utility methods that are defined on any collection. In this section we present a brief listing of these methods, with the understanding that many of these will be revisited in greater detail in Chapter 8.

The first group represents methods for finding the maximum and minimum values in any collection:

`public static Object min(Collection collObject)`—This method returns the smallest member of the collection defined by the parameter, based on the default order relation.

An alternative version of this is defined by

`public static Object min(Collection collObject, Comparator comp)`—This version returns the smallest version of the collection defined by the first parameter, defined for the order relation given by the second parameter.

`public static Object max(Collection collObject)`—This method returns the largest value of the collection defined by the parameter, based on the default order relation.

The last has an alternative version:

`public static Object max(Collection collObject, Comparator comp)`—This version returns the largest value of the collection defined by the first parameter, defined for the order relation given by the second parameter.

EXAMPLE 5.10   Suppose we apply each of `max` and `min` to `intSet`, where `intSet` is implemented as a `HashSet` object and currently contains the `Integer` values represented as

```
intSet = [8, 7, 3, 2, 12, -1, 0]
```

If we apply `max` and `min` using the natural ordering of `Integer` values, and we apply

```
System.out.println("The minimum value of intSet is: " +
                   Collections.min(intSet));
  System.out.println("The maximum value of intSet is: " +
                   Collections.max(intSet));
```

the output is

The minimum value of intSet is: -1
The maximum value of intSet is: 12

Note that although `max` and `min` are `static` methods, we were required to use the *qualified references* `Collections.min(intSet)` and `Collections.max(intSet)`—otherwise, a compile error occurs. In fact, this must be done for each method in the `Collections` class.

In addition, it is important to observe that these methods are restricted to the members of the `Collection` hierarchy (as described in Figure 5.13), and therefore they cannot be applied directly to any `Map` object. Thus, for example, if we attempt to apply `Collections.min(stringFrequency)` or `Collections.max(stringFrequency)` for `stringFrequency` defined as the `HashMap` object of Example 5.4, a compile error results. However, if we apply either of

```
Collections.min(stringFrequency.keySet())
```

or

```
Collections.max(stringFrequency.keySet())
```

the respective results are

I

and

think

What is the advantage to using predefined methods? The programmer is otherwise obliged to write his or her own code for these methods. For example, if we wish to design a method for finding the minimum value of any `Collection` object, we can write the following code:

```
public static Object min(Collection collObject)
{
 Iterator iter = collObject.iterator();
 Comparable smallest = (Comparable)iter.next();
 for(; iter.hasNext();)
 {
  Comparable nextValue = (Comparable)iter.next();
  if(smallest.compareTo(nextValue) > 0)
    smallest = nextValue;
```

```
  }
  return smallest;
} // terminates text of min method.
```

This code would have to be designed and then tested for correctness and efficiency. As well, such code might contain unforeseen bugs and represents needless effort in the presence of methods in an already-existing `Collections` class designed for correctness and efficiency. Furthermore, if a programmer-defined version of any of the methods of `Collections` is used as a replacement for the predefined version appearing in `Collections`, the qualified reference is dropped. For example, if we wish to apply the version of `min` just coded to `stringFrequency.keySet()`, we would use `min(stringFrequency.keySet())` instead of `Collections.min(stringFrequency.keySet())`

In addition to the `max` and `min` methods just described, `Collections` contains a number of other general utility methods—such as methods for reversing the order of appearance of members in any list and randomly shuffling the values in any list, as well as methods for copying, sorting, and applying a form of binary search to any list. These will be studied in the next chapter and in Chapter 8.

Another predefined class called `Arrays` provides a number of utility methods for dealing with the processing of arrays. Most of these methods are definable for arrays of values of each primitive type (except for searching and sorting using `boolean`-valued arrays) and one for `Object`-valued arrays. Each method has two variants: one applies the method to the entire array, while the other has two extra `int`-valued parameters, that define the initial and final indices of a section of the entire array to which the method is to be applied. The general categories of the methods of the `Arrays` class are

1. `sort`—This is a general sort method for arrays and was introduced in Section 3.19.
2. `binarySearch`—This searches a sorted array for a given value and was also introduced in Section 3.19. No subarray version for this method is defined.
3. `equals`—This involves two array parameters and is `boolean`-valued. This method returns `true` just when the two array objects are either both `null` or when both have the same size and equivalent contents.
4. `fill`—This fills the array parameter with a specific value.
5. `asList`—This takes a single array parameter and returns the corresponding `List` object.

As stated earlier, each of these methods defined for `Arrays` requires the qualified reference. Many of these will be discussed in greater detail in Chapter 8.

5.10 **Chapter Summary**

The `java.util` package was originally designed to contain several utility classes that are valuable in a large number of commercial-scale programming environments. Before the emergence of Java 2, the list of predefined classes in `java.util` implementing the data structures and abstract data types commonly used in Java applications were `BitSet`, `Dictionary`, `Enumeration`, `Hashtable`, `Stack`, and `Vector`. Collectively, these classes represent what is now termed Java's *Legacy Collections*. Each of these classes will be studied in detail in Chapters 4 through 10.

The release of the Java 2 platform in 1998 was influenced by C++'s Standard Template Library (STL), but the approach provided by `java.util` was different. For example, `java.util` takes advantage of the distinction between interface and implementation, and it makes heavier and explicit use of inheritance. The `java.util` package thus contains a number of interfaces and classes that provide a general framework for processing well-defined collections of objects. This is known as the Java Collections Framework. This framework is an extremely well-planned aggregate of interfaces together with efficient and correct implementations of these interfaces. In addition, these interfaces and implementations represent reusable software tools.

The primary goals influencing the design of the Java Collections Framework, and the result of implementing the classes and methods defined in this framework, are:

- to minimize the programming effort of the software development team
- to enhance the efficiency of the methods developed for the underlying application
- to promote and encourage software reuse

A major consequence of the Java Collections Framework are the `Collection` and `Iterator` interfaces. The `Collection` interface represents the hub for a number of interfaces and concrete classes such as those for processing lists, using the `List` interface and the `LinkedList` and `ArrayList` implementations. A brief account of `LinkedList` was given in this chapter; a detailed account of these topics appears in Chapter 6. Another segment of the `Collection` hierarchy involves the `Set` interface and the `HashSet` implementation, and the `SortedSet` interface and its `TreeSet` implementation.

A key distinction exists between objects implementing the `List` interface and those implementing the `Set` and `SortedSet` interfaces. `List` objects allow the presence of duplicate values, with these values appearing in the order in which they were introduced. On the other hand, `Set` and `SortedSet` objects do not permit any duplication of values. If a `Set` object is implemented using `HashSet`, a hash function is applied to permit the proper positioning of the values in the object. On the other hand, if `Sort-edSet` is used (and implemented by `TreeSet`), not only is there no duplication of values in the object, but also these values appear in sorted order. The ordering depends on whether the default "less than" order, or an order defined by the programmer using a `Comparator` object, is applied.

It is important that the values of any `Collection` object be traversed in some specific order, and that these values be processed in some well-defined manner. Java supports this functionality by defining iterators and an `Iterator` interface. Iterators possess a behavior that is similar to, but not identical with, `Enumeration` objects. For example, iterators can be used to remove members of a collection, whereas `Enumeration` objects simply traverse the values in a collection without the functionality of removing any such value.

A `Map` object has no direct inheritance relationship with members of the `Collection` hierarchy. Instead, `Map` objects store their values as *keyValue*, *dataValue* pairs. In fact, the *dataValue* component of any pair can be retrieved in any `Map` object, provided that the user supplies the proper form of a search key in the form of a well-defined instance of *keyValue*.

The `java.util` package supplies two general-purpose `Map` implementations: `HashMap` and `TreeMap`. A `HashMap` object hashes the *keyValues* in some way, and a `TreeMap` object orders the *keyValues* so that the *key-Value*, *dataValue* pairs are placed as the information components of nodes on some efficient form of a search tree. The hash map (in the case of `HashMap` objects) and the order relation (in the case of `TreeMap` objects) is applied only to the *keyValue* of the pair—no hashing or comparison is done on the associated *dataValue*.

Although a `Map` object is not classified as a collection in the Java Collections Framework, we can obtain *views* of the `Map` object as objects implemented in the `Collection` hierarchy. There are three possible views:

- the *set* of *keyValues* stored in the `Map` object
- the *collection* of *dataValues* stored in the `Map` object
- the *set* of *keyValue*, *dataValue* pairs

Methods defined in the `Map` interface support returning each of these views.

Our discussion of Java's Legacy Collections in this chapter concentrated on the `BitSet` class, because the remaining legacy members are treated elsewhere in this text. We noted that any `BitSet` object stores a finite sequence of *bits*, which are represented internally as `false` (for the 0 bit) and `true` (for the 1 bit). `BitSet` objects and their associated instance methods provide efficient ways of solving certain key programming problems for which other alternatives are either inefficient or do not give a complete solution of the underlying problem.

The Collections class is also part of the java.util package. It contains a number of static methods applicable to any Collection object. Two of these are max and min, which return the largest and smallest value, respectively, of the collection to which it is applied. Besides these, Collections contains utility methods for reversing the order of appearance of any finite sequence of values appearing as members of a List object, a method for the random shuffling of values stored in a List object, and methods for copying, sorting, and applying a binary search for any value, for List objects. It is important to note that the syntax used for invoking any of these methods requires the use of a *qualified reference,* such as,

```
Collections.min(stringFrequency.keySet())
```

This is used to specify the min method that is predefined in Collections rather than some programmer-defined version.

The package java.util also supports another predefined class of utility methods called Arrays. These were mentioned briefly in the summary at the end of Chapter 3 and will be discussed at length in Chapter 8. The static methods described in the Arrays class involve sorting, binary search, testing arrays for equality, and a method that fills the components of an array with a specific value. In addition to these, Arrays has a method called asList, whose functionality is to return a List object using an ordinary array parameter. As was the case for each of the methods defined in the Collections class, each of the methods just described for Arrays requires the use of the qualified reference.

EXERCISES

1. Give the exact form of the output for the following program:

```
public static void main(String [] args)
{
 // Input values stored in a conformant array.
 int intArr[] = {2,3,4,7,8,1};
 // Construct associated Integer-valued array.
 Integer intValues[] = new Integer[intArr.length];
 // Copy values of intArr into intValues.
 for(int index = 0; index < intValues.length; ++index)
  intValues[index] = new Integer(intArr[index]);
 // Construct LinkedList, HashSet, and TreeSet objects.
 Collection intList = new LinkedList();
 Collection hashedIntegers = new HashSet();
 Collection treesetIntegers = new TreeSet();
```

```
// Copy values of intValues into each of intList, hashedIntegers, and
// treesetIntegers:
for(int index = 0; index < intValues.length; ++index)
{
 intList.add(intValues[index]);
 hashedIntegers.add(intValues[index]);
 treesetIntegers.add(intValues[index]);
}


// Output the results:
System.out.println("intList: " + intList);
System.out.println("hashedIntegers: " + hashedIntegers);
System.out.println("treesetIntegers: " + treesetIntegers);
} // terminates text of main method
```

2. Explain the output provided by the program

```
public static void main(String [] args)
{
    int [] intArr = {2,3,5,2,6,2};
    Integer [] intValues = new Integer[intArr.length];
    LinkedList intList = new LinkedList();

    for(int index = 0; index < intValues.length; ++index)
     intValues[index] = new Integer(intArr[index]);

    for(int index = 0; index < intValues.length; ++index)
     intList.add(intValues[index]);

    Collection noDuplicates = new HashSet(intList);

    System.out.println(intList);
    System.out.println(noDuplicates);
}
```

In particular, explain the processing performed by the constructor

```
Collection noDuplicates = new HashSet(intList);
```

3. a. Write a program that sorts a finite list `intList` of `Integer` values by first constructing an `Integer`-valued array `intValues` containing these `Integer` values. After doing this, pour the components, in order of appearance in `intValues`, into `intList` and display the members of `intList`. Then use `clear()` to empty `intList` and invoke `Arrays.sort(intValues)`, after which the components of `intValues` are poured back into `intList`. Finally, display the contents of `intList`.

b. Do we obtain the same result by constructing

```
Set sortedList = new TreeSet(intList);
```

after initializing `intList` with the values of `intValues`?

4. Write the complete program using the `TreeMap` interface for the program described in Example 5.4.

5. Write the equivalent version for the driver method for Example 5.5, now using the `TreeMap` implementation.

6. Apply `stringFrequency.putAll(newstringFrequency)` and display the results, where `stringFrequency` is the HashMap object of Example 5.4, and `newstringFrequency` is the `HashMap` object whose `keyValues` are derived from the sentence `"I think what I think and I am what I am"`.

7. Using the input of Exercise 6, now apply

```
newstringFrequency.putAll(stringFrequency);
```

and compare the result with that of Exercise 6.

8. Write, compile, and execute a program similar to that for Example 5.6, but now the iterator traverses the *dataValue* components of the `HashMap` object.

9. Write programs similar to those of Examples 5.6 and 5.7 and Exercise 8, but replace the `HashMap` implementation with `TreeMap`.

10. Write a program that constructs the `HashMap` object of Example 5.4 called `stringFrequency` and that increments the `dataValue` component of the member whose `keyValue` is the string `"am"` from its current value of `1` to `2`.

11. a. Find the exact form of the output for the program

```
public static void main(String [] args)
 {
  // Construct array of input strings as a conformant array.
  String arr[] = {"I","think","therefore","I","am"};


  // Construct Map object whose members are pairs with keyValue
  // component is the String value, and whose dataValue component
  // is its frequency of occurrence in the text.
  Map stringFrequency = new HashMap();


  // Initialize frequency of occurrence of each member of arr
  // from conformant array.
  for(int index = 0; index < arr.length; ++index)
  {
   Integer intFreq = (Integer)stringFrequency.get(arr[index]);
   if(intFreq == null)
    intFreq = new Integer(1);
   else
```

```
  {
   int value = intFreq.intValue();
   intFreq = new Integer(value + 1);
  }
  stringFrequency.put(arr[index],intFreq);
 } // terminates text of for-loop
 // Now we wish to iterate over the keyValue parts of
 // stringFrequency -- uses Collection views, and an iterator
 // defined on the keySet.
 for(Iterator iter =
         stringFrequency.entrySet().iterator();iter.hasNext();)
 {
  Map.Entry entry = (Map.Entry)iter.next();
  System.out.println(entry.getKey() + "," + entry.getValue());
 } // terminates for-loop

 Iterator iter = stringFrequency.entrySet().iterator();
 for(int count = 0; count < 2; ++count)
 {
  Map.Entry entry = (Map.Entry)iter.next();
  Integer intFreq = (Integer)entry.getValue();
  int value = intFreq.intValue();
  intFreq = new Integer(value + 1);
  stringFrequency.put(arr[count],intFreq);
 }

 System.out.println("The revised version of stringFrequency is:");
 System.out.println(stringFrequency);

} // terminates text of main method
```

In particular, explain the result of executing the last `for`-loop.

b. What changes (if any) in the output would occur if, instead, `stringFrequency` is declared as

```
Map stringFrequency = new TreeMap();
```

12. a. Find and explain the exact output obtained when executing

```
public static void main(String [] args)
{
 Collection integerSet = new HashSet();
 // Conformant array of int values.
 int intArr[] = {2,3,4,7,8,1,1,-1,7,1};
 // Corresponding array of Integer values.
 Integer intValues[] = new Integer[intArr.length];
```

```
   // Copy values of intArr into intValues:
   for(int index = 0; index < intArr.length; ++index)
    intValues[index] = new Integer(intArr[index]);


   // Install the values in intValues into integerSet.
   for(int index = 0; index < intValues.length; ++index)
    integerSet.add(intValues[index]);


   // Display the current contents of integerSet
   System.out.println("The current contents of integerSet are:");
   System.out.println(integerSet);


   // We now have [8,7,4,3,2,-1,1]
   // Increment second value by 2 and display new result


   Iterator iter = integerSet.iterator();
   Integer intVal = new Integer(0);
   for(int count = 0; count < 2; ++count)
     intVal = (Integer)iter.next();


   integerSet.remove(intVal);
   int value = intVal.intValue();
   intVal = new Integer(value + 2);


   integerSet.add(intVal);


   // Display new results.
   System.out.println("The revised contents of integerSet are:");
   System.out.println(integerSet);

 } // terminates text of main method
```

     b. Explain any changes in the execution of the program when the declaration of `integerSet` is changed to

```
   Collection integerSet = new TreeSet();
```

13. a. Given the program

```
public static void main(String [] args)
 {

  Collection intColl = new LinkedList();
  Collection newColl = new LinkedList();
  int intArr[] = {7,3,-1,4,1,5,1};  // conformant array
```

```
for(int index = 0; index < intArr.length; ++index)
 intColl.add(new Integer(intArr[index]));

System.out.println("intColl = " + intColl);

// Note: the array returned by the toArray() method was created
// as an Object[] array, and the type cannot be changed to
// Integer[].  Instead, we need to use a variant of the toArray()
// method.  Declare an array of length 0 of Integer type.  Then
// the returned array is constructed and is of type Integer[].
// Use the following definition:

Integer [] intValues = (Integer[])intColl.toArray(new Integer[0]);

for(int index = 0; index < intValues.length; ++index)
 System.out.println("intValues[" + index + "] = " + intValues[index]);

Integer [] newValues = new Integer[intValues.length];

for(int index = 0; index < intValues.length; ++index)
 newValues[intValues.length - index - 1] = intValues[index];

for(int index = 0; index < newValues.length; ++index)
 newColl.add(newValues[index]);

System.out.println("newColl = " + newColl);

}
```

find the exact form of the output. What useful functionality concerning list processing is displayed in this program?

b.   Explain any changes in the output that result by changing the definition of `newColl` to

```
Collection newColl = new HashSet();
```

c.   Explain any changes in the output that result by changing the definition of `newColl` to

```
Collection newColl = new TreeSet();
```

14.   Write a program that uses the `HashMap` implementation of `stringFrequency` of Example 5.4 and that performs the following tasks in the order described: Remove the key value of `"I"`, then use `containsKey` to test whether the latest version of `stringFrequency` contains the key value of `"I"`, then use `containsValue` to test whether the current version of `stringFrequency` contains a data value of 2. Finally, reinstall the pair `"I"`,

new `Integer(1)` into `stringFrequency` and output this latest revision of `stringFrequency`.

15. a. Suppose `stringFrequency` is given as in Example 5.4, and `new-stringFrequency` is its counterpart formed using the `String`-valued array formed as a conformant array using the initial values

`{"I","think","what","I","think","therefore","I","am","what","I","am"}`.

Suppose also that `stringFrequency` and `newstringFrequency` are implemented using `HashMap`. Use the `entrySet()` and `containsAll()` methods to test whether `stringFrequency.entrySet()` is contained in `newstringFrequency.entrySet()`.

b. Use the same methods as described in (a) to test whether `stringFrequency.keySet()` is contained in `newstringFrequency.keySet()`.

16. Obtain the same result seen in Example 5.8, now using a combination of the methods `keySet()` and `values()`.

17. a. Design a similar program to that for Example 5.9, but now replace `BitSet` objects by ordinary one-dimensional arrays of `char` values, replacing `true` by `'t'` and `false` by `'f'`.

b. Redo (a) but now replace each `BitSet` object by a corresponding `boolean`-valued array.

c. Comment on the relative efficiency of each implementation, including the `BitSet` version of Example 5.9.

18. Show that the `max` and `min` methods defined in Section 5.9 also work for `stringFrequency.values()`, for `stringFrequency` as defined in Example 5.4.

19. a. Write code similar to that for `min` in Section 5.9 for `max`.

b. Test each of the programmer-defined versions of `min` and `max` on `stringFrequency.keySet()` and on `stringFrequency.values()` as defined in Example 5.4.

20. Given the main method

```
public static void main(String [] args)
{
  // String array as a conformant array.
  String [] stringArray = {"I","think","therefore","I","am"};
  // Echo components of stringArray:
  System.out.println("The components of stringArray are:");
  for(int index = 0; index < stringArray.length; ++index)
   System.out.println("stringArray[" + index + "]= " +
      stringArray[index]);
  // Echo corresponding list.
  System.out.println("Use asList method to convert to list of Strings");
  List stringList = new LinkedList();
  stringList = Arrays.asList(stringArray);
```

```
        System.out.println("stringList = " + stringList);

} // terminates text of main method
```

     a. Find the exact form of the output when this executes.

     b. Describe the details of the computation.

PROGRAMMING PROJECT

1. a. Sort a `List` object using the methods `toArray`, `Arrays.sort`, and `Arrays.asList`. It is important that the final result be the same `List` object defined initially.

     b. Write a program that searches for a value in a `List` object in two different ways. One way is to apply the `contains` method appearing in `Collection` directly to the `List` object, viewing the `List` class as a member of the `Collection` hierarchy. The second way is to use `toArray` on the `List` object, sorting the array using `Arrays.sort`, and then applying `Arrays.binarySearch` to the sorted array. Which, in your opinion, produces the more time-efficient code?

     c. There is a third way to conduct binary search. After sorting the `List` object, as in part (a), apply `Collections.binarySearch` directly to the `List` object, similar to the way `Arrays.binarySearch` applies to arrays. Apply this version of the algorithm and compare its efficiency to the versions described in part (b).

     d. As an alternative to part (a), sort a `List` object directly using `Collections.sort`, where we view the `List` object as a member of the `Collection` hierarchy. Compare the efficiency of this to the algorithm described in part (a).

REFERENCES

Arnold, Ken, James Gosling, and David Holmes. 2000. *The Java Programming Language, Third Edition.* Reading, MA: Addison-Wesley.

Campione, Mary, Kathy Walrath, and Alison Huml. 2001. *The Java Tutorial, Third Edition.* Reading, MA: Addison-Wesley.

De Lillo, Nicholas J. 2002. *Object-Oriented Design in C++ Using the Standard Template Library.* Pacific Grove, CA: Brooks/Cole.

Horstmann, Cay S., and Gary Cornell. 2000. Core Java 2, Volume II—Advanced Features. Englewood Cliffs, NJ: Prentice-Hall.

CHAPTER 6

Vibrators and Lists

Vectors and Lists

CHAPTER OBJECTIVES

- To introduce vectors and lists as useful data structures.
- To present the `Vector` class as a member of `java.util`.
- To continue the study of the `List` interface and its `LinkedList` and `ArrayList` implementations.
- To describe and examine a number of specific applications of vectors and lists.

6.1 Introduction

An important consideration for the program designer is the choice of the most appropriate type of container to use for storing data when solving a specific software problem. For certain problems, the most appropriate choice is an array or vector; for others, a list, stack, or a member of Java's `Collection` or `Map` hierarchy might be the most convenient. In brief, the choice of the most appropriate container type depends heavily on the problem to be solved and the functionality of the structures required for that solution.

This chapter discusses two of the more popularly used container classes: the `Vector` legacy class and the `List` interface, including the `LinkedList` and `ArrayList` implementations.

6.2 The `Vector` Class

One of the most valuable and useful classes in Java's Legacy Collections is the `Vector` class. Objects of the `Vector` class (that is, vectors) are data structures that are assigned a contiguous block of storage in a manner identical to the allocation of storage for an ordinary one-dimensional array. In fact, the behavior of vectors is similar to that for arrays, in that the components of a vector are accessed using methods that are $O(1)$. This is due primarily to the fact that storage allocated for vectors and arrays is contiguous. The distinction between arrays and vectors lies primarily in the observation that vectors have a size that grows dynamically. This simply means that, on occasion and automatically, a larger block of storage is allocated for the elements of that vector, after which the current elements are copied into that new block and the old block is reclaimed by garbage collection. This dynamic growth is usually triggered by an attempt to insert a new element into the vector. Thus, we can insert new elements into a vector, and the vector grows automatically to contain these new elements. This is not possible for an ordinary array. As well, a vector can shrink in size; an ordinary array cannot.

Before proceeding any further, it is important to make an important observation about the instance methods appearing in `Vector` in the presence of the Java 2 platform. These instance methods are *synchronized,* causing the execution of any of these to be inordinately slow if the vector is accessed from a single processing thread. Thus, if processing speed is a major factor of the design, one should consider an alternative to the use of vectors. As it turns out, a recommended alternative is to use objects and instance methods defined in the `ArrayList` class, to be discussed later in this chapter. The objects and instance methods defined for `ArrayList` have essentially the same functionality as those for `Vector`, but without any additional support or concession to synchronized concurrent processing.

When we first discussed the `Collection` hierarchy in Chapter 5, we omitted a number of classes appearing in the hierarchy; the `Collection` hierarchy actually also includes a number of abstract classes.[1] For example, `java.util` defines two abstract classes that are part of the `Collection` hierarchy: `AbstractCollection` and `AbstractList`. In Section 5.3, we defined a number of methods appearing in the `Collection` interface. Some of these are classified as *basic operations* and depend only on the way in which the `Collection` interface is implemented, while others are expressible in terms of these basic operations. For instance, the `size()` method is basic and thus depends only on the specific implementation of `Collection`. As a consequence, `size()` is defined as an `abstract` method in `AbstractCollection`. On the other hand, `isEmpty()` is a method that is definable in terms of `size()`:

```
public boolean isEmpty()
{
  return (this.size() == 0);
}
```

---

[1] See Section 2.6 for a formal treatment of abstract classes.

The presence of such abstract classes reduces the effort required to implement a class in the `Collection` hierarchy, because the implementation effort is limited to the implementation of these abstract methods. The `AbstractList` class works similarly for the `List` interface. Figure 6.1 provides

FIGURE 6.1

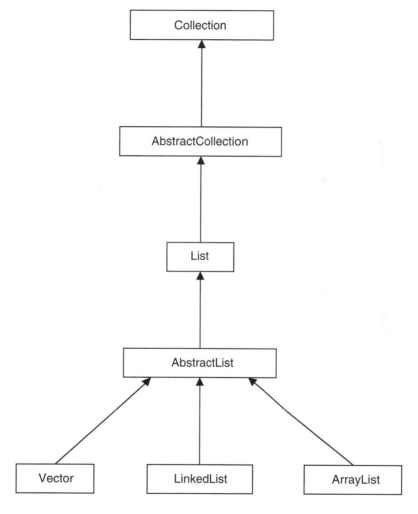

a hierarchical diagram for these classes, including `Vector`, `ArrayList`, and `LinkedList`.

The figure shows that, although `Vector` is a legacy class, it is designed (in the Java Collections Framework) to implement `List` and thus can be viewed as a descendant of `Collection`. As a consequence, `Vector` inherits instance methods from `List` and from `Collection`. As well, `Vector` has its own set of constructors and instance methods.

Each vector has an initial *size* and *capacity*. The size of a vector is defined as the number of elements present in the current vector, and the capacity is defined as the number of storage components allocated to the current vector.

The default constructor has the signature

```
public Vector();
```

This constructs a vector that is initially empty with a default size of 0 and a default capacity of 10.

The second version of the constructor is given by

```
public Vector(int initialCapacity);
```

This version constructs a vector whose initial size is 0 and whose initial capacity is specified by the value of the parameter. Thus, suppose initialCapacity currently stores a value of 14, and this version is invoked. Then the resulting vector will be empty with a default size of 0 and an initial capacity of 14.

In general, if a vector's current capacity is greater than its current size, then a new element can be inserted into the vector without having to wait for an adjustment of storage. In fact, any readjustment of new storage to accommodate the growth of a vector depends on three factors: its current size, its capacity, and a third factor called the *capacity increment*. This last is an int-valued parameter used to allocate exactly the amount of new storage units given by its current value. Thus, if we construct a vector with a capacity of 7 and a capacity increment of 4, then after the first seven components of the vector are filled the capacity grows in jumps of four units to 11, then to 15, and so on. This is reflected in the definition of the third form of the constructor:

```
public Vector(int initialCapacity, int capacityIncrement);
```

The final version of the constructor takes the form

```
public Vector(Collection collObject);
```

This version is analogous to a copy constructor from C++, in which the contents of the parameter are copied, in order of appearance, into the vector. The current size and capacity of the vector under construction are determined by the current size and capacity defined for collObject.

Indeed, suppose List1 is a LinkedList object, where currently List1 = [2,3,7,8,2,8]. If we then define

```
Vector vect1 = new Vector(List1);
```

then vect1 = [2,3,7,8,2,8] and has size and capacity equal to six.

The next method inserts a value at the end of the current vector:

```
void addElement(Object obj);
```

If currently `vect1 = [2,3,7,8,2,8]` and if `IntegerVal` is an `Integer` object whose `intVal` is 10, then `vect1.size() = 6`. If we then apply `vect1.addElement(IntegerVal)`, the result is `vect1 = [2,3,7,8,2,8,10]`, and `vect1.size() = 7`.

Because `Vector` inherits instance methods from `Collection`, we get the same result as that for `vect1.addElement(IntegerVal)` using `vect1.add(IntegerVal)`.

`Vector` contains a number of insertion methods where the programmer must specify the position in the vector where the value is to be inserted. One of these is

```
void add(int index, Object obj);
```

This method inserts `obj` at position `index` after first shifting down one position all the values stored in the current vector after position `index`, in order to make room for the insertion of `obj`. For example, if `vect1 = [2,3,7,8,2,8]`, and if `IntegerVal` is as just described, then the result of executing `vect1.add(5,IntegerVal)` is `vect1 = [2,3,7,8,2,10,8]`.

Another instance method of `Vector` that produces the same result is

```
void insertElementAt(Object obj,int index).
```

The next two methods assign a new value to a component of a vector at a given position. The first of these has the signature

```
Object set(int index,Object obj);
```

This version assigns `obj` to the component of the vector referenced by `index` (assuming `index` is in the subscript range of the current vector) and returns the value of the previous occupant of that position of the vector. If `index` is not in the current range of subscripts of the vector, an `ArrayIndexOutOfBoundsException` exception is thrown. For example, if currently `vect1 = [2,3,7,8,2,8]`, then executing `vect1.set(5,IntegerVal)` yields `vect1 = [2,3,7,8,2,10]`.

The second method has the signature

```
void setElementAt(Object obj,int index);
```

If `vect1 = [2,3,7,8,2,8]`, then `vect1.setElementAt(IntegerVal,5)` produces `vect1 = [2,3,7,8,2,10]`.

`Vector` also has a number of retrieval instance methods. The first of these is inherited from `List`, and has the signature

```
Object get(int index);
```

This version returns the `Object` value currently stored at position `index`, if the value of `index` is within the subscript range of the vector; otherwise an `ArrayIndexOutOfBoundsException` exception is thrown. As an example, suppose `vect1 = [2,3,7,8,2,8]`, and suppose we apply `vect1.get(5)`. The result is `8`.

A similar version appears among the instance methods of `Vector`. Its signature is

```
Object elementAt(int index);
```

We thus obtain the same result as earlier by using `vect1.elementAt(5)`.

Two other special retrieval instance methods appear in `Vector`. The first returns the first member of the vector when the vector is not empty; otherwise a `NoSuchElementException` is thrown. Its signature is

```
Object firstElement();
```

The second method returns the last element of the vector in case the current vector is not empty; otherwise a `NoSuchElementException` exception is thrown.

For `vect1` as defined earlier, `vect1.firstElement()` is 2 and `vect1.lastElement()` is 8.

The final retrieval method appearing in `Vector` is inherited from `List` and has the signature

```
List subList(int first,int last);
```

When `subList` is applied to a vector with `first < last`, and each of `first`, `last` is in the subscript range of the current vector, the result is the `List` object containing members of the vector from positions `first` to `last - 1`. This is *not* a copy of the original vector—in fact, if we make any changes in the values of this list, these changes also appear in the underlying vector from which this list was constructed. Furthermore, if the value of `last` is less than that of `first`, an `IllegalArgumentException` exception is thrown; if either the value of `first` or that of `last` is out of range, an `ArrayIndexOutOfBoundsException` exception is thrown.

`Vector` contains several instance methods for removing objects. The first two are inherited from `List` and have the signatures

```
boolean remove(Object obj);
```

and

```
Object remove(int index);
```

The first of these removes the first occurrence (if it exists) of `obj` in the current vector and returns `true` if `obj` is a member of that vector; otherwise `false` is returned. As an example, suppose `vect1 = [2,3,7,8,2,8]`. Then the result of applying `vect1.remove(new Integer(8))` is `vect1 = [2,3,7,2,8]`.

The second method removes the object at the position given by the value of the parameter, assuming that value lies in the subscript range of the vector. Otherwise, an `ArrayIndexOutOfBoundsExecption` exception is thrown. Indeed, if `vect1` is as given earlier, then the result of applying `vect1.remove(4)` is `vect1 = [2,3,7,8,8]`.

The next instance method appears in `Vector`. Its signature is given by

```
boolean removeElement(Object obj);
```

Its functionality is identical with that of `remove(Object obj)`. Similarly, the method `removeElementAt` is an instance method of `Vector` with signature

```
void removeElementAt(int index);
```

It is similar in functionality to `remove(int index)`.

The next instance method is inherited from `Collection`. Its signature is

```
boolean contains(Object obj);
```

When applied to a vector, it returns `true` if the vector contains the object described by `obj`; otherwise it returns `false`.

The next method is actually an instance method appearing in `List`. Its signature is

```
int indexOf(Object obj);
```

When applied to a vector, the method returns the subscript of the first object whose value is identical with `obj`. If no such match exists, the value returned is -1. Thus, if `vect1` is as described earlier, `vect1.indexOf(new Integer(8))` is 3 and `vect1.indexOf(new Integer(5))` is -1.

A variant of `indexOf(Object obj)` is given by

```
int indexOf(Object obj,int index);
```

When this variant is applied to a vector, it returns the subscript of the first occurrence of `obj` in the vector, with the search for `obj` beginning at the position given by the value of the second parameter. If no such value exists, the method returns -1. Thus, if we apply `vect1.indexOf(new Integer(8),4)`, the value returned is 5. Note also that `indexOf(obj,0)` is the same as `indexOf(obj)` for any choice of `obj`.

Two remaining instance methods in `Vector` are used for searching for a value in a vector. These are described by the signatures

```
int lastIndexOf(Object obj);
```

and

```
int lastIndexOf(Object obj,int index);
```

The first of these returns the subscript of the last occurrence of `obj` in the vector, if such an occurrence exists. Otherwise, -1 is returned. For example, `vect1.lastIndexOf(new Integer(8))` is 5 and `vect1.lastIndexOf(new Integer(5))` is -1.

The second method returns the subscript of the last occurrence of `obj` in the vector, using a backward linear search beginning at the position indicated by the value of the second parameter, if such an occurrence exists. If not, the value -1 is returned. Thus, `vect1.lastIndexOf(new`

`Integer(8),4) = 3` and `vect1.lastIndexOf(new Integer(5),4) = -1`.
Note that, when applied to any vector `vect` and for any object `obj`,
`vect.lastIndexOf(obj) = vect.lastIndexOf(obj,vect.size() - 1)`.

`Vector` also supports a number of bulk operations, inherited from `Col-`
`lection`. These are

```
boolean addAll(Collection otherCollection);
boolean containsAll(Collection otherCollection);
boolean removeAll(Collection otherCollection);
```

and

```
boolean retainAll(Collection otherCollection);
```

The only difference is that now we emphasize that each of these apply to
a vector. For example, suppose `vect1` is as given earlier, and suppose
`intList` is the `List` object given as `intList = [3,5,8,2,6]`. Then

`vect1.addAll(intList)` yields `vect1 = [2,3,7,8,2,8,3,5,8,2,6]`
`vect1.removeAll(intList)` yields `vect1 = [7]`
`vect1.retainAll(intList)` yields `vect1 = [2,3,8,2,8]`

and

`vect1.containsAll(intList)` is `false`

The `Vector` class contains a useful `copyInto` method with the
signature

```
void copyInto(Object [] copyArray);
```

its functionality is similar to that for `toArray` described in Chapter 5 for
`Collection`. However, there is one subtle but important difference between these: If the array parameter does not contain enough components
to store every element of the vector, `toArray` allocates new storage for an
array whose size is large enough to accommodate all of these elements.
When `copyInto` is used in this situation, however, an `ArrayIndexOutOf-`
`BoundsException` will be thrown.

For example, suppose `vect1 = [2,3,7,8,2,8]`, and the `Integer-`
valued array `copyArr` is declared by

```
Integer [] copyArr = new Integer(vect1.size());
```

then the result of executing

```
vect1.copyInto(copyArr);
```

is described in Figure 6.2.

We now present three instance methods of `Vector` that are designed to
improve the efficiency of processing when vectors are involved. The first of
these is `ensureCapacity`, with the signature

```
void ensureCapacity(int cap);
```

When applied to a vector, its capacity is extended to a minimum of `cap` elements, provided the current size of the vector is less than `cap`; on the

FIGURE 6.2   copyArr

```
┌─────────┐
│    2    │
├─────────┤
│    3    │
├─────────┤
│    7    │
├─────────┤
│    8    │
├─────────┤
│    2    │
├─────────┤
│    0    │
└─────────┘
```

other hand, if the current size of the vector is greater than `cap`, no operation is performed. As an example, suppose we have

```
Vector vect2 = new Vector(2,3);
```

As a result, the initial capacity of `vect2` is 2, and its capacity increment is 3. When a third value is inserted into `vect2`, its capacity jumps to 5. If we then invoke

```
vect2.ensureCapacity(7);
```

the capacity of `vect2` is automatically raised to 8 because of the value of the capacity increment; this guarantees (at least) a capacity of 7.

What if no capacity increment is supplied? That is, suppose (for example) we have

```
Vector vect3 = new Vector(2);
```

Here, `vect3` is constructed with an initial capacity of 2, and no specified capacity increment. Suppose further processing of `vect3` raises its current capacity to 8 (by doubling twice). If such is the case at the point where

```
vect3.ensureCapacity(9);
```

is processed, the capacity of `vect3` is doubled once again from 8 to 16.

Note that `ensureCapacity` applies only to the capacity of a vector and not to its size or content.

The next method is `setSize`, with the signature

```
void setSize(int objSize);
```

When this is applied, the size of the underlying vector is set to the value of `objSize`. If the current size of the vector is greater than `objSize`, the new version of the vector is "padded" with `null` objects; if the current size is smaller than `objSize`, the vector is truncated.

For example, suppose `vect1` = [2,3,7,8,2,8] as before, with current size and capacity both equal to 6, and we apply

```
vect1.setSize(10);
```

The result is `vect1` = `[2,3,7,8,2,8,null,null,null,null]`. The respective size and capacity of the resulting `vect1` is `10` and `12`.

On the other hand, suppose we had applied

```
vect1.setSize(4);
```

The result is `vect1` = `[2,3,7,8]`, with respective values of size and capacity given by `4` and `6`.

It might happen that using `ensureCapacity` provides too much storage, particularly if the doubling process is used when no capacity increment is specified, or when little of the additional storage is used when a capacity increment is supplied. For example, suppose we declare `vect3` as before, with an initial capacity of `2` and with no specified capacity increment. Suppose also that subsequent processing of `vect3` uses no more than nine of the components. Because the doubling process produces a capacity of `16` when the ninth element is added, seven extra components of `vect3` will never be involved in any computation. To respond to this and similar situations, `Vector` supports an instance method called `trimToSize`, with the signature

```
void trimToSize();
```

When applied to any vector, this reduces its current capacity to its current size. In the case of `vect3`,

```
vect3.trimToSize();
```

will reduce the capacity of `vect3` from `16` to `9`.

Finally, `Vector` supports the construction of an `Enumeration` object called `elements()`, with the signature

```
Enumeration elements();
```

Its functionality is similar to its counterpart for the `Hashtable` legacy class described in Section 4.7. That is, `elements()` is an `Enumeration` object that enumerates all of the objects currently stored in the underlying vector. For example, if `vect1` = `[2,3,7,8,2,8]`, then the code sequence

```
for(Enumeration e = vect1.elements(); e.hasMoreElements(); )
  System.out.print(e.nextElement() + "   ");
System.out.println();
```

outputs

```
2   3   7   8   2   8
```

The `Enumeration` method `vect1.elements()` places the elements of `vect1` in an `Enumeration` object parametrized by `e`. Then `e.hasMoreElements()` and `e.nextElement()` are used to control the traversal of these elements in an orderly fashion, yielding the output as described. This sequence works equally well for any legacy class of `java.util`.

6.3 **An Application of the** vector **Class**

We wish to solve the following problem:

Given any finite sequence of integers and any selected positive integer (called the modulus), classify the remainders of the values of the sequence when divided by the chosen modulus.

For example, suppose we select 7 as the modulus and input the sequence

```
343
119
43
12
601
120
1134
215
```

Our algorithm classifies the values of the sequence as follows:

```
Component 0 has entries [343, 119, 1134]
Component 1 has entries [43, 120]
Component 2 is empty
Component 3 is empty
Component 4 is empty
Component 5 has entries [12, 215]
Component 6 has entries [601]
```

Our algorithm assumes a value of 7 for the modulus and prompts the user for the length of the input sequence of nonnegative integer values. The user responds with a value for the length and is then prompted for the actual values of the sequence. We declare 7 Integer-valued vectors vect0, vect1, vect2, vect3, vect4, vect5, vect6 to contain the members of the input sequence. The classification that applies is that each value of the input sequence is stored in exactly one of these vectors. Because there is no way of determining in advance the number of sequence members sharing the same remainder when divided by the modulus, Integer-valued vectors represent very efficient structures to contain these values.

The formal program for solving this problem appears in Example 6.1.

EXAMPLE 6.1

```
// Sample program of solution of problem classifying positive integers
// modulo 7 for interactive nonnegative integer input.
```

```
public static void main(String [] args) throws IOException
{
 BufferedReader intIS = new BufferedReader(
                            new InputStreamReader(System.in));
 // Prompt user for the number of values to be processed:
 System.out.println("Please input the number of nonnegative
     integers");
 System.out.println("you wish to classify:");
 int numberOfIntegers;
 numberOfIntegers = Integer.parseInt(intIS.readLine());

 // Value for the modulus
 int modulus = 7;

 // Construct 7 Vector-valued arrays:
 Vector vect0 = new Vector();
 Vector vect1 = new Vector();
 Vector vect2 = new Vector();
 Vector vect3 = new Vector();
 Vector vect4 = new Vector();
 Vector vect5 = new Vector();
 Vector vect6 = new Vector();

 // Declare integer variable to hold input:
 int integerInput;

 // Input and classify:
 System.out.println("Please input " + numberOfIntegers);
 System.out.println("nonnegative integers:");

 for(int index = 0; index < numberOfIntegers; ++index)
 {
  integerInput = Integer.parseInt(intIS.readLine());
  int result = integerInput%modulus;
  Integer value = new Integer(integerInput);
  if(result == 0) vect0.add(value);
  else if(result == 1) vect1.add(value);
  else if(result == 2) vect2.add(value);
  else if(result == 3) vect3.add(value);
  else if(result == 4) vect4.add(value);
  else if(result == 5) vect5.add(value);
  else vect6.add(value);
 }
```

```
// Output the final form of the components of vect0, . . . , vect6
if(vect0.isEmpty()) System.out.println("Component 0 is empty");
else if(!vect0.isEmpty())
   System.out.println("Component 0 has entries " + vect0);
if(vect1.isEmpty()) System.out.println("Component 1 is empty");
else if(!vect1.isEmpty())
   System.out.println("Component 1 has entries " + vect1);
if(vect2.isEmpty()) System.out.println("Component 2 is empty");
else if(!vect2.isEmpty())
   System.out.println("Component 2 has entries " + vect2);
if(vect3.isEmpty()) System.out.println("Component 3 is empty");
else if(!vect3.isEmpty())
   System.out.println("Component 3 has entries " + vect3);
if(vect4.isEmpty()) System.out.println("Component 4 is empty");
else if(!vect4.isEmpty())
   System.out.println("Component 4 has entries " + vect4);
if(vect5.isEmpty()) System.out.println("Component 5 is empty");
else if(!vect5.isEmpty())
```

FIGURE 6.3

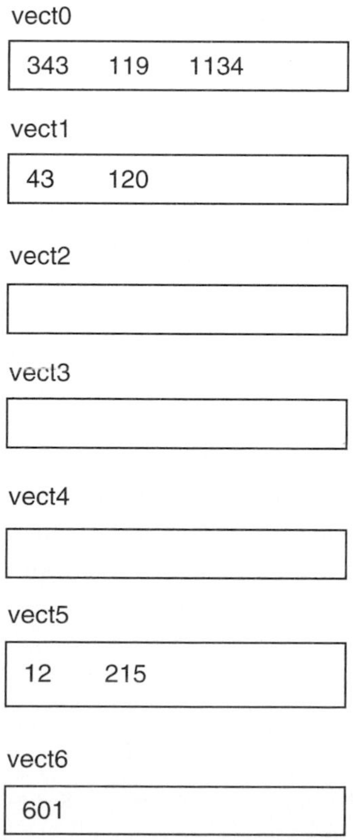

vect0

| 343 | 119 | 1134 |

vect1

| 43 | 120 |

vect2

| |

vect3

| |

vect4

| |

vect5

| 12 | 215 |

vect6

| 601 |

```
    System.out.println("Component 5 has entries " + vect5);
 if(vect6.isEmpty()) System.out.println("Component 6 is empty");
 else if(!vect6.isEmpty())
    System.out.println("Component 6 has entries " + vect6);


} // terminates text of main method
```

Figure 6.3 illustrates the state of each of vect0, vect1, vect2, vect3, vect4, vect5, vect6 after processing the eight input values.

6.4 An Introduction to the `List` ADT and Its Implementations in `java.util`

We begin by describing the concept of *linked storage* and how it differs from storage maintained in an array. When declaring an array, the programmer must specify its size and the type of data to be stored in its components.[2] When defining a vector, an initial size and capacity is assigned, either explicitly or by default, depending on the form of the constructor. In the conventional case, the original size allotted to the array is fixed, and the only way to change it is left to the programmer. He or she must define a new array of a different size and then copy the contents of the original into the new array. In using vectors, the new allocation is automatic and applied as needed, as already described.

For the moment, we will be content with enumerating key distinctions between ordinary arrays and linked storage. In an array, any component is accessed using an *index* or *subscript*. This provides *random access* in the sense that passage from any component to another is accomplished in constant time, simply by jumping to the desired component from the current component. That is to say, access to any array component is an O(1) operation. In linked storage, no such indexing is available: The array (or vector) is replaced by a different data structure in which each component stores the location of the next value along with the current value. Access to any value follows a one-directional linear path, visiting every component in the path, from the current component to the desired component. This combination of a value stored with a reference to the location of the next value (if it exists) is called a *node*. A typical node has the structure of Figure 6.4 and can be formally defined (in the generic case) by

```
class Node
{
  // Constructor.  Copies the info component and the link
```

---

[2]Arrays can be defined as *conformant arrays* whose size is specified by the number of initial values.

FIGURE 6.4

info   next

```
// to the next node.
Node(Object d, Node n)
{
 info = d;
 next - n;
}
Object info;
Node next;
} // Terminates text of Node class.
```

As an example, the sequence of integers 3, -1, 6, 8 can then be represented as shown in Figure 6.5.

FIGURE 6.5

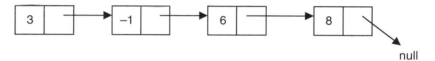

null

Here, any reference to a node can move forward, one node at a time, until it reaches the end of the list. A structure with nodes constructed in this way is called a (one-directional) *linked list*. For convenience, we will adopt the less formal alternative description pictured in Figure 6.6.

FIGURE 6.6

EXAMPLE 6.2   The following code sequence can be used to construct the list of `Integer` values described in Figures 6.5 and 6.6:

```
Integer intVal = new Integer(3);
Node list = new Node(intVal,null);
Node ptr = null;
intVal = new Integer(-1);
ptr = new Node(intVal,null);
list.next = ptr;
Node ptr1 = ptr;
intVal = new Integer(6);
```

```
ptr = new Node(intVal,null);
ptr1.next = ptr;
ptr1 = ptr;
intVal = new Integer(8);
ptr = new Node(intVal,null);
ptr1.next = ptr;
```

We can use the next code sequence to output the info components of any nonempty list:

```
ptr = list;
while(ptr != null)
{
 System.out.print(ptr.info + "  ");
 ptr = ptr.next;
}
System.out.println();
```

Suppose we wish to delete the first node of the current list with an info component of 6, if such a node exists. We can use the code sequence

```
ptr = list;
ptr1 = null;

while(!(ptr.info.equals(new Integer(6))))
{
 ptr1 = ptr;
 ptr = ptr.next;
} // ends while-loop
// This last while-loop finds node with an info component of 6,
// (if it exists), and ptr refers to that node. Also, ptr1
// refers to its immediate predecessor.
// Now remove node from list by executing next instruction:
ptr1.next = ptr.next;
```

What characterizes a List abstract data type (ADT)? That is, what admissible operations should be present as basic operations on lists? Our intuitive view of a list is that of an *ordered finite collection* of objects, if not empty. Any list is an example of a fundamental container for a finite collection of elements. In addition, we can define the following collection of admissible operations definable on any list:

- add a new element to an existing list
- retrieve an element from an existing list
- remove an element from an existing list
- test whether the current list is empty

Besides these, we wish to have some way of traversing the values of any given list, in some specified order.

We have the option of coding these admissible operations by hand. In fact, we can consider designing a generic class for constructing and manipulating lists based on these admissible operations, where these operations appear as instance methods of the underlying class. In fact, our earlier discussions in this section, including Example 6.2, provide enough details as to the design of such a class. Instead, however, we choose to describe the facilities that are predefined in `java.util` with the added assurance of efficiency of design and execution.

As we observed in Section 5.4, the `List` interface extends `Collection` to enable the construction of collections whose elements appear in a specific order. That is, each element of a list exists in a specific position in the list, indexed from 0 to `list.size()` - 1. Because `List` extends `Collection` (see Figure 5.2 and Figure 6.1), `List` inherits all of the methods defined in `Collection`. In particular, `List` inherits the `add` method that, in the presence of ordered collections, places the new element at the end of the current list. We describe this for `Integer`-valued lists in Figure 6.7.

FIGURE 6.7   intList

(before applying intList.add(new Integer(12))**)**

intList

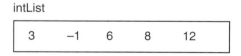

(after applying intList.add(new Integer(12))**)**

When the nth element is removed from a list, where n lies within the range of subscripts of the list, each of the elements of the list from the n + 1th position to the end are shifted over one position to avoid gaps.

The `List` interface can be described by

```
public interface List
{
 // Retrieves the value appearing in the position given by
 // the value of the parameter.
 Object get(int index);
```

```
// Sets the element of the current list in the position given by
// value of the first parameter to the value of the second
// parameter, replacing the current element by this value.
Object set(int index,Object obj);

// Adds the entry given by the value of the second parameter
// to the current list in the position given by the value of
// the first parameter, shifting every element in the current list
// from index down one position.
void add(int index,Object obj);

// Removes the element in the current list in the position given by
// the value of the parameter, shifting all elements in the list past
// the current value of the parameter one position to avoid gaps.
Object remove(int index);

// Returns the index of the first element in the current list
// that is equal to the value of the parameter, or null if that
// parameter is null.  Returns -1 if no match is found.
int indexOf(Object obj);

// Returns the index of the last element in the current list
// that is equal to the value of the parameter, or null if that
// parameter is null.  Returns -1 if no match is found.
int lastIndexOf(Object obj);

// Returns the list that is a view of the current list over the
// range from the value of the first parameter to one less than
// the value of the second parameter.
List subList(int first,int last);

}
```

Each of the methods get, set, add, and remove takes an int-valued parameter index. If the value of index is either less than zero or greater than or equal to the size of the current list, an ArrayIndexOutOfBounds- Exception is thrown.

As already indicated in Section 5.4, the ListIterator interface extends the Iterator interface, allowing for each of the methods hasNext(), next(), and remove() to be applied to any list. As a matter of fact, besides iterating forward through the elements of a list, ListIterator also supports iteration backwards through any list, using methods hasPrevious() (in place of hasNext()) and previous() (in place of next()). The following code segment outputs `intList` as described in the "before" picture of Figure 6.7 in backwards order:

```
for(ListIterator backIter = intList.listIterator(intList.size());
        backIter.hasPrevious(); )
    System.out.print(backIter.previous() + " ");
System.out.println();
```

`listIterator(intList.size())` is a `ListIterator` method returning a `ListIterator` object that has the functionality of traversing all of the values of the current list. This `ListIterator` object is initially positioned one location beyond the end of the current list. This iterator then backs up through the elements of the list, one at a time, outputting each value horizontally followed by a single blank space. Because `List` objects are indexed by position from 0 through `list.size()` - 1, we can apply `nextIndex()` or `previousIndex()` to obtain the index of the element of the list when `next()` or `previous()` is invoked. In the case of a forward traversal through the values of the current list, the final value of the list index will be `list.size()`; in the case of a backwards traversal, the final value of the iterator is -1.

`java.util` supports two implementations of the `List` interface: `ArrayList` and `LinkedList`. In Section 5.4, we investigated `List` and `LinkedList` as they apply to a number of situations, with the assurance that their functionality would be explained in this chapter. With this in mind, we can observe that any `LinkedList` object assumes the form of a *doubly linked list*. Thus, each node of such a list is designed with `previous`, `info`, and `next` components, where `previous` and `next` hold references to other similar nodes, or are `null`, and where `info` is the component holding the data. The structure of any such node is described as in Figure 6.8:

FIGURE 6.8

previous   info   next

The formal definition of such nodes can be defined by the class `doubleNode`, defined for the generic case by

```
class doubleNode
{
    // Constructor.  Copies the info component and links.
    public doubleNode(Node prev, Object d, Node nxt)
    {
```

```
    info = d;
    previous = prev;
    next = nxt;
  } // terminates text of constructor
  Object info;
  doubleNode previous, next;
} // terminates text of doubleNode
```

The sequence of integers 3,-1,6,8 can be represented as a `LinkedList` object, as in Figure 6.9.

FIGURE 6.9

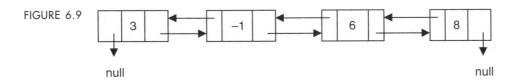

null   null

For convenience, we will once again adopt the less formal alternative description for doubly linked lists as pictured in Figure 6.6, where the context will determine whether that representation is for a `LinkedList` object or otherwise.

What advantages exist in performance based on implementing `List` as `LinkedList`? Adding an element at the end of a `LinkedList` object (using `add`) is an $O(1)$ operation. However, if we wish to either add or remove an element currently appearing in the list at some position other than at the end, a swap is executed to put that element at the end, and then the appropriate operation is applied to that element. This is followed by a reverse swap to maintain the current list. In summary, adding or removing an element of a `LinkedList` object is $O(1)$. On the other hand, retrieving an element from the list requires traversing the list from one end and moving through the list until arriving at the desired position.

The `LinkedList` interface implements all of the methods in `List`, along with two constructors, and methods that enhance the efficiency of implementation for doubly linked lists.

The first constructor has the signature

```
public LinkedList();
```

This constructs an initially empty `LinkedList` object.

The second constructor is a form of a copy constructor

```
public LinkedList(Collection collObject);
```

This version constructs a new `LinkedList` object whose initial contents are those of `collObject`, with a predefined order given by the actual specification of `Collection` (whether the `Collection` is a `List`, `Vector`, or `Set`).

The following sequence represents methods that are useful and efficient when applied to `LinkedList` objects, and they appear as instance methods in the `LinkedList` class.

```
// Returns the first element in a LinkedList
public Object getFirst();


// Returns the last element in a LinkedList
public Object getLast();


// Removes the first element in a LinkedList
public Object removeFirst();


// Removes the last element in a LinkedList
public Object removeLast();


// Adds obj to the current LinkedList as its new first element
public Object addFirst(Object obj);


// Adds obj to the current LinkedList as its new last element
public Object addLast(Object obj);
```

In direct contrast, the `ArrayList` implementation uses a one-dimensional array as its basic container. Unlike an ordinary array, however, and similar to a vector, an `ArrayList` object can grow and shrink. In fact, although both `ArrayList` objects and vectors have similar behaviors, vectors support concurrent programming while `ArrayList` objects do not. This distinction is a key reason why we suggested earlier that programs using vectors should be used only sparingly, because there is a considerable overhead in supporting concurrency. That is, when a design decision requires choosing between vectors and `ArrayList` objects, and it does not involve any use of concurrent processing, the decision should be to use `ArrayList` objects.

For `ArrayList`, adding and removing elements at either end is $O(1)$; also retrieving a value anywhere in an `ArrayList` object is $O(1)$, because the reference to the element is through the underlying array subscript. This provides random access to any member of the `ArrayList` object, making the retrieval operation $O(1)$. The only drawback to using `ArrayList` objects is when a substantial number of additions and deletions of elements in the middle is anticipated. Such operations are essentially of order $O(n)$, where n is the number of elements currently stored in the container, because $n - i$ elements have to be moved down one position, where $0 < i < n$. Because $n - i$ elements of the list have to be shifted after the current element at position i to close up the resulting list, removals near the center of the list are not very efficient.

An `ArrayList` object has a *capacity*, with a default value of 10. The programmer has the option of overriding this default capacity using an appropriate form of a constructor, and with other methods available for managing capacity. As elements are added to the list, they are actually stored in the underlying array. As was the case with vectors, when the number of elements exceeds the current capacity, a new replacement array is allotted to accommodate the increasing size of the list.

`ArrayList` has three constructors. The first of these is the default constructor, with the signature

```
public ArrayList();
```

This constructs an `ArrayList` object with a default capacity of 10. The second has the signature

```
public ArrayList(int initialCapacity);
```

This constructs an `ArrayList` object whose initial capacity is the value of the parameter. The third constructor is a copy constructor, whose signature is

```
public ArrayList(Collection collObject);
```

When invoked, this form constructs an `ArrayList` object whose contents, in some order, are those of `collObject`. The capacity of the constructed `ArrayList` object is 110 percent of the current capacity of `collObject`, to allow for some growth of the newly constructed `ArrayList` object before it has to resize.

`ArrayList` also includes two methods to manage the capacity of its objects:

```
public void trimToSize();
```

and

```
public void ensureCapacity(int cap);
```

The functionality of each of these is similar to their `Vector` counterpart; consequently, we omit any further discussion of these methods here.

What should guide the programmer in deciding whether to implement `List` using either `LinkedList` or `ArrayList`? If the programmer needs the functionality of a linked list whose processing activity is not necessarily confined to a single end, the recommendation is to implement the list using `LinkedList`. This is particularly true in implementing the queue ADT or the deque ADT, where the bulk of processing is concentrated at both ends of the sequence.[3] On the other hand, if we anticipate an implemen-

---

[3] We will introduce the deque ADT later in this chapter in Sections 6.5 and 6.6; the queue ADT in Chapter 7.

tation of a data structure where processing is concentrated at a single end, such as for stacks, and we wish to use the List interface, the more sensible and efficient choice would be to use ArrayList. This is due primarily to the observations that processing objects require considerable more processing overhead and that LinkedList implementations treat each node of the list as an object, whereas the array is viewed as a single object. Thus, fewer objects are required using ArrayList instead of LinkedList.

In Chapter 7, we will observe that java.util supports a predefined implementation of the stack ADT called Stack, which is a subclass of Vector.

We close this section with Example 6.3. The main method described performs the same operations as those of Example 6.2 but now applies the ArrayList implementation.

EXAMPLE 6.3   The following method constructs the same list as that described in Example 6.2, and then outputs the result. Following this, the program removes the first node with an info component of 6, and then outputs the revised list.

```java
public static void main(String [] args)
 {
  // Construct an initially empty ArrayList object.
  List list = new ArrayList();
  // Add the sequence 3,-1,6,8 to list:
  list.add(new Integer(3));
  list.add(new Integer(-1));
  list.add(new Integer(6));
  list.add(new Integer(8));
  // Now output current list:
  System.out.println("Current list is now = ");
  for(ListIterator iter = list.listIterator();iter.hasNext();)
   System.out.print(iter.next() + "  ");
  System.out.println();
  // Now remove the first node in the list holding a 6
  // and then output the contents of the revised list.
  //int value = list.indexOf(new Integer(6));
  list.remove(list.indexOf(new Integer(6)));
  System.out.println("Revised list is = ");
  for(ListIterator iter = list.listIterator();iter.hasNext();)
     System.out.print(iter.next() + "  ");
  System.out.println();
 }
```

The output is

```
Current list is now =
3  -1  6  8
Revised list =
 -1  8
```

6.5 An Application of Lists: The deque ADT

We can define a *deque* as a sequence that is either empty or supports efficient insertions and removals of elements from both ends. In essence, deques possess a functionality similar to that of vectors. The essential difference is that deques allow for constant-time insertions and removals from *either end* of the sequence. Unlike vectors, deques are not predefined in java.util as part of the Collection hierarchy.

As an ADT, deque should contain the following methods:

- addFirst, used to insert an element at the front of the current deque as its new first element
- addLast, used to insert an element at the rear of the current deque as its new last element
- removeFirst, used (whenever possible) to remove an element at the front of the current deque
- removeLast, used (whenever possible) to remove an element at the rear of the current deque
- getFirst, used (whenever possible) to retrieve the element at the front of the current deque
- getLast, used (whenever possible) to retrieve the element at the rear of the current deque
- isEmpty, which tests whether the current deque is empty

We choose to implement deque as ArrayList, because ArrayList objects have exactly the functionality described for deque objects. In fact, there is no need to define a separate deque class as a subclass of ArrayList because, as we have already observed, the entire functionality for any deque is contained within the scope of the instance methods for ArrayList.

6.6 An Application of Deques: Sifting Random Numbers

We consider a simply stated problem whose solution varies in complexity with the choice of the container used to store the data. Its statement is

Given any finite sequence of positive integers, we wish to "sift" its members so that the even members precede the odd members.

We will solve this problem for randomly generated integers between 1 and 30,000, inclusive. It is not necessary that the sequence is sorted. For example, if our sequence is

24444   20691   28507   15708   3506   19535

then the result of sifting these values is

3506   15708   24444   20691   28507   19535

The algorithm for solving this problem is quite straightforward:

Input the size of the random sequence of integers to be generated,
Construct the container to be used for the sifting process;
Generate the random sequence:
 for *each sequence member:*
  if *(member is even) insert it at the front of the container;*
 else *insert it at the rear of the container;*

How do we generate the random sequence? We cannot use any algorithm for this purpose because an algorithm is *deterministic* by its very definition. That is, each step of an algorithm determines exactly one successor. Thus, in generating any finite sequence of random numbers, the next random number cannot depend in any combinatorial way on the values of any of its predecessors. Conceding this, we can accomplish the next best thing: Generate a *pseudorandom* sequence of integers, applying functions whose output gives the appearance of random sequences. A thorough and comprehensive discussion of generating pseudorandom sequences is found in Knuth (1981) in the References section at the end of this chapter.

The Math class contains a method called random(). The value returned is a pseudorandom number of type double with a plus sign, greater than or equal to 0.0 but less than 1.0. To obtain a number in a different range we can perform arithmetic operations to convert it to this range and use an appropriate cast if necessary. For example, if we wish to generate a single random number between 1 and 100, we can use

```
int intValue = (int)(Math.random() * 100 + 1);
```

If it is necessary to generate a *sequence* of random numbers, java.util defines a Random class for that purpose. For example, if we need to generate a sequence of ten random integers with values between 1 and 100, inclusive, we can execute the code sequence

```
// Construct Random object RandObj
Random RandObj = new Random();
int value;
for(int index = 0; index < 10; ++index)
{
 value = Math.abs(RandObj.nextInt()) % 100 + 1;
```

```
  System.out.println();
}
```

The object `RandObj` constructed in the `Random` class is a random number generator. The initial value generated from this object (called the *seed*) is provided by using an *internal clock* present in any computer system. The application of the instance method `nextInt()` present in `Random` produces a pseudorandom number lying between the smallest negative `int` value `Integer.MIN_VALUE` and the largest positive `int` value `Integer.MAX_VALUE`, inclusive, supported by Java. The `Math.abs` function described in the earlier code sequence converts any negative number to its positive counterpart using the absolute value. The expression

```
Math.abs(RandObj.nextInt()) % 100 + 1;
```

generates an `int` value between 1 and 100, inclusive. (See Arnold, Gosling, and Holmes [2000] in the References section, especially pages 470–71, for a detailed treatment of the `Random` class.)

Implementing the Sifting Algorithm

We seek an efficient solution of the sifting problem that is independent of the size of the sequence. This necessarily rules out the choice of an ordinary one-dimensional array as a candidate for the container used to store the sifted randomly generated integers, because the size of the array would have to conform to the size of the input sequence. As a matter of fact, even if we were to agree to a maximum possible size for the random sequence, and then "overdimension" the array to this maximum size, the resulting situation would involve an array that, in most situations, contains needless extra components. This results in a proposed solution that is space inefficient. Even if we were to concede this factor of space inefficiency, shifting down the array subscripts one additional position to make room at one end for the next value to be placed properly involves this shifting operation, which is `O(n)` where n is the size of the sequence. For these reasons, as well as others, we conclude that ordinary arrays are not the best choice for the underlying container.

What about vectors? They are a better choice than arrays, because vectors have a size and capacity whose values can change during the course of execution. However, vectors are not the best possible choice because vectors support concurrency, slowing down the speed of computation. Besides this, insertions performed at the front of the vector turn out to be `O(n)` operations.

A deque, implemented as an `ArrayList` object, is the best possible choice because it permits equally efficient insertions at both front and rear. This is exactly what we require to implement the solution of the sifting problem.

EXAMPLE 6.4   The final coding of this solution is given by

```java
public static void main(String [] args) throws IOException
{
 List sifter = new ArrayList();
 BufferedReader intIS = new BufferedReader(
                        new InputStreamReader(System.in));
 // Prompt user for the number of random integers to sift:
 System.out.println("Input the number of integers to sift:");
 int number;
 number = Integer.parseInt(intIS.readLine());
 System.out.print("Generate " + number + " random integers with ");
 System.out.println("values");
 System.out.println("between 1 and 30,000, inclusive:");
 Integer IntArr[] = new Integer[number];

 // Construct Random object RandObj
 Random RandObj = new Random();
 int value;
 for(int index = 0; index < number; ++index)
 {
  value = Math.abs(RandObj.nextInt())%30000 + 1;
  IntArr[index] = new Integer(value);
 }

 // Display contents of IntArr before the sifting process:
 System.out.println("Before the sifting, the contents of IntArr are:");
 for(int index = 0; index < number; ++index)
  System.out.print(IntArr[index] + "  ");
 System.out.println();

 // Begin the sifting:
 System.out.println("Begin the sifting:");
 for(int index = 0; index < IntArr.length; ++index)
  if(IntArr[index].intValue() % 2 == 0) sifter.add(0,IntArr[index]);
  else sifter.add(sifter.size(),IntArr[index]);
 // terminates for-loop.

 // Display sifted values
 System.out.println("The sifted values are:");
 for(ListIterator iter = sifter.listIterator();iter.hasNext();)
  System.out.print(iter.next() + "  ");
 System.out.println();
} // terminates text of main method
```

Suppose `IntArr` is illustrated as in Figure 6.10.

FIGURE 6.10 IntArr

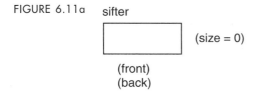

24444	20691	28507	15708	3506	19535
[0]	[1]	[2]	[3]	[4]	[5]

If we were to trace the execution of

```
for(int index = 0; index < IntArr.length; ++index)
 if(IntArr[index].intValue() % 2 == 0) sifter.add(0,IntArr[index]);
 else sifter.add(sifter.size(),IntArr[index]);
```

we observe that `sifter` is initially empty, as shown in Figure 6.11a.

FIGURE 6.11a sifter

	(size = 0)
(front) (back)	

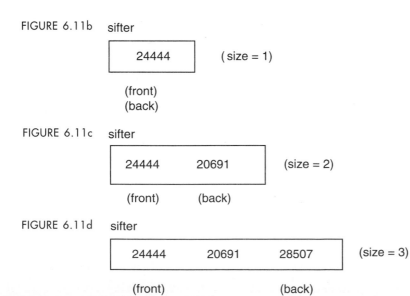

The next sequence of figures—Figures 6.11b through 6.11g—traces the progress of the sifting process as it applies to the values in `IntArr`, scanned rightward from `IntArr[0]`:

FIGURE 6.11b sifter

24444	(size = 1)
(front) (back)	

FIGURE 6.11c sifter

24444	20691	(size = 2)
(front)	(back)	

FIGURE 6.11d sifter

24444	20691	28507	(size = 3)
(front)		(back)	

FIGURE 6.11e sifter

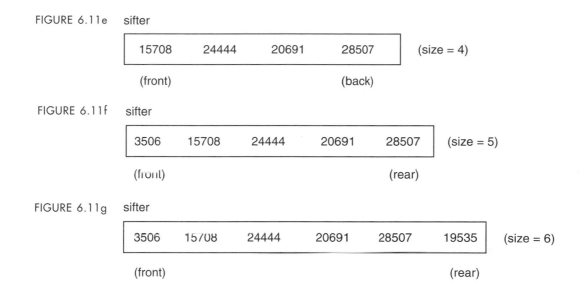

FIGURE 6.11f sifter

FIGURE 6.11g sifter

We can display this trace by inserting an additional statement in the for-loop:

```
for(int index = 0; index < IntArr.length; ++index)
{
 if(IntArr[index].intValue() % 2 == 0) sifter.add(0,IntArr[index]);
 else sifter.add(sifter.size(),IntArr[index]);
 for(ListIterator iter = sifter.listIterator(); iter.hasNext(); )
  System.out.print(iter.next() + "   ");
 System.out.println();
}
```

6.7 **Sorting Randomly Generated Odd and Even Positive Integers**

This section describes a problem whose solution illustrates the interaction of lists illustrated by `ArrayList` objects and `TreeSet` objects used for sorting. The problem to be solved can be stated as follows:

*Given any finite sequence of positive integers, we wish to convert it into
a sequence beginning with the odd integers in the sequence, sorted in order
of increasing size, and ending with the even numbers in the sequence, also
sorted in order of increasing size.*

To illustrate this, suppose we generate the following random sequence:

1952   17453   23065   23858   16091   16105   16991

Our solution would then involve rearranging the sequence as

16091   16105   16991   17453   23065   1952   23858

How do we design an algorithm for solving this? The algorithm would begin by storing the integers in some integer-valued array `IntArray` and then constructing two initially empty `TreeSet` objects `oddIntegers` and `evenIntegers`. `oddIntegers` and `evenIntegers` are constructed as `TreeSet` objects, exploiting their sorting functionality. As each random integer is scanned in `IntArr`, it is tested as to whether it is odd or even and then inserted in either `oddIntegers` or `evenIntegers`, whichever is appropriate. When this completes, we construct the corresponding `ArrayList` objects `oddList` and `evenList`. Then we insert the values, one at a time, from the front of `evenList` to the rear of `oddList`. The resulting `oddList` contains the sequence solving the original problem.

A preliminary version of the formal algorithm to solve the problem can then be given as

Begin by determining the number of random integers to generate;
Construct an `Integer`*-valued array* `IntArr` *whose components hold*
 the sequence of random integers generated;
Construct two initially empty collections of `Integer` *values: one for storing*
 the odd integers generated, and the other for storing the even numbers generated;
Generate the values of the random sequence;
`for` *(each sequence member generated)*
 Decide whether that number is even or odd;
 `if` *(number is odd) insert that number in* `oddIntegers`*;*
 `else` *insert that number in* `evenIntegers`*;*
// this completes execution of the `for`*-loop.*
Sort each of `oddIntegers` *and* `evenIntegers` *in order of increasing size;*
Adjoin the list of even integers, one member at a time, at the rear of the list of
 odd integers;
// The result of this adjoining operation produces the list of odd integers as the list
// of the sorted odd integers, followed by the sorted even integers.
Display the contents of the list of odd integers;

EXAMPLE 6.5   We generate a sequence of random integers between 1 and 30,000, inclusive. The programmed solution of the problem can then be given by

```
public static void main(String [] args) throws IOException
{
 BufferedReader intIS = new BufferedReader(
                    new InputStreamReader(System.in));
 // Prompt user for number of random integers to generate.
 System.out.println("How many random integers do you wish to
     generate?");
```

```
int numberOfIntegers;
numberOfIntegers = Integer.parseInt(intIS.readLine());
System.out.println("Generate " + numberOfIntegers + " random
     integers");
System.out.println("with values between 1 and 30,000, inclusive:");
Integer IntArr[] = new Integer[numberOfIntegers];
int value;

// Construct Random object RandObj:
Random RandObj = new Random();
for(int index = 0; index < numberOfIntegers; ++index)
{
 value = Math.abs(RandObj.nextInt()) % 30000 + 1;
 IntArr[index] = new Integer(value);
}

// Display contents of IntArr before the sorting.
System.out.println("Before the sorting, the contents of IntArr are:");
for(int index = 0; index < numberOfIntegers; ++index)
  System.out.print(IntArr[index] + "  ");
System.out.println();

// Construct two initially empty TreeSet objects.  One to store the
// sorted even members of the sequence, and the other to store the
// sorted odd members of the sequence.
Set oddIntegers = new TreeSet();
Set evenIntegers = new TreeSet();

// Now place each value of IntArr in its appropriate TreeSet object:
for(int index = 0; index < IntArr.length; ++index)
  if(IntArr[index].intValue() % 2 == 0)
    evenIntegers.add(IntArr[index]);
  else oddIntegers.add(IntArr[index]);

// Display current contents of evenIntegers and oddIntegers:
System.out.println("The current contents of evenIntegers are:");
System.out.println(evenIntegers);
System.out.println("The current contents of oddIntegers are:");
System.out.println(oddIntegers);

// Now we wish to form a single list with the sorted odd integers
// preceding the sorted even integers.
```

```
// First create oddList as an ArrayList object, using the
// copy constructor.
ArrayList oddList = new ArrayList(oddIntegers);

// Then create evenList as an ArrayList object, using the
// copy constructor.
ArrayList evenList = new ArrayList(evenIntegers);

// Now add each member of evenList, one at a time, to the back
// of oddList:
for(ListIterator iter = evenList.listIterator(); iter.hasNext(); )
 oddList.add(iter.next());

// Now display the contents of the final list:
System.out.println("The final sorted list is:");
System.out.println(oddList);

} // terminates text of main method
```

Why did we choose to construct `oddList` and `evenList`? Why didn't we adjoin the values, one at a time, of the `TreeSet` object `evenIntegers` to the rear of `oddIntegers`? The answer lies in the observation that, in the latter case, the resulting `TreeSet` object `oddIntegers` would sort the *entire collection*—the odd integer values of `oddIntegers` would be sorted among the even values of `evenIntegers`, resulting in a single sorted sequence of integers. Thus, for example, for the random sequence

| 1952 | 17453 | 23065 | 23858 | 16091 | 16105 | 16991 |

the resulting `oddIntegers` `treeSet` object would output its elements as

| 1952 | 16091 | 16105 | 16991 | 17453 | 23065 | 23858 |

which is not what we want.

6.8 **Some Important Predefined `List` Methods**

The basic `List` access methods `get`, `set`, `add`, and `remove` have a functionality that is similar to their respective counterparts `elementAt`, `setElementAt`, `insertElementAt`, and `removeElementAt` found in `Vector`. However, there are subtle differences between the two: the `List` methods `set` and `remove` return the old value being overwritten or removed, while the corresponding `Vector` methods `setElementAt` and `removeElementAt` are `void` and hence have no return value. On the other hand, the search methods `indexOf` and `lastIndexOf` of `List` have exactly the same behavior, as well as name, as those of `Vector`.

The predefined `get` and `set` methods of `List` permit the definition of a `static` `swapList` method, that we can code in generic form as

```
public static void swapList(List listValue, int i, int j)
{
 Postcondition: the elements in the list named by listValue
 at position i and j are interchanged.
 Object tempHolder = listValue.get(i);
 listValue.set(i,listValue.get(j));
 listValue.set(j,tempHolder);
}
```

This method swaps values in any `List` object, whether that object is implemented as a `LinkedList` or an `ArrayList`. As an example, suppose `intList` is implemented as an `ArrayList` object whose current state is shown in Figure 6.12a.

FIGURE 6.12a   intList

If we then execute `swapList(intList,0,intList.size() - 1)`, the result is shown in Figure 6.12b.

FIGURE 6.12b   intList

This is primarily because, no matter what the implementation of `List`, the members of any `List` object are *indexed*. Thus, Java "knows" what elements lie in positions `i` and `j`. On the other hand, if one or both values of `i` and `j` lie outside the range of subscripts of the `List` object, an `IndexOutOfBoundsException` exception is thrown.

We stated earlier, in Section 5.9, that a number of the algorithms specified in the `Collections` class apply specifically to `List` objects. Although we will provide a detailed study of these algorithms in Chapter 8, we give a brief description of several of these in this section because they apply specifically to `List` objects. These have the following signatures:

- `sort(List listValue)`—This sorts `listValue` in order of increasing size using `mergeSort`, which is a stable sort.
- `reverse(List listValue)`—This reverses the order of appearance of the elements of `listValue`.

- fill(List listValue, Object obj)—This overwrites every element of listValue with obj.
- copy(List destinationList, List sourceList)—This copies sourceList into destinationList.
- binarySearch(List listValue, Object obj)—This searches for obj in the sorted list listValue, using the binary search algorithm.

Each of these methods requires the use of the qualified reference using Collections. Thus, for example, if we wish to sort intList as described in Figure 6.12a, we use

```
Collections.sort(intList);
```

We end this section by noting that we can now consider an important and alternative solution to the problem stated in Section 6.7. This new version does not require the TreeSet objects evenIntegers and oddIntegers. All that needs to be done here is to construct the two initially empty ArrayList objects oddList and evenList and then insert the odd (respectively, even) randomly generated positive integers directly into oddList (respectively, evenList). Although neither of oddList and evenList is sorted at this point, we now apply sort to each of these and then merge the sorted versions of oddList and evenList, as before. Finally, the resulting oddList solves the original problem. Example 6.6 displays the complete coded solution.

EXAMPLE 6.6

```java
public static void main(String [] args) throws IOException
{
 BufferedReader intIS = new BufferedReader(
                          new InputStreamReader(System.in));
 // Prompt user for number of random integers to generate.
 System.out.println("How many random integers do you wish to
                      generate?");
 int numberOfIntegers;
 numberOfIntegers = Integer.parseInt(intIS.readLine());
 System.out.println("Generate " + numberOfIntegers + " random
                      integers");
 System.out.println("with values between 1 and 30,000, inclusive:");
 Integer IntArr[] = new Integer[numberOfIntegers];
 int value;

 // Construct Random object RandObj:
 Random RandObj = new Random();
 for(int index = 0; index < numberOfIntegers; ++index)
```

```
{
 value = Math.abs(RandObj.nextInt()) % 30000 + 1;
 IntArr[index] = new Integer(value);
}

// Display contents of IntArr before the sorting.
System.out.println("Before the sorting, the contents of IntArr are:");
for(int index = 0; index < numberOfIntegers; ++index)
 System.out.print(IntArr[index] + "  ");
System.out.println();

// Construct two initially empty ArrayList objects.  One to store the
// sorted even members of the sequence, and the other to store the
// sorted odd members of the sequence.
List oddList = new ArrayList();
List evenList = new ArrayList();

// Now place each value of IntArr in its appropriate ArrayList object:
for(int index = 0; index < IntArr.length; ++index)
 if(IntArr[index].intValue() % 2 == 0) evenList.add(IntArr[index]);
 else oddList.add(IntArr[index]);

// Display current contents of evenList and oddList:
// They are not sorted.
System.out.println("Before applying Collections.sort to");
System.out.println("each list:");
System.out.println("The current contents of evenList are:");
System.out.println(evenList);
System.out.println("The current contents of oddList are:");
System.out.println(oddList);

// Now sort each list, using the predefined Collections.sort method:
Collections.sort(oddList);
Collections.sort(evenList);

// Display current contents of evenList and oddList:
// They are sorted.
System.out.println("After applying Collections.sort to");
System.out.println("each list:");

System.out.println("The current contents of evenList are:");
System.out.println(evenList);
System.out.println("The current contents of oddList are:");
```

```
System.out.println(oddList);

// Now we wish to form a single list with the sorted odd integers
// preceding the sorted even integers.

// Now add each member of evenList, one at a time, to the back
// of oddList:
for(ListIterator iter = evenList.listIterator(); iter.hasNext(); )
 oddList.add(iter.next());

// Now display the contents of the final list:
System.out.println("The final sorted list is:");
System.out.println(oddList);


} // terminates text of main method
```

Let us trace an execution of this program.

How many random numbers do you wish to generate?
6
Generate 6 random integers
With values between 1 and 30,000, inclusive:
Before the sorting, the contents of IntArr are:
14399 17995 1733 18141   438   25475
Before applying Collections.sort to
each list:
The current contents of evenList are:
[438]
The current contents of oddList are:
[14399, 17995, 1733, 18141, 25475]
After applying Collections.sort to
each list:
The current contents of evenList are:
[438]
The current contents of oddList are:
[1733, 14399, 17995, 18141, 25475]
The final sorted list is:
[1733, 14399, 17995, 18141, 25475, 438]

We should observe that the solution of this problem, given by the method described in Example 6.5, contains a subtle flaw. Although the problem is certainly solved by this method, the remote possibility exists that the sequence of random integers generated may contain *duplicate values*. Because we use TreeSet objects evenIntegers and oddIntegers to produce the sorting of the respective even and odd random integers generated, any duplicate values are removed, as `TreeSet` objects do not include duplicate elements. On the other hand, because no `TreeSet` objects are used in the solution given in Example 6.6, duplicates are counted in the `ArrayList` objects `oddList` and `evenList`. The stable sorting performed by applying `Collections.sort` to each of `oddList` and `evenList` is actually performed on the underlying array—hence, duplicate values are counted.

6.9 **Chapter Summary**

This chapter introduced the `Vector` class from Java's Legacy Collections, as well as the `List` interface and the `LinkedList` and `ArrayList` implementations of `List`. Briefly stated, a vector is an object constructed from the `Vector` class and is capable of storing a finite sequence of elements. The size of the vector is permitted to change while the application program in which it is defined is executing.

Three different constructors are defined for `Vector`. The first is a default constructor, constructing a `Vector` object with an initial size of `0` and an initial capacity of `10`. A second version constructs a vector with an initial size of `0` and an initial capacity specified by the value of the single parameter. The third version is a copy constructor in which the collection specified by the parameter is copied, element by element, into the vector whose initial size and capacity become those of the parameter.

We can think of a vector as a generalization of an ordinary one-dimensional array, except that the array has a fixed size when compiled and cannot vary during the course of execution. In fact, we observed that a number of key processing problems in searching and sorting now either appear as instance methods of `Vector` or exploit the fact that `Vector` is a member of the `Collection` hierarchy, as described in Figure 6.1.

Although the use of vectors is appealing, it is important to observe that their instance methods are *synchronized,* causing the execution of many of these to be inordinately slow if the vector is being processed from a single processing thread. Thus, our design might have to take into account whether processing speed is a major factor. If such is the case, an alternative to vectors should be considered. A popular choice is to use objects constructed from the `List` interface, particularly using the `ArrayList` implementation. The instance methods defined in `List` have essentially the same functionality as the corresponding instance methods defined in `Vector` but without any additional support for synchronized concurrent processing.

The `List` interface has two implementations supported by Java 2: `LinkedList` and `ArrayList`. The `LinkedList` implementation views any object as a doubly linked list, with iterators than can move either forward or backward (bidirectional movement). Thus, each node of such a list is designed with `previous`, `info`, and `next` components, where `previous` and `next` hold references to similar nodes or are `null`, and where `info` is the component holding the data. Adding an element to the end of a `LinkedList` object is an `O(1)` operation. If it is necessary to add or remove an element in the list at some other position, however, more effort is required. In fact, retrieving an element from the list requires a traversal of the list beginning at one end. This is because traversal of a `LinkedList` object is bidirectional (that is, not random access).

In direct contrast, the `ArrayList` implementation views its objects as generalizations of one-dimensional arrays. Like an ordinary array, an `ArrayList` object permits random access to any of its elements. That is, any component of an `ArrayList` object can be accessed in constant time—accessing any of the components of an `ArrayList` object is a `O(1)` operation. Unlike ordinary arrays, `ArrayList` objects are constructed with an initial capacity—the size of the underlying array. This capacity changes automatically during the course of computation. Thus the underlying array grows or shrinks dynamically during the course of computation. Insertions and removals from either end of the array are efficient—in fact, `O(1)`—because relatively few shifts of array components are required in order to properly place the new element being inserted, or to remove the element, at either end. When insertions and removals are to be performed toward the middle of the `ArrayList` object, however, the shifting of components approaches `O(n)`.

In most applications involving lists, we recommend using the `ArrayList` implementation because it offers constant time access to any element in the list. This is partly due to the fact that the `ArrayList` implementation does not need to spend any processing time to allocate storage for a new doubly linked node object as the repository for a new item of data being added to the current list. In addition, if a number of consecutive elements have to be added at once to the list, `ArrayList` can apply certain predefined and efficient array methods such as `System.arraycopy` to accomplish this.

One useful application of the `List` interface is the implementation of the `deque` ADT. A deque is a fundamental linear container admitting efficient insertions and removals from either end—its *front* and *rear*. A deque is the candidate of choice for the container needed to solve the problem of *sifting* the elements of a finite list of randomly generated positive integers so that the even values precede the odd values. In addition, we also showed how predefined generic methods appearing in Java's `Collections` hierarchy are used to sort lists. A particularly valuable application solves the problem of rearranging a finite sequence of randomly generated positive integers so that the even numbers, sorted in order of increasing size, precede the odd numbers, also sorted in order of increasing size. A number of variations of these problems appear in the following exercises, as well as in the Programming Project section.

EXERCISES

1. Suppose we have the declaration

    ```
    Collection Set1 = new HashSet();
    ```

    and suppose currently Set1 = [0,7,3,2].
    Suppose we also define the constructor

    ```
    Vector vect1 = new Vector(Set1);
    ```

    a. What are the current contents, in order, of vect1?
    b. What is the current size of vect1?
    c. What is the current capacity of vect1?

2. If vect1 is the Integer-valued vector whose current value is [2,3,7,8,2,8], and if IntegerVal is the Integer-valued object whose intVal() value is 12, show that the result of executing vect1.add(IntegerVal) produces vect1 = [2,3,7,8,12].

3. Start with vect1 = [2,3,7,8,2,8] and apply the code sequence

    ```
    List newList = new LinkedList();
    newList = vect1.subList(1,5);
    newList.set(2,new Integer(10));
    System.out.println("newList = " + newList);
    System.out.println("vect1 = " + vect1);
    ```

    Find the exact form of the output.

4. a. For vect1 = [2,3,7,8,2,8], show that vect1.removeElement(new Integer(8)) produces the same vect1 as vect1.remove(new Integer(8)).
    b. Furthermore, show that vect1.removeElementAt(4) produces the same vect1 as vect1.remove(4).

5. a. Assume vect1 is the Vector object whose current value is vect1 = [2,3,7,8,2,8]. Show that the code sequence

    ```
    Vector vect2 = new Vector();
    for(ListIterator iter = vect1.listIterator(); iter.hasNext(); )
        vect2.add(iter.next());
    ```

    produces vect2 = [2,3,7,8,2,8].

    b. Show that the same result as that of (a) can be obtained using the code sequence

    ```
    Vector vect2 = new Vector();
    for(Enumeration e = vect1.elements(); e.hasMoreElements(); )
        vect2.add(e.nextElement());
    ```

      c.   Show that the code sequence

```
Vector vect2 = new Vector();
for(ListIterator backIter = vect1.listIterator(vect1.size());
        backIter.hasPrevious(); )
    vect2.add(backIter.previous());
```

            produces `vect2` = `[8,2,8,7,3,2]`.

6. Solve the sifting problem similar to that described in Example 6.6, in Section 6.8, but now the generated even integers appear in reverse sorted order following the odd integers sorted in increasing order.

7. Suppose the current contents of the `Integer`-valued `Vector` object `vect1` is `[2,3,7,8,2,8]`. Using this, trace the following code sequence:

```
Integer [] IntArr = new Integer[vect1.size()];
IntArr = (Integer [])vect1.toArray(new Integer[0]);
Arrays.sort(IntArr);
vect1.clear();
for(int index = 0; index < IntArr.length; ++index)
  vect1.add(IntArr[index]);
```

What are the contents of `vect1` after this code sequence completes execution?

8. Use `Random` to generate random sequences of lowercase alphabet letters. The length of the sequence is supplied by the user.

9. Write a version of the sifter program of Section 6.6 that rearranges any sequence of randomly generated lowercase alphabet letters, so that all of the vowels of the sequence precede all of the consonants.

10. a.   Implement the stack ADT using vectors. Show that the method

```
public static void main(String [] args) throws IOException
 {
 BufferedReader intIS = new BufferedReader(
                 new InputStreamReader(System.in));
 // Construct empty stack:
 Vector stack = new Vector();
 int howMany;
 // Prompt user for the number of Integer values to push
 //onto stack.
 System.out.println("How many integers do you wish to");
 System.out.println("push onto the stack?");
 howMany = Integer.parseInt(intIS.readLine());
 System.out.println("Push " + howMany + " integers onto stack:");
 for(int index = 0; index < howMany; ++index)
 {
  int value;
  value = Integer.parseInt(intIS.readLine());
```

```
    System.out.println("Pushing " + value + " onto stack");
    stack.add(new Integer (value));
  }
  //Display contents of current stack:
  System.out.println("Current stack is:");
  for(int index = stack.size() - 1; index >= 0; --index)
    System.out.print(stack.get(index) + " ");
  System.out.println();

  // Pop stack until empty and show top value:
  System.out.println("Show top of current stack, and pop until empty:");
  while(!stack.isEmpty())
  {
    System.out.println("Top of current stack is " + stack.lastElement());
    stack.removeElementAt(stack.size() - 1);
  }
  if(stack.isEmpty())
    System.out.println("Current stack is empty.");
  else
    System.out.println("Current stack is not empty.");
}
```

   tests the basic admissible operations push, pop, isEmpty, and top.

 b. Write an equivalent form of (a), now implementing stacks using ArrayList objects.

 c. Which of these two versions of stack implementations is regarded as the more efficient? Give reasons for your decision.

11. Describe the initial size and capacity for each of the following. Assume v is a vector whose current value is v = [0,1,2,3].

```
Vector vect1 = new Vector();
Vector vect2 = new Vector(5);
Vector vect3 = new Vector(5,3);
Vector vect4 = new Vector(v);
```

 Give the size and capacity of each of vect2 and vect3 after six values have been added to each.

12. Give the exact form of the output for

```
public static void main(String [] args)
{
  Vector v = new Vector();
  for(int index = 0; index < 4; ++index)
    v.add(new Integer(index));
  List list1 = new ArrayList();
  List list2 = new ArrayList(5);
```

```
List list3 = new ArrayList(v);

System.out.println("size of list1 = " + list1.size());
System.out.println("size of list2 = " + list2.size());
System.out.println("size of list3 = " + list3.size());

// Now add 6 values to each of list2, list3:
for(int index = 0; index < 6; ++index)
{
 list2.add(new Integer(index));
 list3.add(new Integer(index));
}

// Output new size of each of list2 and list3:
System.out.println("After adding 6 values to each of list2, list3:");

System.out.println("new size of list2 = " + list2.size());
System.out.println("new size of list3 = " + list3.size());

}
```

13. Find the exact form of the output for

```
public static void main(String [] args)
 {
   String st1 = "Hello, there!";
   List helloList = new ArrayList();
   for(int index = 0; index  < st1.length(); ++index)
   {
    char chValue = st1.charAt(index);
    helloList.add(new Character(chValue));
   }

   Collections.reverse(helloList);

   System.out.println("helloList = " + helloList);
 }
```

14. Find the exact form of the output for

```
public static void main(String [] args)
 {
   String st1 = "Celeste Aida";
   List aidaList = new ArrayList();
   for(int index = 0; index  < st1.length(); ++index)
   {
```

```
    char chValue = st1.charAt(index);
    aidaList.add(new Character(chValue));
   }

   Collections.sort(aidaList);

   System.out.println("aidaList = " + aidaList);
  }
```

15. Find the exact form of the output for

```
public static void main(String [] args)
 {
  String st1 = "Celeste Aida, forma divina!";
  List ls1 = new ArrayList();
  List ls2 = new ArrayList();

  for(int index = 0; index < st1.length(); ++index)
  {
   char chValue = st1.charAt(index);
   ls1.add(new Character(chValue));
  }

  for(int index = 0; index < ls1.size(); ++index)
   ls2.add(index,ls1.get(ls1.size() - index - 1));

  System.out.println("ls1 = " + ls1);
  System.out.println("ls2 = " + ls2);

 }
```

PROGRAMMING PROJECT

Solve the problem similar to that posed in Section 2.7, but now the prime numbers in the sequence of random integers precede, in order of increasing size, the nonprimes in the sequence, also sorted in order of increasing size.

REFERENCES

Arnold, Ken, James Gosling, and David Holmes. 2000. *The Java Programming Language, Third Edition*. Reading, MA: Addison-Wesley.

Knuth, Donald E. 1981. *The Art of Computer Programming, Volume 2, Seminumerical Algorithms*. Reading, MA: Addison-Wesley.

CHAPTER 7

··

Stacks, Queues, and Priority Queues

CHAPTER OBJECTIVES

- To introduce the `Stack` class predefined in `java.util`.
- To define the `Queue` ADT.
- To implement the `Queue` ADT using the resources available in the Java Collection Framework.
- To investigate several key uses of stacks and queues in a number of important application areas, such as language analysis, compiler design, and operating systems.
- To introduce the priority queue abstraction and to study several of its important applications.

···

7.1 Introduction

In Chapter Six we studied the properties of vectors, deques, and lists. In fact, we observed that Java's Collection Framework provided the predefined `Vector` class and `List` interface, implemented using either `ArrayList` or `LinkedList`. Together with ordinary one-dimensional arrays, these form a category of data types called *sequence containers*. These are characterized as containers whose structure permits any finite collection of values to be stored in a strictly linear configuration.

As early as Section 1.2, we defined a stack as a specific kind of sequence container that permits insertions and removals of elements from one end only, called the *top* of the stack. In fact, in Chapter Six, we noted how the stack ADT can be implemented using vectors, `ArrayList` objects, or `LinkedList` objects. This chapter will introduce yet another implementation: the predefined `Stack` class in `java.util`, emerging as a derived class of `Vector`.

266

In addition, we will introduce another important ADT for application: the Queue ADT. At present, there is no predefined Queue class in the Java Collection Framework. As a consequence, we will study implementation of the Queue ADT using lists.

7.2 **The Stack Abstraction**

In Section 1.2, we defined a *stack* as a data structure that is either empty or consists of a finite sequence of values of some specific type, for which we define the following finite collection of admissible operations:

- push, which inserts a new value onto the stack
- pop, which removes a value from the current stack (whenever possible)
- isEmpty, which tests whether the current stack is empty
- top, which retrieves the value currently at the top of the stack (whenever possible)

We observed that a stack is an example of an abstract data type (ADT), which is an aggregate consisting of a (nonempty) collection of entities, together with a finite collection of well-defined admissible operations applicable to these entities. Other examples of ADTs that we have already studied are hash tables, vectors, deques, lists, sets, and maps. Implementing an ADT in Java involves defining a class whose instance methods implement the admissible operations, along with constructors for creating specific instances or entities (objects) of that type. If we use predefined classes from the Java Collection Framework, much of the internal structural details of the abstraction are already defined. This is one of the key advantages of using the Java Collection Framework: We avoid the burden of having to provide code for the implementation of the structure by hand and are assured of the optimal level of efficiency attached to that implementation.

In any case, we wish to use the abstraction in applications without having to be concerned about how it is implemented. Thus, for example, when we use stacks in a specific application, we must be able to apply any of the admissible operations for stacks without worrying whether the stack is implemented using arrays (Sections 1.3, 1.6, 1.7), vectors (Exercise 6.10[a]), lists (Exercises 6.10[b],[c]), or some other underlying structure. These implementation details are hidden from the user by applying encapsulation and information hiding.

Examples of stacks abound in everyday life, and they all have a common characteristic: We allow items to "stack up" on top of one another in such a way that, when we need one of the stacked items, we gain access to the item that was placed last. In addition, access to the items currently placed on the stack is permitted only for the one currently on top—the one most recently placed ("pushed") onto the stack. Furthermore, the only item eligible to be removed ("popped") from the current stack (if not empty) is the item on top. For example, if we allowed newspapers to be stacked in this manner, we'll gain access to the most recently placed one (although the stack may contain some very old newspapers). The key idea is that stacks allow access to the data items they store in a *last-in, first-out* (LIFO) manner.

7.3 Implementation of Stacks Using the stack Class

As previously mentioned, we defined the stack ADT as early as Chapter One. This definition included an implementation of stacks using ordinary one-dimensional arrays, and one of the programming projects at the end of that chapter presented a second implementation using linked lists. These implementations share a common property: The implementation details are the responsibility of the programmer, and none of the facilities of java.util are used.

In this section, we look at the first of several implementations of the stack ADT using java.util. This version is the Stack class, which is completely predefined in java.util. The Stack class is a subclass of Vector and thus is part of the Java Collections Framework. We then have a hierarchy such as the one shown in Figure 7.1.

FIGURE 7.1

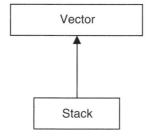

The Stack class contains a single constructor and five instance methods. The methods in java.util.Stack have the signatures

- Stack()—Constructs an initially empty Stack object.
- boolean empty()—Returns true if the current stack is empty, and false if not.
- Object peek()—Returns the value at the top of the current stack if the current stack is not empty, and otherwise throws an EmptyStack-Exception.

- Object pop()—Removes the top element of the current stack and returns that value; throws an EmptyStackException if the current stack is empty.
- Object push(Object value)—Inserts the current contents of value at the top of the current stack and returns that value.[1]
- Int search(Object value)—Returns the position of value relative to the top of the current stack in the case of a successful search. The value -1 is returned in the case of an unsuccessful search.

Note that this implementation uses peek as the name of the method returning the value at the top of the current stack. This is used in place of top in our array implementation of Chapter One. In addition, Stack contains a search method that is included in our implementation. The return value of search uses the fact that elements of any stack implemented this way associate with a nonnegative integer index, indicating its relative location from the bottom of the stack. Consequently, to search for a value not on the stack produces a value of -1. This clearly indicates an unsuccessful search, because no value on the stack corresponds to an index of -1.

Example 7.1 is a driver for Stack.

EXAMPLE 7.1

```
public static void main(String [] args) throws IOException
{
 BufferedReader intIS = new BufferedReader(
                         new InputStreamReader(System.in));

 Stack intStack = new Stack();

 System.out.print("Initially, size of intStack = ");
 System.out.println(intStack.size() + " and has capacity =");
 System.out.println(intStack.capacity());

 int howMany;
 System.out.println("How many integers do you wish to push");
 System.out.println("onto intStack?");
 howMany = Integer.parseInt(intIS.readLine());
 System.out.println("Pushing " + howMany + " integers onto
     intStack:");
 for(int index = 0; index < howMany; ++index)
```

[1]The return value defined for pop and push can be suppressed. See Example 7.1.

```
    {
      int value = Integer.parseInt(intIS.readLine());
      System.out.println("Pushing " + value + " onto intStack");
      intStack.push(new Integer(value));
    }
    System.out.println("The current contents of intStack, from");
    System.out.println("bottom to top are");
    System.out.println(intStack);

    while(!intStack.empty())
    {
      System.out.println(intStack.peek() + " is popped from current
                  intStack");
      intStack.pop();
      System.out.println("After this pop, intStack is ");
      System.out.println(intStack);
    }
    if(intStack.empty())
      System.out.println("intStack is currently empty");
    else
      System.out.println("intStack is not currently empty");

} // terminates text of main method
```

A sample run of this program follows.

```
Initially, size of intStack = 0 and has capacity
10
How many integers do you wish to push
onto intStack?
6
Pushing 6 integers onto intStack:
34
Pushing 34 onto intStack
65
Pushing 65 onto intStack
134
Pushing 134 onto intStack
-229
Pushing -229 onto intStack
1032
Pushing 1032 onto intStack
12
```

```
Pushing 12 onto intStack
The current contents of intStack, from
bottom to top are
[34, 65, 134, -229, 1032, 12]
12 is popped from current intStack
After this pop, intStack is
[334, 65, 134, -229, 1032]
1032 is popped from current intStack
After this pop, intStack is
[34, 65, 134, -229]
-229 is popped from current intStack
After this pop, intStack is
[34, 65, 134]
134 is popped from current intStack
After this pop, intStack is
[34, 65]
65 is popped from current intStack
After this pop, intStack is
[34]
34 is popped from current intStack
After this pop, intStack is
[]
intStack is currently empty
```

This implementation has a number of drawbacks. First, because `Stack` is a subclass of `Vector`, all of the instance methods of `Vector` are inherited by `Stack`. Some of these methods support synchronized concurrent processing, causing their execution to be unusually slow if the stack is accessed from a single processing thread. This idea was already discussed in Section 6.2. Second, a major drawback due to the inheritance of `Stack` from `Vector` is that any of the instance methods defined in `Vector` can be applied to any stack. However, some of these have no meaning with respect to the actions of a stack as defined, for example, by the stack ADT. As an example, it makes no sense to apply any of

```
void insertElementAt(Object obj, int index);
Object setElementAt(Object obj, int index);
Object elementAt(int index);
void removeElementAt(int index);
```

for any value of `index` besides `<stack_identifier>`.size() - 1. This is completely at odds with the very concept of a stack, yet this implementation compels us to maintain these methods in this general form.

7.4   **Implementing the `Stack` ADT as a Subclass of `ArrayList`**

This version is not completely predefined; it requires some coding by the programmer. Here, we supply our own code for the `Stack` class, viewed as a subclass of `ArrayList`, as shown in Figure 7.2.

FIGURE 7.2

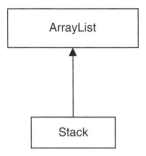

This current design avoids one problem inherent in the stack implementation defined by looking at `Stack` as a subclass of `Vector`, that is, we are no longer affected by the synchronization problem. Despite this, a number of `ArrayList` methods do not apply to stacks. Many of these are inherited from the `Collection` interface.[2] Some that we do not wish to support in this new design are all of the methods defined in `Collection` except for `isEmpty()`. In addition, the only instance methods we need are actually defined in `List`, where we redefine `get`, `add`, and `remove` for the `size()` - 1 entry, viewed in our abstraction as the location of the top of the current stack. We will also have to account for handling an underflow exception, caused by attempting to either pop or retrieve the value at the top of a stack that is currently empty.

In Figure 7.3, we picture the abstraction of a specific instance of an `Integer`-valued stack `intStack`, together with our planned implementation of `intStack` using `ArrayList`.

How do we implement this design in Java? We use the `StackException` class coded in Example 1.5 and define the class `ArrStack` as a subclass of `ArrayList` as follows

```
class ArrStack extends ArrayList
{
 // Data field.
 protected ArrayList st;
```

[2]See Section 5.3.

FIGURE 7.3

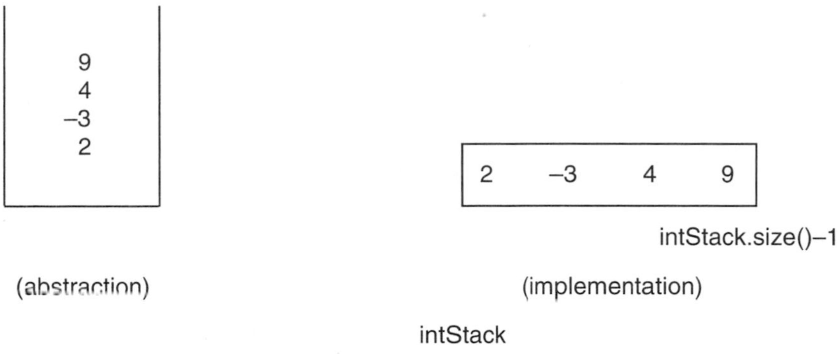

(abstraction)   (implementation)

intStack

```
// Constructor. Constructs empty stack.
public ArrStack()
{
 st = new ArrayList();
}


// Tests whether the current stack is empty.
public boolean isEmpty()
{
 return st.isEmpty();
}


// Push operation. Pushes parameter value on the current stack.
public void push(Object obj)
{
 st.add(obj);
}


// Pop operation.  Removes value at the top of the current stack.
// Precondition: Current stack is not empty.
public void pop() throws StackException
{
 if(!st.isEmpty())
  st.remove(st.size() - 1);
 else
  throw new StackException("Error -- underflow");
}


// Top operation. Retrieves value at the top of the current stack.
// Precondition: Current stack is not empty.
public Object top() throws StackException
{
```

```
  if(!st.isEmpty())
   return st.get(st.size() - 1);
  else
   throw new StackException("Error -- underflow");
 }


} // terminates text of ArrStack class
```

This class definition contains the functionality given in our original description of the stack ADT. Besides this, we are assured of the same level of efficiency for the instance methods described in `ArrStack` as those defined in `ArrayList`.

The definition

```
protected ArrayList st;
```

assures that any object constructed in the `ArrStack` class is actually an object inherited from `ArrayList`. Thus, any method applied to any such object is actually an adaptation of a method acting on that object when viewed as an `ArrayList` object. This is evident from the coding of the constructor for `ArrStack`. This is similar to what is done in the Standard Template Library (STL) in C++ for `stack` objects, where objects of the predefined `stack` class in STL are viewed as an adaptation of vectors, deques, or lists.

A number of major differences exist between STL and `java.util` in this regard. First, `stack` is predefined in STL, whereas `ArrStack` has to be designed by the programmer. Second, the user functions defined in the user interface in STL's version of `stack` are the only operations applicable to any `stack` object. In Java, by contrast, by using inheritance it is possible to apply any instance method defined in `ArrayList`, or in the `List` or `Collection` interfaces, to any `ArrStack` object. In order to prevent the application of any "unwanted" instance method to an `ArrStack` object, it is necessary to override them, for example, by including each as an `ArrStack` instance method, but now have each throw a `StackException` exception when invoked. As an example, we would override `indexOf` by

```
int indexOf(Object obj) throws StackException
{
 throw new StackException("Error - undefined operation");
}
```

Each of these has to be included in the text of the `ArrStack` class. We now look at a driver for `ArrStack` similar to that defined in Example 7.1 for `Stack`.

EXAMPLE 7.2

```
public static void main(String [] args) throws IOException
{
```

```
BufferedReader intIS = new BufferedReader(
                        new InputStreamReader(System.in));
// Construct empty stack.
ArrStack intStack = new ArrStack();
// Prompt user for number of Integer values to push
// onto intStack
System.out.println("How many integers do you wish to");
System.out.println("push onto the stack?");
int howMany = Integer.parseInt(intIS.readLine());
System.out.println("Push " + howMany + " integers onto stack:");
for(int index = 0; index < howMany; ++index)
{
 int value = Integer.parseInt(intIS.readLine());
 System.out.println("Pushing " + value + " onto stack.");
 intStack.push(new Integer(value));
}

// Now pop stack until empty and show top value each time:
System.out.println("Show top of current stack, and pop until empty:");
while(!intStack.isEmpty())
{
 System.out.println("Top of current stack is " + intStack.top());
 intStack.pop();
}
if(intStack.isEmpty())
 System.out.println("Current stack is empty.");
else
 System.out.println("Current stack is not empty.");

} // terminates text of main method.
```

A sample run of this program is

```
How many integers do you wish to
push onto the stack?
6
Push 6 integers onto stack:
34
Pushing 34 onto stack.
65
Pushing 65 onto stack.
134
Pushing 134 onto stack.
-229
Pushing -229 onto stack.
```

```
1032
Pushing 1032 onto stack.
12
Pushing 12 onto stack.
Show top of current stack, and pop until empty:
Top of current stack is 12
Top of current stack is 1032
Top of current stack is -229
Top of current stack is 65
Top of current stack is 34
Current stack is empty.
```

7.5 Implementing the `Stack` ADT as a Subclass of `LinkedList`

In a manner similar to that described for `ArrStack` in the previous section, we can implement the stack ADT as a subclass of `LinkedList`. More precisely, we can define the class `LinkedStack` as

```
class LinkedStack extends LinkedList
{
 protected LinkedList st;

 // Constructor. Constructs empty stack.
 public LinkedStack()
 {
  st = new LinkedList();
 }


 // Tests whether the current stack is empty.
 public boolean isEmpty()
 {
  return st.isEmpty();
 }


 // Push operation. Pushes parameter value on the current stack.
 public void push(Object obj)
 {
  st.addLast(obj);
 }


 // Pop operation.  Removes value at the top of the current stack.
```

```
// Precondition: Current stack is not empty.
public void pop() throws StackException
{
 if(!st.isEmpty())
  st.removeLast();
 else
  throw new StackException("Error -- underflow");
}


// Top operation. Retrieves value at the top of the current stack.
// Precondition: Current stack is not empty.
public Object top() throws StackException
{
 if(!st.isEmpty())
  return st.getLast();
 else
  throw new StackException("Error -- underflow");
}

} // terminates text of LinkedStack class
```

Each of the `ArrayList` and `LinkedList` implementations provide constant-time efficiency when applying the basic stack operations `push`, `pop`, `top`, and `isEmpty`. Again, as was the case when implementing the stack ADT using `ArrayList`, inheritance causes any method defined in `Collection`, `List`, and `LinkedList` to be applied to any `LinkedStack` object. Each of these "unwanted" instance methods would have to be accompanied by code throwing a `StackException` exception.

Suppose we wish to combine an interface with an implementation that extends an already existing class. For example, suppose we combine the `Stack` interface defined in Example 1.6 with `LinkedStack` as just defined. Then the code for `LinkedStack` would have to be written using the following syntax[3]:

```
class LinkedStack extends LinkedList implements Stack
{
        .

        .

        .
    // body of LinkedStack as before
```

[3]Actually, there is a change in the coding of the `Stack` interface. The `push` method no longer is involved with a `StackException` exception, because an overflow condition no longer applies when implementing stacks using either `ArrStack` or `LinkedStack`.

.

.

.

```
}
```

7.6 **Applications of the `Stack` ADT**

We present several key applications of the stack ADT in this section. Each of the applications is solvable by any implementation of the stack ADT. For this reason, we do not commit to any specific stack implementation unless it is necessary to do so.

Application 1: Balanced Parentheses, Brackets, and Braces

The first application involves testing any character string of finite length for the occurrence of balanced parentheses (and), brackets [and], and braces { and }. Let `str` be a character string of finite length. We say `str` is *balanced* (with respect to parentheses, brackets, and braces) if

1. `str` is empty (that is, `str` contains no characters and has length zero) or has no occurrences of (and), or [and], or { and }
2. `str` contains as many occurrences of right parentheses) as there are left parentheses (, as many occurrences of right brackets] as there are left brackets [, and as many occurrences of right braces } as there are left braces {
3. the occurrences of the corresponding right parenthesis, right bracket, or right brace occurs later in `str` than its matching left parenthesis, left bracket, or left brace
4. a right parenthesis matches only a left parenthesis, a right bracket matches only a left bracket, and a right brace matches only a left brace
5. any right parenthesis, bracket, or brace must match the closest corresponding left parenthesis, bracket, or brace occurring earlier in `str`

Thus, each of the following character strings is balanced:

```
((a + b) + c) + [d + {e}]
a + (b * c)
{{}}
```

and each of the following is not balanced:

```
([a + b] + c
{a + {b + c
({)}
```

The ability to detect balanced parentheses, brackets, and braces is critical in the design of compilers for the most popular high-level programming languages (such as C, C++, Scheme, Ada, and Java) because each of the underlying syntax structures defined in any of these languages requires balanced characters of this type. Therefore, one of the components used in writing a compiler for any of these languages is a test for balanced parentheses, brackets, and braces. Character-valued stacks are particularly useful in this regard because they represent a relatively simple tool for testing any such string for balance.

The efficiency of push, pop, top, and isEmpty depends on the implementation of the underlying container (whether the stack is implemented as a subclass of Vector or as an ArrStack or LinkedStack object). Accordingly, we design a solution to this problem that is independent of the implementation chosen for the stack ADT. We will therefore define a charvalued stack charStack for the purpose of solving the problem, and we execute the steps described in the following proposed algorithm:

Scan the input string character by character from left to right;
If a left parenthesis, left bracket, or left brace is scanned, push it onto charStack;
If a right parenthesis, right bracket, or right brace is scanned, compare it to the
 character currently at the top of charStack (*if such exists*);
if (*the character currently at the top of* charStack *is a left parenthesis, left bracket,*
or left brace matching the right character currently being scanned)
 apply charStack.pop();
else
 signal a "mismatch" error;
In the case of a "mismatch" error, reject the input string as unbalanced;
if (*the entire character string is scanned and the final stack is empty*)
 accept the input string as balanced;
else
 reject the input string as unbalanced;

Mismatches also occur if charStack is empty before the entire input string is scanned and that string has a further occurrence of a right parenthesis, right bracket, or right brace before an occurrence of a left parenthesis, left bracket, or left brace. This happens as a consequence of an oversupply of right characters. A mismatch also occurs by attempting to pop from a currently empty stack, scanning a right character before a left character, or if the entire character string is scanned and the final stack is not empty. This last situation occurs when there is an oversupply of left characters. Finally, if the string contains other characters besides parentheses, brackets, or braces, scan that character but perform no action on charStack.

Let us test the algorithm on several input strings. Suppose the input string is (a + b) + c) + [d + {e}]. Each of the first two characters scanned is pushed onto charStack and then a, +, and b are scanned, with no action taken on charStack. The next character scanned is), which is the right character corresponding to the character (currently at the top of charStack. Accordingly, charStack is popped once, leaving charStack with a single character (. The characters + and c are scanned, with no action taken on charStack. The next character scanned is), which prompts a pop action on charStack because its current top is (. At this point, charStack is empty. The + character is scanned, with no action taken on charStack. The next character scanned is [, which is pushed onto charStack. The next two characters d and + are scanned, with no action performed on charStack. Then a left brace is scanned and pushed onto charStack. The next character scanned is e, prompting no action on charStack. The next character scanned is a right brace, which is a match with the left brace currently at the top of charStack; thus, charStack is popped, leaving charStack with the single character [. The final character (which is]) is scanned, matching the left bracket currently at the top of charStack. Therefore, charStack is popped; because the entire input string has been scanned, the algorithm accepts the entire input string as balanced.

Now look at the input string ({)}. Push the first two characters (and { onto charStack. The next character scanned is a right parenthesis. Because) is not the matching right symbol for the left brace currently at the top of charStack, the decision is to reject the input string as unbalanced.

Finally, suppose the input string is ([a + b] + c. The first two characters (and [are scanned and pushed in that order onto charStack. The next three characters a, +, and b are scanned, with no change in charStack. The next character scanned is], matching the [currently at the top of charStack. Consequently, charStack is popped once, leaving it holding the single character (. The remaining characters of the input string are scanned, with no further action performed on charStack. Because charStack is not empty after the entire input string has been scanned, it is unbalanced.

The following boolean-valued method, called checkBalance, implements the algorithm using a string and a char-valued stack.

EXAMPLE 7.3

```
public static boolean checkBalance(String str, ArrStack charStack)
{
   // Input string is balanced until proven to be unbalanced.
   boolean running = true;
   for(int index = 0; index < str.length(); ++index)
```

```
     {
      char chValue = str.charAt(index);
      // If current character is a left parenthesis, left bracket,
      // or left brace, push its wrapper equivalent onto charStack.
      if(chValue == '(' || chValue == '[' || chValue == '{')
       charStack.push(new Character(chValue));
      // Now seek matches of left characters with the corresponding
      // right characters.
      else if(!charStack.isEmpty() && chValue == ')'
               && charStack.top().equals(new Character('(')))
        charStack.pop();
      else if(!charStack.isEmpty() && chValue == ']'
               && charStack.top().equals(new Character('[')))
        charStack.pop();
      else if(!charStack.isEmpty() && chValue == '}'
               && charStack.top().equals(new Character('{')))
        charStack.pop();
      // If have oversupply of left parentheses, left brackets,
      // or left braces, declare an imbalance and exit.
      else if(charStack.isEmpty() &&
         (chValue == '(' || chValue == '[' || chValue == '{'))
      {
         running = false;
         break;
      } // terminates last if-clause
      // If have oversupply of right parentheses, right brackets,
      // or right braces, declare an imbalance and exit.
      else if(charStack.isEmpty() &&
          (chValue == ')' || chValue == ']' || chValue == '}'))
      {
         running = false;
         break;
      } // terminates last if-clause

    } // terminates text of for-loop
   return (running && charStack.isEmpty());
 } // terminates text of checkBalance
```

Note that the second parameter of checkBalance is of type ArrStack. We could just as well use any of the other implementations of the stack ADT described in the text as a replacement, with very little modification of the code. Also, observe that any other characters in the input string, such as a, b, c, and + in (a + b) + c, fall through the cracks—these are scanned but do not effect any processing action on charStack. Indeed, after any such character is scanned, control of execution passes to the next character of `str`. Processing of the `for`-loop either continues until all of the characters of `str` are scanned or exits early due to a detected imbalance.

The caller invokes `checkBalance` using

`checkBalance(strValue,characterStack)`

with a `boolean` value returned. We leave the coding of a driver for `check-Balance` as an exercise. (See Exercise 3 at the end of this chapter.)

Application 2: Evaluating Postfix Expressions

When we write arithmetic expressions, we use *infix form;* that is, we place a binary operator symbol between its two operands. With *postfix form,* the operator immediately follows its two operands. Conversely, in *prefix form,* the operator immediately precedes its two operands. Table 7.1 shows the infix form and the corresponding prefix and postfix forms for several arithmetic expressions.

Table 7.1 shows that prefix and postfix expressions do not require parentheses. Instead, the order of appearance of the symbols in each of

TABLE 7.1 **Prefix and Postfix Forms for Some Arithmetic Expressions**

Infix	Prefix	Postfix
a+b	+ab	ab+
a+b*c	+a*bc	abc*+
(a+b)*c	*+abc	ab+c*
(a+b)*(c−d)	*+ab−cd	ab+cd−*
(b*b − 4*a*c)/(2*a)	/−*bb**4ac*2a	bb*4ac*−2a*/

these expressions dictates the order of application of the underlying operations. This is particularly valuable in automating the evaluation of arithmetic expressions, as is done in programming-language compilers.

Many hand-held calculators perform their computations by first converting the expression into postfix form and then evaluating the resulting postfix expression. Furthermore, compilers for the conventional high-level programming languages convert arithmetic expressions appearing in the source code into their equivalent postfix form before generating lower-level code to evaluate the expression. This application describes how stacks are valuable tools for evaluating postfix expressions. We will design and code a `static` method for evaluating postfix expressions with single-digit operands.

We look at several examples. Suppose we wish to evaluate 23+7*, which is the postfix equivalent of the infix expression (2 + 3) * 7. The parentheses are needed because the evaluation of this expression calls for the + operation to be executed before *. Indeed, if we consider the evaluation of 2 + 3 * 7 instead with the usual precedence rules in effect, the multiplication of 3 and 7 is executed first, followed by the sum of that product with 2, yielding an answer of 23. The equivalent postfix form for 2 + 3 * 7 is 237*+.

How do we evaluate 23+7*? We first scan 2, then 3, and push these values in succession onto an initially empty stack st. We can assume that st is either int-valued (if we use the class intArrayStack as defined in Section 1.3) or Integer-valued (if we use any of the generic stack implementations, including those that are completely predefined in java.util as in Section 7.3, or ArrStack or LinkedStack from Sections 7.4 and 7.5). Any of these implement the abstraction seen in Figure 7.4. Indeed, Figure 7.4a shows the result of pushing 2, then 3, onto st.

FIGURE 7.4

(a) (b) (c) (d)

Then we scan the operator symbol +. This prompts a popping of st twice, producing the values of the two operands opnd1 and opnd2, in that order. In this case, opnd1 has value 3 and opnd2 has value 2. Then + is applied to opnd1 and opnd2, producing an answer of 5, which is then pushed onto st, as in Figure 7.4b. The next step is to scan the next character in the postfix expression. This character is the digit 7, which is now pushed onto st, as in Figure 7.4c. The next character * is scanned, prompting two successive pops of st, with opnd1 now storing 7 and opnd2 now storing 5. Then opnd1 * opnd2 is computed, yielding 35, which is now pushed onto st, as in Figure 7.4d. At this point, the entire postfix expression has been scanned, prompting a final popping of st; its only value (35) represents the value of the postfix expression.

We compare this to the result of evaluating 237*+. We trace this evaluation as well, observing the changes in st viewed in the various forms of Figure 7.5. The first three characters, each a single numeric digit, are scanned and pushed onto st in order, as in Figure 7.5a. Then the operator symbol * is scanned, prompting two successive pops of st, with opnd1 holding 7 and opnd2 holding 3. Their product is computed and pushed onto st, as in Figure 7.5b. Then the operator + is scanned, once again causing

FIGURE 7.5

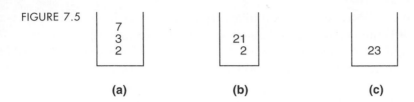

(a) (b) (c)

two successive pops of st, with opnd1 now holding 21 and opnd2 now holding 2. The sum opnd1 + opnd2 is computed and the result (23) is pushed onto st, as in Figure 7.5c. The result is popped, and because there are no further characters to scan the value popped is the value of the post-fix expression.

We wish to design a formal algorithm for evaluating postfix expressions. We note first that any postfix expression serving as input to this algorithm is simply a special form of a character string. Hence, any numeric digit appearing in the string is a character that must be converted into its integer-valued equivalent so as to enable arithmetic computations to be performed. These converted integer values are pushed onto the operand stack. Similarly, even if we restrict the computations to involve only the five integer-valued binary operations +, -, *, /, and %, each of these symbols appears as a character value in the postfix expression. When any one of these operator symbols is scanned, it prompts the popping of the operand stack twice and then the application of the operation to these operands. For -, /, and %, it is particularly important to observe that the operation is not commutative; hence the proper order of the operands must be observed. In each such case, the second value popped (opnd2) appears in front of the operator, and the first popped (opnd1) appears after the operator. Thus, we have

- opnd2 - opnd1 when '-' is scanned
- opnd2 / opnd1 when '/' is scanned
- opnd2 % opnd1 when '%' is scanned

If the original postfix string is well defined, the scanning process terminates with the entire postfix string scanned and with a final operand stack containing a single integer value. This value is popped from the final stack and represents the value of the original postfix string.

The algorithm can be represented as

for(*each character in postfix string scanned successively from left to right*)

{
  if(*the character is a numeric digit*)
  push the corresponding integer onto st;

```
  else
  {
   pop st for the value of opnd1;
   pop st for the value of opnd2;
   switch(operator symbol currently scanned)
   {
    case '+': push opnd1 + opnd2 onto st and exit;
    case '-': push opnd2 - opnd1 onto st and exit;
    case '*': push opnd1 * opnd2 onto st and exit;
    case '/': push opnd2 / opnd1 onto st and exit;
    case '%': push opnd2 % opnd2 onto st and exit;
   } // ends switch
  } // ends for-loop
 // At this point, there should be a single integer value on st
 // if the postfix string is well-defined. Pop that value and return it
 // as the value of the original postfix expression.
 return the result of popping st;
```

We will assume that we are using a stack of `Object` values. Therefore, any integer digit in the original postfix string will be converted to its equivalent `Integer` value by the `static` method `convert`, coded as

```
// Convert character digit to its corresponding Integer value.
public static int convert(char chValue)
{
 switch(chValue)
 {
  case '0': return new Integer(0);
  case '1': return new Integer(1);
  case '2': return new Integer(2);
  case '3': return new Integer(3);
  case '4': return new Integer(4);
  case '5': return new Integer(5);
  case '6': return new Integer(6);
  case '7': return new Integer(7);
  case '8': return new Integer(8);
  case '9': return new Integer(9);
  default:
  {
   System.out.println("Error in evaluation");
   return new Integer(-1);
  } // terminates default
 } // terminates switch
} // terminates text of convert
```

Finally, to implement the algorithm, we code an `Integer`-valued method `evalPostfix` with two parameters. The first parameter is `str`, a `String` value whose successive characters are those of the postfix expression to be evaluated, and the second is an `Integer`-valued[4] stack `opndStack` (implemented here as an `ArrStack` object). The elements of `opndStack` are used to store the operands as the evaluation process progresses. The return value is the result of the evaluation of the postfix expression passed as the value of the first parameter. The code for `evalPostfix` is

```
public static Integer evalPostfix(String str,ArrStack opndStack)
 {
  for(int index = 0; index < str.length(); ++index)
  {
   // if current character is an integer digit
   char chValue = str.charAt(index);
   if('0' <= chValue && chValue <= '9')
   // Push the converted integer digit onto operand stack.
    opndStack.push(convert(chValue));
   else
   {
    Integer opnd1 = (Integer)opndStack.top();
    opndStack.pop();
    Integer opnd2 = (Integer)opndStack.top();
    opndStack.pop();
    switch(chValue)
    {
     case '+':{
               int value = opnd1.intValue() + opnd2.intValue();
               opndStack.push(new Integer(value));
               break;
              }
     case '-':{
               int value = opnd2.intValue() - opnd1.intValue();
               opndStack.push(new Integer(value));
               break;
              }
     case '*':{
               int value = opnd1.intValue() * opnd2.intValue();
```

---

[4]Actually, the stack stores `Object` values. We cast the `Integer` objects when processing their values.

```
                    opndStack.push(new Integer(value));
                    break;
                }
      case '/':{
                    int value = opnd2.intValue() / opnd1.intValue();
                    opndStack.push(new Integer(value));
                    break;
                }
      case '%':{
                    int value = opnd2.intValue() % opnd2.intValue();
                    opndStack.push(new Integer(value));
                    break;
                }
      } // terminates text of switch
    } // terminates else clause
    // Monitoring stack action by disclosing top of stack
    // value during each loop cycle.
    System.out.println("Top of stack is now: " +
                            (Integer)opndStack.top());

  } // terminates for-loop
  Integer result = (Integer)opndStack.top();
  opndStack.pop();
  return result;
} // terminates evalPostfix
```

This version of evalPostfix also monitors the activity of the operand stack as the evaluation progresses by outputting the value at the top of the stack for each cycle of the for-loop. The results obtained are consistent with our design. To illustrate, suppose we apply evalPostfix to 23+7*. The execution of evalPostfix then produces

Top of stack is now: 2
Top of stack is now: 3
Top of stack is now: 5
Top of stack is now: 7
Top of stack is now: 35

If, instead, we input the postfix string 237*+, evalPostfix yields

Top of stack is now: 2
Top of stack is now: 3
Top of stack is now: 7
Top of stack is now: 21
Top of stack is now: 23

Application 3: Converting Infix Expressions to Postfix

We can view the evaluation of postfix expressions in Application 2 as the second step of a two-step process performed in the compilation of higher-level source code into lower-level code. The first step of the process is the transition of any arithmetic expression written in infix form to its postfix equivalent. This application provides that step.

Again, stacks provide the necessary computational tool for this transition. However, several key differences are seen in the stacks used for this step. Here, the stacks are `Character`-valued, and binary operator symbols as well as left parentheses are capable of being pushed onto the stack. Other members of the infix string will be either single-digit numeric characters or (possibly) right parentheses. The binary operator symbols will be the same as in Application 2.

Let us consider several applications before formulating a general conversion algorithm. Suppose we begin with the infix expression 2 + 3. Its corresponding postfix form is clearly 23+. But how do we automate this transition process? We define three objects:

1. a `Character`-valued stack of operators (and possibly left parentheses), initially empty, called `operatorStack`
2. a `Character`-valued string, initially empty, called `postfixString`
3. a `String` variable holding the original infix expression, called `infixString`

We scan the character in `infixString` from the leftmost character to the end, as usual. Referring to the infix expression 2 + 3, the first character (`'2'`) is scanned; because it is an operand, it is inserted at the rear of `postfixString` and the next character (`'+'`) is scanned. This is pushed onto `operatorStack` and the next character is scanned. This is the numeric character `'3'`, which is inserted at the rear of `postfixString`. This completes the scan of the infix string, so the computation completes by popping `operatorStack` until empty and inserting each character popped at the rear of `postfixString`. This results in the final version of `postfixString` as 23+, the desired postfix equivalent. We trace this sequence of actions in Figure 7.6a.

What about 2+3*7? Here we have two operators `'+'` and `'*'`, with `'*'` having a higher precedence than `'+'`. We begin as before, inserting `'2'` at the rear of `postfixString`, and continue by scanning `'+'`. As before, `'+'` is pushed onto `operatorStack`, and we resume by scanning `'3'`, which is again inserted at the rear of `postfixString`. Now `'*'` is scanned. At this point, we examine the current status of `operatorStack`. If this stack contains other operator symbols whose precedence is the same as `'*'`, such as `'*'`, `'/'`, or `'%'`, we systematically pop `operatorStack` and insert each

FIGURE 7.6a

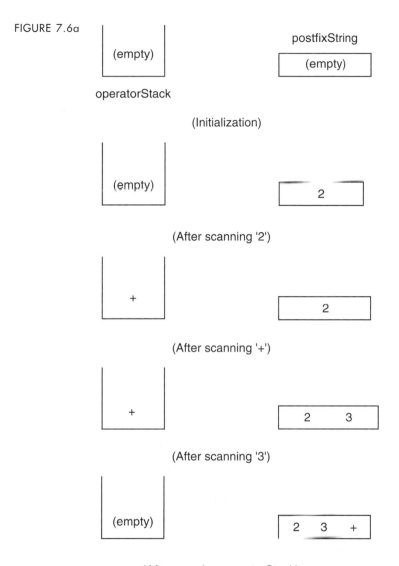

operatorStack

(Initialization)

(After scanning '2')

(After scanning '+')

(After scanning '3')

(After popping operatorStack)

such operator symbol at the rear of postfixString until either opera-torStack empties or the top of operatorStack contains either '+' or '-', of lower precedence. Then the current operator symbol being scanned ('*' in this case) is pushed onto operatorStack. At this point, opera-torStack is read from bottom to top as '+', '*'. We then scan the character '7' of the infix string and insert it at the rear of postfixString. Because this completes the scan of the entire infix expression, we systematically pop operatorStack and insert each such character at the rear of postfixString, producing the result 237*+. The steps are illustrated in Figure 7.6b.

FIGURE 7.6b

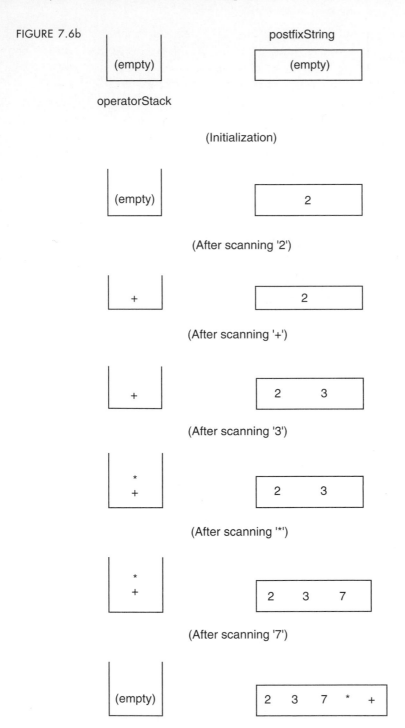

postfixString

operatorStack

(Initialization)

(After scanning '2')

(After scanning '+')

(After scanning '3')

(After scanning '*')

(After scanning '7')

(After popping operatorStack until empty)

How are enclosing parentheses handled, as in `(2 + 3)* 7`? Here the enclosing parentheses emphasize that the usual precedence rules between operators are to be superseded and that the evaluation of the expression `2 + 3` is to be done before operating on the result with `'7'` using `'*'`. We begin by pushing `'('` onto `operatorStack` and continue by scanning `'2'`. As usual, `'2'` is inserted at the rear of `postfixString`, and `'+'` is now scanned. This is pushed onto `operatorStack`, and `'3'` is scanned next and inserted at the rear of `postfixString`. Then `')'` is scanned. This prompts a sequence of pops of `operatorStack` and insertions at the rear of `postfixString` up to but not including the first occurrence of `'('`. The symbol `'('` is popped from `operatorStack` but not inserted at the rear of `postfixString`. Scanning the infix expression resumes by pushing `'*'` onto `operatorStack`. The character `'7'` is then scanned and inserted at the rear of `postfixString`. This completes the scan of the infix string, so the remaining character on `operatorStack` (only `'*'` in this case) is popped and inserted at the rear of `postfixString`, yielding `23+7*`. This sequence of actions is traced in Figure 7.6c.

FIGURE 7.6c

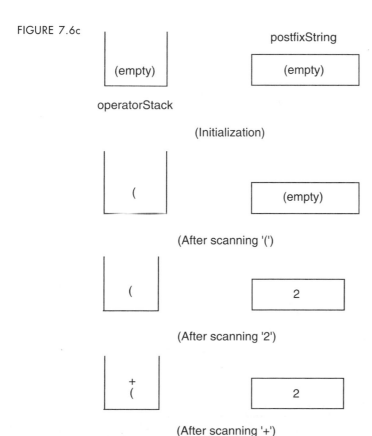

operatorStack

(Initialization)

(After scanning '(')

(After scanning '2')

(After scanning '+')

(continued)

FIGURE 7.6c
Continued

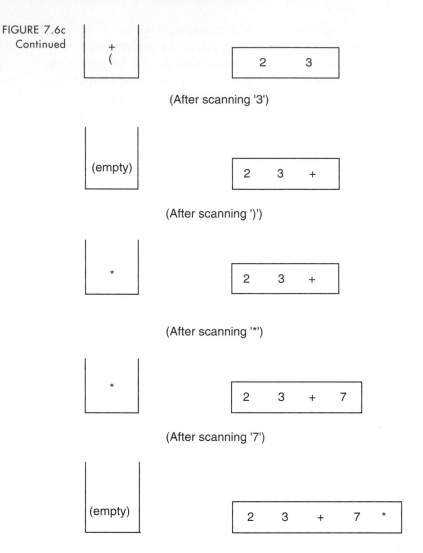

(After scanning '3')

(After scanning ')')

(After scanning '*')

(After scanning '7')

(After popping operatorStack until empty)

We can now state the algorithm under the assumption that the current infix expression is well defined with operators +, -, *, /, % and (possibly) (and).

Initialize operatorStack *and* postfixString *as empty;*
for(*each character in* infixString *scanned successively from left to right*)
{
if(*character is* '(')
push that character onto operatorStack;

else if(*the character is* ')')
{
pop operatorStack *of each operator symbol and insert each of these
at the rear of* postfixString *until the first occurrence of* ')' *is
located on* operatorStack;
pop operatorStack *once more (but do not insert* '(' *at the rear of*
postfixString);
}
else if(*the character is either* '+' *or* '-')
{
pop operatorStack *of all symbols down to (but not including) the first
occurrence of* '(' *(if it appears at all) and insert each such symbol at the
rear of* postfixString;
push the operator symbol currently being scanned onto operatorStack;
}
else if(*the character is either* '*', '/', *or* '%')
{
pop operatorStack *of all* '*', '/', *or* '%' *up to but not including
(if such exist) the first occurrence of* '+' *or* '-';
insert each such character at the rear of postfixString;
push the operator symbol currently being scanned onto operatorStack;
}
// *If the character currently being scanned is none of the above, it is an operand.*
// *Append this value at the rear of* postfixString.
else
insert character at the rear of postfixString;
} // *ends* for-*loop.*
Now pop remaining operators from operatorStack *and append each at the
rear of* postfixString;
Return contents of postfixString;

The implementation of this algorithm in Java uses a method whose return value is of the String type, representing the final version of post-fixString. The method is called toPostfix and has a single formal String parameter infixString whose value is the infix expression to be converted to its equivalent postfix form. This implementation is given in Example 7.5.

EXAMPLE 7.5   The formal code for the conversion from infix to postfix is given by

```
public static String toPostfix(String infixString)
{
 // Operator stack initialized.
```

```
      ArrStack operatorStack = new ArrStack();

// Postfix string initialized as empty.
String postfixString = "";

// Scan infixString and take appropriate action.
for(int index = 0; index < infixString.length(); ++index)
{
 char chValue = infixString.charAt(index);
 // If chValue is a '(' push it onto operatorStack.
 if(chValue == '(') operatorStack.push(new Character('('));
 // If chValue is a ')' then pop all operators from
 // operatorStack until matching '(' is found.
 else if(chValue == ')')
 {
  Character oper = (Character)operatorStack.top();
  while(!(oper.equals(new Character('(')))
        && !(operatorStack.isEmpty()))
  {
   postfixString += oper.charValue();
   operatorStack.pop();
   oper = (Character)operatorStack.top();
  }
  // After this is done, pop operatorStack once more
  // to remove the matching '('.
  operatorStack.pop();
 } // closes else.
 // If chValue is either '+' or '-', pop all operators
 // from operatorStack and append each to postfixString.
 // Then push current character onto operatorStack.
 else if(chValue == '+' || chValue == '-')
 {
  // If current operatorStack is empty, push character
  // onto operatorStack without any popping.
  if(operatorStack.isEmpty())
    operatorStack.push(new Character(chValue));
  else // Current operatorStack is not empty.
  {
   Character oper = (Character)operatorStack.top();
   while(!(operatorStack.isEmpty()
         || oper.equals(new Character('('))
         || oper.equals(new Character(')'))))
   {
```

```
      operatorStack.pop();
      postfixString += oper.charValue();
     } // ends while.
     // Push current '+' or '-' onto operatorStack
     operatorStack.push(new Character(chValue));
    } // closes last else.
  } // closes else if(chValue == '+' || chValue == '-')
   // If chValue is either '*','/',or '%', pop all
   // operators from operatorStack until a '+' or '-'
   // is found
  else if(chValue == '*' || chValue == '/' || chValue == '%')
   {
     // If current operatorStack is empty, push character
     // onto operatorStack without any popping.
     if(operatorStack.isEmpty())
      operatorStack.push(new Character(chValue));
     else // Current operatorStack is not empty.
     {
      Character oper = (Character)operatorStack.top();
      while(!oper.equals(new Character('+'))
           && !oper.equals(new Character('-'))
           && ! operatorStack.isEmpty())
      {
       operatorStack.pop();
       postfixString += oper.charValue();
      } // ends while.
      // Then push current operator onto operatorStack.
      operatorStack.push(new Character(chValue));
     } // closes inner else.
    } // closes outer else.

    // If chValue is none of '(',')','+','-','*','/',
    // or '%', it must be an operand.  Append the chValue to
    // postfixString.
   else
    postfixString += chValue;
  } // ends for-loop.

  // Now pop remaining operators from operatorStack
  // and append to postfixString.
  while(!operatorStack.isEmpty())
  {
   Character oper = (Character)operatorStack.top();
```

```
    if(!oper.equals(new Character('(')))
    {
     operatorStack.pop();
     postfixString += oper.charValue();
    }  // closes if
  } // closes while


  return postfixString;
 } // terminates text of toPostfix.
```

It is useful to comment on a number of statements appearing in the text of `toPostfix`. First, we observe that `chValue` is of type `char`. Hence when we compare the contents of `chValue`, we use the primitive comparative operator ==, as in `chValue == '+'`. On the other hand, `operatorStack` is a stack of objects. Thus, if we wish to test whether the `Character` variable `oper` has a specific value, such as `'('`, we must express this as `oper.equals(new Character('('))`.

Furthermore, `postfixString` is a `String` variable. To append a value popped from `operatorStack` at the rear of `postfixString`, we use

```
postfixString += oper.charValue();
```

The += operator accumulates (by concatentation) `char` values at the rear of `postfixString`, and `oper.charValue()` is used to convert the `Character` value of `oper` into its equivalent primitive `char` form.

If we apply `toPostfix` with `infixString` equal to `(2 + 3)*7`, and with `operatorStack` and `postfixString` initially empty, the return value is the postfix string `23+7*`.

7.7 The `Queue` Abstraction

A *queue* is a data structure that differs from a stack in that the values are inserted at one end (called the *base* or *rear*) and removed from the other end (called the *front*). Instead of the last-in, first-out (LIFO) behavior characterizing a stack, a queue stores and processes its contents in a first-in, first-out (FIFO) manner.

As an ADT, queues are generally identified by the following list of admissible operations:

- an insertion operation, inserting a new value at one end[5]
- a removal operation, removing (whenever possible) the value stored at the front of the queue[6]

---

[5]Besides using the identifier "insert" to describe this operation, many computer scientists commonly refer to this as "add" or "enqueue."
[6]This is often referred to as "delete" or "dequeue."

- a Boolean-valued operation testing whether the current queue is empty
- an operation retrieving (whenever possible) the value stored at the front

7.8 **Implementing the Queue ADT**

Unlike the situation with stacks, Java does not provide any predefined implementation of queues in java.util. Therefore, any implementation of queues requires some original design by the programmer.

We begin this design by coding a public interface that captures the essence of the queue ADT described in Section 7.7. This design uses the description of the Node class presented in Section 6.4 and also includes a description of a QueueException class for the purpose of handling exceptions that might arise during processing with queues. The QueueException class is defined as

```
class QueueException extends RuntimeException
{
 // Constructor.
 public QueueException(String str)
 {
  super(str);
 } // terminates text of constructor
} // terminates text of QueueException class.
```

The formal coding of the Queue interface is given by

```
interface Queue
{
 // Tests whether current queue is empty.
 // Returns true if so, false if not.
 public boolean isEmpty();

 // Inserts a value at the rear of the current queue.
 public void insert(Object value);

 // Removes value at the front of the current queue.
 // Precondition: current queue is not empty.
 public void remove() throws QueueException;

 // Retrieves value at the front of the current queue.
 // Precondition: current queue is not empty.
 public Object front() throws QueueException;
} // terminates text of Queue interface.
```

Our first implementation of `Queue` does not use any of the classes or facilities predefined in the Java Collections Framework. Instead, it represents a completely programmer-defined implementation of `Queue` using linked lists. It is described by the class `LinkedQueue`, whose code is given by

```
class LinkedQueue implements Queue
{
 private Node frontRef, rearRef;
 // References to front and rear, respectively, of current queue.

 // Constructor. Initializes queue as empty.
 public LinkedQueue()
 {
  frontRef = null;
  rearRef = null;
 } // terminates text of constructor

 // Code for admissible queue operations.
 // Tests whether current queue is empty
 public boolean isEmpty()
 {
  return (frontRef == null) && (rearRef == null);
 } // terminates text of isEmpty

 // Insert method.
 public void insert (Object value)
 {
  // Construct the new node.
  Node newNode = new Node(value,null);
  // Now insert new node at the rear of the current queue.
  if(isEmpty()) // Current queue is empty
  {
   frontRef = newNode;
   rearRef = newNode;
  }
  else  // Insertion into non-empty queue
  {
   rearRef.next = newNode;
   rearRef = newNode;
  }
 } // terminates text for insertion operation.

 // Remove method.
```

```
public void remove() throws QueueException
{
  if(!isEmpty()) // Current queue is not empty.  Remove element
                 // at the front of the current queue.

    // Suppose current queue contains only one node.
    if(frontRef == rearRef)
    {
      frontRef = null;
      rearRef = null;
    }
    else // more than one node in current queue
    {
      frontRef = frontRef.next;
    }
  else // current queue is empty.  Throw QueueException.
    throw new QueueException("Removal aborted.  Queue is empty");
} // terminates text of remove method.


// Retrieves value at front of the current queue.
// Precondition: current queue is not empty.
public Object front() throws QueueException
{
  if(!isEmpty()) // Current queue is not empty
    return frontRef.info;
  else // Current queue is empty.  Throw QueueException.
    throw new QueueException("Front reference aborted. Queue is empty");
} // terminates text of front() method.
} // terminates text of class LinkedQueue.
```

An example of an Integer-valued queue using the LinkedQueue implementation is pictured in Figure 7.7.

You should write a driver that constructs this queue and then outputs and removes each value until the queue is empty. (See Exercse 7 at the end of the chapter.)

A second implementation uses ArrayList from java.util. Because queues are defined as data structures in which processing is performed exclusively at each end, an efficient implementation is to adapt ArrayList to queues. This is due primarily to the observation that, in any ArrayList object, insertions and removals at either end are of complexity O(1). (See Section 6.4.) The following class gives the details of the formal adaptation of queues using ArrayList.

```
class ArrQueue extends ArrayList implements Queue
{
```

FIGURE 7.7

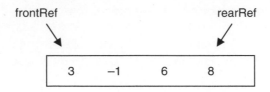

abstraction

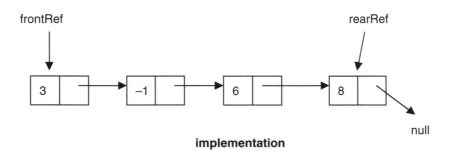

implementation

```
// Data field.
protected ArrayList qu;

// Constructor.  Constructs empty queue.
public ArrQueue()
{
 qu = new ArrayList();
}

// Tests whether current queue is empty.
public boolean isEmpty()
{
 return qu.isEmpty();
}

// Insert operation.  Inserts parameter value at the rear
// of the current queue.
public void insert(Object obj)
{
 qu.add(obj);
}

// Removal operation.  Removes value at the front of the
// current queue.
```

```
// Precondition. Current queue is not empty.
public void remove() throws QueueException
{
 if(!qu.isEmpty())
  qu.remove(0);
 else
  throw new QueueException("Error -- underflow");
}

// Front operator. Retrieves value at the front of the
// current queue.
// Precondition: Current queue is not empty.
public Object front() throws QueueException
{
 if(!qu.isEmpty())
  return qu.get(0);
 else
  throw new QueueException("Error -- underflow");
}

} // terminates text of ArrQueue class.
```

As was seen earlier in the context of implementing stacks using ArrayList, it is possible to apply any instance method defined in ArrayList to any ArrQueue object other than those explicitly defined in the Queue interface. Again, to prevent the application of any such "unwanted" instance method to an ArrQueue object, we must override each of these in a manner similar to that already discussed for ArrStack.

Using this ArrQueue implementation, we can write a driver that constructs the queue of Figure 7.7 and then removes each value in succession until the queue is empty. (See Exercise 8.)

We can also use the LinkedList class defined in java.util to implement queues. We will call the underlying class LinkedQueue1, coded as follows:

```
class LinkedQueue1 extends LinkedList implements Queue
{
// Data field.
protected LinkedList qu;

// Constructor.  Constructs empty queue.
public LinkedQueue1()
{
```

```
      qu = new LinkedList();
    }

    // Tests whether current queue is empty.
    public boolean isEmpty()
    {
     return qu.isEmpty();
    }

    // Insert operation.  Inserts parameter value at the rear
    // of the current queue.
    public void insert(Object obj)
    {
     qu.addLast(obj);
    }

    // Removal operation.  Removes value at the front of the
    // current queue.
    // Precondition. Current queue is not empty.
    public void remove() throws QueueException
    {
     if(!qu.isEmpty())
      qu.removeFirst();
     else
      throw new QueueException("Error -- underflow");
    }

    // Front operator. Retrieves value at the front of the
    // current queue.
    // Precondition: Current queue is not empty.
    public Object front() throws QueueException
    {
     if(!qu.isEmpty())
      return qu.getFirst();
     else
      throw new QueueException("Error -- underflow");
    }

} // terminates text of LinkedQueues class.
```

In a manner similar to that for LinkedQueue and ArrQueue, we can write a driver that constructs the queue of Figure 7.7, systematically outputs the value at the front of the current queue, and then removes that value until the queue is empty. (See Exercise 9.)

7.9 **Applications of the Queue ADT**

We see many instances of queues in our everyday experience. Examples include a group of individuals waiting to enter a theater for a performance, a group of customers waiting in a bank for teller services, or a group of individuals waiting to renew their driver's license. There are also a number of applications of queues in various areas in computer science. One of these is the use of queues either in a timesharing system or in a local network of jobs waiting to acquire the services of a shared line printer. A second application used in timesharing systems involves a queue of processes waiting to be executed in a single shared multiprogrammed central processing unit (CPU).

Application 1: Simulating a Finite Sequence of Processes on the Ready Queue in a Multiprogrammed Environment

In the earliest days of computing, through the mid-1960s, computing was performed using *single-stream batch processing*, which simply means that data and programs were submitted for execution in groups called *batches*, with a single job submitted for processing at any given time. All other jobs were delayed until the current job completed execution. Of course, this represented a highly inefficient way to operate, because it is rarely the case that any single job uses all of a system's resources. Even at this early stage of development, operating systems programmers observed that when a given job in execution was waiting for the completion of the execution of an external service, such as acquiring new input data or by depositing newly computed data in a permanent storage device (a segment of magnetic tape or a sector of a disk), the CPU remained idle. It would therefore be extremely important for this idle time for a process to be better utilized by having a second process submitted to the CPU to begin executing. In fact, the outcome of this analysis was the observation that submitting more than one job to the CPU at any given time, with the mixture of submitted jobs representing a diversity of computing activities, was the best way to minimize the idle time of the processor. This also had the very desirable side effect of optimizing the active time of the CPU and increasing system *throughput*, defined as the amount of data generated by the computer for a fixed and given period of time.

As a consequence, operating system designers developed the concept of *multiprogramming*, in which several jobs are kept in main memory at one time. The processor then switches from one job to another as is necessary to minimize the processor's idle time. More advanced operating systems followed in the early 1970s and were designed to serve a number of *interactive users*, namely users who communicate with the computer via terminals.

Because the user is present and interacting directly with the computer, the operating system must be designed with the objective of responding as quickly as possible to the users' requests. The fulfillment of this objective optimized the system's productivity. Thus, *timesharing systems* were designed as a response to this, where "timesharing" refers to the fact that several processes are permitted to share processing time in the CPU, with one process currently executing and the rest in a state of "readiness" waiting to execute.[7]

The first example we present shows how queues are used to simulate a multiprogrammed system in an elementary setting. The version offered here is one in which a fixed number of processes are submitted for execution by a single timeshared CPU, with the first being the only one in the "running" state. This form maintains a process queue in which each entry is an integer value representing the number of processing steps required for that job to complete its execution. Every process runs to completion, its execution beginning when its predecessor in the queue completes execution. As that process completes execution, it is purged (popped) from the queue, with its successor in the queue being the next process to execute. This version does not allow any new process to be added during the course of execution: only those processes submitted originally are permitted to execute, in the order of their submission into the queue. Thus, these processes execute in a FIFO order.

How do we design the simulator? We will design an *interactive* version, which first prompts the user for the number of processes to be monitored. The int value returned will be stored in a variable called size. We will also construct an Object-valued queue called processQueue, initially empty, to store the number of execution steps for each process. At this point, the user will be prompted to supply the number of such steps for each process. The values are inserted into processQueue using the sequence

```
steps = Integer.parseInt(intIS.readLine());
process_queue.insert(steps);
```

where steps is an int-valued variable storing the number of execution steps for any single process. This sequence is actually the body of a for-loop that cycles size times. When this loop completes execution, processQueue holds size values in the order of their appearance in the input sequence.

The following discussion describes the key steps of the simulation. We begin by describing the execution, one step at a time, of the processes

---

[7]We distinguish between a *job* and a *process* by observing that when a job is admitted to the CPU for execution, it assumes the internal form of a process. The queue then holds a finite sequence of processes in the "ready" state awaiting execution by the CPU.

whose steps are stored in processQueue beginning at the front, because this describes a FIFO environment. In our simulator, this is done by invoking the method monitorQueue, whose signature is given by

```
monitorQueue(ArrQueue procQueue, int[] counter);
```

where counter keeps track of the process number.

The first step initializes counter at 1. Control of execution now transfers to a while-loop whose entry condition depends on whether the current contents of procQueue are empty. If procQueue is not empty, this signifies that there are processes remaining to be monitored; consequently, the while-loop is reentered. On the other hand, if procQueue is empty, entry into the while-loop is blocked and represents the termination of the monitoring process. The monitoring process itself consists of a description of the number of the process currently executing (that is, in the running state) and the step number in that process. After the process completes execution, the value of counter is incremented, and the process currently at the front of procQueue is removed. This loop terminates when procQueue eventually becomes empty.

The complete text of monitorQueue is given by

```
public static void monitorQueue(ArrQueue procQueue,int[] counter)
{
  counter[0] = 1;
  while(!procQueue.isEmpty())
  {
   System.out.println("Process " + counter[0] + " is executing.");
   for(int index = 0; index < ((Integer)procQueue.front()).intValue();
         ++index)
   {
    System.out.print("Process " + counter[0] + " is executing Step");
    System.out.println(index + 1);
   }
   System.out.println("Process " + counter[0] + " terminates
                   execution.");
   // Go to the next process.
   ++counter[0];
   // Purge procQueue of the completed process.
   procQueue.remove();
  } // terminates while-loop
  // At this point, simulation process terminates.
  // Prepare to exit.
  System.out.println("Entire execution shuts down.");
 } // terminates text of monitorQueue.
```

The driver is used primarily to set up `processQueue` by prompting the user for the number of processes to be inserted into `processQueue` and the number of execution steps for each such process:

```
public static void main(String [] args) throws IOException
 {
  BufferedReader intIS = new BufferedReader(
                        new InputStreamReader(System.in));
  int[] processCounter = new int[1]; // Stores the process number.
  int size, // stores the number of processes
      steps; // stores the number of executable steps of
             // any process.
  // Prompt user for the number of processes:
  System.out.println("Input the number of processes:");
  size = Integer.parseInt(intIS.readLine());
  // Construct queue holding the number of processing steps
  // for each process.
  ArrQueue processQueue = new ArrQueue();
  // Prompt user for contents of processQueue:
  System.out.println("Input " + size + " integers, representing");
  System.out.println("the execution steps of the ");
  System.out.println(size + " processes");
  // Input these values into processQueue:
  for(int index = 0; index < size; ++index)
  {
   steps = Integer.parseInt(intIS.readLine());
   processQueue.insert(new Integer(steps));
  }
  // Echo the initial size of processQueue after loading.
  System.out.println("The process queue now has " + size);
  System.out.println("members");

  // Monitor the action of processQueue:
  monitorQueue(processQueue,processCounter);
 } // terminates text of main method.
```

The following represents the result of a test run of this program:

```
Input the number of processes:
4
Input 4 integers, representing the execution
steps of each of the 4 processes.
3
3
4
```

2

```
The queue now has 4 members
Process 1 is executing.
Process 1 is executing Step1
Process 1 is executing Step2
Process 1 is executing Step3
Process 1 terminates execution.
Process 2 is executing.
Process 2 is executing Step1
Process 2 is executing Step2
Process 2 is executing Step3
Process 2 terminates execution.
Process 3 is executing.
Process 3 is executing Step1
Process 3 is executing Step2
Process 3 is executing Step3
Process 3 is executing Step4
Process 3 terminates execution.
Process 4 is executing.
Process 4 is executing Step1
Process 4 is executing Step2
Process 4 terminates execution.
Entire execution shuts down.
```

Application 2: Simulating a Finite Sequence of Processes in a Multiprogrammed Environment Using a Time Quantum

In Application 1, we simulated the activity of a multiprogrammed system of processes residing simultaneously in main memory, which executes in sequence until completion. In that setting, once a specific process begins executing, it continues to execute until completion, regardless of the number of processing steps required. Thus, for example, if Processes 1, 2, 3 currently reside in memory with respective steps 7, 2048, 5, these complete execution in the order presented. Consequently, Process 3, having only 5 steps, must wait until Process 1 and Process 2 terminate to begin executing. We might not judge this as a major hardship, but it certainly represents a significant delay in the presence of Process 2. This is particularly emphasized if Process 3 is time critical—that is, must execute as soon as possible.

Our simulation in Application 1 makes no accommodation for such a situation. In practice, however, there are several ways to cope with this situation. One way is to place a *priority* on each process submitted for execution, with those of highest priority placed in the ready queue before those of any lower priority to ensure their rapid completion. The type of container used to implement this is a *priority queue,* discussed in the next section. Another strategy commonly used to cope with such situations employs ordinary queues and is the method described in this application. It is often used in conjunction with priorities and involves the implementation of a *quantum.* Each process is inserted initially on the queue of ready processes and gradually moves to the front of the queue. When the process arrives at the front and when the CPU becomes available, the state of the process changes from "ready" to "running," and the CPU begins executing the steps of that process. The act of assigning the CPU to the process currently at the front of the queue is known as *dispatching* and is performed by special operating systems software called the *dispatcher.* To prevent any lengthy process from monopolizing the CPU for any significant amount of time, such as that just described for the processes 1, 2, and 3, it is possible for the hardware to set an *interval timer* to allow this process to execute during a preset time interval (or *quantum*). If the number of steps does not exceed the quantum, the process completes execution and is purged from the system. Otherwise, the process executes as many steps as the value of the quantum permits and is removed from the queue, going from the "running" to the "ready" state, after which it is inserted onto the queue once again with the remaining steps required for it to complete execution. It again moves gradually to the front, gains the CPU once again, and continues in this way until it finally completes execution.

We will again design software to simulate this situation, using a queue to store the sequence of ready processes. Our first task is to design a way of identifying the distinct processes. Unlike the situation in the simulator described in Application 1, it is no longer necessarily true that a process, once executing, goes to completion. Therefore, we must include the process number in our naming convention, along with the number of execution steps remaining for that process to complete. Thus, the queue will not contain single `Integer` values as it did before. Instead, it will be replaced by two `int`-valued queues: one for the process number and a second for the remaining steps. It also follows that in this case a process cannot be identified simply by locating its position in the queue. In fact, it could be the case that, at some point of execution of the simulator, a value in the queue of process numbers is smaller than that of a predecessor.

How do we implement this design in software? We will take a practical approach, using `int`-valued replacements for many of the formal implementations defined in Section 7.8. For example, we replace the `Queue` interface by

```
interface intQueue
{
  // Tests whether current queue is empty.
```

```
 // Returns true if so, false if not.
 public boolean isEmpty();

 // Inserts a value at the rear of the current queue.
 public void insert(int value);

 // Removes value at the front of the current queue.
 // Precondition: Current queue is not empty.
 public void remove() throws QueueException;

 // Retrieves value at the front of the current queue.
 // Precondition: Current queue is not empty.
 public int front() throws QueueException;

} // terminates text of intQueue interface.
```

The QueueException class is identical with that defined in Section 7.8. In addition, nodes are int-valued—that is, our nodded contain int-valued info components:

```
class Node
{
 // Constructor. Copies the info component and the link
 // to the next node.
 Node(int d, Node n)
 {
  info = d;
  next = n;
 }
 int info;
 Node next;
} // Terminates text of Node class.
```

Using these preliminaries, we can define a class intLinkedQueue implementing intQueue. This is done by taking the text of LinkedQueue seen in Section 7.8 and replacing each reference to Object by int and every reference to Node objects using Object-valued info components to those using info components that are int-valued.

Because a process is defined in this context as a pair of int values, one for the process number and the second for the remaining execution steps, we can view any process as a single object of the class Process defined as

```
class Process
{
 int procNumber;
```

```
    int steps;
}
```

Finally, we can define two corresponding `int`-valued queues. The first is the queue holding the currently active process numbers, defined as

```
intLinkedQueue procNumberQueue = new intLinkedQueue();
```

The second holds the corresponding steps needed for each process to complete execution, defined as

```
intLinkedQueue stepsQueue = new intLinkedQueue();
```

Our contact with the `Process` class applies only at initialization. All that is required from the user is the number of processes to be simulated and the number of processing steps involved in each. The initial forms of `procNumberQueue` and `stepsQueue` will still be in the usual sequential order so far as the naming of processes is concerned. As the simulation progresses, however, it is important to maintain the same sequential order on both queues if it involves removal from the front with possible reinsertion of values at the rear.

We illustrate these ideas with the following example. Suppose `size` is an `int`-valued variable whose value is input by the user and represents the number of ready processes originally submitted to the system. Our version will prompt the user for the value of `size`. Assume that value is 3. Then the user will be prompted for three `int` values representing the respective number of processing steps involved initially for each of the three processes. Suppose, in response, the user inputs the sequence

2

12

4

The resulting initial number of steps is 2 for `Process 1`, 12 for `Process 2`, and 4 for `Process 3`. These pairs of values will be placed in order into `procNumberQueue` and `stepsQueue`, as described in Figure 7.8.

FIGURE 7.8   procNumberQueue   stepsQueue

| 1 | 2 | 3 |

(front)   (back)

| 2 | 12 | 4 |

(front)   (back)

Suppose the declaration

```
final int quantum = 3;
```

defines the size of the quantum, and the constructor

```
Process proc = new Process();
```

constructs a new `Process` object for each process to be simulated, responding to the prompt

```
Input 3 integers, representing the
execution steps of each of the 3
processes.
```

The input operation is then accomplished using

```
for(int k = 0; k < size; ++k)
{
 proc.procNumber = k + 1;
 proc.steps = Integer.parseInt(intIS.readLine());
 procNumberQueue.insert(proc.procNumber);
 stepsQueue.insert(proc.steps);
} // terminates for-loop
```

If the number of remaining steps does not exceed the value of the quantum, the process completes execution during this cycle, and the current values at the front of each of procNumberQueue and stepsQueue is removed. Otherwise, the value of proc.steps is adjusted to reflect the fact that another cycle has terminated without completing the execution of the process. In its adjusted form, the value of each of proc.procNumber and proc.steps is inserted at the rear of the respective queues procNumberQueue and stepsQueue. This key processing step can be implemented using

```
public static void monitorQueue(
                          intLinkedQueue procNumberQueue,
                          intLinkedQueue stepsQueue,
                          Process proc,
                          int quantum)
{
  while((!procNumberQueue.isEmpty())&&(!stepsQueue.isEmpty()))
  {
   System.out.print("Process " + procNumberQueue.front() + " is");
   System.out.println(" executing.");
   int counter = stepsQueue.front(); // Counts number of remaining
                                     // processing steps.
   if(counter > quantum) // Process does not complete on this cycle.
   {
     System.out.print("Process " + procNumberQueue.front() +
                      " executes ");
     System.out.println("for the complete quantum of " + quantum);
     System.out.println("steps and does not terminate on this cycle");
     counter = counter - quantum;
     proc.procNumber = procNumberQueue.front();
     proc.steps = counter;
     procNumberQueue.insert(proc.procNumber);
```

```
      stepsQueue.insert(proc.steps);
  } // completes if-clause.
  else // Process at front completes execution on this cycle
       // because counter <= quantum.
  {
     System.out.print("Process " + procNumberQueue.front());
     System.out.println(" completes execution in this cycle in ");
     System.out.println(counter + " steps.");
  } // completes else-clause.
  procNumberQueue.remove();
  stepsQueue.remove();
  } // completes while-loop.
  // At this point, procNumberQueue and stepsQueue are empty.
  // Indicate that this signifies shutdown.
  System.out.println("Entire system shuts down.");
} // terminates text of monitorQueue.
```

At the point of completion of the `while`-loop, all processes have executed to completion, `procNumberQueue` and `stepsQueue` are empty, and our monitor terminates with the message

Entire system shuts down.

The version we have presented assumes a quantum value of 3. However, this value can be chosen to be any nonnegative integer. The complete form of the method serving as the driver for the simulator can be given as

```
public static void main(String [] args) throws IOException
 {
  BufferedReader intIS = new BufferedReader(
                         new InputStreamReader(System.in));
  int size; // number of processes

  final int quantum = 3;

  // queue holding process numbers.
  intLinkedQueue procNumberQueue = new intLinkedQueue();

  // queue holding corresponding steps:
  intLinkedQueue stepsQueue = new intLinkedQueue();

  Process proc = new Process();

  // Prompt user for the number of processes to monitor:
  System.out.println("Input the number of processes:");
  size = Integer.parseInt(intIS.readLine());
```

```
System.out.println("Input " + size + " integers, representing the");
System.out.println("execution steps of each of the " + size);
System.out.println("processes.");

// Input initial data for each process.
for(int k = 0; k < size; ++k)
{
 proc.procNumber = k + 1;
 proc.steps = Integer.parseInt(intIS.readLine());
 procNumberQueue.insert(proc.procNumber);
 stepsQueue.insert(proc.steps);
} // terminates for-loop

// Describe activity of the execution sequence by invoking
// monitorQueue.
monitorQueue(procNumberQueue, stepsQueue, proc, quantum);

} // terminates text of main method
```

Let us examine a trace of the execution of the while-loop using the input information and initial description of procNumberQueue and stepsQueue as described in Figure 7.8. Process 1 executes to completion in two steps; consequently, its process number is removed from procNumberQueue and the number of remaining steps (2) is removed from stepsQueue. This results in procNumberQueue and stepsQueue as described in Figure 7.9.

FIGURE 7.9   procNumberQueue   stepsQueue

| 2 | 3 | | 12 | 4 |
|---|---| |----|---|

(front)   (rear)   (front)   (rear)

Now Process 2 is at the front of procNumberQueue, and 12 (the number of executable steps remaining to complete Process 2) is at the front of stepsQueue. Process 2 executes for the entire quantum without completion, leaving the number of steps left to complete at 9. These values are removed from the front of the respective procNumberQueue and stepsQueue and then reinserted, as in Figure 7.10:

FIGURE 7.10   procNumberQueue   stepsQueue

| 3 | 2 | | 4 | 9 |
|---|---| |---|---|

(front)   (rear)   (front)   (rear)

Process 3 then begins execution for the first time and runs for the entire quantum without completion, leaving one remaining processing step to complete execution. These values are removed and reinserted into the respective queues, with the result as described by Figure 7.11.

FIGURE 7.11

procNumberQueue

2	3

(front)   (rear)

stepsQueue

9	1

(front)   (rear)

Process 2 resumes execution for the entire quantum and again does not complete on this cycle, with 6 processing steps remaining to complete execution. The result of this is as in Figure 7.12.

FIGURE 7.12

procNumberQueue

3	2

(front)   (rear)

stepsQueue

1	6

(front)   (rear)

Process 3 then resumes and completes execution in this cycle in one step. Thus 3 is removed from procNumberQueue and 1 is removed from stepsQueue without any further reinsertion. This is described in Figure 7.13.

FIGURE 7.13

procNumberQueue

2

(front)
(rear)

stepsQueue

6

(front)
(rear)

This indicates that Process 2 is the only remaining process, with 6 steps left to complete execution. Thus, Process 2 resumes execution and executes for the entire quantum without completion, with its process number and the number of steps remaining to complete execution removed and reinserted at the rear of the respective procNumberQueue and stepsQueue, as described in Figure 7.14.

FIGURE 7.14

procNumberQueue

2

(front)
(rear)

stepsQueue

3

(front)
(rear)

Finally, `Process 2` resumes execution and completes on this cycle, resulting in empty queues for each of `procNumberQueue` and `stepsQueue`.

The output for this sample run is

```
Input the number of processes:
3
Input 3 integers, representing the
execution steps of each of the 3
processes.
2
12
4
Process 1 is executing.
Process 1 completes execution in this cycle in
2 steps.
Process 2 is executing.
Process 2 executes for the complete quantum of 3
steps and does not terminate on this cycle
Process 3 is executing.
Process 3 executes for the complete quantum of 3
steps and does not terminate on this cycle
Process 2 is executing.
Process 2 executes for the complete quantum of 3
steps and does not terminate on this cycle
Process 3 is executing.
Process 3 completes execution in this cycle in
1 steps.
Process 2 is executing.
Process 2 executes for the complete quantum of 3
steps and does not terminate on this cycle
Process 2 is executing.
Process 2 completes execution in this cycle in
3 steps.
Entire system shuts down.
```

We chose to design the simulator using two queues: `procNumberQueue`, storing the process numbers submitted to the system, and `stepsQueue`, storing the number of remaining executable steps of each of the processed. As we observed, this led to an efficient implementation of the problem of simulating a finite sequence of processes in a multiprogrammed environment using a time quantum. However, several alternative implementations are possible. One such is to first define the class `Process` as we have already done, but instead of identifying two "parallel" int-valued queues we could define a *single* queue of int-valued pairs (m,n), where m is the current process number and n is the number of executable steps remaining for that process to complete execution. Such a queue of pairs can then be defined as an instance using `LinkedList` or `ArrayList`. In either case, insertions and removals in the underlying list involve individual *pairs* (instead of two matching operations—one for the process number and the other for the number of remaining processing steps). The downside of this implementation is that insertions and removals involve generic operations and conversions from `int` to `Object` and back, causing a significant amount of processing overhead. The details of this implementation is left as an exercise. (See the Programming Projects section at the end of this chapter.)

7.10   **The `PriorityQueue` Abstraction**

A *priority queue* is a data structure differing from stacks and ordinary queues in that the value to be removed next is the "highest" value contained in the structure. Thus, we can characterize a priority queue either as empty or as a finite sequence of values of some well-defined data type `T`, where

- a binary relational operator < is defined for any two elements of `T`
- the value in the sequence immediately available for removal (or retrieval) is the value of "highest priority" in the sense of <

In this sense, a priority queue does not necessarily classify either as a LIFO or FIFO container. As an ADT, priority queues are identified by the following list of admissible operations:

- an `insert` operation, admitting a new value `v` into the priority queue
- a `remove` operation, removing (whenever possible) the value of highest priority in the current priority queue
- a `boolean`-valued operation `isEmpty`, testing whether the current priority queue is empty—returning `true` if so, and `false` if not
- a `front` operation, retrieving (whenever possible) the value of highest priority currently in the priority queue

Unlike its counterpart in C++ and similar to ordinary queues in Java, `java.util` does not provide any predefined implementation of priority queues. Therefore, just as was the case for ordinary queues, any implementation of priority queues has to be designed to some extent by the programmer.

We begin this design by defining a `PriorityQueueException` class for the purpose of handling exception, should such arise in the processing of priority queues. The code for this class is nearly identical with that for ordinary queues:

```
class PriorityQueueException extends RuntimeException
{
```

```
// Constructor.
public PriorityQueueException(String str)
{
 super(str);
} // terminates text of constructor.
} // terminates text of PriorityQueueException class.
```

The formal coding of the `PriorityQueue` interface can be given in generic form as described in the following. Note that `Comparable` is used instead of `Object` because priority queues are defined only for those data types for which any two of its members are comparable.

```
interface PriorityQueue
{
 // Tests whether current priority queue is empty.
 // Returns true if so, false if not.
 public boolean isEmpty();

 // Inserts a value into the current priority queue.
 public void insert(Comparable value);

 // Removes value with the highest priority from the
 // current priority queue, whenever possible.
 // Precondition: current priority queue is not empty.
 public void remove() throws PriorityQueueException;

 // Retrieves value of highest priority currently stored
 // in the priority queue.
 // Precondition: current priority queue is not empty.
 public Comparable front() throws PriorityQueueException;
} // terminates text of PriorityQueue interface.
```

EXAMPLE 7.6

Assume we have constructed an `Integer`-valued priority queue `prQueue` that is currently empty, and suppose we insert the following sequence of values into `prQueue`:

2   3   -1   7   9

If we then remove values from `prQueue` until it is empty, we obtain the output sequence

9   7   3   2   -1

Here we associate the value inserted into the priority queue with its priority. Thus, 9 has a priority of 9, 3 has a priority of 3, -1 has a priority of -1, and so on.

7.11 **Implementing the `PriorityQueue` ADT**

How are priority queues implemented in Java? We will design an implementation of the `PriorityQueue` interface using `ArrayList` and two predefined `List` methods `sort` and `reverse` from Java's Collections Framework that were first defined in Section 6.8. Our design includes an `insert` method that sorts the values of the priority queue in reverse order each time a new value is inserted. This will assure that, in the case of a nonempty priority queue, the value in the queue of that highest priority will always appear at the front.

The following is a class implementing the `PriorityQueue` interface using `ArrayList`.

```
class ArrPriorityQueue extends ArrayList implements PriorityQueue
{
 // Data field.
 protected ArrayList prq;

 // Constructor.  Constructs empty priority queue.
 public ArrPriorityQueue()
 {
  prq = new ArrayList();
 }

 // Tests whether current priority queue is empty.
 public boolean isEmpty()
 {
  return prq.isEmpty();
 }

 // Insert operation.  Inserts parameter value at its
 // proper position in the priority queue.
 public void insert(Comparable value)
 {
  // Add new value at rear.
  prq.add(value);
  // Now sort new sequence in ascending order.
  Collections.sort(prq);
  // Reverse the values of the sequence.
  Collections.reverse(prq);
 }

 // Removal operation.  Removes value of highest priority
 // from the current priority queue.  By construction, that
```

```
// value appears at the front of the current priority queue.
// Precondition: Current priority queue is not empty.
public void remove() throws PriorityQueueException
{
 if(!prq.isEmpty()) prq.remove(0);
 else
   throw new PriorityQueueException("Error -- underflow");
}


// Retrieves value of highest priority currently stored
// in the priority queue.
// Precondition: Current priority queue is not empty.
public Comparable front() throws PriorityQueueException
{
 if(!prq.isEmpty()) return (Comparable)prq.get(0);
 else
   throw new PriorityQueueException("Error -- underflow");
}


} // terminates text of class ArrPriorityQueue
```

The main method described below is used to execute the result described in Example 7.6.

```
public static void main(String [] args)
 {
  // Construct Integer-valued priority queue using ArrPriorityQueue.
  ArrPriorityQueue prQueue = new ArrPriorityQueue();
  // Insert five Integer values into prQueue:
  prQueue.insert(new Integer(2));
  prQueue.insert(new Integer(3));
  prQueue.insert(new Integer(-1));
  prQueue.insert(new Integer(7));
  prQueue.insert(new Integer(9));

  System.out.println("Empty out current prQueue:");
  while(!prQueue.isEmpty())
  {
   System.out.print(prQueue.front() + "   ");
   prQueue.remove();
  }

 }  // terminates text of main method
```

The explicit output obtained from executing this method is

```
Empty out current prQueue:
9   7   3   2   -1
```

Another possible implementation of the `PriorityQueue` interface mimics the implementation just described but now uses `LinkedList` instead of `ArrayList`. We leave the formal details of the coding of this implementation as an exercise.

7.12   **Applications of the `PriorityQueue` ADT**

Priority queues have many useful applications. For example, we can observe that priority queues are often used in designing operating systems to choose the next process waiting in the ready queue to obtain the services of the CPU.

Application 1: Simulating the Ready Queue of Processes in a Multiprogrammed Environment

In practice, the ready queue of processes awaiting the services of the CPU takes the form of a priority queue because these processes are generally classified according to several different levels of priority. Usually, processes initiated by those systems programmers whose primary duty is to monitor and improve the efficiency of the system's operations have a significantly higher priority than those of other members of the staff. Consequently, such processes execute earlier than those of other users. This is accomplished by implementing the ready queue of processes as a priority queue.

We begin the simulation by prompting the user for the number of processes to be inserted into the priority queue and then prompt for the priority of each process. We assume the priority of each process will be a positive integer, with larger integers indicating processes of higher priority. As before, we will not allow any new processes to be inserted into the priority queue after the initial input, and in this particular case we will not output the number of processing steps nor involve a quantum. These additional attributes may be treated in later applications.

The simulator can be designed with a main method prompting the user for the number of processes and the priority of each. The activity of the priority queue will be handled by the method `monitorPriorityQueue`, with the signature

```
static void monitorPriorityQueue(ArrPriorityQueue prQueue);
```

Our design calls for `monitorPriorityQueue` to provide a step-by-step account of the progress of the processes execution with the designated priority values. Its code is given by

```
static void monitorPriorityQueue(ArrPriorityQueue prQueue)
 {
  while(!prQueue.isEmpty())
   {
    System.out.print("Process with priority " + prQueue.front());
    System.out.println(" is executing.");
    System.out.println("This process terminates execution.");
    prQueue.remove();
   } // terminates while-loop
   // At this point, simulation process terminates.
   // Prepare to exit.
   System.out.println("Entire execution shuts down.");
  } // terminates text of monitorPriorityQueue
```

A driver for `monitorPriorityQueue` is given as

```
public static void main(String [] args) throws IOException
 {
  BufferedReader intIS = new BufferedReader(
                          new InputStreamReader(System.in));

  int size,  // stores the number of processes
    priority; // stores the priority of each process.

  // Prompt user for the number of processes.
  System.out.println("Input the number of processes:");
  size = Integer.parseInt(intIS.readLine());

  // Construct priority queue storing the priority of each process.
  ArrPriorityQueue processQueue = new ArrPriorityQueue();

  // Prompt user for the contents of processQueue:
  System.out.println("Input " + size + " integers, representing the");
  System.out.println("respective priorities of each of the");
  System.out.println(size + " processes:");

  // Input these values into processQueue:
  for(int index = 0; index < size; ++index)
  {
   priority = Integer.parseInt(intIS.readLine());
```

```
   processQueue.insert(new Integer(priority));
 }

// Echo initial size of processQueue after loading.
//System.out.print("processQueue now has " + processQueue.size());
//System.out.println(" members.");

// Monitor the activities of processQueue:
monitorPriorityQueue(processQueue);

} // terminates text of main method.
```

Here is a sample run of the program:

```
Input the number of processes:
5
Input 5 integers, representing the
respective priorities of each of the
5 processes:
7
6
3
4
7
Process with priority 7 is executing.
This process terminates execution.
Process with priority 7 is executing.
This process terminates execution.
Process with priority 6 is executing.
This process terminates execution.
Process with priority 4 is executing.
This process terminates execution.
Process with priority 3 is executing.
This process terminates execution.
Entire execution shuts down.
```

Thus, the output indicates that five processes were inserted into the priority queue with the respective priorities 7, 6, 3, 4, 7, and the activity of the priority queue is to execute the two processes with priority 7 first, followed in order by those of priorities 6, 4, and 3.

Application 2: Simulating the Ready Queue of Processes in a Multiprogrammed Environment, Counting Processing Steps

The simulator for the priority queue of ready processes described in Application 1 is fine as far as it goes, but it does not give a description of the number of steps executed by each process whenever that process acquires the running state. To provide for this, we must give a more detailed description of each process, defining the specific process number, number of executable steps for that process, and its priority. Part of the description includes a definition of the "less" relationship existing between any two processes. This relationship is used as the basis of the `sort` method executed in the `insert` instance method defined in the `ArrPriorityQueue` implementation of the `PriorityQueue` interface. We will accomplish this by designing a class `Process` that involves three data members: its process number, number of remaining executable steps, and its priority. We will also define a separate object constructed from the predefined `Comparator` class formalizing the "less" relationship comparing two such processes (`Process` objects), serving as a basis for the `sort` method described earlier. Thus, we view each process as an object constructed from the `Process` class expressed as an ordered triple of `Integer` values: The first value is the process number, the second is the number of remaining executable steps, and the third is the priority of the process.

The definition of the `Process` class is given by

```
class Process
{
 // Data members.
  Integer processNumber;
  Integer steps;
  Integer priority;
}
```

In order to define the "less" relationship, we first note that the objects that are to appear on the priority queue will be objects constructed from the `Process` class, which we can view as *ordered triples* of `Integer` values. Consequently, when sorting the objects on this priority queue, we must create a way to compare two `Process` objects and then decide which comes first. This comparison is not predefined in any class in Java's library. To deal with such situations, Java provides the `Comparator` interface. This interface defines two abstract methods, given as

```
// Returns a negative integer, or zero, or a positive integer, to
// indicate that, respectively, o1 is less than o2, or o1 and o2
// are equal, or o1 is greater than o2.
public abstract int compare(Object o1, Object o2);


// Returns true if the current object is equal to obj; otherwise false.
public abstract boolean equals(Object obj);
```

The `compare` method is similar to the more familiar `compareTo`, except that it involves two arguments instead of only one. In addition, although `equals` has been defined explicitly as an instance method of `Comparator`, it is hardly ever used because `equals` already appears as an instance method of the `Object` class. Thus, there is no need to invoke this explicit form in our discussion.

The definition of `insert` for `ArrPriorityQueue` involves a call to `Collections.sort`. The version we have used up to now assumes a default "less than" relationship `<` applied to individual `Integer` values, because these were stored on the priority queues used so far. This is no longer the case—instead, ordered triples of `Integer` values appear on this priority queue. To accommodate this, we must make a number of changes in the `PriorityQueue` interface and its implementation class `ArrPriorityQueue` after designing a "less" relationship applicable to `Process` objects.

We first design the "less" relationship. This relationship must order `Process` objects in order of decreasing priority. The definition of a `Comparator` object we seek can be done using

```
static final Comparator less = new Comparator()
{
 public int compare(Object o1, Object o2)
 {
  Process p1 = (Process)o1;
  Process p2 = (Process)o2;
  return p2.priority.compareTo(p1.priority);
 }
};
```

The reason for including the semicolon in the last line is that the formal definition of `less` is given within the text of the specific form of `compare`, along with the fact that `less` is being constructed as a specific `Comparator` object.

The formal definition of the `PriorityQueue` interface now recognizes that objects appearing on the priority queue are `Process` objects rather than `Comparable` objects:

```
 interface PriorityQueue
{
 // Tests whether current priority queue is empty.
 // Returns true if so, false if not.
 public boolean isEmpty();

 // Inserts a value into the current priority queue.
 public void insert(Process value);

 // Removes value with the highest priority from the
 // current priority queue, whenever possible.
```

```
// Precondition: current priority queue is not empty.
public void remove() throws PriorityQueueException;

// Retrieves value of highest priority currently stored
// in the priority queue.
// Precondition: current priority queue is not empty.
public Process front() throws PriorityQueueException;
} // terminates text of PriorityQueue interface.
```

So far as the revisions of the implementation class `ArrPriorityQueue` are concerned, the only changes appear in the text of `insert` and `front`, as follows:

```
public Process front() throws PriorityQueueException
{
  if(!prq.isEmpty()) return (Process)prq.get(0),
  else
    throw new PriorityQueueException("Error - underflow");
}
```

The `insert` method involves a new version of `Collections.sort` with a second `Comparable` parameter directly invoking `less`, in the form

```
public void insert(Process value)
{
  prq.add(value);
  Collections.sort(prq,less);
}
```

Unlike the version of `insert` discussed earlier, there is no need to include `Collections.reverse(prq)` in this text, because `Collections.sort(prq,less)` already rearranges the triples on this priority queue in order of decreasing priority.

As we will see in greater detail in Section 8.3, this version of `Collections.sort` sorts any list of `Process` objects according to decreasing priority values. This is exactly what was needed to formally define a priority queue of `Process` objects.

Once these processes are inserted into the priority queue, its behavior is monitored by the following method, which indicates which of the submitted processes is currently executing, its priority, and the current execution steps. The code for this monitor is given by

```
static  void monitorPriorityQueue(ArrPriorityQueue prQueue)
{
 while(!prQueue.isEmpty())
 {
   System.out.println("Process " + (prQueue.front().processNumber).intValue()
                  + " is executing.");
```

```
System.out.println("This process has priority " +
                        (prQueue.front().priority).intValue() );
for(int index = 1; index1 <= (prQueue.front().steps).intValue();
            ++index)
System.out.println("Process " +
            (prQueue.front().processNumber).intValue()
                " is executing step: " + index);
// terminates text of for-loop
System.out.println("Process " +
            (prQueue.front().processNumber).intValue()
                + " terminates execution.");
// Go to the next process.
prQueue.remove();
} // terminates text of while-loop.
// At this point, simulation process terminates.
// Prepare to exit.
System.out.println("Entire execution shuts down.");
} // terminates text of monitorPriorityQueue.
```

Finally, the main method drives the monitor after it has prompted the user for the necessary input information and after the priority queue has been constructed.

```
public static void main(String [] args) throws IOException
{
BufferedReader intIS = new BufferedReader(
                        New InputStrreamReader(System.in));
ArrPriorityQueue processQueue = new ArrPriorityQueue();
int size;  // Number of processes submitted to priority queue.
Process proc = new Process(); // Constructs object proc from
                                // Process class.
System.out.println("Input the number of processes to be monitored:");
size = Integer.parseInt(intIS.readLine());
System.out.println("Input the number of executions of each of the "
                + size + " processes,");
System.out.println("followed by the priority of each of the "
                + size + " processes.");
for(int index = 0; index < size; ++index)
{
proc.processNumber = new Integer(index + 1);
System.out.println("Process Number " +
                        (proc.processNumber).intValue());
System.out.println("---------------");
System.out.print("Number of steps: ");
```

```
    int stepValue = Integer.parseInt(intIS.readLine());
    proc.steps = new Integer(stepValue);
    System.out.print("Priority: ");
    int priorityValue = Integer.parseInt(intIS.readLine());
    proc.priority = new Integer(priorityValue);
    System.out.println();
    processQueue.insert(proc);
  } // terminates text of for-loop.

 monitorPriorityQueue(processQueue);
} // terminates text of main method.
```

A sample run of the main method follows, with diagrams illustrating the current form of the priority queue during the progress of execution.

```
Input the number of processes to be monitored:
4
Input the number of executions of each of the 4 processes,
followed by the priority of each of the 4 processes.
Process Number 1
---------------
Number of steps: 5
Priority: 4
Process Number 2
---------------
Number of steps: 3
Priority: 6
Process Number 3
---------------
Number of steps: 4
Priority: 4
Process Number 4
---------------
Number of steps: 6
Priority: 3
```

After inserting these processes into `processQueue`, the priority queue can be pictured as in Figure 7.15a.

FIGURE 7.15a   processQueue

(2,3,6)	(1,5,4)	(3,4,4)	(4,6,3)

(front)   (rear)

Here each process can be described as an ordered triple whose first component is the process number, with the second component describing the number of remaining executable steps, and the third component giving the priority. Execution of the monitor continues with the output

```
Process 2 is executing.
This process has priority 6
Process 2 is executing step: 1
Process 2 is executing step: 2
Process 2 is executing step: 3
Process 2 terminates execution.
```

At this point, the triple currently at the front of `processQueue` is removed, producing the result shown in Figure 7.15b.

FIGURE 7.15b   processQueue

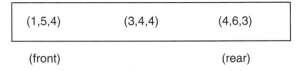

(front)   (rear)

The steps of execution continue as

```
Process 1 is executing.
This process has priority 4
Process 1 is executing step: 1
Process 1 is executing step: 2
Process 1 is executing step: 3
Process 1 is executing step: 4
Process 1 is executing step: 5
Process 1 terminates execution.
```

At this point, the triple currently at the front of `processQueue` is removed, yielding the description given in Figure 7.15c.

FIGURE 7.15c   processQueue

(3,4,4)	(4,6,3)

(front)   (rear)

The output for the monitor continues as

```
Process 3 is executing.
This process has priority 4
Process 3 is executing step: 1
```

```
Process 3 is executing step: 2
Process 3 is executing step: 3
Process 3 is executing step: 4
Process 3 terminates execution.
```

The triple at the front of the current `processQueue` is removed, yielding the description of `processQueue` given by Figure 7.15d.

FIGURE 7.15d   processQueue

```
┌─────────────┐
│   (4,6,3)   │
└─────────────┘
```

(front)
(rear)

Processing in the monitor continues with the output

```
Process 4 is executing.
This process has priority 3
Process 4 is executing step: 1
Process 4 is executing step: 2
Process 4 is executing step: 3
Process 4 is executing step: 4
Process 4 is executing step: 5
Process 4 is executing step: 6
Process 4 terminates execution.
```

The triple at the front of the current `processQueue` is removed, causing `processQueue` to become empty. This terminates execution of the `while`-loop in `monitorPriorityQueue`, leading to the execution of the final output statement

```
Entire execution shuts down.
```

7.13 **Chapter Summary**

This chapter provided a detailed and extensive study of three major data structures used extensively in contemporary data processing: stacks, queues, and priority queues. In each case, we showed how each of these structures can be defined using already existing structures from Java's Collection Framework. In each case, the instance methods provided in the class implementing the ADT is defined in terms of one of the already existing classes from the Collection Framework.

For stacks, the underlying class can be chosen either as `Vector`, `ArrayList`, or `LinkedList`, as well as the specific `Stack` class. We also described in some detail how stacks aid in the solution of a number of key problems in several distinct application areas:

- balanced parentheses, brackets, and braces: useful in formal languages and complier construction
- evaluating an arithmetic expression in postfix form: useful in syntax analysis in compiler construction
- converting an arithmetic expression from infix form to its equivalent in postfix form: useful in compiler construction

Although each of these problems requires the application of stacks, whether predefined by the implementation (as was shown using Java's Collection Framework) or completely designed by the programmer, our solutions used the former approach. The advantage in doing so is that we were relieved of the further burden of having to design and implement the fundamental stack operations "by hand." We exploited the fact that the implementations provided at least in part by the use of a class from the Collection Framework is guaranteed to be both correct and as efficient as possible. This is due to the observation that the design of the classes provided throughout `java.util` are aimed at optimizing efficiency.

For queues, the underlying class was either `ArrayList` or `LinkedList`, because inserting values at one end and removing values from the other end is most efficient when implemented in Java as either an `ArrayList` or `LinkedList` object. Our applications of queues concentrated on some of the fundamental ideas coming from the study of operating systems. We used queues as the basic structure for solving the problem of monitoring the activity of a finite sequence of ready processes waiting to execute in a timeshared CPU in a multiprogrammed operating system. Similar simulators can be designed for processes in a local area network waiting to acquire the services of a single line printer attached to that network.

Priority queues were first introduced as an ADT and then implemented using `ArrayList`, although we observed that `LinkedList` is a viable alternative choice as the background structure. Our applications of priority queues concentrated on their use in monitoring the activity of processes in a multiprogrammed timesharing operating system. The use of priority queues in this application area provides a realistic simulation because processes submitted for execution in a real-life timesharing environment involve a priority system that depends on the position of the individual who submits the process for execution. Certain personnel, such as system programmers or network operators, submit processes of the highest possible priority because these processes are generally intended to upgrade and/or improve the quality of system performance.

EXERCISES

1. Implement the stack ADT manually as a subclass of `Vector`. Use the design of `ArrayStack` and `LinkedStack` as guides.

2. Run the same driver for `LinkedStack` as that displayed in Example 7.2 for `ArrStack`.

3. Write a driver for `checkBalance` as decribed in Section 7.6.

4. Test each of the following for balanced parentheses, brackets, and braces. Show your results in two ways: by hand and by using `checkBalance`.

    a.   `(x + (y    (z ⊦ w))]`
    b.   `x + (y - (z * (w + u)))`
    c.   `x + (y - [z + (w + u)]])}`
    d.   `x * y/(z + w)`

5. Evaluate each of the following postfix expressions. Show your result for each in two ways: by hand and by executing `evalPostfix`.

    a.   `xy+zw-*pr-/` with x = 6, y = 4, z = 3, w = 1, p = 2, r = 1
    b.   `xyzw+-*` with x = 4, y = 3, z = 3, w = 2

6. Convert each of the following to its equivalent postfix form. Show your result in two ways: by hand and by using `toPostfix`.

    a.   `(x + y) * (c - d/e) % f`
    b.   `(x + y) - (z + w)) * u`

7. Using the `LinkedQueue` implementation of `Queue`, write a driver that constructs the queue of Figure 7.7 and then outputs and removes each value until the queue is empty.

8. Solve Exercise 7 above, now using the `ArrQueue` implementation of queues.

9. Redo 8, but now use the `LinkedQueue1` implementation of queues.

10. Implement the following algorithm using `Character`-valued stacks to test for palindromes:

Construct three `Character`-valued stacks `stack1`, `stack2`, `stack3`. Push the character string to be tested, one character at a time, onto each of `stack1` and `stack2`. Pop the contents of `stack2`, and push each of the characters popped from `stack2` onto `stack3`. If the contents of `stack1` and `stack3` are identical, then the original input string is a palindrome; otherwise, it is not a palindrome.

11. Design and write code for a `void static` method that swaps the two topmost values on a stack.

12. Design and write code for a `void static` method that appends the contents of one stack to the top of a second stack of values of the same data type. The appended stack begins with its bottom value directly on top of the top value of the second stack.

13. Write a `boolean`-valued method testing whether two queues of values of the same type are identical.

14. Design a void static method that adds 1 to each prime positive integer in an int-valued queue and adds 5 to every other integer.

15. Design a method that reverses the sequence of values currently stored in a queue.

16. Change the value of the quantum from 3 to 4 and then to 6 in Application 2 of Section 7.9. Compare the results of each simulator on the same input sequence. Is any general conclusion derivable from these observations?

17. Implement the PriorityQueue interface using LinkedList. Call the resulting class LinkedPriorityQueue and design a driver producing the same results as those of Example 7.6, now using LinkedPriorityQueue.

18. Suppose we add the following method to the PriorityQueue interface:

```
// Returns size of the current priority queue.
 public int size();
```

and add the following implementation of this method to ArrPriority-Queue:

```
// Returns size of the current priority queue.
 public int size()
 {
  return prq.size();
 }
```

Use these changes to find the exact form of the output for the main method given by

```
public static void main(String [] args)
 {
 // Construct Integer-valued priority queue using ArrPriorityQueue.
 ArrPriorityQueue prQueue = new ArrPriorityQueue();
 // Insert five Integer values into prQueue:
 prQueue.insert(new Integer(2));
 prQueue.insert(new Integer(3));
 prQueue.insert(new Integer(-1));
 prQueue.insert(new Integer(7));
 prQueue.insert(new Integer(9));

 System.out.println("Empty out current prQueue:");
 while(!prQueue.isEmpty())
 {
  System.out.println("Current size of prQueue = " + prQueue.size());
  System.out.println(prQueue.front() + "   ");
  prQueue.remove();
 }

 } // terminates text of main method
```

Is it possible to inherit the size method from List or ArrayList?

PROGRAMMING PROJECTS

1. Rewrite `toPostfix` using a `switch` statement to replace the nested `if-else` statements in the code currently in Example 7.5.

2. Implement the solution of the problem of simulating a finite sequence of processes in a multiprogrammed environment using a time quantum, now using a single queue of pairs of `int` values `(m,n)`, where `m` is the current process number and `n` is the number of processing steps remaining for `Process m` to complete execution.

CHAPTER 8

Generic Algorithms and the `StringTokenizer` Class

CHAPTER OBJECTIVES

- To describe the concept and purpose of generic algorithms and their use in the problem-solving environment.
- To classify generic algorithms into categories reflecting their functionality.
- To investigate each generic algorithm from the standpoint of efficiency.
- To provide specific examples of the use of generic algorithms in a number of key applications areas.
- To introduce the `StringTokenizer` class and describe its value in a number of major problem-solving areas.

8.1   Introduction

Algorithms can be viewed as methods that perform useful computations, such as sorting and searching, on objects that implement a number of different interfaces from Java's Collection Hierarchy. These algorithms are therefore classified as *generic* in the sense that their implementation is not necessarily restricted to a single class of containers. We can also characterize each of these algorithms as *polymorphic* in that the same method is applicable to several different implementations of the same collection interface. This implies that programmers using these generic algorithms are no longer required to redesign and encode these algorithms to fit the specific implementation. In this sense, such algorithms are regarded as *reusable software tools*. Therefore, the programmer need only choose the appropriate predefined generic algorithm with the assurance that the algorithm has been designed for optimal efficiency and correctness. This assurance is one of the major goals to be fulfilled in the design of each component of Java's Collection Framework.

8.2   An Overview of Java's Generic Algorithms for the `Collections` Class

Most of the generic algorithms provided by `java.util` apply to `List` objects, although two of these (`max` and `min`) apply as well to any object definable in the `Collection` interface. Because all of these algorithms are listed in the `Collections` class, each must be preceded by the qualified reference as displayed by the syntax

```
Collections.<identifier>(<argument_list>);
```

where `<identifier>` names the generic algorithm (such as `sort`, `reverse`, `max`, and `min`) and `<argument_list>` is a finite list of arguments to which the algorithm applies, separated by commas.

We can classify these algorithms as

- the `sort` algorithm
- the `shuffle` algorithm
- the `reverse` algorithm
- the `fill` algorithm
- the `copy` algorithm
- the `binarySearch` algorithm
- the `max` and `min` algorithms
- the `nCopies` algorithm
- Singleton algorithms

In Section 3.19 we introduced a number of generic algorithms that apply specifically to arrays. These are provided by Java in a special `Arrays` class and require the inclusion of `Arrays` as a qualified reference. Thus, in a similar manner to that for `Collections`, these must be used according to the syntax

```
Arrays.<identifier>(<argument_list>);
```

The `Arrays` class contains two major algorithms:

- `sort`, which sorts the values of the array in order of ascending size
- `binarySearch`, which performs a binary search on an array of values for a specific value

The remainder of this chapter gives a thorough and detailed account of the functionality of each of these generic algorithms.

8.3   Generic Sorting Algorithms Applicable to `List` Objects

In Section 5.9, we began a discussion of Java's `Collections` class. We observed that it contains a wide range of `static` methods that apply primarily to objects constructed in any implementation of the `List` interface. This means that any implementation of `List`, such as `ArrayList` or `LinkedList`, can invoke any of these algorithms, knowing that the result will be correct and highly optimized with respect to efficiency.

The `sort` Algorithm

The `sort` algorithm rearranges the elements in any `List` object[1] so that they appear in order of ascending size, according to some well-defined order relation existing on the underlying data type. This is an example of a *nonmutating sequence algorithm*, because it applies to a finite sequence, and none of the existing values are changed to new values by virtue of applying this algorithm; at worst, the current values are rearranged so that they appear in ascending order, counting any possible repetitions.

This algorithm has two forms. The first sorts a `List` object according to the natural ordering existing among its elements. For example, if `intList` is a finite nonempty list of `Integer` values, then applying `sort` to `intList` automatically rearranges its values in order of increasing size. The formal syntax for this version is

```
Collections.sort(<identifier>);
```

where `<identifier>` names the `List` object whose elements are to be sorted.

We illustrate this with the following sequence of examples.

EXAMPLE 8.1   The following main method initializes `intList` as `[2,3,1,0,8]` and applies `sort` to obtain the result `[0,1,2,3,8]`.

```
public static void main(String [] args)
 {
  int intArr[] = {2,3,1,0,8};
  List intList = new ArrayList();

  for(int index = 0; index < intArr.length; ++index)
   intList.add(new Integer(intArr[index]));

  System.out.println("Before applying sort, intList is:");
  System.out.println(intList);
```

---

[1]We use this terminology to describe any object that is constructed using either the `ArrayList` or `LinkedList` implementation.

```
System.out.println("Now apply Collections.sort(intList):");
Collections.sort(intList);

System.out.println("After applying sort, intList is:");
System.out.println(intList);

} // terminates text of main method
```

The output derived from running this is

```
Before applying sort, intList is:
[2,3,1,0,8]
Now apply Collections.sort(intList):
After applying sort, intList is:
[0,1,2,3,8]
```

Example 8.2 shows the polymorphic nature of the sort algorithm, applying sort to a LinkedList object with String values.

EXAMPLE 8.2   Suppose we consider the execution of the following main method:

```
public static void main(String [] args)
 {
  String strArray[] = {"Vivian","Josephine","Patrizia","Angela"};

  LinkedList strList = new LinkedList();

  for(int index = 0; index < strArray.length; ++index)
   strList.add(strArray[index]);

  System.out.println("Before applying sort, strList is:");
  System.out.println(strList);

  System.out.println("Now apply Collections.sort(strList):");
  Collections.sort(strList);

  System.out.println("After applying sort, strList is:");
  System.out.println(strList);

} // terminates text of main method
```

This method has output

```
Before applying sort, strList is:
[Vivian, Josephine, Patrizia, Angela]
Now apply Collections.sort(strList):
```

```
After applying sort, strList is:
[Angela, Josephine, Patrizia, Vivian]
```

The sort algorithm implements a variation of mergesort, as discussed in detail in Section 3.17. Two major features influenced this design choice:

1. The algorithm optimizes speed of execution. For a list of n elements, this algorithm is O(n log n) and runs substantially faster on lists that are almost completely sorted. Experimental results show that this version executes as quickly as a highly optimized version of quicksort. However, we already know that there are "worst possible cases" where quicksort is $O(n^2)$.

2. This implementaion of sort is *stable*. It maintains the same order of succession as the original unsorted list as it applies to equal elements of the sequence.

The second version of sort passes a Comparator[2] object as a second parameter. Its general syntax is given by

```
Collections.sort(<list_identifier>,<Comparator_identifier>);
```

The result of executing this version produces a rearrangement of the List object identified by <list_identifier> according to the ordering identified by <Comparator_identifier>. As an example of this, suppose we wish to sort intList as defined in Example 8.1 in order of *descending* size. Then we might use the static method Collections.reverse-Order(). The result is a comparator that reverses the values in the compareTo() method. In fact, when we invoke

```
Collections.sort(intList,Collections.reverseOrder());
```

The result is the list [8,3,2,1,0].

This version of sort is flexible enough to allow programmers to construct their Comparator objects. As an example of this, let us consider a variation of some of the ideas first presented in Application 2 of Section 7.12. Recall that this application provided a simulator for the priority queue of ready processes in a multiprogrammed environment, counting processing steps.

EXAMPLE 8.3   We begin the example by giving a more detailed definition of the Process class, which now includes a constructor and a number of data retrieval instance methods.

```
class Process
{
```

---

[2]Comparator objects were defined in Section 5.6.

```
// Data members
Integer processNumber;
Integer steps;
Integer priority;

// Constructor.  Constructs Process object with the given
// processNumber, steps, and priority.
public Process(int pNum,int s,int pr)
{
 processNumber = new Integer(pNum);
 steps = new Integer(s);
 priority = new Integer(pr);
}
// Retrieval methods
public int getprocessNumber()
{
 return processNumber.intValue();
}
public int getSteps()
{
 return steps.intValue();
}
public int getPriority()
{
 return priority.intValue();
}
} // terminates text of Process class.
```

The following text is an example of the second version of `sort`, using a `Comparator` object to define a binary order relationship among any two `Process` objects, defined by their respective `priority` components. The `Process` object with the higher priority value appears before that with the lower priority. The formal definition of this sort method is given by

```
new Comparator()
 {
  public int compare(Object obj1,Object obj2)
  {
   return ((Process)obj2).getPriority() -
                          ((Process)obj1).getPriority();
  }
 }
```

The complete program is given by

```
public static void main(String [] args)
 {
  Process p1 = new Process(1,2,3);
  Process p2 = new Process(2,2,8);
  Process p3 = new Process(3,1,4);

  System.out.println("Priority for p1 = " + p1.getPriority());
  System.out.println("Priority for p2 = " + p2.getPriority());
  System.out.println("Priority for p3 = " + p3.getPriority());

  // Now construct list of processes.
  List processList = new ArrayList();
  // Insert p1,p2,p3 into processList:
  processList.add(p1);
  processList.add(p2);
  processList.add(p3);

  // Define sort on processList, using priorities:

 Collections.sort(processList,new Comparator()
 {
  public int compare(Object obj1,Object obj2)
  {
   return ((Process)obj2).getPriority() - ((Process)obj1).getPriority();
  }
 }
 );

 //  Output priorities of the members of processList, after sorting.
for(ListIterator iter = processList.listIterator(); iter.hasNext();)
{
 Process proc = (Process)iter.next();
 System.out.print(proc.getPriority() + "  ");
 }
 System.out.println();
 } // terminates text of main
```

The output is

```
            Priority for p1 = 3
            Priority for p2 = 8
            Priority for p3 = 4
                 8   4   3
```

8.4 **The `shuffle` Algorithm**

The `Collections` class contains an algorithm called `shuffle` whose behavior is the complete opposite of that of `sort`. Indeed, given any `List` object, the result of applying `shuffle` is a reordering of its elements. This is another example of a nonmutating sequence algorithm, because the result of applying `shuffle` does not change any of the values in the list but only their order of appearance. The algorithm is useful from the standpoint of simulating the action of games of chance. As an example, we will show how `shuffle` can be used to simulate the shuffling of an ordinary deck of playing cards.

This algorithm has two versions. The first is a `void` method with a single `List` parameter. Its syntax can be expressed as

```
Collections.shuffle(<identifier>);
```

where `<identifier>` names the `List` object whose elements are to be shuffled. This algorithm uses the predefined `random` method defined in the `Math` library to generate a random ordering of the elements in the list named by `<identifier>`.

The method illustrated here fills an `ArrayList` object with the first 52 nonnegative integers, representing the cards in an ordinary deck of playing cards. The deck is shuffled and the first five cards are drawn. The result is a numeric display of the five cards drawn. Note that the randomness assures that a different display of values occurs each time the program executes. The formal text of the program is given by

```
public static void main(String [] args)
 {
  List playingCards = new ArrayList(52);
  for(int index = 0; index < 52; ++index)
   playingCards.add(new Integer(index));

  Collections.shuffle(playingCards);
  List fiveCardHand = playingCards.subList(0,5);

  System.out.println("The five-card hand dealt was:");
  System.out.println(fiveCardHand);

 } // terminates text of main method
```

The second version of the algorithm assumes the form

```
Collections.shuffle(<list_identifier>,<Random_identifier>);
```

where `<list_identifier>` names the list to be shuffled and `<Random_identifier>` names the `Random` object to be used in the shuffling process.[3]

---

[3]The `Random` class was described in Section 6.6.

Let us consider the following variation of the program:

```
public static void main(String [] args)
  {
   List playingCards = new ArrayList(52);
   for(int index = 0; index < 52; ++index)
    playingCards.add(new Integer(index));

   // Construct Random object RandObj:
   Random RandObj = new Random();

   // Apply second version of shuffle:
   Collections.shuffle(playingCards,RandObj);
   List fiveCardHand = playingCards.subList(0,5);

   System.out.println("The five-card hand dealt was:");
   System.out.println(fiveCardHand);

  } // terminates text of main method
```

8.5 The reverse Algorithm

The reverse method reverses the order of appearance of the elements stored in any List object. The syntax is quite simple:

```
Collections.reverse(<identifier>);
```

where <identifier> names the List object whose elements are to be reversed.

Suppose, for example, we construct charList as

```
List charList = new ArrayList();
```

And suppose charList becomes [r,o,s,a,l,i,e]. Then the result of executing the code sequence

```
System.out.print("The result of applying");
System.out.println("Collections.reverse(charList)");
System.out.print("to " + charList + " is ");
Collections.reverse(charList);
System.out.println(charList);
```

is

```
The result of applying Collections.reverse(charList)
to [r,o,s,a,l,i,e] is [e,i,l,a,s,o,r]
```

Here is another application of the reverse algorithm, used to test for palindromes.

EXAMPLE 8.4   The following `static` method uses `Collections.reverse` to test for palindromes:

```
static boolean isPalindrome(String str)
 {
  String strCopy = str;

  // Create List objects for each of str, strCopy:
  List strList = new ArrayList();
  List strCopyList = new ArrayList();

  for(int index = 0; index < str.length(); ++index)
   strList.add(new Character(str.charAt(index)));

  for(int index = 0; index < strCopy.length(); ++index)
   strCopyList.add(new Character(strCopy.charAt(index)));

  // After this, strCopyList is an exact copy of strList.

  // Now apply Collections.reverse to strList.
  Collections.reverse(strList);

  // Now test two lists for palindrome matches.
  for(int index = 0; index < strList.size(); ++index)
   if(!strList.get(index).equals(strCopyList.get(index)))
    return false;
  return true;

 } // terminates text of isPalindrome
```

8.6 **The `fill` Algorithm**

This algorithm has the syntax

```
Collections.fill(<list_identifier>,<value>);
```

where `<list_identifier>` names a `List` object and `<value>` is an object whose type does not necessarily match those elements of the list named by `<list_identifier>`. Thus, `fill` overwrites every element currently appearing in the list named by `<list_identifier>` with `<value>`. This operation is particularly useful if the application requires reinitializing a list during the course of a computation.

As an example, if the current contents of `intList` are `[2,3,8,0,4,1]`, then the result of applying `Collections.fill(intList,new Integer(0))` is `[0,0,0,0,0,0]`.

8.7 **The `copy` Algorithm**

This algorithm copies all of the elements, in order, from an already existing source `List` object to the same positions in a new target `List` object. The target list must be at least as long as the source list. The syntax for this method can be given by

```
Collections.copy(<target_identifier>,<source_identifier>);
```

where <source_identifier> names the source list and <target_identifier> names the target list.

If we apply this algorithm, the elements of the source overwrite, position by position, the corresponding elements of the target. If the target is properly larger than the source, the leftover values of the target remain the same. As an example, suppose `targetList = [a,n,t,h,o,n,y]` and `sourceList = [r,o,c,c,o]`. Then the result of applying `Collections.-copy(targetList,sourceList)` is `targetList = [r,o,c,c,o,n,y]` and `sourceList` remains `[r,o,c,c,o]`.

Another way to make an exact copy of the elements from an already existing `List` object `strList` is to follow the next sequence of actions. First create a string of blanks whose size matches that of `strList`. This is done by executing

```
String strCopy;
for(int index = 0; index < strList.size(); ++index)
 strCopy.charAt(index) = ' ';
```

Then construct a `List` object `strCopyList` whose size matches that of `strList` and that consists entirely of blanks. This is done by executing the code sequence

```
List strCopyList = new ArrayList();
for(int index = 0; index < strCopy.length(); ++index)
 strCopyList.add(new Character(' '));
```

Finally, copy the contents of `strList` into `strCopyList`, using

```
Collections.copy(strCopyList,strList);
```

8.8 **Binary Search on Lists**

The `binarySearch` algorithm searches for a specified object in a sorted list.[4] The `Collections` class implements this algorithm for `List` objects and provides two separate versions. The first version takes the form

```
index = Collections.binarySearch(<list_identifier>,<value>);
```

[4]Binary search for arrays was discussed in Section 3.11.

where `index` is an `int`-valued variable, `<list_identifier>` is an identifier naming the `List` object whose elements are sorted in ascending order where the binary search is to be conducted, and `<value>` identifies the value sought.

In the case of a successful binary search, `index` is a nonnegative `int` value indicating the location in the list named by `<list_identifier>` where an occurrence of `<value>` is found. If the value of `index` is negative, however, this indicates that there is no element in `<list_identifier>` matching `<value>`. In this case, the return value is - `index` - 1 and represents the location in the list where `<value>` should be inserted to maintain the ordering.

As an example, suppose `intList` = `[-1,4,9,12,56]` and `value-Sought` stores the `Integer` value 12. Then the result of applying `Collections.binarySearch(intList,valueSought)` is 3, because the search successfully located an instance of `valueSought` at position 3. In fact, if we were to execute `intList.get(index)`, where `index` = 3, the `Integer` value returned is 12.

On the other hand, suppose `intList` is as above, but now `value-Sought` is the `Integer` value 3. Then the result of applying `Collections.binarySearch(intList,valueSought)` is -2, because - (-2) - 1 = 1 is the proper insertion position for the value 3 in `intList` that maintains the ordering of its elements. That is, `intList.add(- index - 1, valueSought)` = `intList.add(-1,new Integer(3))` produces the ordered list object `intList` = `[-1,3,4,9,12,56]`.

The second version of `binarySearch` adds a third parameter of type `Comparator` and has the syntax

```
index = Collections.binarySearch(<list_identifier>,<value>,
                              <Comparator_identifier>);
```

where `index`, `<list_identifier>`, and `<value>` are as in the first version, and where `<Comparator_identifier>` names a `Comparator` object specified by the programmer.

For example, suppose `valueSought` is the `Integer` value 12, and suppose `<Comparator_identifier>` is `Collections.reverseOrder()`. Then `intList` = `[56,12,9,4,-1]` and `Collections.binarySearch(intList, valueSought,Collections.reverseOrder())` returns -1.

On the other hand, suppose `intList` is again `[56,12,9,4,-1]`, but now `valueSought` is the `Integer` value 3. Then

```
Collections.binarySearch(intList,valueSought,
                         Collections.reverseOrder())
```

returns the value -6.

8.9 **The max and min Algorithms**

The next pair of algorithms defined in the Collections class are extremely useful and simple to apply. In addition, they are unusual because they are applicable to any object defined in the Java Collection Framework. For instance, these are applicable to TreeMap and HashSet objects, as well as List objects.

The first of these is the max algorithm. When applied, max returns the maximum element appearing in a specified Collection object. This algorithm appears in two versions. The first version is the simpler form, because it takes a single Collection parameter and returns the maximum element in the object specified by the parameter, according to the default ordering for that parameter. Its syntax is given by

```
Collections.max(<Collection_identifier>);
```

where <Collection_identifier> names the specific Collection object whose maximum value is sought.

We look at two examples. Suppose we have the List object list1, implemented using ArrayList, and the Set object set1, implemented using HashSet. Suppose list1 = [8,0,9,-1,5,12] and set1 = [a,l,i,s,h,o,c,n]. Then

```
Collections.max(list1) = 12
```

and

```
Collections.max(set1) = 's'.
```

The second form takes a second Comparator parameter and has the syntax

```
Collections.max(<Collection_identifier>,<Comparator_identifier>);
```

where <Collection_identifier> is defined exactly like the first version, and where <Comparator_identifier> names a Comparator object that orders the members of the data type defined for the Collection object named by <Collection_identifier>. When applied, Collections.max(<Collection_identifier>,<Comparator_identifer>) will return the largest element in the Collection object named by <Collection_identifier> in the sense of the ordering named by <Comparator_identifier>.

As an example, assume that <Comparator_identifier> is Collections.reverseOrder(), and list1 and set1 are defined as above. Then

```
Collections.max(list1,Collections.reverseOrder()) = -1
```

and

```
Collections.max(set1,Collections.reverseOrder()) = 'a'.
```

The min algorithm is similar in behavior to max. The only difference is that when min is applied it returns the minimum element in a specified

Collection object. It also comes in two versions. The first (and simpler) version takes a single Collection parameter and returns the minimum element in the object specified by the parameter, according to the default "natural" ordering. Its syntax is given by

```
Collections.min(<Collection_identifier>);
```

where <Collection_identifier> names the specific Collection object whose minimum value is sought.

If we apply min to each of list1 and set1 as defined earlier, the respective results are

```
Collections.min(list1) = 1
```

and

```
Collections.min(set1) = 'a'.
```

The second version of min takes an additional Comparator-valued parameter and has syntax

```
Collections.min(<Collection_identifier>,<Comparator_identifier>);
```

Indeed, suppose list1 and set1 are as defined earlier. Then

```
Collections.min(list1,Collections.reverseOrder()) = 12
```

and

```
Collections.min(set1,Collections.reverseOrder()) = 's'.
```

How do max and min apply to Map objects? Here we can use each of the instance methods keySet() and values(), because these permit any Map object to be viewed as a collection. To illustrate this, suppose we revisit Examples 5.4 and 5.5 and apply the first version of max to each of stringFrequency.keySet() and stringFrequency.values(). This is summarized in Example 8.5.

EXAMPLE 8.5   Suppose we consider the main method

```
public static void main(String [] args)
 {
  // Construct array of input strings as a conformant array.
  String arr[] = {"I","think","therefore","I","am"};

  // Construct Map object whose mambers are pairs with keyValue
  // component is the String value, and whose dataValue component
  // is its frequency of occurrence in the text.
  Map stringFrequency = new HashMap();

  // Initialize frequency of occurrence of each member of arr
  // from conformant array.
  for(int index = 0; index < arr.length; ++index)
```

```
  {
   Integer intFreq = (Integer)stringFrequency.get(arr[index]);
   if(intFreq == null)
    intFreq = new Integer(1);
   else
   {
    int value = intFreq.intValue();
    intFreq = new Integer(value + 1);
   }
   stringFrequency.put(arr[index],intFreq);
  } // terminates text of for-loop
  System.out.println("The input sentence contains " +
       stringFrequency.size());
  System.out.println("distinct words.");
  System.out.println("stringFrequency = " + stringFrequency);

  // Now apply Collections.max to stringFrequency.keySet():
  System.out.println("Collections.max(stringFrequency.keySet()) = ");
  System.out.println(Collections.max(stringFrequency.keySet()));

// Now apply Collections.max to stringFrequency.values():
  System.out.println("Collections.max(stringFrequency.values()) = ");
  System.out.println(Collections.max(stringFrequency.values()));

 } // terminates text of main method
```

The output obtained from executing this is

```
The input sequence contains 4
distinct words.
stringFrequency = {I=2,therefore=1,am=1,think=1}
Collections.max(stringFrequency.keySet()) =
think
Collections.max(stringFrequency.values()) =
2
```

8.10 **The** nCopies **Algorithm**

Despite its name, this algorithm does not copy an existing list to a second target list. Instead, it creates a new list from an existing Object element and a positive integer n. The resulting list contains exactly n elements, each of which is the designated element. The syntax for this is

```
<list_identifier> = Collections.nCopies(<expression>,<element>);
```

where <list_identifier> names the resulting list, <expression> is an int-valued expression whose value is a positive integer giving the number of copies to be made, and <element> names the element to be copied. As an example, the code sequence

```
List targetList = new ArrayList();
TargetList = Collections.nCopies(10,new Integer(4));
System.out.println("targetList = " + targetList);
```

produces output

```
targetList = [4,4,4,4,4,4,4,4,4,4]
```

8.11 **Singleton Algorithms**

This section describes three algorithms accomplishing similar results on List, Set, and Map objects. Each of the algorithms creates an object of the appropriate type containing a single element.

Java provides a singletonList algorithm to enable the construction of a List object with a single Object-valued parameter. Its syntax can be expressed as

```
<list_identifier> = Collections.singletonList(<element>);
```

where <list_identifier> names the list with a single element and <element> describes that element. For example, the following code sequence constructs the List object sList with the single Character value 'j' as its single element:

```
List sList = new ArrayList();
sList = Collections.singletonList(new Character('j'));
```

To construct a singleton Set object, Java provides the singleton algorithm in Collections, with the syntax

```
<set_identifier> = Collections.singleton(<element>);
```

where <set_identifier> names the Set object with a single element whose value is provided by <element>. The following code sequence constructs the Set object singSet using the TreeSet implementation, with the single Character value 'j' as its only element:

```
Set singSet = new TreeSet();
SingSet = Collections.singleton(new Character('j'));
```

Java also defines a singletonMap algorithm in Collections, requiring the programmer to provide a value for keySet() and a value for values(). The syntax for this is

```
<map_identifier> = Collections.singletonMap(<keySet,<values>);
```

where <map_identifier> names the singleton Map object, <keySet> is the value of that object's keySet() component, and <values> is the value assigned to that object's `values()` component. To create a singleton `Map` object, all that needs to be done is to first construct it as initially empty and then provide a value for each of that object's `keySet` and `values` component.

As an example, the code sequence

```
// Construct empty Map object.
Map singMap = new HashMap();

// Create singleton map.
singMap = Collections.singletonMap("Hello",new Integer(5));

// Output results.
System.out.println("singMap.keySet() = " + singMap.keySet());
System.out.println("singMap.values() = " + singMap.values());
```

produces output

```
singMap.keySet() = [Hello]
singMap.values() = [5]
```

8.12 Predefined `final static` Fields in the `Collections` Hierarchy

The `Collections` class also contains three `static` and `final` fields called `EMPTY_LIST`, `EMPTY_SET`, and `EMPTY_MAP`. These were included in the `Collections` class because, in a number of applications, it is useful to provide an empty `List`, `Set`, or `Map` object without compromising the efficiency of execution of these "emptying" operations.

As a simple example, let us trace the following code sequence, where we first construct a `List` object called `list1`, then insert two `Integer` values into `list1`, and then empty out `list1`. Note that the "emptying out" process is accomplished by assigning the value `Collections.EMPTY_LIST` to `list1`. Specifically,

```
List list1 = new ArrayList();
list1.add(new Integer(2));
list1.add(new Integer(3));
System.out.println("list1 = " + list1);
list1 = Collections.EMPTY_LIST;
System.out.println("list1 = " + list1);
```

The output obtained by executing this code is

```
list1 = [2,3]
list1 = []
```

EMPTY_SET and EMPTY_MAP perform similar actions on Set and Map objects, respectively. See the Exercises at the end of this chapter.

8.13   **The `Arrays` Utility Class**

We began a discussion of the `Arrays` class in Section 3.19. In brief, the `Arrays` class is part of the `java.util` library and contains a number of predefined efficient `static` methods for processing ordinary one-dimensional arrays. Several of these have versions similar to their counterpart for `Collections`. Others have versions that apply either to the entire array or to a segment of the array whose respective lower and upper boundaries are specified by the programmer. Similar to the `Collections` class, each method appearing in the `Arrays` class must be preceded by the `Arrays` modifier as a qualified reference, using the syntax

```
Arrays.<identifier>(<argument_list>);
```

where `<identifier>` again names the generic algorithm to be applied and `<argument_list>` is a finite list of arguments to which the algorithm applies, separated by commas.

Four major algorithms are listed in the `Arrays` class:

- `sort`
- `binarySearch`
- `equals`
- `fill`

The `sort` Algorithm

The `sort` method provided by `Arrays` sorts the array using a technique whose complexity is `O(n log n)`. There are two versions of `sort`. The first assumes a default "natural" ordering existing among its elements. Its syntax takes the form

```
Arrays.sort(<identifier>);
```

where `<identifier>` names the `Object`-valued array to be sorted.

To illustrate this, suppose we execute the code sequence

```
// Conformant array.
   int [] intArr = {2,3,-1,7,1};

   Integer[] IntArr = new Integer[intArr.length];

   // Fill IntArr with Integer versions of components of intArr:
   for(int index = 0; index < intArr.length; ++index)
```

```
IntArr[index] = new Integer(intArr[index]);

// Sort IntArr:
Arrays.sort(IntArr);

// Output results:
System.out.println("The sorted IntArr is:");
for(int index = 0; index < IntArr.length; ++index)
 System.out.println("IntArr[" + index + "] = " + IntArr[index]);
```

The output is

```
The sorted IntArr is:
IntArr[0] = -1
IntArr[1] = 1
IntArr[2] = 2
IntArr[3] = 3
IntArr[4] = 7
```

The second version of sort takes the form

```
Arrays.sort(<array_identifier>,<Comparator_identifier>);
```

where <array_identifier> names the array to be sorted, according to the Comparator object named by <Comparator_identifier>. As an example, suppose we apply the same code sequence as above, with one noteworthy replacement: Arrays.sort(IntArr) is replaced by Arrays.sort(Int-Arr,Collections.reverseOrder()). The result of this change produces the output

```
IntArr[0] = 7
IntArr[1] = 3
IntArr[2] = 2
IntAtt[3] = 1
IntArr[4] = -1
```

It is possible to apply the sort algorithm to sort an array segment that is part, but not necessarily all, of the underlying array. Assuming the "natural" ordering of its elements, this new version has the syntax

```
Arrays.sort(<identifier>,<low>,<high>);
```

where <identifier> names the array to be sorted and <low>, <high> are int-valued expressions, with the value of <low> less than or equal to that of <high>. The result of applying this version is a sorting of a portion of the array named by <identifier> for the segment beginning at <low> up to but not including <high>. As an example, suppose intArr and IntArr are defined as before. Then the result of applying

```
Arrays.sort(IntArr,1,4);
```

is

```
IntArr[0] = 2
IntArr[1] = -1
IntArr[2] = 3
IntArr[3] = 7
IntArr[4] = 1
```

A final version of sort involves sorting a portion of the array using a Comparator object supplied by the programmer from the component occupying position <low> up to but not including the component occupying position <high>. The syntax for this version is given by

```
Arrays.sort(<array_identifier>,<low>,<high>,<Comparator_identifier>);
```

As a specific example of this, note that

```
Arrays.sort(IntArr,1,4,Collections.reverseOrder());
```

produces

```
IntArr[0] = 2
IntArr[1] = 7
IntArr[2] = 3
IntArr[3] = -1
IntArr[4] = 1
```

The binarySearch Algorithm

The behavior of binarySearch is exactly the same for arrays as for lists. That is, several versions of binarySearch are applicable to arrays, with a functionality that imitates their respective counterpart for lists. The first (and simplest) assumes the default "natural" ordering of the components of the array and takes the form

```
index = Arrays.binarySearch(<array_identifier>,<value>);
```

where index is an int-valued variable, <array_identifier> names the array where the binary search is to be conducted, and <value> identifies the value sought. It is understood that the components of the array are sorted in ascending order, counting any possible repetitions. Again, the return value is a subscript of the array where an occurrence of <value> was found in the case of a successful search, and otherwise returns a subscript where <value> can be inserted in order to preserve the order of the components of the array.

For example, suppose IntArr is the Integer-valued array given in Figure 8.1.

Then the result of applying Arrays.binarySearch(IntArr,new Integer(9)) is index = 5. If instead we apply Arrays.binarySearch (IntArr,new Integer(0)), the result is index = -3, because - index -

FIGURE 8.1   IntArr

[0]	−3
[1]	−1
[2]	2
[3]	4
[4]	8
[5]	9
[6]	23

`1 = -(-3) - 1 = 2`, the proper location for the insertion of `new Inte-ger(0)` in the sorted `IntArr`.

The second version of `binarySearch` for arrays mimics the corresponding second version for lists. This version assumes an ordering of the array provided by the `Comparator` object serving as the additional parameter. Thus, the syntax for this version takes the form

```
index = Arrays.binarySearch(<array_identifier>,<value>,
                            <Comparator_identifier>);
```

Now assume `IntArr` is the `Integer`-valued array sorted by the `Comparator` object `Collections.reverseOrder()`, as pictured in Figure 8.2.

FIGURE 8.2   IntArr

[0]	23
[1]	9
[2]	8
[3]	4
[4]	2
[5]	−1
[6]	−3

Then

```
Arrays.binarySearch(IntArr,new Integer(9),
                    Collections.reverseOrder())
```

is

index = 1,

and

Arrays.binarySearch(IntArr,new Integer(0),
                              Collections.reverseOrder())

is

index = -6.

Unlike sort, Arrays does not support any version of binarySearch for smaller segments of arrays.

The equals Algorithm

The Arrays class supports a static boolean-valued method called equals, having two Object-valued array parameters. equals returns true just when the two array objects are the same, either because both are null or they have the same size and identical components. The syntax for this is

Arrays.equals(<array_identifier1>,<array_identifier2>);

where <array_identifier1>, <array_identifier2> name the two array objects.

For example, suppose we examine the following code segment, where we assume IntArr1, IntArr2 are two Integer-valued arrays:

```
if(Arrays.equals(IntArr1,IntArr2))
 System.out.println("Arrays are equal");
else
 System.out.println("Arrays are not equal");
```

If IntArr1, IntArr2 are the same object, the output is

Arrays are equal

but if otherwise the output is

Arrays are not equal

This algorithm is defined only for entire arrays—no version is applicable to proper segments of either array.

The fill Algorithm

This is the direct analogue for arrays for the version for List objects studied earlier in this chapter in Section 8.6. Its syntax is given by

Arrays.fill(<array_identifier>,<value>);

where <array_identifier> names an array and <value> names the object whose type matches that of the array named by <array_identifier>.

As a result of executing fill, every element currently in <array_identifier> is overwritten by <value>. For example, suppose the current contents of the Integer-valued array IntArray is as in Figure 8.3a.

The result of applying Arrays.fill(IntArray,new Integer(0)) is seen in Figure 8.3b.

FIGURE 8.3

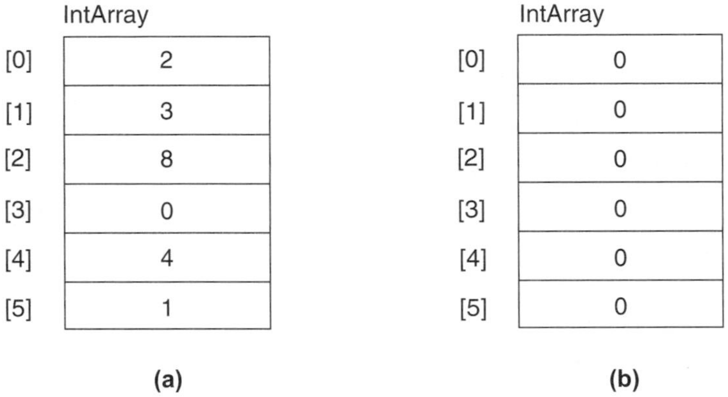

IntArray

[0]	2
[1]	3
[2]	8
[3]	0
[4]	4
[5]	1

(a)

IntArray

[0]	0
[1]	0
[2]	0
[3]	0
[4]	0
[5]	0

(b)

8.14 **Moving between Arrays and Lists**

The Arrays.asList algorithm takes a single array parameter and returns a List object whose elements, in order of appearance, are those of the argument. The syntax for this is

<list_identifier> = Arrays.asList(<array_identifier>);

where <array_identifier> names the array whose elements are to become members of the list named by <list_identifier>. The asList method differs from any of the other methods we have looked at in the Arrays class, because this provides a transition from Arrays objects to Collections objects (in the form of List objects). The size of the list is that of the underlying array and cannot be changed during the course of any subsequent computation. That is, if either of the add or remove is attempted on the resulting list, an UnsupportedOperationException exception is raised.

However, several operations are permitted, so long as the size of the array or list is not changed. The following is an illustration of the movement between the array and its associated list that involves sorting. The result is somewhat indirect and clearly inefficient in the face of other sorting techniques we have already studied, but the point here is that sorting represents a permissible operation in the presence of movement between arrays and associated lists, using `asList` and `toArray`.

```java
public static void main(String [] args)
 {
  // Conformant int-valued array.
  int [] intArr = {2,3,1,7,9};
  // Equivalent Integer-valued array:
  Integer [] IntArray = new Integer[intArr.length];
  for(int index = 0; index < IntArray.length; ++index)
   IntArray[index] = new Integer(intArr[index]);
  // Display contents of IntArray:
  System.out.println("Current contents of IntArray:");
  for(int index = 0; index < IntArray.length; ++index)
   System.out.println("IntArray[" + index + "] = " + IntArray[index]);

  // Now apply asList:
  List IntList = new ArrayList();
  IntList = Arrays.asList(IntArray);

  // Display contents of IntList.
  System.out.println("IntList = " + IntList);

  // Now attempt to sort the list.
  Collections.sort(IntList);

  // Display contents of IntList.
  System.out.println("IntList = " + IntList);

  // Now use toArray to pour this sorted list into IntArray:
  IntArray = (Integer [])IntList.toArray(new Integer[0]);

  // Display contents of IntArray:
   System.out.println("New contents of IntArray:");
   for(int index = 0; index < IntArray.length; ++index)
    System.out.println("IntArray[" + index + "] = " + IntArray[index]);

 } // terminates text of main method.
```

The output is

```
Current contents of IntArray:
IntArray[0] = 2
IntArray[1] = 3
IntArray[2] = 1
```

```
IntArray[3] = 7
IntArray[4] = 9
IntList = [2,3,1,7,9]
IntList = [1,2,3,7,9]
IntArray[0] = 1
IntArray[1] = 2
IntArray[2] = 3
IntArray[3] = 7
IntArray[4] = 9
```

8.15 Some Applications of Generic Algorithms

This section examines a number of ways to apply generic algorithms when solving some processing problems. The first of these involves using singleton sets in removing a number of elements from an already existing Map object. Specifically, suppose we construct a Map object called stringFrequency using

```
Map stringFrequency = new TreeMap();
```

and then proceed to fill stringFrequency using

```
String names[] = {"Rocco","Anthony","Lorenzo","Angela","Vivian"};
String occupation[] = {"Engineer","Doctor","Lawyer","Engineer",
                              "Lawyer"};
for(int index = 0; index < names.length; ++index)
  stringFrequency.put(names[index],occupation[index]);
```

The result of executing this last code sequence is

```
stringFrequency = {Angela=Engineer, Anthony=Doctor, Lorenzo=Lawyer,
                Rocco=Engineer, Vivian=Lawyer}
```

We can view the result of executing this last code sequence as a Map of the names listed in names[] to the corresponding occupations [Doctor,Engineer,Lawyer]. Suppose we are interested in removing all of the current elements of this map that associate with [Lawyer]. We can do this using the singleton set whose only member is the string "Lawyer". This will be used in conjunction with the Collection instance method removeAll, which removes all objects in stringFrequency.values() involving "Lawyer". We can do this by applying

```
stringFrequency.values().removeAll(Collections.singleton("Lawyer"));
```

The result is

```
stringFrequency = {Angela=Engineer, Anthony=Doctor, Rocco=Engineer}
```

Another application involves removing all occurrences of a specific value from a list. For example, suppose IntList is an Integer-valued list currently taking the form

IntList = [2,3,1,7,3,1,2,1].

Suppose we wish to remove all occurrences of the Integer value 1 from IntList. This can be done quite easily using a combination of removeAll and singleton. The actual removal is performed using

IntList.removeAll(Collections.singleton(new Integer(1)));

After executing this, the result is

IntList = [2,3,7,3,2].

A third application begins with an already existing list of Integer values such as

IntList = [2,3,1,7,3,1,2,1].

However, rather than removing all occurrences of a single element from this list, we now wish to insert a fixed number of copies of a specific Integer value at random locations in the list. Specifically, suppose we wish to insert five copies of the Integer value 5 at randomly chosen positions in IntList. The following code sequence accomplishes this, using addAll, nCopies, and shuffle:

```
List value = new ArrayList();
value = Collections.nCopies(5,new Integer(5));
IntList.addAll(value);
Collections.shuffle(IntList);
```

The representation of IntList after adding the five copies of new Integer(5) will change each time this code sequence is executed.

8.16 **The StringTokenizer Utility Class**

A program in any programming language begins as a long character string. This string is commonly referred to as the program's *source code*. The task of interpreting and grouping the consecutive characters in the source code into basic language units is done by a program called a *compiler* or *interpreter*. Depending on the specific language, some of the character sequences will be strings identifying variables, keywords, operators, or punctuations used to separate one group of consecutive characters from another. These form the *lexical elements* of the underlying language. Perhaps the first phase of compiling source code into a form that is executable by the computer's hardware involves the *lexical scanning* of the source code, resulting in a sequence of *tokens*. This phase usually ignores blanks and any comments appearing in the text of the source code. The tokens are distinguished from one another because some represent keywords, others represent variables, still others represent operator symbols or punctuations, and so forth.

One of the useful facilities of the `java.util` library is the `StringTokenizer` class, which provides a way to break down a `String` object into a sequence of tokens. The decomposition of the string into tokens here is completely determined by the programmer, unlike the situation existing in any language compiler or interpreter. The method of decomposing an input string into tokens is straightforward, compared to the default `StreamTokenizer` class that is part of the `java.io` library. The `StreamTokenizer` class is used to break down Java source code into tokens for the purpose of generating executable Java programs. In contrast, a `StringTokenizer` object is completely controlled by the programmer—it does not automatically distinguish among identifiers, numbers, and quoted strings, nor does it ignore inline comments, as is the case with `StreamTokenizer`.

Specifically, objects constructed from the `StringTokenizer` class break down a character string into a sequence of tokens, using specified *delimiters*. The tokens that emerge represent what we might view as an *ordered enumeration* of these tokens. Consequently, `StringTokenizer` implements the `Enumeration` interface.[5] In particular, `StringTokenizer` objects allow the programmer to control and select which characters are to serve as delimiters by providing a character string whose members are the specified delimiters. Because `StringTokenizer` implements the `Enumeration` interface, a `StringTokenizer` object can be used as an `Enumeration` object. This observation will prove to be very useful in the following discussion.

Consider an example. Suppose we declare

```
String strValue = "I think, therefore I am!";
```

and we invoke the constructor

```
StringTokenizer tokens = new StringTokenizer(strValue," ,!");
```

By specifying a blank, comma, and exclamation point as delimiters in this constructor, the tokenizer uses each to separate the input string into tokens. These tokens are then simply the individual words seen in `strValue`.

The `StringTokenizer` class can then be described as

```
public class StringTokenizer implements Enumeration
{
  // Constructor.  Constructs a StringTokenizer object on str, using
  // delim as the delimiter set.  The returnTokens parameter determines
  // whether the delimiters are returned as tokens.  If returnTokens is
```

---

[5]The `Enumeration` interface was discussed in Section 4.7.

```
// true, each delimiter character is returned separately.
public StringTokenizer(String str,String delim,boolean returnTokens);

// Constructor.  Its behavior is identical with
// StringTokenizer(str,delim,false).
public StringTokenizer(String str,String delim);

// Constructor.  The only delimiters are blanks, which are skipped.
public StringTokenizer(String str);

// Returns true if more tokens exist.
public boolean hasMoreTokens();

// Returns the next token of the string.  If no further tokens exist,
// a NoSuchElementException exception is thrown.
public String nextToken();

// Switches the set of delimiters to the characters appearing in
// the parameter, and returns the next token.
public String nextToken(String delim);

// Returns the number of tokens remaining in the string after the
// current position, using the current set of delimiter characters.
public int countTokens();
} // terminates text of StringTokenizer
```

Because a StringTokenizer object can serve as an Enumeration object, we can use the next for-loop to output all of the tokens of strValue above in a single column.

```
for(StringTokenizer e = tokens;e.hasMoreTokens();)
    System.out.println(e.nextToken());
```

The resulting output is

I
think
therefore
I
am

EXAMPLE 8.6 We can apply the StringTokenizer class as an alternative to the methodology applied in Chapter Seven to solve a number of problems that are critical in formal language design and compiler construction. In particular, we studied three major problems in this area: balanced parentheses, brackets, and braces; evaluating postfix arithmetical expressions; and the conversion of an arithmetical expression from infix form to its equivalent postfix form. This example shows how using StringTokenizer objects proves to be extremely valuable in the solution of the evaluation of postfix expressions. In fact, we will show how using the StringTokenizer class might prove to be a better choice in solving the problem of how to evaluate postfix expressions. The use of StringTokenizer objects to solve the other two problems are left as exercises. (See the Exercises and Programming Project at the end of this chapter.)

In particular, suppose we wish to evaluate the string "7 15 + 3 *", noting that we use blanks as delimiters. In this case, five tokens emerge: "7", "15", "+", "3", and "*", in that order. How do we design a solution using StringTokenizer objects to evaluate postfix expressions? We begin by anticipating the existence of a number of runtime exceptions that might occur during the course of evaluating a postfix expression. Notable among these is either an insufficient supply of operator symbols or an oversupply of these symbols. In either case, it makes sense to design a PostfixException class whose code in its simplest form can be given as

```
class PostfixException extends RuntimeException
{
  // Constructor
public PostfixExpression(String str)
  {
   super(str);
  } // terminates text of constructor
} // terminates text of PostfixException
```

Because stack processing is involved, we can apply any implementation of stacks; we choose the version ArrStack described in Section 7.4. Having dispensed with these preliminaries, we can now implement the algorithm described in Application 2 of Section 7.6, using the StringTokenizer class as follows:

```
public static Integer evalPostfix(String str)
 {
  // Construct initially empty operand stack opndStack.
  ArrStack opndStack = new ArrStack();

  // Auxiliary int-valued variables.
  int value, opnd1, opnd2;
  int result = 0;

  // Auxiliary Integer-valued variable
  Integer IntValue, topResult;
```

```
// Current token as a String value.
String token;

// Construct StringTokenizer object with only blank delimiters.
StringTokenizer tokens = new StringTokenizer(str," ");

// Parse input postfix string into individual tokens.
while(tokens.hasMoreTokens())
{
 token = tokens.nextToken();
 if(!isOperator(token))
 {
    // Process an integer-valued operand
    value = Integer.parseInt(token);
    IntValue = new Integer(value);
    opndStack.push(IntValue);
 }
 else // process an operator symbol
 {
    opnd2 = ((Integer)opndStack.top()).intValue();
    opndStack.pop();
    opnd1 = ((Integer)opndStack.top()).intValue();
    opndStack.pop();
    if(token.equals("+"))
     result = opnd1 + opnd2;
    else if(token.equals("-"))
     result = opnd1 - opnd2;
    else if(token.equals("*"))
     result = opnd1 * opnd2;
    else if(token.equals("/"))
     result = opnd1 / opnd2;
    else if(token.equals("%"))
     result = opnd1 % opnd2;

    opndStack.push(new Integer(result));
 } // terminates else-clause
} // terminates while-loop

if(opndStack.isEmpty())  // Signals error:  not enough operands.
 throw new PostfixException("Error: insufficient number of operands");
else // opndStack not empty
{
```

```
    topResult = (Integer)opndStack.top();
    opndStack.pop();
    if(!opndStack.isEmpty())  // Signals error: too many operands.
     throw new PostfixException("Error: too many operands");
    else // Exactly one operand on final stack.
        // That operand is the value of the postfix expression.
     return topResult;
  } // terminates text of outer else-clause
 }  // terminates text of evalPostfix


// Method testing whether current token is an operator symbol.
 // Returns true if so, false if not.
 private static boolean isOperator(String st)
 {
  return (st.equals("+") || st.equals("-") || st.equals("*")
          || st.equals("/") || st.equals("%"));
 } // terminates text of isOperator
```

We trace an execution of evalPostfix using str = "7 15 + 3 *". (Note the presence of blanks between the arguments in the input string.) The StringTokenizer object tokens is constructed and the while-loop is entered because tokens.hasMoreTokens() is true. The initial token "7" is formed by virtue of executing the assignment token = tokens.nextTo-ken(). Because "7" is not an operator symbol, its Integer value is pushed onto the initially empty opndStack, as described in Figure 8.4a.

FIGURE 8.4a   opndStack

The while-loop is reentered, with the token value as "15". Because isOperator is false once again, the Integer equivalent of "15" is pushed onto opndStack, producing the result seen in Figure 8.4b.

The while-loop is entered once again, with token = "+". Because isOperator is true for "+", the else clause executes, with opnd2 holding the int value 15; opndStack is popped again, followed by an evaluation of opnd1 holding the int value 7, also emptying opndStack. Because token holds the string "+", the int value result is computed, using the assign-

FIGURE 8.4b   opndStack

ment result = opnd1 + opnd2. Then opndStack.push(new Integer(result)) executes, pushing the Integer value 22 onto opndStack, which now looks like Figure 8.4c.

FIGURE 8.4c   opndStack

The while-loop is entered once again, with token = "3". As before, this is converted to Integer form and pushed onto opndStack, producing the result seen in Figure 8.4d.

FIGURE 8.4d   opndStack

The while-loop is reentered, with token = "*". Because isOperator is true, the else-clause executes, producing int values of opnd2 = 3 and opnd1 = 22. Then result = opnd1 * opnd2 executes and the Integer equivalent of result is pushed onto opndStack, producing the result seen in Figure 8.4e.

FIGURE 8.4e   opndStack

This terminates execution of the `while`-loop; because the current `opndStack` contains exactly one element, `topResult` stores the `Integer` value 66, which is returned to the caller.

This version of `evalPostfix` has a number of advantages over the version described in Section 7.6. First, the operand stack is coded as a local entity: It was unnecessary to pass it as an additional parameter. A more significant observation is that this version is *not* restricted to single-digit operands, because a token representing an integer-valued operand can be any `String` value—even a value with more than a single digit. While it is certainly possible to recode `evalPostfix` from Section 7.6 to handle multidigit operands, it involves coding that is substantially more complex than that presented there. Finally, this version of `evalPostfix` is closer to the spirit of how an actual postfix expression is evaluated in a typical language compiler, because compilers and interpreters make heavy use of tokens in the process leading from source code to machine-executable code. Thus, we can say that this version of `evalPostfix` is a better and closer simulation of the process actually performed by the computer in evaluating an arithmetic expression, without any sacrifice in efficiency.

8.17 **Chapter Summary**

This chapter was devoted to a detailed summary of two major components of the `java.util` library: generic algorithms and the `StringTokenizer` class. The algorithms presented in this chapter are characterized as generic because they apply to a wide variety of objects defined in the Java Collection Framework. Many of these algorithms are applicable to `List` objects, and several of these apply as well to `Set` and `Map` objects, regardless of the specific implementation of these interfaces. Another group apply to the `Arrays` utility class—these algorithms are useful in processing ordinary one-dimensional arrays.

The algorithms applicable to `List`, `Set`, or `Map` objects are listed in the `Collections` class and must use a qualified reference with syntax

```
Collections.<identifier>(<argument_list>);
```

where `<identifier>` names the generic algorithm and `<argument_list>` is a finite list of arguments to which the algorithm applies, separated by commas. The algorithms in this group can be classified as

- `sort`, which rearranges the elements appearing in the collection in some specific order
- `shuffle`, which returns a randomly generated rearrangement of the elements in the collection
- `reverse`, which reverses the current listing of the elements in the collection
- `fill`, which overwrites the current elements of the collection with a specific value
- `copy`, which duplicates the elements appearing in a collection to form a second collection
- `binarySearch`, which performs a binary search for a specific value on any list whose elements are already sorted
- `max` and `min`, which return the largest and smallest element, respectively, of a specific collection
- `nCopies`, which appends n copies of a specific element to a given collection
- Singleton algorithms, which construct new lists consisting of a single element specified by the programmer

These algorithms are extremely useful in solving a number of diverse programming problems, ranging from problems originating from ordinary business-related data processing to those involved with timeshared multiprocessing using priority queues. With the notable exception of `max` and `min`, the algorithms listed here are applicable to any `List` object, whether implemented using `ArrayList` or `LinkedList`.

Several of the algorithms listed have a number of different versions:

- a default version, assuming a default ordering of the elements of the collection
- a second version, prompting the programmer to specify other parameters, such as specific `Comparator` objects, or a `Random` identifier, or others

Java also provides an `Arrays` utility class, containing a number of useful implementations of algorithms applicable to ordinary one-dimensional arrays. The algorithms in this class can be accessed by using

```
import java.util.Arrays;
```

or

```
import java.util.*;
```

Four major processing algorithms are listed in the `Arrays` class:

- `sort`
- `binarySearch`
- `equals`
- `fill`

Each of these must be preceded by the `Arrays` modifier as a qualified reference, using the syntax

```
Arrays.<identifier>(<argument_list>);
```

where `<identifier>` and `<argument_list>` are defined exactly as for `Collections`.

The `sort` algorithm has four different versions. Besides the default version, there are versions using a `Comparator` parameter and versions with parameters specifying the low and high subscripts of an array segment to be sorted. The `binarySearch` algorithm behaves in exactly the same manner for arrays as for lists but does not have a version that is applicable to a properly smaller segment of the sorted array. The `fill` algorithm is the direct analogue of the `List` version whereas `equals` applies to two arrays, returning `true` just when both arrays are identical, and `false` if otherwise.

In addition, there are algorithms enabling movement between array and `List` objects. The `Arrays.asList` method takes a single array parameter and returns a `List` object whose elements, in order of their appearance, are those of the array argument. The size of the list is that of the underlying array and cannot be changed during the course of the subsequent computation. The reverse movement is also possible: We have already discussed the `toArray` method, converting a `Collection` object to an ordinary one-dimensional array.[6]

The primary design objective for including generic algorithms is to provide predefined and highly efficient versions of a number of implementations of algorithms that are frequently used in commercial software design. Their inclusion into the Java Application Programming Interface (the Java API) helps to lift the burden, to a large extent, of coding these algorithms from the shoulders of the programmer: All the programmer has to do is to retrofit the existing generic algorithm to suit the environment of the specific problem to be solved.

One of the useful facilities of the `java.util` library is the `StringTokenizer` class, whose objects break down a character string into a sequence of *tokens*. This decomposition is completely governed by the programmer, who specifies a finite number of *delimiters*. Some of the advantages in using `StringTokenizer` objects include providing a highly efficient alterna-

---

[6]See Section 5.3 for details of the use of `toArray()`.

tive to the solution of a number of significant problems that arise in formal language design and compilation, while very closely simulating the behavior of a compiler or interpreter of a high-level general purpose programming language. Some of the more important problems that are solvable using the StringTokenizer class also involve stacks—such as the problem of balanced parentheses, brackets, or braces, as well as the problem of evaluating an arithmetic expression in postfix form or the problem of converting an arithmetic expression in infix form to its equivalent in postfix form.

EXERCISES

1. Define a Comparator object similar to the application defined in Example 8.4 for priorities, but now define it for increasing processNumber.

2. Redo Exercise 1, but now for steps.

3. Use the reverse algorithm to write any character string backwards.

4. Show that the following code sequence can be used to test for palindromes:

```
BufferedReader intIS = new BufferedReader(
                    new InputStreamReader(System.in));
String inputString = intIS.readLine();
List charList = new ArrayList();
for(int index = 0; index < inputString.length(); ++index)
{
 char chValue = inputString.charAt(index);
 charList.add(new Character(chValue));
}
Collections.reverse(charList);
String reverseString = ""; // reverseString is initially empty.
for(int index = 0; index < charList.size(); ++index)
{
 Character value =  (Character)(charList.get(index));
 char cValue = value.charValue();
 reverseString = reverseString + cValue;
}
if(reverseString.equals(inputString))
 System.out.println(inputString + " is a palindrome");
else
 System.out.println(inputString + " is not a palindrome");
```

5. Suppose we declare

```
List list1 = new ArrayList(10);
```

and currently list1 = [2,5,3,5]. What is the result of applying Collections.fill(list1,new Integer(10)) ?

What is the result of executing `Collections.fill(list1,new Integer(10))` if instead we have the declaration

```
List list1 = new ArrayList(4);
```

and currently `list1 = [2,5]` ?

6. Apply `Collections.fill(intList,new Character('X'))` to the `Integer`-valued `intList = [2,3,1,7,8]` and explain the consequences of the result.

7. Justify or refute: For any `<Collection_identifier>` naming a well-defined `Collection` object,

   a. `Collections.max(<Collection_identifier>,Collections.reverseOrder()) = Collections.min(<Collection_identifier>)`

   b. `Collections.min(<Collection_identifier>,Collections.reverseOrder()) = Collections.max(<Collection_identifier>)`

8. Recode and execute Example 8.5, but now construct `stringFrequency` as a `TreeMap` object.

9. Create similar code sequences to that seen in Section 8.12 for `Set` and `Map` objects to illustrate the use of `EMPTY_SET` and `EMPTY_MAP`.

10. Show how to reverse the values of the components of an `Integer`-valued array by reversing the contents of the associated list using `asList` and `toArray`.

11. Use `Character`-valued arrays `Arrays.asList`, `Arrays.equals`, and `toArray` to test any character string for palindromes.

12. Suppose `list1 = [Vivian,Angela,Patrizia,Josephine]`.

    a. Describe the result of applying

       ```
       list1.addAll(Collections.nCopies(4,"Michela"));
       ```

    b. Compare this to the result of applying

       ```
       list1.addAll(1,Collections.nCopies(4,"Michela"));
       ```

13. Suppose `stringFrequency` is described as in Section 8.15, now using the `Map` constructor

    ```
    Map stringFrequency = new HashMap();
    ```

    Describe any changes, if they exist, occurring in the representation of `stringFrequency`, `stringFrequency.keySet()`, and `stringFrequency.values()` before and after invoking

    ```
    stringFrequency.values().removeAll()(Collections.singleton("Lawyer"));
    ```

14. Suppose `list1`, `list2` are the `Integer`-valued lists initialized as follows:

    ```
    list1 = [2,3,1,7,8,2,8]
    list2 = [4,0,4,9]
    ```

    Find the values of each of `list1` and `list2` after executing each of the code sequences listed below:

a. `Collections.copy(list1,list2);`

b. `Collections.reverse(list1);`
   `Collections.reverse(list2);`
   `Collections.copy(list1,list2);`

c. `Collections.reverse(list2);`
   `Collections.fill(list2,new Integer(3));`

d. `Collections.copy(list1,list2);`
   `Collections.sort(list1);`

e. `Collections.copy(list1,list2);`
   `Collections.sort(list1,Collections.reverseOrder());`

15. What is the exact form of the output when the following main method executes?

```java
public static void main(String [] args)
{
 String [] strArray = {"Vivian","Patrizia","Angela","Josephine",
   "Michela","Rosalie"};
 for(int index = 1; index <= strArray.length; ++index)
 {
  System.out.println("Sorting from position 0 to position "
                          + (index-1));
  Arrays.sort(strArray,0,index);
  for(int i = 0; i < strArray.length; ++i)
    System.out.println("strArray[" + i + "] = " + strArray[i]);
 } // terminates text of outer for-loop
} // terminates text of main method
```

16. Compute and explain the output generated by

```java
public static void main(String [] args)
{
 // Input string to be parsed into tokens.
 String strValue = "I think, therefore I am!";
 StringTokenizer tokens = new StringTokenizer(strValue," ,!");
 while(tokens.hasMoreTokens())
 {
  System.out.println(tokens.nextToken());
  System.out.println(tokens.countTokens());
 }
} // terminates text of main method
```

17. Write a driver for `evalPostfix`, using the input strings `"2 3 + 4 *"` and `"25 13 - 4 %"`.

18. Rewrite the method `checkBalance` from Section 7.6, now using String-Tokenizer.

PROGRAMMING PROJECT

Rewrite the code for toPostfix for converting an arithmetic expression in infix form to its equivalent in postfix form, now using tokens generated from an appropriate version of StringTokenizer.

CHAPTER 9

....

Sets and Maps

CHAPTER OBJECTIVES

- To extend the study of the Set ADT begun in Chapter Five.
- To describe the HashSet and TreeSet implementations of the Set interface in greater detail.
- To examine several key applications of the Set interface.
- To continue the study of the Map ADT.
- To provide a deeper study of the HashMap and TreeMap implementations of the Map interface.
- To compare the SortedSet and SortedMap interfaces.

....

9.1 Introduction

In Section 5.5 we defined a *set* as a special kind of collection, in that a set does not allow for the storage of duplicate elements. In other words, if we attempt to add two equal elements of a set (in the sense of the equals method defined in Object), the first invocation of the add method will add the element to the set (if that element is not already present in the set) and the second will return false, to indicate that the element is already present. Thus, the Set interface, defined as a subclass of Collection, is faithful in this respect to the mathematical abstraction of a set.

If we compare the Collection and Set interfaces from Chapter Five, we note that Set contains no methods other than those inherited from Collection—the only distinction between these is that a Set object, no matter what implementation is used, does not support duplicate objects. We also see that it is possible to compare any two Set objects, even if their respective implementations differ.

In direct contrast, the Map interface does *not* represent a subclass of Collection. A Map object does not consist of single entities—instead, any

Map object consists of a pair, involving a key and its corresponding value. Several restrictions are observed: A map cannot contain duplicate keys; that is, each key maps to no more than one value. A value, however, can correspond to one or more distinct keys. Again, as was the case for sets, this definition of a map is in perfect accord with its formal mathematical counterpart. As an example, it is possible to use a Map object to store a correspondence between a person's surname and his or her current profession. Although there may well be more than one surname corresponding to a single profession (for example, "Miller" and "Ross" may both map to "physician"), the map may well return the same profession for more than one surname.

This chapter is devoted to an extended study of the Set and Map interfaces, along with their various implementations. Special attention will be given to related design issues in which the choice between a Set or Map solution might occur. The decision as to which is the more appropriate and efficient choice will be influenced, at least in part, by the description of the application domain. More precisely, our solution will attempt to respond effectively to the following question:

What implementation is best for optimizing the speed and efficiency of the storage and retrieval of data?

One implementation might involve sorting the keys in some specific order, such as ascending numeric order (if the keys are numeric) or ascending lexicographic order (if the keys are character strings). Another implementation might involve the application of some hash function, as defined initially in Chapter Four. In Java, the first is handled by the SortedSet or SortedMap interface; the second requires the use of the HashSet or HashMap implementation. We will study each of these in this chapter.

9.2   **The Set Interface and the HashSet and TreeSet Implementations**

One of the key reasons why software designers using Java choose Set objects is because of their efficiency in searching. With this in mind, the designer might choose between two possible implementations of the Set interface: HashSet and TreeSet. The construction of Set objects implemented using HashSet uses a predefined hash function that promotes highly efficient searches and retrievals of its elements. In fact, we have already noted that hashing is usually of order O(1). The only drawback is that using the HashSet implementation provides no guarantee that such objects will store its elements in any specific order. On the other hand, if a sorted version of the Set object is crucial for the application, or (as we will see later) if the methods present in the SortedSet interface are needed, the choice of TreeSet is more appropriate. In fact, TreeSet is the only implementation offered in Java for SortedSet. At this point, it is enough for us to observe that implementing Set using TreeSet produces a representation of the underlying object with elements that are sorted according to the default "natural" ordering. The representation of the object using TreeSet outputs its elements using an *inorder iterator*. This is because the TreeSet implementation of any object stores its elements using a balanced form of a binary search tree.[1] Thus, the application of a traversal of this tree using an inorder iterator produces the natural sorted order of its elements.

Example 9.1 illustrates the distinctions between representations of the same finite collection of Integer values as a HashSet object and as a TreeSet object.

EXAMPLE 9.1

```java
public static void main(String [] args)
 {
    // Conformant array holding input data.
    int [] intArr = {2,3,7,-1,4,8};

    // Construct two Set objects, one implemented using HashSet
    // and the other implemented using TreeSet.
    Set hashSet = new HashSet();
    Set treeSet = new TreeSet();

    // Install the values of intArr into each of
    // hashSet and treeSet.
    for(int index = 0; index < intArr.length; ++index)
    {
     hashSet.add(new Integer(intArr[index]));
     treeSet.add(new Integer(intArr[index]));
    }

    // Output contents of each.
    System.out.println("hashSet = " + hashSet);
    System.out.println("treeSet = " + treeSet);

 } // terminates text of main method
```

The output derived from executing this program is

hashSet = [8,7,4,3,2,-1]
treeSet = [-1,2,3,4,7,8]

[1]Implementation details for sets are discussed in Section 9.5.

We noted in Section 5.5 that the `HashSet` and `TreeSet` implementations each define four constructors. The constructors defined for `HashSet` use capacity and load factor, while those defined for `TreeSet` pay special attention to the ordering of the elements present in the `Set` object. So far as defaults are concerned, for `HashSet` objects the default initial capacity is `101`. For `Set` objects using the `HashSet` implementation, the capacity of the object is determined by the number of "buckets" present in the underlying hash table. If the programmer wishes to optimize performance using the `HashSet` implementation, we suggest that the programmer design a constructor that overrides this default capacity. This is because, in most cases, the default initial capacity is far too large for the specific application, resulting in a loss of storage and processing speed. For example, if a `HashSet` object with an initial capacity of `35` is required, we suggest using the constructor

```
Set hSet = new HashSet(35);
```

The `TreeSet` class implements `SortedSet`. The hierarchical diagram describing the relationship among `Set`, `SortedSet`, and `TreeSet` was given in Figure 5.12. In contrast to `HashSet`, `TreeSet` is not concerned with hashing. Hence, no initial capacity value nor capacity increment value is involved in the construction of `TreeSet` objects. Instead, `TreeSet` provides constructors whose objects have elements that are sorted using a default "less than" ordering or that are defined by the programmer either by specifying a `Comparator` parameter or by specifying a specific `SortedSet` parameter.

9.3 `Set` **Operations**

`Set` objects share a behavior that is similar to finite sets in pure mathematics in a number of ways. In fact, we have already shown that, if not empty, any `Set` object stores a finite collection of elements in some order, whether optimal for hashing (in the case of `HashSet` objects) or sorted (in the case of `TreeSet` objects). We can observe that the instance methods defined in the `Set` interface might be used to mimic the fundamental set-theoretic operations of set inclusion and membership, union, intersection, difference, and symmetric difference.

Set Membership and Inclusion

The `Set` interface supports a `boolean`-valued instance method `contains` that returns `true` if the `Set` object contains an element whose value matches that of the parameter; otherwise, the return value is `false`. This involves the set membership relationship that is commonly denoted by $\in$. For instance, if `S` is a set and `x` is a value of the same type as the elements of `S`, then $x \in S$ means that `x` is an element of `S`. Thus, if `S` is the `Integer-`

valued set represented as `[2,3,1,4,7]`, then $7 \in S$ is true but $5 \in S$ is false.[2]

The syntax for `contains` is given by

```
boolean contains(Object obj);
```

If we have already constructed `S` as the `Integer`-valued set just given, and if we execute the code sequence

```
S.contains(new Integer(7));
```

the result is `true`, whereas the code sequence

```
S.contains(new Integer(5));
```

produces a result whose value is `false`.

The set-theoretical relationship of set inclusion is defined by observing that, if `S`, `T` are sets, then `S` is *included* in `T` (or `S` is a *subset* of `T`) if and only if every element of `S` is also a member of `T`. The notation $S \subseteq T$ is used to denote the fact that `S` is included in `T`. In mathematics, we can show that two sets are *equal* (that is, they have the same elements) if we can show that each is included in the other.

In Java, we can observe that set inclusion is implemented in the `Set` interface by the "bulk" method `containsAll`, with the signature

```
boolean containsAll(Collection otherCollection);
```

This method returns `true` just when the `Collection` object whose value is given by the parameter is included in the current `Set` object. That is, if `S`, `T` are `Set` objects, then `S.containsAll(T)` returns `true` just when every element of `T` also appears as an element of `S`.

As an example, if `S` is the `Integer`-valued set `[2,3,1,4,7]` and `T` is the `Integer`-valued set `[2,4,1]`, then `S.containsAll(T)` returns `true`. If `S` is instead defined as above and `T` = `[2,3,5]`, then `S.containsAll(T)` is `false`.

Set Union

If `S`, `T` are sets, then the *union* of `S`, `T`, commonly denoted by $S \cup T$, is simply the set whose elements appear in at least one of `S`, `T`. Thus, for example, if `S` is the `Integer`-valued set `[2,3,1,4,7]` and `T` is the `Integer`-valued set `[5,0,2,9]`, then $S \cup T$ is the `Integer`-valued set `[2,3,1,4,7,5,0,9]`.

Each of the following represents a true statement about set unions:

- `S` $\cup$ `S` = `S`
- `S` $\cup$ `T` = `T` $\cup$ `S`
- If `S` $\subseteq$ `T`, then `S` $\cup$ `T` = `T`

---

[2]An alternative notation for such statements as "$5 \in S$ is false" is "$5 \notin S$."

The `Set` interface defines a bulk method `addAll` simulating the set-theoretical operation of set union. Its syntax was given in Section 5.5 by

```
boolean addAll(Collection otherCollection);
```

In fact, we can see that the parameter can be any well-defined `Collection` object. In our implementation of set union, however, the parameter will be a `Set` object. Recalling the definition given in Section 5.5, if `S,T` are `Set` objects, then `S.addAll(T)` returns `true` just when `S` is changed as a result of executing `addAll`, and `false` if otherwise. As a side result, the new version of `S` is the result of applying `S.addAll(T)`. Thus, for example, if `S,T` are the `Integer`-valued sets given earlier, then the code sequence

```
if(S.addAll(T))
   System.out.println("The union of S and T is " + S);
else
   System.out.println("T is a subset of S. Consequently S did not change");
```

produces output

The union of S and T is [0,1,2,3,4,5,7,9][3]

This simulation of union by `retainAll` works only if the sets involved contain elements of a common data type, as was the case for the example of `Integer`-valued sets `S,T` given above. If not, a `ClassCastException` is thrown.

Set Intersection

If `S,T` are sets, then the *intersection* of `S` and `T`, commonly denoted by $S \cap T$, is the set whose elements appear in both `S` and `T`. For example, if `S` is the `Integer`-valued set `[2,3,1,4,7]` and `T` is the `Integer`-valued set `[5,0,2,9]`, then $S \cap T$ is the set `[2]`.

Each of the following is a property of set intersections:

- $S \cap S = S$
- $S \cap T = T \cap S$
- If $S \subseteq T$, then $S \cap T = S$

How do we simulate intersection using `Set` objects whose elements share a common data type? We will show how this is possible for `Integer`-valued sets, with the understanding that this can be imitated for any other wrapper class. Assuming `S,T` have already been constructed and initialized, we then use the `Iterator` class and execute the following code sequence:

```
// Set constructed to store intersection.
Set intST = new TreeSet();
```

---

[3]Here we assume the `TreeSet` implementation of `Set`.

```
for(Iterator iter = S.iterator(); iter.hasNext(); )
{
 Integer value = (Integer)iter.next();
 if(T.contains(value)) intST.add(value);
}
```

```
System.out.println("Intersection of S,T is: " + intST);
```

We construct the Set object intST to hold the elements present in the intersection of S and T. The iterator moves through the elements of S, when the iterator also scans an element of T, that element is in the intersection of S and T. Consequently, that element is added to intST. The output derived by executing the code sequence on S, T defined earlier is

Intersection of S,T is: [2]

Set Difference and Symmetric Difference

Suppose S, T are Set objects whose elements share the same data type. The *difference* of S and T is defined as the set of elements in S with all of those elements that are also in T removed. The notation used for this is S - T. As an example, suppose S is the Integer-valued set given by [1,2,4,5,7] and T is the Integer-valued set [3,4,5,9]. Then S - T is [1,2,7].

Several implementations are possible in Java to compute S - T. One such implementation uses the predefined instance method removeAll defined in Section 5.5 with the signature

```
boolean removeAll(Collection otherCollection);
```

This method removes all objects in the collection (Set object in this case) described by the parameter from the current Set object, returning true if the set was changed as a result of invoking this method, and false if not.

If we apply this method to compute S - T for S, T as above, we would use

```
if(S.removeAll(T))
  System.out.println("S - T is: " + S);
else
  System.out.println("S was not changed by using S.removeAll(T)");
```

A second alternative is to apply an Iterator object in a way that is similar to the computation yielding the intersection of two sets. More specifically, let us consider the code sequence

```
// Set defined to store S - T.
Set diffST = new TreeSet();

for(Iterator iter = S.iterator(); iter.hasNext();)
```

```
{
  Integer value = (Integer)iter.next();
  if(!T.contains(value)) diffST.add(value);
}

System.out.println("S - T is: " + diffST);
```

In either case, the output is

S - T is: [1,2,7]

Note that set difference is not a symmetric operation because T - S, defined as those elements in T that are not elements in S, is [3,9].

The following are properties of set difference, where we again assume S,T are Set objects whose elements are from the same data type:

- S - ∅ = S, where ∅ denotes the empty set
- S - S = ∅
- S - T ⊆ S

If S,T are Set objects whose elements share a common data type, we define the *symmetric difference* of S and T as the union of S - T and T - S. For example, if S is the Integer-valued set [1,2,4,5,7] and T is the Integer-valued set [3,4,5,9], then the symmetric difference of S and T is [1,2,3,7,9] and can be computed using diffST.addAll(diffTS).

At this point, we should observe that each of the set operations defined in this section is O(n). Executing each of these involves an iterator that compares the elements in S with those of T in order to choose those to be included in the new set being built.

9.4   **The Methods of the SortedSet Interface**

The SortedSet interface extends Set by including a number of extra methods that use the sorted nature of the underlying object. The TreeSet class implements SortedSet—thus, any Set object constructed using the TreeSet implementation is automatically a SortedSet object.

We will illustrate the functionality of these methods using the Integer-valued SortedSet object S = [1,2,4,5,7]. We also assume the default "less than" ordering. The first method we will consider has the syntax described by the signature

```
public Object first();
```

This returns the first (smallest) object in the current sorted set. Thus, S.first() applied to S as defined above yields the Integer value 1.

The next method has the syntax

```
public Object last();
```

This returns the last (largest) object in the current sorted set. Thus, when applied to S as defined above, S.last() yields the Integer value 7.

The signature of the next method is

```
public SortedSet subSet(Object minValue, Object maxValue);
```

The result of applying this method to a SortedSet object is the subset of that object whose elements are at the same time greater than or equal to the first parameter but also strictly less than the value of the second parameter. It is also understood that the two parameters share the same data type as the elements of the SortedSet object. As an example, if we apply S.subSet(new Integer(2),new Integer(5)), the result is [2,4]. Note that the value(s) of the parameters need not necessarily be elements to which subSet is being applied. Thus, if we apply S.subSet(new Integer(3),new Integer(5)), the result is [4].

The next method has the signature

```
public SortedSet headSet(Object value);
```

When applied to a SortedSet object, the return result is a representation of the subset of that object whose elements are strictly less than the value of the parameter. Again, as before, we assume that the parameter has a data type that is shared by the elements of the SortedSet object. Thus, for example, S.headSet(new Integer(5)) returns [1,2,4].

Finally, the last method we will discuss in this section has the signature

```
public SortedSet tailSet(Object value);
```

This returns a representation of that object consisting of the subset of all elements in that object that are greater than or equal to the value of the parameter. Again, the parameter is assumed to share the same data type as that of the elements appearing in the object. For example, S.tailSet(new Integer(5)) is [5,7].

By virtue of the inheritance relationship existing among Set, Sorted-Set, and TreeSet, as illustrated in Figure 5.12, any TreeSet object automatically inherits each of the methods described in SortedSet. This also includes the definition of an alternative Comparator object if the design decision is to use a Comparator object that differs from the default.

9.5 Implementation Details: Binary Search Trees and Red-Black Trees

This section gives a brief description of how TreeSet objects are implemented in software. As stated earlier, Set objects (whether implemented using `HashSet` or `TreeSet`) should be used whenever we wish to store and retrieve values in an efficient and speedy manner using some type of key. As we will see, the choice of the underlying data structure is also motivated by the attempt to minimize as many worst-case situations as possible for the operations of searching for and retrieving a value, inserting a new value, and removing values from the underlying container. For readers who are familiar with the data structures described in this section or who do not require this information for their work, the topics presented here can be easily skipped without interrupting the presentation of the remaining topics presented in this chapter.

We begin by defining the concept of a *binary tree*. A binary tree is a nonlinear data structure that either is empty or consists of a finite sequence of *nodes,* each of which consists of three components called `left`, `info`, and `right`, described as follows:

- `left` and `right` store references to other nodes or are `null`
- `info` stores the data (of some given type) to be maintained at that node

If we view this superficially, there seems to be no distinction between the basic structure of nodes presented here and those defined for `LinkedList` objects in Section 6.4. However, there are significant differences between the way binary tree nodes are linked to others, and the way nodes are linked for the `LinkedList` implementation of `List`. In the case of binary tree nodes, there is a uniquely determined *root node,* representing the only entry point into the tree. Once access is established at the designated root, passing to other nodes in the tree (if such nodes exist) is possible *in one direction only:* from the root node to no further than a *leaf node*. A *leaf* (or *leaf node*) in a tree is a node for which no further downward movement is possible. Nodes that are not leaf nodes are called *interior nodes*.

Binary trees are characterized by the property that, if not empty, a maximum of two nonempty nodes come from any node. If the `left` component of the node is not empty, the node referenced by `left` is the *left child* (or *left descendant*) of the node. Similarly, if the `right` component of the node is not empty, the node referenced by `right` is called the *right child* (or *right descendant*) of the node. Each of the left and right descendants can be viewed as the root node of a binary tree called the *left subtree* and *right subtree,* respectively, of the original binary tree. Because the left and right subtrees are binary trees in their own right, the definitions of left and right descendants, left and right subtrees, root and leaf nodes, and others to follow are recursive in nature.

A *binary search tree* (sometimes called a *BST*) is a special form of a binary tree in which the `info` component of any node (assuming the "less than" comparison operator) is greater than the value of the `info` component of any node in the designated left subtree (referenced by the `left` component of the current node) and less than the value of the `info` component of any node in its designated right subtree (referenced by the `right` component of the current node). Our definition of BST precludes the possibility of any duplicate values.

We also define the *level* of any node recursively, as follows: The level of the root node is `0`, and the level of either child of any node is `1 + level` of its uniquely determined "parent" node. As an illustration of these ideas, consider the BST of integer values given in Figure 9.1.

FIGURE 9.1

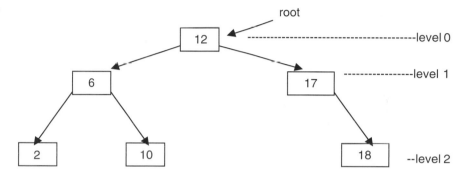

Here, the root node `12` and the nodes containing the values `6` and `17` are interior nodes, and the nodes containing the values `2`, `10`, and `18` are leaf nodes. The left child of the root is the node holding the value `6`, and the right child of the node holding `17` is the node holding `18`, and so on. We can then characterize any leaf node as one whose left and right subtrees are empty—that is, a leaf node is one having no children. The implementation of the abstraction of Figure 9.1 displaying the complete layout of each node is shown in Figure 9.2.

FIGURE 9.2

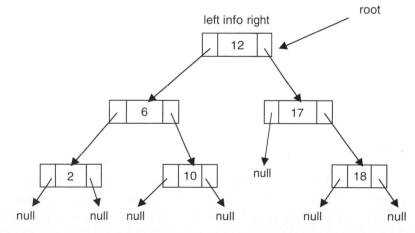

If the data type of the `info` components is more complicated, the basic structure of the binary search tree is maintained by defining a key from the values of the data type defined for the `info` components of the nodes and then comparing the values of the corresponding keys. Each wrapper type defined in Java has a default "less than" operator that allows any two of its values to be compared using `compareTo`. If we require an alternate comparison operator, however, we can define it as a `Comparator` object. In our presentation, unless we explicitly specify otherwise, we will assume the "less than" operator.

Not every binary search tree has the "symmetric" (perhaps better termed "short and thick") representation given in Figure 9.1. In fact, Figure 9.3 is also a BST containing the same values as those of Figure 9.1.

 FIGURE 9.3

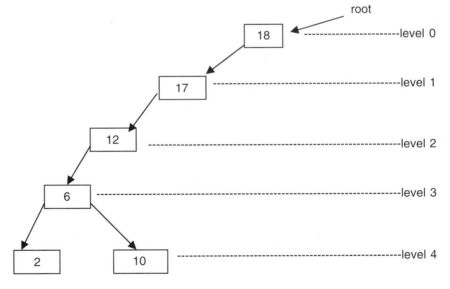

What causes such differences? Using binary search trees as the implementation of sorted containers involves a heavy dependence on the *order of insertion* of values into the container. For example, the binary search tree depicted in Figure 9.1 implements the input sequence 12, 6, 17, 10, 18, 2, whereas the binary search tree of Figure 9.3 uses the input sequence 18, 17, 12, 6, 10, 2. So far as retrieval is concerned, because entry into the tree is possible only through the root, it would require, for example, only 3 comparisons to determine that 10 appears in the tree in Figure 9.1, but 5 comparisons are required to arrive at the same conclusion for the tree in Figure 9.3. Thus, we see in a real and elementary sense that "symmetric" binary search trees are better suited for efficient retrieval of values and other related operations. This is primarily due to the fact that search and retrieval operations done in trees such as that depicted in Figure 9.3 are of nearly linear complexity, while those of trees such as Figure 9.1 are approximately of order $O(\log n)$.

We define a *full* binary tree as one whose leaves are all at the same level k, for some nonnegative integer k, and for which each possible position at level k is occupied by a (leaf) node. Thus, the tree described in Figure 9.4 is an example of a full binary search tree, while those described in Figures 9.1 and 9.3 are not. In addition, the definition of a full tree is extendable in a natural way to more general trees. We leave the formal details of this extended form of the definition as an exercise for the reader.

How can we guarantee that the binary search tree is symmetric? The fact is, we cannot! This is quite obvious from the way the binary search trees in Figures 9.1 and 9.3 were constructed. We can conclude that what is needed is a different form of a search tree where the order of complexity of the operations usually attributed to sorted containers is independent of the order of insertion of values in the associated container. A step in the direction of constructing a more suitable tree uses the definition of a *2-3-4 tree*. A 2-3-4 tree is a search tree that is no longer binary but rather extends the idea of a search tree to those whose nodes might contain exactly one, two, or three values and have subtrees (if they exist) defined as follows:

1. If a node contains exactly one data value, it is called a *2-node* and has exactly two (possible empty) subtrees, defined exactly as in the case of a binary search tree.
2. If a node contains exactly two values `val1` and `val2`, with `val1` "less than" `val2` (such a node is called a *3-node*), then three (possibly empty) subtrees exist: one whose nodes have values "less than" `val1` (designated as the *left subtree*), the next whose nodes have values "between" those of `val1` and `val2` (designated as the *middle subtree*), and the last consisting of nodes all of whose values are "no less than" that of `val2` (designated as the *right subtree*).
3. If a node contains exactly three values `val1`, `val2`, and `val3`, where `val1` is "less than" `val2` and `val2` is "less than" `val3`, it is called a *4-node*. It has four (possibly empty) subtrees, representing the natural extension of the definition of subtrees for a 3-node as defined in (2).
4. The last row of the tree containing all of the leaves is completely filled.

We define a search tree to be *complete* if all of its leaves are at the same level and there are no gaps in the row of the tree in which all of its leaves appear or at any earlier level, when such rows are scanned steadily from left to right. In other words, a binary search tree is complete if, for every node having a nonvoid right child, that same node already has a nonvoid left child. Thus, we can conclude that the binary search trees of Figures 9.1 and 9.3 are not complete, whereas the binary search tree of Figure 9.4 is complete.

FIGURE 9.4

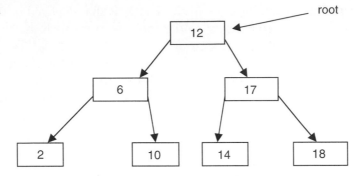

We define the *height* of the left (or right) subtree of any node in a BST as the maximum length (number of distinct nodes) of any path in the left (or right) subtree beginning with that node and ending at a leaf. Thus, the height of the node of the left subtree of Figure 9.1 containing the value 17 is zero, and the height of the left subtree of the same node in Figure 9.3 is 3. We define a binary tree as *balanced* if the height of any node's right subtree differs from the height of its corresponding left subtree by at most one. The binary trees of Figures 9.1 and 9.4 are balanced, whereas that of Figure 9.3 is not. The tree in Figure 9.5 is an example of a balanced binary search tree with leaves at different levels:

FIGURE 9.5

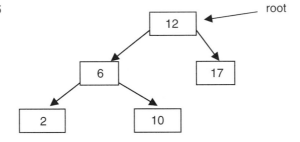

The motivation behind the idea of 2-3-4 trees is to keep the level of the tree nodes as minimal as possible. In addition, the ideas of level, height, and completeness extend to 2-3-4 trees with little extra effort. In summary, the idea behind 2-3-4 trees is to be able to maintain the same level for a node as long as possible, until the insertion of new values into the tree "saturates" the current node to the extent that the only remaining alternative is to increase the height of the tree. As an example, consider the 2-3-4 tree of Figure 9.6 with no 4-nodes, constructed as the result of applying the insertion operation to the input sequence 18, 17, 12, 6, 10, 2.

Thus, we go from a binary search tree of level 4 in Figure 9.3 to a 2-3-4 tree of level 1 in Figure 9.6. We can then conclude that the 2-3-4 tree

FIGURE 9.6

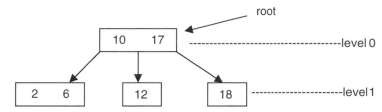

is more efficient because the processing time required to compare several values at a single node is substantially less than that required to progress to a lower level of the tree; following a pointer is slower than comparing values. Therefore, the efficiency of processing operations commonly attributed to sorted containers is generally enhanced when the 2-3-4 tree is used as an alternative to the corresponding BST. To illustrate this, look at the 2-3-4 tree of Figure 9.7. This tree is constructed from the same input sequence as that used to construct the tree in Figure 9.6. Although it is different from that of Figure 9.6, it is in no way less efficient.

FIGURE 9.7

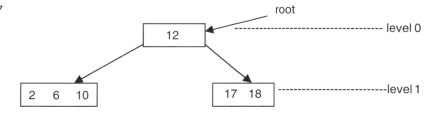

There is, however, one major drawback to using 2-3-4 trees. Designing and coding efficient algorithms for searching and retrieving values, as well as inserting and deleting values, is substantially more complicated than the corresponding code for binary search trees. What we require, then, is some form of compromise between the ease of processing afforded by binary search trees and the efficiency of operations for 2-3-4 trees. This compromise is provided by using *red-black trees.*

A red-black tree is a binary search tree representing the following adaptation of 2-3-4 trees:

1. If we have a 2-node in the 2-3-4 tree, we make no changes in the corresponding red-black tree.
2. If we have a 3-node in the 2-3-4 tree, as in Figure 9.8a, convert this either to Figure 9.8b or Figure 9.8c.

The (red) designation of a node in the red-black tree is for a newly constructed node to complete the correspondence with the underlying 2-3-4 tree.

FIGURE 9.8a

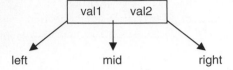

FIGURE 9.8b

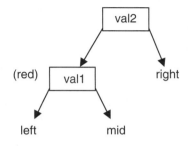

FIGURE 9.8c

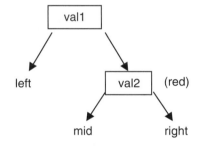

3. If we have a 4-node such as that described in Figure 9.9a, convert this to the red-black tree structure given in Figure 9.9b.

FIGURE 9.9a

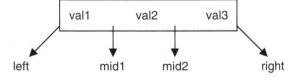

FIGURE 9.9b

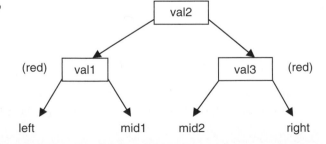

The idea is to reconstruct each 3- or 4-node as a sequence of nodes and links in a binary tree in such a way that the ordering of the nodes' values is preserved; that is, so that the corresponding binary tree is a binary search tree. As item (2) in the previous list shows, this representation is not necessarily unique. As an example, the 2-3-4 tree of Figure 9.7 can be converted to the red-black tree of Figure 9.10, and the 2-3-4 tree of Figure 9.7 can be converted into the red-black tree of Figure 9.11.

FIGURE 9.10

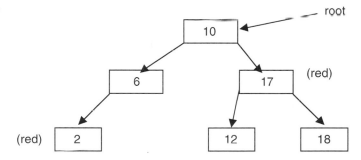

FIGURE 9.11

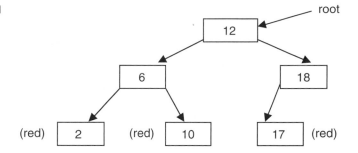

As Figure 9.10 shows, the corresponding red-black tree is not necessarily complete. In the conversion rules stated earlier, the original node in the 2-3-4 tree is designated a *black node*, as is the case of the root node. The only nodes that become red nodes are those in the corresponding red-black tree to which the earlier conversion rules (2) and (3) have been applied.

In summary, we observe that the design of the TreeSet class is based on red-black trees. That is, when a TreeSet object is constructed and elements of the appropriate data type are added to the object, it has the internal representation of a red-black tree. Because a red-black tree is balanced, any operation performed on the elements of the object (that is, elements of the tree) is of order O(log n). This attests to the efficiency of searching for a value and modifying the object when constructed using TreeSet. In addition, the sorted nature of the tree is evident by a TreeSet iterator in order traversal of its elements.

9.6 The `Map` Interface and its `HashMap` and `TreeMap` Implementations

Section 5.7 provided us with a brief but accurate description of the purpose of including the `Map` interface in the fundamental design of the `java.util` library. Recall that a `Map` object is not technically a member of a class in the Java Collection Framework. Instead, `Map` forms the hub of a separate class hierarchy with such interfaces and concrete classes as `Map`, `SortedMap`, `HashMap`, and `TreeMap`. The principal idea is that when a `Map` object is constructed, a single data element is *not* added to this object—instead, a *pair* of data objects is added in the form of a *keyValue, dataValue* combination. Stated in other words, a `Map` object stores only *keyValue, dataValue* pairs. This exploits the intuitive idea that it is ordinarily not the case, nor is it absolutely necessary, to retrieve an entire block of data about a single individual or item by knowing *every* component of the data in advance. Instead, to retrieve every component of data involving that individual or item, it is sufficient to know only certain information about that item—that information supplied in a *key*.

Analogous to the situation with `Set`, `SortedSet`, `HashSet`, and `TreeSet` studied in Chapter Five and earlier in this chapter, there is a similar relationship existing between the `Map` and `SortedMap` interfaces and between the `HashMap` and `TreeMap` implementations. The hierarchy is described in Figure 5.14. In brief, we can comment that the situation for `Map` is the analog for that of `Set`, in the following sense: If `SortedMap` methods are required for the application, it is advisable to construct `TreeMap` objects in order to take advantage of the `Collection` views afforded by that construction. Otherwise, a more efficient alternative would involve constructing `HashMap` objects.

An important observation about `HashMap` or `TreeMap` objects is that the hash function (for `HashMap` objects) or the comparison operator (for `TreeMap` objects) is applied *only* to the `keyValue` component of any element. The `dataValue` component is never hashed or compared—it simply goes along with the `keyValue` component. In addition, `keyValue` components of elements of a `Map` object must be unique, regardless of the implementation. Thus, it is impossible to store distinct elements of the same `Map` object with the same `keyValue` component.

To see the distinction existing between the representation of `HashMap` and `TreeMap` objects, let us reexamine the `names[]` and `occupation[]` arrays from Section 8.15, where we have

```
String names[] = {"Rocco","Anthony","Lorenzo","Angela","Vivian"};
```

and

```
String occupation[] = {"Engineer","Doctor","Lawyer","Engineer","Lawyer"};
```

Suppose we now construct `Map` objects as

```
Map stringFrequency1 = new TreeMap();
Map stringFrequency2 = new HashMap();
```

and then initialize `stringFrequency1, stringFrequency2` by

```
for(int index = 0; index < names.length; ++index)
{
  stringFrequency1.put(names[index],occupation[index]);
  stringFrequency2.put(names[index],occupation[index]);
}
```

The result of executing this code sequence is

```
stringFrequency1 = {Angela=Engineer, Anthony=Doctor, Lorenzo=Lawyer,
  Rocco=Engineer, Vivian=Lawyer}
```

and

```
stringFrequency2 = {Angela=Engineer, Lorenzo=Lawyer, Rocco=Engineer,
  Anthony=Doctor, Vivian=Lawyer}
```

Thus, we see the distinction in representing the object using `TreeMap` and `HashMap`. Note the lexicographic ordering of the `keySet` components of the `TreeMap` version `stringFrequency1`.

The design of the `TreeMap` class emulates the processing performed in red-black trees. Again, applying an inorder traversal of the `keySet` components of any `TreeMap` object results in the sorted representation of its elements. As the representation of `stringFrequency1` shows, the entire pair is displayed although the `keySet` components of the pair are sorted in lexicographic order.

9.7 An Application of Maps to Prime Numbers: The Sieve of Eratosthenes

This section is dedicated to the presentation of an application of `Map` objects to the solution of a classical problem in number theory.

Given any two distinct integers greater than or equal to two, find and count the primes lying between these two integers, inclusive.

We design a solution that begins by prompting the user for two distinct integers greater than or equal to two, with the smaller integer being the first value input. We will store these input variables in `smaller` and `larger`, respectively. After this is done, we design a `TreeMap` object with `number-Size = larger - smaller + 1` elements. Each element is a pair of the form given as *keyValue, dataValue,* where *keyValue* is an `Integer` whose value lies in the range between smaller and larger, inclusive, and whose *dataValue* component is a Character value that is either 'p' (if the *keyValue* is a prime) or 'n' (if the *keyValue* is not a prime).

We define a char-valued array testArray, indexed from 0 to larger - smaller and whose components are either 'p' or 'n'. In this way, once adjusted to initiate at smaller, the index is tested as to whether it is a prime.

The coding of the underlying algorithm begins with the construction of the TreeMap object

```
Map primeFrequency = new TreeMap();
```

We choose TreeMap instead of HashMap because TreeMap maintains the sequential order of the integers between smaller and larger. (We could just as well have constructed primeFrequency as a HashMap object. This is left as an exercise for the reader.)

The values of testArray are computed using the for-loop

```
for(int index = smaller; index <= larger; ++index)
 if(isPrime(index)) testArray[index - smaller] = 'p';
 else testArray[index - smaller] = 'n';
```

These are then converted to their Character wrapper form and placed into primeFrequency as the respective *dataValue* components, using

```
for(int index1 = 0; index1 < numberSize; ++index1)
 primeFrequency.put(new Integer(index1), new Character(testArray[index1]));
```

We also define an int-valued variable used to count the number of primes between smaller and larger, using the loop

```
for(int index = smaller; index <= larger; ++index)
{
 int index1 = index - smaller;
 if((primeFrequency.get(new Integer(index1))).equals(new Character('p')))
 {
  ++primeCount;
  System.out.println(index + " is a prime");
 } // terminates if-clause; no else-clause.
} // terminates for-loop.
```

The method isPrime is the usual boolean-valued method with a single int-valued parameter returning true just when the parameter is a prime, and false if not. The complete text of the main method is given next.

EXAMPLE 9.2   The main method used for this prime counter is given as

```
public static void main(String [] args) throws IOException
 {
```

```
// Establish interactive input stream file.
BufferedReader intIS = new BufferedReader(new
  InputStreamReader(System.in));

// Construct associated TreeMap object.
Map primeFrequency = new TreeMap();

// Prompt user for two positive integers:
System.out.println("Please input two integers greater than");
System.out.println("or equal to two, the smaller one first:");
int smaller = Integer.parseInt(intIS.readLine());
int larger = Integer.parseInt(intIS.readLine());

int numberSize = larger   smaller + 1;
// Establish char-valued array:
char [] testArray = new char[numberSize];

// Fill in values of testArray: 'p' if prime, 'n' if not.
for(int index = smaller; index <= larger; ++index)
 if(isPrime(index)) testArray[index - smaller] = 'p';
 else testArray[index - smaller] = 'n';

// Prime counter initialized at zero:
int primeCount = 0;

// Assign values to primeFrequency:
for(int index1 = 0; index1 < numberSize; ++index1)
 primeFrequency.put(new Integer(index1), new Character(testArray[index1]));

// Count and determine primes using primeFrequency:
for(int index = smaller; index <= larger; ++index)
{
 int index1 = index - smaller;
 if((primeFrequency.get(new Integer(index1))).equals(new Character('p')))
 {
   ++primeCount;
   System.out.println(index + " is a prime");
 } // terminates if-clause; no else-clause.
} // terminates for-loop
System.out.println("There are " + primeCount + " primes");
System.out.println("between " + smaller + " and " + larger + ",");
System.out.println("inclusive.");
} // terminates text of main method.
```

To illustrate a sample run of this program, suppose the user responds to the prompt by inputting the respective values **11** and **19.** Then `number-Size = 19 -11 + 1 = 9`; thus `testArray` is allotted 9 `char`-valued components as in Figure 9.12.

FIGURE 9.12

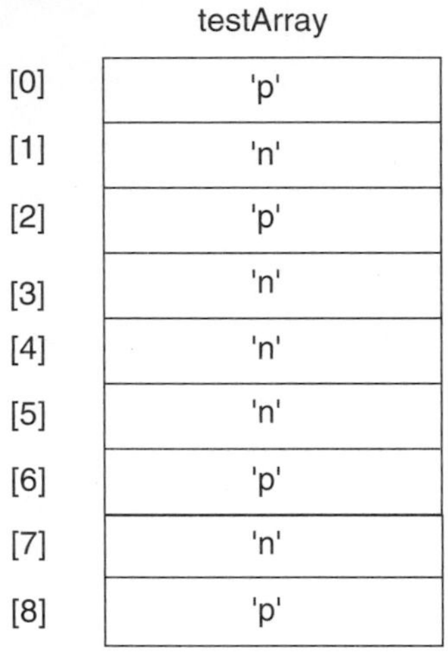

testArray

[0]	'p'
[1]	'n'
[2]	'p'
[3]	'n'
[4]	'n'
[5]	'n'
[6]	'p'
[7]	'n'
[8]	'p'

The components are filled in with the `char` valued displayed as the result of executing the first `for`-loop. The establishment of the `TreeMap` object `primeFrequency` is the result of executing the next `for`-loop, displayed as

```
primeFrequency = {11='p', 12='n', 13='p', 14='n', 15='n', 16='n', 17='p',
  18='n', 19='p'}.
```

(See Figure 9.13.)

FIGURE 9.13

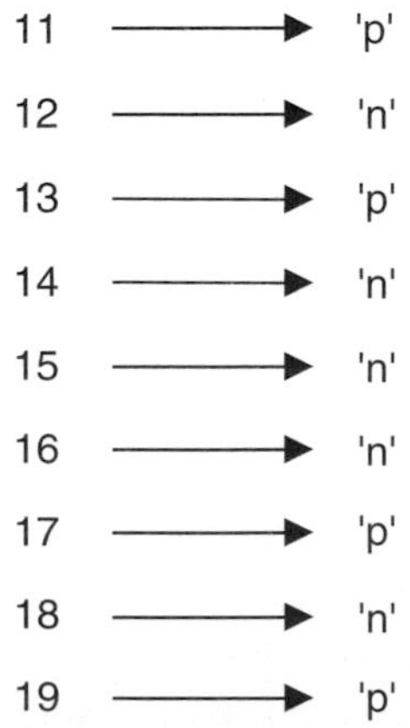

11 ⟶	'p'
12 ⟶	'n'
13 ⟶	'p'
14 ⟶	'n'
15 ⟶	'n'
16 ⟶	'n'
17 ⟶	'p'
18 ⟶	'n'
19 ⟶	'p'

The counting and determination of the primes is done using the last of the `for`-loops, where `primeCount` is incremented for each element of `primeFrequency` whose *dataValue* component has the value `'p'`.

countPrimes

4

and output

```
11 is a prime
13 is a prime
17 is a prime
19 is a prime
There are 4 primes
between 11 and 19,
inclusive.
```

The *sieve of Eratosthenes* is an algorithm that can be adapted and used to solve this problem. The idea is to, first, list all of the integers between `smaller` and `larger`, inclusive. We will illustrate this for `smaller` = 11 and `larger` = 19. The listing is given in Figure 9.14a.

FIGURE 9.14a
11	12	13	14	15	16	17	18	19
smaller								larger

Then the integers divisible by 2 lying in the list are deleted. This is indicated by underlining these integers and is illustrated in Figure 9.14b.

FIGURE 9.14b
11	12	13	14	15	16	17	18	19
smaller								larger

Because 3 is the next prime after 2, all surviving integers in the list that are divisible by 3 are deleted. The result of this is seen in Figure 9.14c.

FIGURE 9.14c
11	12	13	14	15	16	17	18	19
smaller								larger

The next prime to be tested is 5—all integers in the list that are divisible by 5 have already been deleted as integers that are also divisible by 3. We continue by observing that the next prime to test is 7, and again we observe that the only integer in the list that is divisible by 7 (namely, 14) has already been deleted because it is also divisible by 2. The surviving integers in the list represent the primes lying between `smaller` and `larger`, inclusive.

How do we implement the Sieve of Eratosthenes using the facilities available in `java.util`? We begin by constructing `primeFrequency` as an initially empty `TreeSet` object:

```
Set primeFrequency = new TreeSet();
```

Then the user is prompted as before for two distinct integers called `smaller` and `larger`. These play identical roles as their counterpart in the method described in Example 9.2. The list of all integers between `smaller` and `larger`, inclusive, constitute the complete set of initial values assigned to `primeFrequency`. This is accomplished by the `for`-loop

```
for(int index = smaller; index <= larger; ++index)
    primeFrequency.add(new Integer(index));
```

The next step is to apply the Sieve of Eratosthenes. This is done by eliminating all prime multiples lying between the values of `smaller` and `larger`, inclusive, that appear as current elements of `primeFrequency`. The next pair of nested `for`-loops accomplish this:

```
for(int index = smaller; index <= larger; ++index)
{
 for(int index1 = 2; index1 < larger/2 + 1; ++index1)
  if(isPrime(index1) && (index % index1 == 0))
   primeFrequency.remove(new Integer(index));
  // no else-clause
  if(primeFrequency.contains(new Integer(index)))
   System.out.println(index + " is a prime");
}
```

The surviving elements of `primeFrequency` are the primes lying between `smaller` and `larger`, inclusive. Their count is provided next.

```
System.out.println("There are " + primeFrequency.size() + " primes");
System.out.println("between " + smaller + " and " + larger + ",");
System.out.println("inclusive.");
```

The complete text of the main method implementing the Sieve of Eratosthenes is given in Example 9.3.

EXAMPLE 9.3

```
public static void main(String [] args) throws IOException
 {
  // Establish interactive input stream file.
  BufferedReader intIS = new BufferedReader(new
    InputStreamReader(System.in));
```

```
// Construct associated TreeSet object.
Set primeFrequency = new TreeSet();

// Prompt user for two positive integers:
System.out.println("Please input two integers greater than");
System.out.println("or equal to two, the smaller one first:");
int smaller = Integer.parseInt(intIS.readLine());
int larger = Integer.parseInt(intIS.readLine());

// Assign initial values to primeFrequency:
for(int index = smaller; index <= larger; ++index)
 primeFrequency.add(new Integer(index));

// Apply Sieve of Eratosthenes:
for(int index = smaller; index <= larger; ++index)
{
 for(int index1 = 2; index1 < larger/2 + 1; ++index1)
  if(isPrime(index1) && (index % index1 == 0))
   primeFrequency.remove(new Integer(index));
  // no else-clause

  // The surviving elements of primeFrequency are the primes
  // lying between smaller and larger, inclusive.
  if(primeFrequency.contains(new Integer(index)))
   System.out.println(index + " is a prime");
}

System.out.println("There are " + primeFrequency.size() + " primes");
System.out.println("between " + smaller + " and " + larger + ",");
System.out.println("inclusive.");

} // terminates text of main method
```

If we run this program for the same input values as those for Example 9.2, the output obtained for this version is identical. A trace of the execution of this version shows how the nested for-loops eliminate the non-primes lying between the values of smaller and larger, inclusive.

9.8   **The Methods of the SortedMap Interface**

We stated in Section 5.7 that the SortedMap interface extends the Map interface by requiring that its objects store elements whose *keyValue* components are sorted in a specific order, either by the default "less than" ordering or by a `Comparator` object that is defined when the `SortedMap` is constructed. The concrete class `TreeMap` implements `SortedMap`—thus, any `Map` object constructed using the `TreeMap` implementation is automatically a `SortedMap` object and any of the instance methods defined in `SortedMap` are applicable to this object.

We will illustrate the functionality of each instance method of `Sorted Map` on the `TreeMap` object `stringFrequency1 = {Angela=Engineer, Anthony=Doctor, Lorenzo=Lawyer, Rocco=Engineer, Vivian=Lawyer}` defined in Section 9.6.

The first method has the signature

```
public Object firstKey();
```

This returns the first (smallest) `keyValue` component of any object in the current sorted map. Thus, `stringFrequency1.firstKey()` returns `Angela`.

The next method has the syntax described by the signature

```
public Object lastKey();
```

This returns the last (largest) `keyValue` component of any object in the current sorted map. Consequently, `stringFrequency1.lastKey()` returns `Vivian`.

The signature of the next method is

```
public SortedMap subMap(Object minKey, Object maxKey);
```

When this is applied to a `SortedMap` object, it returns a view of that object whose `keyValue` components have values greater than or equal to the value of the first parameter and strictly less than the value of the second parameter. When we apply `stringFrequency1.subMap("Anthony", "Vivian")`, the result is `{Anthony=Doctor, Lorenzo=Lawyer, Rocco=Engineer}`.

The next method has the syntax

```
public SortedMap headMap(Object minKey);
```

This returns a view of that portion of the current `SortedMap` object whose `keyValue` is strictly less than the `keyValue` of the parameter. Therefore, the result of applying `stringFrequency1.headMap("Rocco")` is `{Angela=Engineer, Anthony=Doctor, Lorenzo=Lawyer}`.

The last of these is the method whose syntax is provided by the signature

```
public SortedMap tailMap(Object minKey);
```

This returns a view of the current `SortedMap` object whose `keyValue` components have values that are greater than or equal to the value of the `keyValue` component of the parameter. As a result, `stringFrequency1.-tailMap("Rocco") = {Rocco=Engineer, Vivian=Lawyer}`.

The inheritance relationship existing among `Map`, `SortedMap`, and `TreeMap` is diagrammed in Figure 5.14. This shows that any `TreeMap` object automatically inherits each instance method just described. As was the case for `TreeSet` objects in Section 9.4, it is also possible to define an alternative `Comparator` object instead of the default, if the design requires this alternative.

9.9   A Commercial Application of Maps: Processing Employee Records

Chapter Four was devoted to the discussion of processing employee records using the idea of hashing, which was implemented in two ways. The first implementation was programmer defined, where a `hashTable` class was defined and hashing was implemented using open addressing and separate chaining. The second approach introduced the `java.util` library, with special emphasis placed on implementing the predefined `Hashtable` class.[4]

This section describes yet another alternative, in which we describe the construction of a `HashMap` implementation of the `Map` interface. This technique also defines a class from which objects representing individual employee records can be constructed, with instance methods enabling the computation and retrieval of pertinent employee data. We also observe how iterator objects are used as important and useful tools in this respect.

We begin the discussion by outlining the design of an `employeeRecord` class, begun in Section 4.2. The current version describes a constructor for objects whose components are listed in the "data members" section. In addition, we describe an instance method retrieving the surname of each employee. This also suggests the possible coding of other useful and relevant instance methods, such as the computation of gross pay, net pay, and the itemizing of deductions from the gross pay, for each employee. We leave these extensions as exercises.

The `employeeRecord` class can be defined as

```
class employeeRecord
{
 // Constructor.
 public employeeRecord(String s,String n,char c,String d,int i, double r)
 {
  surname = s;
  name = n;
  mi = c;
  dob = d;
  hrsWorked = i;
```

---

[4]Note the distinction between the programmer-defined `hashTable` class and the predefined `Hashtable` class.

```
  hrlyRate = r;
}


// Instance method.
// Retrieve surname
public String getSurname()
{
  return surname;
}


// Other pertinent instance methods.

// Data members.
private String surname;
private String name;
private char mi;
private String dob;
private int hrsWorked;
private double hrlyRate;


}
```

To illustrate how this class is used in conjunction with `HashMap` objects, suppose our key values are the individual social security numbers of the employees. The map defined on any such key produces the individual's unique employment record, with data components defined by the `employeeRecord` class. Because any single social security number cannot map to two or more separate employment records, the concept of a `Map` object is maintained by this design. We therefore construct the `HashMap` object employees using

```
Map employees = new HashMap();
```

Note that this allows for the use of an "internal" hash function, thus relieving the programmer of the concern of the existence of a number of pitfalls inherent in the implementation of programmer-defined hash functions, such as primary and secondary clustering or the implementation of separate chaining.

To further illustrate these ideas, suppose we fill `employees` with three separate *keyValue, dataValue* pairs. This is done using conformant arrays to store the social security numbers (`keyValues`) and employment records (`dataValues`) of three individuals. We do this using

```
String ssNumber[] = {"099364150","086364036","131417018"};
```

and

```
employeeRecord entry[] = new employeeRecord[ssNumber.length];
```

using

```
entry[0] = new employeeRecord("Boccia","Horace",'J',"140739",45,9.00);
entry[1] = new employeeRecord("Procach","Rosalie",'A',"020140",35,8.50);
entry[2] = new employeeRecord("Egan","Walter",'D',"061237",40,10.75);
```

We use these data to fill employees using the for-loop

```
for(int index = 0; index < ssNumber.length; ++index)
  employees.put(ssNumber[index],entry[index]);
```

How do we process this employee data, now that it is stored in the values() component of this HashMap object? To give a simple example, suppose we wish to output the surnames of all of the employees as stored in employees. This is done by defining an iterator on the values() view of employees and executing the loop

```
for(Itcrator iter = (employees.values()).iterator();iter.hasNext();)
{
 employeeRecord value = (employeeRecord)iter.next();
 System.out.println(value.getSurname());
}
```

The output obtained by executing this loop is

```
Egan
Procach
Boccia
```

We leave the processing of other pertinent employee data as exercises. (See the Exercises and Programming Project sections at the end of this chapter.)

9.10   **Sorting Using Nonlinear Structures:** TreeSort **and** HeapSort

One of the major topics of investigation in Chapter Three was the study and analysis of algorithms for sorting a finite sequence of values. Although we noted that these algorithms varied in complexity, all shared a common attribute: The sorting was performed in an array. An array can be characterized as a *linear* data structure, because the components of an array can be viewed as being arranged in a linear path. Another linear structure of note is an ordinary or doubly linked list. In this section, we study two highly efficient sorting algorithms called (binary) *tree sort* and *heap sort*. These differ from the sorting algorithms studied in Chapter Three in one major respect: Although the sequence of values to be sorted are presented in the form of an ordinary one-dimensional array, the underlying data structure used to implement the sort is *nonlinear*. In the case of tree sort, this structure takes the form of a red-black tree; in the case of heap sort, the underlying structure is a special kind of complete binary tree called a *heap.*

Tree Sort

In binary tree sort, the values of the array are sorted, in order, in a specially constructed `TreeSet` object. Because the insertion of values into this object represents the insertion of nodes into a red-black tree, the result is a specially constructed binary search tree. After these values have been inserted into the tree, they are copied back into the array in order of increasing size, using the `toArray` method in the `Collection` interface.

There is one caveat, however—the array cannot contain any repetitive values. This is because the formation of the `TreeSet` object used in the sorting process cannot contain any repetitive values. If we analyze the tree sort algorithm applied to any array of n nonrepeating values of any `Comparable` data type, we can observe that the complexity of the algorithm is `O(n log n)`, because the underlying tree structure takes the form of a "short and fat" tree. Thus, the algorithm is highly efficient. Besides its optimal efficiency, it is also attractive in the sense that the more difficult programming work is performed internally in the insertion of values in a `TreeSet` object. The programmer is thus relieved of having to perform any major programming and design work in setting up the binary search tree used to store the array values. If we cannot guarantee that the array values are not repetitive, however, the only remaining alternative is to design this binary search tree structure by hand and possibly sacrifice the efficiency as a side effect. This is one of the factors that motivated the use of the predefined `Arrays.sort` studied in Chapter Eight to assume the form of a variation of internal mergesort.

The formal coding of the generic version of binary tree sort is given in Example 9.4, as the `static` method `treeSort`.

EXAMPLE 9.4

```
public static void treeSort(Comparable [] arr)
  {
   // Postcondition: Components of arr are sorted in order of
   // increasing size.  Because of the nature of the TreeSet class
   // this will not work if there are any possible repetitions in
   // the array.

   // Construct TreeSet object.
   TreeSet treeValue = new TreeSet();
   for(int index = 0; index < arr.length; ++index)
```

```
    treeValue.add(arr[index]);

  // Convert treeValue components back into arr components.
  treeValue.toArray(arr);
} // terminates text of treeSort.
```

Heap Sort

A *heap* is a complete binary tree in which every node has the property that its info component contains a value that is greater than or equal to the value assigned to the info component of each of its nontrivial children. Because this property is defined recursively, it prevails throughout the entire tree. Consequently, the largest value contained in the heap is found at its root. A simple illustration of an integer-valued heap (assuming the default "less than" relationship) appears in Figure 9.15a.

FIGURE 9.15a

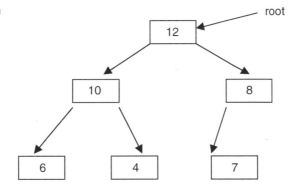

The heap can also be represented by a sequence of values stored in an array. Consequently, if heapArray is an int-valued array used to represent the heap pictured in Figure 9.15a, it assumes the form illustrated in Figure 9.15b.

FIGURE 9.15b   heapArray

0	1	2	3	4	5
12	10	8	6	4	7

Heaps are efficient data structures commonly used in commercial data processing, especially suited for solving the problem of efficiently finding the largest value in a sequence. Because the largest value is always found at the root node of the heap, solving this problem simply amounts to re-trieving this value. In addition, if the root is removed, a new heap can be formed from the surviving values by moving nodes (using a finite sequence of swap operations) from lower levels of the heap upward. This upward movement (commonly known as "trickle up") has complexity $O(\log n)$, owing to the completeness of the heap.

If new values are to be inserted into the heap, they are first inserted as new leaf nodes and are then trickled upward to re-form the heap with the new node properly situated. Deleting values from a heap is accomplished by removing the current root and then re-forming the two surviving sub-trees into a single heap. This technique is used in sorting a sequence of val-ues stored in some array by first inserting each array component to form the initial heap, removing the root each time, and then inserting that value at the end of the array until the heap becomes empty. At that point, the resulting array is a sorted version of the original array.

It is important for us to note several characteristics of heap sort. First, while it is certainly possible to store the original sequence of values to be sorted in a `Vector` or `List` object, it is also possible to implement heap sort without using any of the predefined facilities from `java.util`. Second, we observe that heap sort is an example of an *in-place sort*, because it is un-necessary to perform the actual sorting in a copy of the array to be sorted. Other examples of in-place sorting algorithms that were discussed in ear-lier chapters include selection and insertion sort and quicksort.

How can we implement heap sort in Java? We begin by defining a `Heap` class whose objects are constructed and initialized without any values. The values to be inserted into the heap are done using the instance method `insertHeap`. An additional instance method called `removeHeap` removes the root node from the heap and returns that value to the caller. The `removeHeap` method calls an auxiliary method called `rebuildHeap`, which is used to restore the heap structure when the root is removed. In addition, there is a `boolean`-valued method called `isEmpty`, used to test whether the current heap is empty. The formal details of the `Heap` class are given by

```java
class Heap
{
  private int ArraySize = 10;   // Maximum size of heap.
  private Comparable[] info;     // Stores heap values.
  private int currSize;          // Keeps track of current size of heap.

  // Constructor.  Constructs empty heap with no elements.
  public Heap()
  {
    info = new Comparable[ArraySize];
```

```
 currSize = 0;
} // terminates text of constructor


// Tests whether current heap is empty.
// Returns true if so, false if not.
public boolean isEmpty()
{
 return currSize == 0;
} // terminates text of isEmpty


// Inserts a new value into heap.
public void insertHeap(Comparable value) throws HeapException
{
 // Precondition: value is the value of the info component
 // of the new node to be inserted into the heap.
 // Postcondition: If heap is not already full, value is in its
 // proper position in the heap, otherwise, HeapException is
 // thrown.
 if(currSize < ArraySize)
 {
  // Place new node at the end of the current heap.
  info[currSize] = value;
  // "Trickle up" the new value to its proper position.
  int index = currSize;
  int parent = (index - 1)/2;
  while((parent >= 0) && (info[index].compareTo(info[parent]) > 0))
  {
   // swap info[index] and info[parent].
   Comparable temp = info[parent];
   info[parent] = info[index];
   info[index] = temp;

   index = parent;
   parent = (index - 1)/2;
  } // terminates text of while-loop.
  // Increment currSize
  ++currSize;
 } // terminates text of if-clause.
 else // No room left in heap for insertion of new value
  throw new HeapException("Heap Exception: heap is already full");
} // terminates text of insertHeap.


// Removes root from heap and returns that value whenever possible.
```

```
public Comparable removeHeap()
{
 // Postcondition: if the heap is not empty, the root value
 // is returned and deleted from info array.
 // If the heap is already empty, nothing to remove and null
 // is returned.
 Comparable rootValue = null;
 if(!isEmpty())
 {
  rootValue = info[0];
  info[0] = info[--currSize];
  rebuildHeap(0);
 } // terminates text of if-clause
 return rootValue;
} // terminates text of removeHeap.


// rebuildHeap method.  Use this if root is not a leaf, and if
// the value of the root is less than the larger of the values
// of the children of the root.
public void rebuildHeap(int root)
{
 int child = 2*root + 1; // subscript of root's left child
                         // if root is not a leaf.
 if(child < currSize)
 {
  // root is not a leaf, so it has a left child at position child.
  int rightChild = child + 1; // subscript of right child of root,
                              // if root has a right child.
  // If root also has a right child, find the child with the
  // larger value.
  {
   Comparable temp = info[root];
   info[root] = info[child];
   info[child] = temp;

  // Then transform the new subtree into a heap.
   rebuildHeap(child);
  } // terminates text of last if-clause
 } // terminates text of outer if-clause
 } // terminates text of rebuildHeap
} // terminates text of Heap class.
```

The next class is the HeapException class, invoked whenever a heap exception is thrown. Its coding is similar to that for StackException.

```
// class HeapException
class HeapException extends RuntimeException
{
 // Constructor.
 public HeapException(String str)
 {
  super(str);
 } // terminates text of constructor
} // terminates text of HeapException class.
```

   To illustrate how heap sort is implemented using the Heap class, assume that the values to be sorted appear in an array. For example, consider the (conformant) int-valued array heapArray, defined as

```
int[] heapArray ={6,10,7,12,4,8};
```

Then construct the Heap object heapObject and the Integer-valued array IntegerArr equivalent to heapArray. The sorting will actually be performed in IntegerArr.

```
Heap heapObject = new Heap();
Integer[] IntegerArr = new Integer[heapArray.length];
```

Insert the Integer equivalent of each component of heapArray into IntegerArr, using

```
for(int index = 0; index < IntegerArr.length; ++index)
 IntegerArr[index] = new Integer(heapArray[index]);
```

Then insert the values of the components of IntegerArr into heapObject:

```
for(int index = 0; index < IntegerArr.length; ++index)
 heapObject.insertHeap(IntegerArr[index]);
```

Once heapObject is filled with the current values of IntegerArr, the actual sorting of IntegerArr is performed using

```
for(int index = IntegerArr.length  1, index >= 0; --index)
 IntegerArr[index] = (Integer)heapObject.removeHeap();
```

   Thus, before the sorting, IntegerArr is depicted as shown in Figure 9.16a.

FIGURE 9.16a   IntegerArr

0	1	2	3	4	5
6	10	7	12	4	8

After the sorting, IntegerArr is as in Figure 9.16b.

FIGURE 9.16b   IntegerArr

0	1	2	3	4	5
4	6	7	8	10	12

In analyzing heap sort, note that removeHeap() is invoked in the text of the last for-loop. Thus, in the worst case, removeHeap() executes n times, where n = length of IntegerArr = number of values to be sorted. Each time removeHeap() is invoked, rebuildHeap(0) executes. In the worst case, rebuldHeap(0) requires log n steps. Consequently, heap sort is of complexity O(n log n).

9.11 Chapter Summary

The Set interface is predefined in Java and is part of the java.util library. Its purpose is to provide for the construction of objects used in the speedy and efficient access applied to storing and retrieving data. The description of the Set interface is the same as that for the Collection interface, but it uses methods that do not permit the existence of objects with duplicate values or ignores the order of presentation of the elements appearing in any of its objects. For example, the equals method, defined for Set objects, judges two such objects as identical if they contain exactly the same elements but not necessarily in the same order.

Each concrete class of HashSet and TreeSet implements the Set interface. The HashSet implementation sorts the elements in any of its objects using a predefined hash function whose implementation details are kept hidden from the user, while the TreeSet implementation sorts the elements appearing in any of its objects in order of ascending size (the default) according to some red-black tree whose internal structure is also kept hidden from the user. In addition, the SortedSet interface supports a sequence of instance methods that are applicable to objects that are sorted in some predefined order, whether that ordering is the default "less than" ordering or that provided by the programmer in the form of some specific Comparator object.

Many of the usual set-theoretic operations are definable and easily applicable to Set objects, such as set membership, inclusion, union, intersection, set difference, and symmetric difference. As well, Set objects can be used for providing a highly efficient solution to the problem of the Sieve of Eratosthenes—for determining the number of primes and their respective values lying between two given integers greater than or equal to 2.

The Map interface is used to construct objects for speedy and efficient data retrieval. Superficially, Map objects appear to serve the same needs as Set objects. However, there is one glaring difference between the two. Although Set objects enable the speedy and efficient retrieval of data, it is necessary to have an exact copy of the element to be found when retrieval is performed in a Set object. On the other hand, Map objects store elements using a *keyValue/dataValue* pair. Simply put, an element of a Map object can be retrieved simply by supplying the information provided in the key. This is particularly useful in business applications, where complete employee records can be retrieved simply by supplying the key of an employee's social security number.

The HashMap and TreeMap concrete classes represent the two implementations of the Map interface in java.util. The hash function provided by HashMap and the built-in ordering provided by TreeMap apply exclusively to the keys of the elements present in any Map object. Besides, the SortedMap interface supports a sequence of instance methods that are useful in providing special views of specific Map objects.

TreeSet objects can be constructed for the primary purpose of sorting a sequence of values. However, there is one major restriction in applying binary tree sort using TreeSet objects : No duplicate values are permitted. On the other hand, tree sort is highly efficient when implemented: When applying tree sort to a sequence of n values, its complexity is O(n log n).

A heap is defined as a complete binary tree with the additional property that the value stored in any parent node is greater than or equal to the value stored in any of its children. Constructing a heap is a relatively simple operation, especially when we represent the heap as an ordinary one-dimensional array. Heaps are particularly important tools, because they can be used to produce a highly efficient sorting algorithm called heap sort, whose complexity is always O(n log n). Interestingly enough, heap sort can be implemented using a Heap class that requires little or no use of the facilities present in java.util.

EXERCISES

1. Solve the problem of Example 9.2 using a HashMap implementation of primeFrequency.

2. a. Extend the design of the employeeRecord class of Section 9.9 to include methods for retrieving the first name, number of hours worked weekly, and hourly rate of pay for each employee.

b. Also include two new data members for gross pay and net pay, and methods for computing and retrieving these values, where we understand that there is no extra compensation for overtime hours and net pay is 85 percent of the amount for the gross pay.

3. Test set inclusion for `Character`-valued `Set` objects, using either a `Hash-Set` or a `TreeSet` implementation, where the two `Set` objects S, T are formed from the two conformant arrays defined as

```
char [] charArray1 = {'e','l','e','p','h','a','n','t'};
char [] charArray2 = {'a','a','r','d','v','a','r','k'};
```

4. a. Test set union and set intersection in a manner similar to that done for `Integer`-valued `Set` objects in Section 9.3, but now for the same two `Character`-valued sets formed in Exercise 3.

   b. Compute the set differences S - T and T - S and the symmetric difference for the `Character`-valued sets S, T from Exercise 3.

5. *de Morgan's laws* state that for any sets A, B, C,

A ∩ (B ∪ C) = (A ∩ B) ∪ (A ∩ C)
A ∪ (B ∩ C) = (A ∪ B) ∩ (A ∪ C)

Show that de Morgan's laws apply to the `Integer`-valued `Set` objects formed from the conformant array declarations

```
int [] intArray1 = {2,7,3,9,15};
int [] intArray2 = {-4,0,5,3,6,7,8,10,14,15,20};
int [] intArray3 = {8,0,8,2,4,9,-7,4};
```

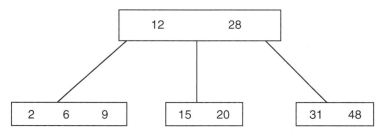

6. Find each red-black tree corresponding to the 2-3-4 tree described as

7. Given the integer-valued input sequence

15, 18, 12, 3, 20, 7, 4, 11

   a. construct the binary search tree associated with this sequence.

   b. compare this to the binary search tree associated with the rearrangement of the sequence given by 12, 3, 20, 18, 15, 4, 7, 11.

   c. what conclusion(s) do you arrive at based on your comparison of the two binary search trees constructed in parts (a) and (b)?

8. Count and determine the primes lying between 371 and 698, inclusive

   a. using the program described in Example 9.2.

   b. using the Sieve of Eratosthenes program described in Example 9.3.

9. Write a program using a `SortedMap` object to store pairs of values whose first component is a `String` value and whose second component is a `double` value. The first component is the surname of each of the eight position baseball players for the New York Mets baseball team who started the game played at Shea Stadium against the Houston Astros on August 1, 2002, and for which the corresponding `double` value is that player's current batting average:

```
"Alomar",0.277
"Perez",0.313
"Piazza",0.288
"Vaughn",0.251
"Alfonzo",0.322
"Burnitz",0.211
"Cedeno",0.258
"Ordonez",0.237
```

    a. Output the contents of the `SortedMap` object formed from these pairs.

    b. Compute the values of `firstKey()` and `lastKey()` for this `SortedMap` object.

    c. Compute `subMap("Burnitz","Piazza")` for this `SortedMap` object.

    d. Compute each of `headMap("Piazza")` and `tailMap("Piazza")` for this `SortedMap` object.

10. a. Compare the `HashMap` and `TreeMap` implementations obtained from constructing the `Map` object formed from the conformant array of key values

```
String [] players = {"Alomar","Perez","Piazza","Vaughn","Alfonzo",
  "Burnitz","Cedeno", "Ordonez"};
```

and data values given by

```
double [] bAvg = {0.277,0.313,0.288,0.251,0.322,0.211,0.258,0.237};
```

    b. In general, is it possible to reverse the definitions of *keyValue* and *dataValue* for surnames of baseball players and their respective current batting averages?

11. Trace execution of heap sort using the code sequence

```
Heap heapObject = new Heap();
Integer[] IntegerArr = new Integer[heapArray.length];
for(int index = 0; index < IntegerArr.length; ++index)
  IntegerArr[index] = new Integer(heapArray[index]);
for(int index = 0; index < IntegerArr.length; ++index)
  heapObject.insertHeap(IntegerArr[index]);
for(int index = IntegerArr.length - 1; index >= 0; --index)
  IntegerArr[index] = (Integer)heapObject.removeHeap();
```

for `heapArray` defined as the conformant `int`-valued array defined as

```
int [] heapArray = {6,7,10,12,4,8};
```

12. a. Trace `heapSort`, now using the `int`-valued `Vector` object `heapVector` initialized as heapVector

6	7	10	12	4	8

b. Redo (a), but now the int-value `ArrayList` object `heapList` is to be sorted, where

heapList

6	7	10	12	4	8

13. Trace execution of heap sort using a code sequence for a `Character`-valued array `heapArray` similar to that used in Exercise 11 for `Integer`-valued arrays. Specifically, let `heapArray` be defined as

```
heapArray = {'r','o','s','a','l','i','e'};
```

14. Redo Exercise 13, now for a `String`-valued array `heapArray` defined as

```
String [] heapArray =
{"Nicholas","Anthony","Lorenzo","Rocco","Rosalie","Vivian",
"Josephine","Angela","Patrizia"};
```

15. Given the current `Integer`-valued `Heap` object `heapObject` described as

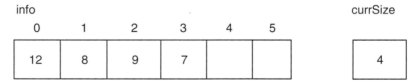

heapObject

info   currSize

0	1	2	3	4	5
12	8	9	7		

currSize

4

Perform and show the result of executing the code sequence

```
heapObject.insertHeap(new Integer(10));
heapObject.insertHeap(new Integer(5));
```

PROGRAMMING PROJECT

Define a *heap* as a complete binary tree with the property that the value stored at any node is now *less than or equal to* the value stored at any of the node's children. Thus, the smallest value stored in the current heap always appears as the value of the current root. Reformulate heap sort using this alternative definition of a heap and show that this version of heap sort proceeds in place, filling in the values of the underlying array in the order of smallest subscripts first.

......

CHAPTER 10

Graphs and Networks

CHAPTER OBJECTIVES

- To introduce graphs as useful data structures.
- To classify graph ADTs.
- To implement graph ADTs in Java.
- To present some of the basic concepts of local area networks and their design and implementation.
- To apply the concepts of object-oriented design and object-oriented programming to produce a simulator of the activity associated with local area networks.

....

10.1 Introduction: Basic Ideas Concerning Graphs

In Chapter Nine we introduced the concept of trees as a specific kind of nonlinear structure. We also observed that certain forms of trees, such as red-black trees and heaps, were very useful in implementing some of the predefined facilities of `java.util` and in solving fundamental sorting problems in an efficient manner. In general, the nodes appearing on any tree share a common characteristic: Either the node is the unique root node or it has exactly one parent.

There are other kinds of useful nonlinear structures, however. For example, we can define a *graph* as a nonlinear structure in which there is no set root node and for which a node can be the child of more than one parent. In fact, graphs are used to represent a finite sequence of data values represented as *points* (or *vertices*), some of which are joined by *edges*. The edges represent relationships existing between pairs of these vertices. Indeed, suppose G names a specific graph. Then G is defined by two sets: a nonempty set V of *vertices* and a set E (possibly empty) of *edges* whose members consist of certain pairs of vertices. The order of appearance of the vertices in an edge might be significant; if so, the graph is called a *directed graph* or simply a *digraph*. In addition, edges with the same vertex at each end are permitted. Because any graph is characterized by V and E, we use the notation G = (V,E). Figure 10.1 is a simple illustration of an (undirected) graph. Here, V = {A_0, A_1, A_2, A_3, A_4} and E = {{A_0,A_1}, {A_0,A_2}, {A_0,A_4}, {A_1,A_2}, {A_2,A_4}}, where, for example, the (undirected) edge with vertices A_0 and A_1 is denoted by {A_0,A_1}. Note also that G has no edge with vertex A_3.

FIGURE 10.1

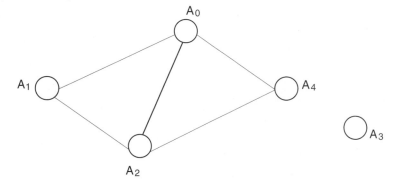

A *path* in any graph G between vertices X and Y is a finite collection of (undirected) edges of G: {X_1,X_2}, {X_2,X_3}, . . . , {X_{k-1},X_k}, where X_1 = X and X_k = Y. For the graph described in Figure 10.1, there is a path between A_0 and A_4 given by {A_0,A_1}, {A_1,A_2}, {A_2,A_0}, {A_0,A_4}. We define a path to be *simple* if the path never passes through any vertex more than once. The previous example of a path was not simple, but the path {A_1,A_2}, {A_2,A_4}, {A_4,A_0} is simple. Furthermore, a *cycle* is a path that begins and ends at the same vertex and otherwise passes through no vertex more than once. The path {A_0,A_1}, {A_1,A_2}, {A_2,A_0} in Figure 10.1 is an example of a cycle. A graph G is *connected* if a path exists between every pair of distinct vertices of G. The graph in Figure 10.1 is not connected because, for example, there is no path joining A_3 to any other vertex. If A_3 were omitted, however, the resulting graph is connected.

A graph is *complete* if there is an edge connecting each distinct pair of vertices. The graph shown in Figure 10.2 is an example of a complete graph.

FIGURE 10.2

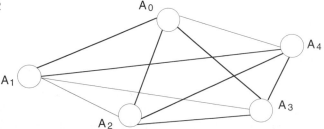

A graph is *directed* if each of its edges has a *direction*, that is, there is a well-defined initial vertex and a terminal vertex. Thus, each edge in a directed graph determines a flow from its initial to its terminal vertex. We can represent a directed graph $G = (V,E)$, where V is the set of vertices defined exactly as above and E is the set of *directed edges* represented as ordered pairs (A_i,A_j), where A_i and A_j are in V. The ordering of the pair is used to indicate that the initial vertex of the pair (A_i,A_j) is given by the left member A_i and the terminal vertex is given by the right member A_j. The graph in Figure 10.3 is an example of a digraph where the arrows describe the direction of flow in each edge.

FIGURE 10.3

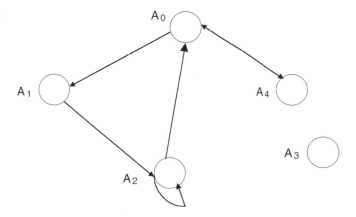

Here $V = \{A_0,A_1,A_2,A_3,A_4\}$ and $E = \{(A_0,A_1),(A_0,A_4),(A_1,A_2),(A_2,A_0),(A_2,A_2),(A_4,A_0)\}$. We define a *cycle* in a digraph as a path $(X_1,X_2),(X_2,X_3),\ \ .\ \ .\ \ .\ \ ,\ (X_{k-1},X_k)$ in which $X_1 = X_k$. A cycle in a digraph is *simple* if X_1 and X_k represent the only pair of common vertices. A digraph is *acyclic* if it contains no cycles; it is commonly referred to as a directed acyclic graph (DAG). The graph in Figure 10.4 is an example of a DAG.

FIGURE 10.4

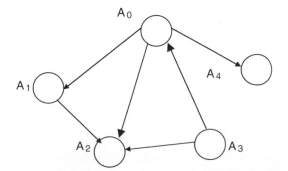

10.2 **Design Issues for Graph ADTs**

We are interested in answering several key questions regarding graphs:

- How do we define a graph abstract data type (ADT)?
- How can we implement graphs using classes in Java?
- How are graphs *traversed*? That is, how do we move around from one vertex to another in a graph? How do we implement these traversals?
- Are there efficient algorithms for graph traversals?

In an object-oriented design, a graph ADT should address the construction and initializations of graph objects. We will define a constructor initializing graph objects with no vertices or edges. In addition, the user interface should contain instance methods allowing for changes in the structure of the graph object, by either inserting or removing vertices or edges or both. Furthermore, we should be able to test whether certain vertices or edges appear in that object. Finally, the design should include the definition and implementation of methods for traversing the vertices of the graph in some particular order from some designated starting vertex.

In brief, our plan is to define interfaces and classes that implement these methods described in interfaces for undirected graphs and for digraphs. The vertices of each graph (digraph) will be of type `Comparable`. In addition, for the sake of simplicity, we assume that the value of each node is integer-valued and matches the subscript assigned to that node. In addition, these classes should possess the following functionality:

1. constructors, allowing for the creation of graph (digraph) objects with vertices storing values of some specific instance of a `Comparable` type
2. insertion methods for new vertices and edges in any graph (digraph) object
3. removal methods for vertices and edges in the current graph (digraph) object
4. a `boolean`-valued method testing whether the current graph (digraph) object is empty—that is, whether the object has any vertices or edges
5. a `boolean`-valued method with two vertex parameters testing whether those vertices are joined by an edge in the current graph (digraph) object
6. a method with a single vertex parameter v returning the collection of all vertices in the current graph (digraph) object that are "adjacent" to v—that is, connected to v by an edge
7. methods implementing traversals of vertices of the current graph (digraph) object beginning with a designated start vertex and terminating with a designated goal vertex, given as parameters

Our design will involve defining two interfaces and consequently two implementation classes, one for a graph class and one for a digraph class. These classes will be related by inheritance. Specifically, these interfaces and their corresponding implementation classes will be related using inheritance with the digraph class as the base class and the (undirected) graph class as the subclass, using some fundamental observations about graphs and digraphs to exploit the inheritance relationship (see Figure 10.5). We describe an inheritance relationship existing between DigraphInterface and GraphInterface that name the respective interfaces for digraph and graph objects.

FIGURE 10.5

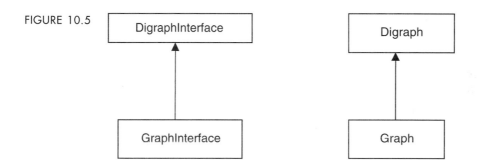

10.3 **Implementation Details of Graph ADTs in Java**

We sketch the coding of DigraphInterface and GraphInterface, leaving some of the formal coding details as an exercise.

```java
public interface DigraphInterface
{
 // Tests whether current digraph is empty.
 // Returns true if so, false if not.
 boolean isEmpty();

 // Returns the number of vertices in the current digraph.
  int size();

  // Returns whether v is joined to w by an edge.
  // Precondition: v, w are vertices in the current digraph.
 boolean isAdjacent(Comparable v, Comparable w);

  // Inserts edge from v to w.
  // Returns true if edge is constructed from v to w, and false if
  // no such edge is constructed.
  //  Precondition: v, w are vertices in the current digraph.
  boolean insertEdge(Comparable v, Comparable w);
```

```
// Inserts vertex into digraph.
// Returns true if new vertex is inserted, and false if no vertex
// is inserted since it is already a vertex of the digraph.
boolean insertVertex(Comparable v);


// Removes vertex from current digraph if present, along with
// all incident edges.  Returns true if erased, false if not.
boolean eraseVertex(Comparable v);


// Removes edge from v to w, if currently present in digraph.
// Precondition: v, w are vetices in current digraph.
boolean eraseEdge(Comparable v, Comparable w);
```

} // terminates text of DigraphInterface.

How do we arrive at the design decision that `GraphInterface` is to be inherited from `DigraphInterface`? The decision is based on an elementary observation: Each edge in an undirected graph can be viewed as a pair of edges in a digraph whose initial and terminating vertices exchange positions. For instance, we can view the edge $\{A_i, A_j\}$ in an undirected graph as a pair of edges (A_i, A_j) and (A_j, A_i) in a digraph. Thus, in particular, inserting and deleting edges in an undirected graph simply amounts to inserting edges in a digraph. Applying this idea and inheritance, we can code `GraphInterface` as

```
public interface GraphInterface extends DigraphInterface
{
// Inserts edge connecting v and w.
// Precondition: v, w are vertices in undirected graph.
 boolean insertEdge(Comparable v, Comparable w);


// Removes edge from v to w, if currently present in graph.
// Precondition: v, w are vertices in current undirected graph.
 boolean eraseEdge(Comparable v, Comparable w);
```

} // terminates text of GraphInterface

How are `Digraph` and `Graph` objects represented internally? In other words, how do we describe the `private` data members implementing `DigraphInterface`? We begin by defining an *adjacency matrix* as a two-dimensional display of `boolean` values whose rows and columns are indexed by the vertices of the underlying digraph (or graph). If the adjacency matrix is to represent a specific undirected graph with vertices $A_0, A_1, \ldots, A_{n-1}$, the adjacency matrix will be a symmetric matrix with n rows and n columns, where `true` appears in position i,j (row index i and column index j) if and only if there is an edge connecting A_i and A_j in the graph. For undirected graphs, the `boolean` value in each location i,j will be the same as that for location j,i. In the case of the undirected graph shown in Figure 10.1, the associated adjacency matrix is that given in Figure 10.6, and the adjacency matrix for the directed graph in Figure 10.3 is given in Figure 10.7. Note that this last matrix is not symmetric.

FIGURE 10.6

		(column index)				
		0	1	2	3	4
	0	false	true	true	false	true
	1	true	false	true	false	false
(row index)	2	true	true	false	false	true
	3	false	false	false	false	false
	4	true	false	true	false	false

FIGURE 10.7

		(column index)				
		0	1	2	3	4
	0	false	true	true	false	true
	1	false	false	true	false	false
(row index)	2	true	false	true	false	false
	3	false	false	false	false	false
	4	true	false	false	false	false

We can use these ideas to fill in the data members of the implementation of `DigraphInterface` by defining a two-dimensional `boolean`-valued matrix type. We leave these formal coding details to the reader as an exercise.

10.4 **Graph Traversals**

To traverse a digraph (or graph) is to systematically probe the structure by examining each vertex and edge. We seek efficient algorithms for graph traversals where we judge such algorithms as efficient if all vertices and edges on the graph are examined (visited) in time proportional to the number of vertices and edges present. If a digraph (graph) has n vertices and m edges, we seek traversal algorithms of order $O(n + m)$.

We will confine our attention to the discussion of traversals of undirected graphs. The results for directed graphs are similar and thus are left as an exercise. The objective in the *depth-first traversal* of a graph is to move as deeply as possible into the graph from a designated initial vertex to a final vertex or goal vertex (presumed to exist in the graph) without having to backtrack to a set of previously visited vertices. Such a search strategy is important in a number of different applications, particularly in finding paths from one vertex to another or finding a *spanning tree* for a connected graph.

Suppose we consider depth-first traversals of the graph given in Figure 10.8, with initial vertex A_0 and final vertex A_4. A depth-first search would

FIGURE 10.8

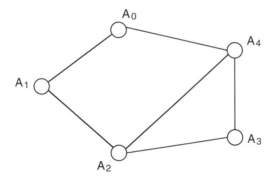

proceed to any vertex joined to A_0 by an edge—in this case, either to A_1 or A_4. Suppose the traversal proceeds to A_1. Then the next vertex to visit is A_2. We eliminate A_0 as a viable candidate because this would involve an early instance of backtracking. After visiting A_2, the next vertex to visit may be either A_3 or A_4. If A_3 is visited first, the remaining vertex to visit without backtracking is A_4. Thus, a result of a depth-first traversal beginning with A_0 and ending with A_4 is expressed as the sequence A_0, A_1, A_2, A_3, A_4 (or, more simply, the sequence of integer subscripts 0, 1, 2, 3, 4). Other depth-first traversals beginning with A_0 and ending with A_4 are A_0, A_4 (or 0, 4) and A_0, A_1, A_2, A_4 (or 0, 1, 2, 4).

In *breadth-first search,* the objective is to list all vertices adjacent to the current vertex before visiting some new vertex. This allows us to determine a path from the initial vertex to the goal vertex by performing a lateral sweep of all paths in the graph with the same number of vertices until finding a candidate with the desired goal vertex before considering candidates with additional vertices. If such a candidate is found, we have the desired result; if no such candidate is found, we conclude that there is no path in the current graph beginning at the designated initial vertex and ending with the desired goal vertex. The proper data structure for holding the paths to be examined is a queue, each member of which represents a path whose first node is the initial vertex.

The first value inserted is a path (in the form of a linked list) consisting of the initial vertex of the traversal. Then this vertex is removed and replaced by all paths (represented as linked lists of vertex subscripts) consisting of the initial vertex and whose remaining vertex subscript is that of any of the members of the *adjacency set* of the initial vertex (the set of all vertices identifying all of the vertices to which the initial vertex is connected by an edge). When a path is removed from the queue, it is replaced by a new path continuing the path just removed by inserting all paths with three vertices consisting of the initial vertex, followed by the vertex of the edge just removed, and then followed by any of the vertices in the adjacency set of the vertex in the path just removed. This process continues until either a path at the front of the queue ends with a terminating vertex equal to the desired goal, or, if the queue becomes empty, an indication that no path is defined in the current graph from the designated initial vertex to the goal.

The underlying idea is that the queue maintains a repository of paths, all of which begin with the desired initial vertex, with the next candidate path at the front and which sweep though the graph breadth-first until the desired path is found or until no further candidate exists. To illustrate, we consider the graph in Figure 10.8 and a breadth-first traversal of the graph with initial vertex A_0 and goal vertex A_4. The algorithm first examines the possibility that the goal is the same as the initial vertex, but this is rejected immediately. The algorithm continues with a sweep of paths at the next level. In this case, there are two candidates: A_0, A_1 and A_0, A_4. The first candidate, presumed placed at the front of the queue, is rejected; after this candidate is removed from the queue, the second candidate is tested and accepted. Thus, the result of the breadth-first search is the path A_0, A_4 (or equivalently, 0, 4).

10.5 Networks: Introductory Ideas

A *network* is a finite set of communications links for connecting a number of terminals, printers, memory devices, and other hardware units used for processing and transmitting data. Every data communications network consists of units for sending and receiving data, computing units, and peripheral devices. Any point in the network where data are either received or transmitted is called a *node* or a *switch*. A *circuit* is a communications path between two nodes through which data can move in a single direction. The peripheral devices might include printers, disk and magnetic tape permanent storage devices, interactive or graphics terminals, or bar code scanners.

In this context, we define a *message* as a single item of communication. For example, if the network is an electronic mail system, a message is a document sent from one node in the network to another. Any message sent through the network consists of a *bitstring*—namely, a finite string of bits. We add other bits to the message as a way of identifying the node for which the message was intended. This ensures reliable communication, correct routing, and avoidance of congestion and delay at some node in the network. Thus, it is generally the case that the messages sent through the network are very long bitstrings that might not be capable of being transmitted all at once in their entirety, due to hardware limitations. Hence, these messages are generally broken down into smaller bitstrings, called *packets*. These packets are sent through the network to their intended destination and are reassembled at that destination to reproduce the original message. We will assume that each node is distinguished from any other by a unique *address*, represented by some positive integer whose value is part of the bitstring sent along in the packet.

We define a *network topology* as the geometrical configuration of its nodes. One such topology is the *ring topology,* in which consecutive nodes are connected by links arranged to form a simple closed path as shown in Figure 10.9.

FIGURE 10.9

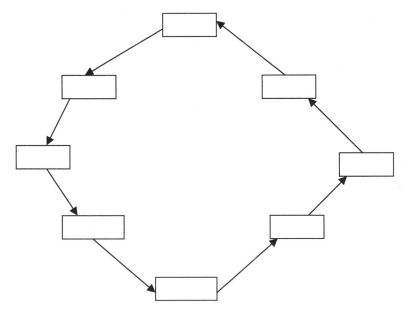

We also assume that the packets are transmitted from one node to another around the ring in a single direction, from the transmitting (or source) node to the receiving (or destination) node, and that the interface at each node has the ability to recognize its own address in a data packet in order to accept messages sent to it. The interface also has the ability to retransmit messages along the network intended for other nodes. At any time, a node can be in any one of three modes: LISTEN, TRANSMIT, and BYPASS. When an interface is in the LISTEN mode, it scans the packet for the destination address and then copies the message into a *buffer* (a memory unit at that node) if the message was intended for that node. If not, the message is retransmitted to the next interface. When the interface is in the TRANSMIT mode, the node involved enters its own data into the ring. Finally, if a node is in the BYPASS mode, it is not fully operational or might be in the process of being removed from the network for maintenance or replacement. In this case, messages are sent through that node as though it were no longer part of the network.

We will assume that exactly one message is allowed to pass through the network at any given time. One possible way to ensure this is to use a *token*, which is a special bitstring that circulates in the network when no message is being sent. When a node is ready to transmit, it removes the token from circulation and stores it. This signifies that the node is now able to transmit its message through the network. It does so by changing its mode from LISTEN to TRANSMIT. In the meantime, the other nodes are continuously monitoring the messages passing through the network, remaining in the LISTEN mode. One key rule we must enforce is that each node must identify any messages passed to it and must transmit messages intended for other nodes. When a node finishes transmitting its message, it switches back to the LISTEN mode and passes the token back into the network. This enables another node to pick up the token and thus pass its message through the network. The type of network we have just described is commonly called a *token ring network*.

Each node of the network is initialized in the LISTEN mode. If a message sent into the network is not accepted by any other nodes, it "laps" the network and is removed after completing one full cycle. This implies that the node for which the message is intended either has not as yet been added to the network or is no longer part of the current network. We will also assume that any network can be in any one of two states: *active* or *inactive*. When *active*, the network is performing its ordinary operations; it is *inactive* when a node is either being removed from or being added to the current network.

10.6 **Basic Design Components for a Network ADT**

How do we implement these introductory ideas about networks in software? We use an object-oriented design in which these ideas are combined in a single abstraction, defining an ADT implemented in a class called Net-work. In order for the methods of Network to operate properly, we will use the List interface and the ArrayList implementation.

Each node in any such network has the internal structure as shown in Figure 10.10.

FIGURE 10.10

address   mode   info   hasToken

The address field contains the unique address of the network node. In addition, the mode field contains a value given by any one of the String values "LISTEN", "TRANSMIT", or "BYPASS". The info field holds a string of fixed size, to be determined using the following observations: We define the size as the value assigned to an int-valued constant MessageLength, because this simulates a typical hardware constraint. Thus, the value of the info field contains the message (in bitstring form) about to be sent by the node into the network, once that node acquires the token or the message received by the node when its address is verified as the proper destination.

We therefore define the value of MessageLength as the maximum length of any packet capable of moving through the network. The first six bits of any packet defined the address of the destination node. Thus, the value of MessageLength must be substantially higher than six. Finally, the hasToken field contains a boolean value that is true just when the current node has the token, and is false otherwise. We capture the definition of MessageLength in formal code as

```
final int MessageLength = some hardware-dependent positive integer;
```

The next definition represents an implementation of the data type (called stringType) characterizing the structure of a packet. We will single out the first six bits as int values 0 or 1 and viewed as the bitstring yielding the address of the node for which the message is intended.[1] The remaining MessageLength - 6 values, each of which is the char value '0' or '1', is a character string whose content is the message in the packet. Using this, we define

```
class stringType
{
  // First six bits are int-valued, initialized as 1.
```

[1]An alternative is to use a BitSet object to represent the first six bits. (See Section 5.8.)

```
int bit0 = 1;
int bit1 = 1;
int bit2 = 1;
int bit3 = 1;
int bit4 = 1;
int bit5 = 1;
// Remaining bits are char-valued, either '0' or '1'.
char [] msg = new char[MessageLength - 6];

} // terminates definition of stringType.
```

Thus, we can view any value of `stringType` as having the structure described in Figure 10.11.

FIGURE 10.11

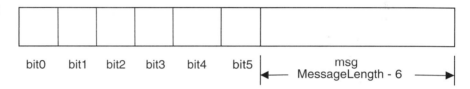

To illustrate these ideas, suppose the value of `MessageLength` is `32` and suppose the message is a `stringType` variable whose current value is `01100111010011001100111100101101`. Then the address of the destination node is the value of the bitstring `011001`, which is `25`. A node of the network can then be defined as an object of the class `NetworkNode` whose formal definition is given as

```
class NetworkNode
{
 // Constructor
 public NetworkNode(int a)
 {
  address = a;
  mode ="LISTEN";
  hasToken = false;
 }

 // Data values.
 int address;
 String mode;
 boolean hasToken;
```

```
      stringType info;
   } // terminates definition of class NetworkNode.
```

Because the implementation uses `ArrayList`, we include the definition

```
List networkObject = new ArrayList();
```

Using these preliminary design concepts, we can describe the interface for a network as

```
public interface NetworkInterface
{
 // Inserts new node into network.
 // Postcondition: New node is inserted at the end of network.
 void insertNode();


 // Removes node with address as parameter from the network.
 // Precondition: The current network has at least one node.
 // Postcondition: Node referenced by parameter is removed from
 //   current network.
 void removeNode(int address);


 // Retrieves the number of nodes in the current network.
 int networkSize();


 // Lists the addresses of the nodes currently active in network.
 // Precondition: The current network contains at least one node.
 void listNetwork();


 // Sends the message from the source node to the destination
 // node if the source and destination addresses are currently
 // active in the network.
 void processMessage();


} // terminates text of NetworkInterface.
```

Once a network object is constructed, the user has access to five instance methods. These all appear in `NetworkInterface` and are listed as follows:

- `processMessage`, used to simulate the sending of a message through the network
- `removeNode`, used for removing any node currently in the network
- `insertNode`, used for inserting a new node in the current network
- `networkSize`, used for retrieving the number if nodes currently active in the network
- `listNetwork`, used for retrieving the addresses of all active nodes in the current network.

10.7   Implementation Details for the Network Simulator

We sketch the code of a `Network` class implementing `NetworkInterface`; in many cases, the code is actual formal code and is not pseudocode. In each case, however, the code as presented is very close to the actual formal code representing the actual formal implementation of `NetworkInterface`.

The implementation of the network simulator with interface `NetworkInterface` has the syntax

```
public class Network implements NetworkInterface
{
 // Constructor.  Constructs a new network with no
 // nodes and designated as active.
 public Network()
 {
  size = 0;
  isActive = true;
 } // terminates text of constructor.


 // Implementation of instance methods described in
 // NetworkInterface.  Described in detail below.


 // Data members.
 private int size;
 private boolean isActive;
} // terminates text of Network class.
```

Each object constructed in the `Network` class is a specific network in the sense just described, whose structure contains two data members: `size` and `isActive`. The `size` field is of type `int`; `isActive` is `boolean`-valued and is `true` just when the current network is active, and `false` if otherwise. In addition, the remaining text of `Network` contains a number of `private` methods that are helpful in simplifying the coding of the `public` methods listed in `NetworkInterface`.

We now present the formal encoding of the following `private` auxiliary methods: `findAddress`, `Powerof2`, `findNode`, and `toBitString`. Each of these plays a pivotal role in simulating the process of sending a message through the network from a designated source node to an appropriate destination node. The purpose of `findAddress` is to convert the first six bits of any packet to its equivalent `int` value.

```
private int findAddress(stringType message)
// Returns the address of the node whose address is
// stored in positions 0 through 5.
```

```
{
 int value = 0;
 if(message.bit0 == 1)
  value += Powerof2(5);
 if(message.bit1 == 1)
  value += Powerof2(4);
 if(message.bit2 == 1)
  value += Powerof2(3);
 if(message.bit3 == 1)
  value += Powerof2(2);
 if(message.bit4 == 1)
  value += Powerof2(1);
 if(message.bit5 == 1)
  value += Powerof2(0);
 return value;
} // terminates text of findAddress.
```

The method `Powerof2` invoked in `findAddress` is coded as

```
private int Powerof2(int i)
// Returns the integer value of 2 raised to the ith power.
// Precondition: i is a non-negative integer.
{
 int base = 1;
 while(i-- > 0)
  base *= 2;
 return base;
} // terminates text of Powerof2.
```

We should note that here we wish to enforce another precondition: The address of any node cannot exceed 63, because 63 is the largest integer value that can be stored in 6 bits. If there is any need to exceed this value, we can alter the design to include more bits in the message for the addresses of nodes.

The auxiliary method `findNode` returns an iterator reference to the node in the network whose address is the value of the parameter, if such a node exists in the current network. Otherwise, `null` is returned. Its formal coding is given by

```
private ListIterator findNode(int addressValue)
// Returns a reference to the node whose address is the value
// of the parameter, if a node exists; otherwise nothing
// is returned.
{
 // Begin the search, moving through current network
 ListIterator iter = this.iterator();
```

```
while(iter.hasNext())
{
 NetworkNode n = (NetworkNode)iter.next();
 // If a node is found with the address sought, return a
 // reference to that node.
 if(n.address == addressValue)
   return iter;
}
 return null;
} // terminates text of findNode
```

Recall that the network object is implemented as an `ArrayList` object. Thus, iterators referencing the nodes of a network object actually take the form of `ListIterator` objects.

The objective of `toBitString` is to produce the bitstring equivalent of the destination address.

```
private stringType toBitString(int destination)
{
 stringType message;
 message.bit0 = 0;
 message.bit1 = 0;
 message.bit2 = 0;
 message.bit3 = 0;
 message.bit4 = 0;
 message.bit5 = 0;
 if(destination >= Powerof2(5))
 {
  message.bit0 = 1;
  destination -= Powerof2(5);
 }
 if(destination >= Powerof2(4))
 {
  message.bit1 = 1;
  destination -= Powerof2(4);
 }
 if(destination >= Powerof2(3))
 {
  message.bit2 = 1;
  destination -= Powerof2(3);
 }
 if(destination >= Powerof2(2))
 {
  message.bit3 = 1;
  destination -= Powerof2(2);
```

```
        }
        if(destination >= Powerof2(1))
        {
         message.bit4 = 1;
         destination -= Powerof2(1);
        }
        if(destination >= Powerof2(0))
        {
         message.bit5 = 1;
         destination.Powerof2(0);
        }
        return message;
    } // terminates text of toBitString.
```

The method `sendMessage` contains all of the formal coding details of the act of sending a message from the source node to the intended destination node. Because any such detail is intended primarily for the successful completion of the sending process and is not of any importance to the user, its code is `private`. With these considerations in mind, we code this as follows.

```
private void sendMessage(NetworkNode source)
// Simulates sending a message through the network from
// a source node to a destination node.  Source node
// must have the token from the network before sending
// the message, and cannot listen to any other message.
// Precondition: Current network contains at least two
// nodes, and the source and destination nodes are distinct.
{
 // Prepare source node for transmitting the message.
 source.hasToken = true;
 source.mode = "TRANSMIT";
 // Use auxiliary iterator to conduct a search through the
 // network, looking for destination node.
 // Initialize position of auxiliary iterator at the initial node.
 ListIterator iter = this.iterator();
 while(iter.hasNext())
 {
  System.out.println("Searching node " + source.address);
  NetworkNode qptr = (NetworkNode)iter.next();
  System.out.println("Destination node " + qptr.address);
  if(findAddress(source.info) == qptr.address)
  {
   System.out.println("Destination node found");
```

```
    // The message is being sent to the proper destination.
    // Set the mode of the destination to TRANSMIT, since it
    // cannot receive any new message until the current
    // message is received.
    qptr.mode = "TRANSMIT";
    // Copy message into the destination's info field.
    qptr.info = source.info;
    // Reset the mode of the destination node to LISTEN.
    qptr.mode = "LISTEN";
   } // terminates text of if-clause.
  } // terminates text of while-loop.
  // Reset mode and hasToken fields of source.
  source.mode = "LISTEN";
  source.hasToken = false;
  // Reset iterator to the beginning node of the current network
  // and return its value.
  iter = this.iterator();
  return iter;
} // terminates text of sendMessage.
```

We use the `static` variable `addressCounter` to maintain an accurate count of the newly created nodes installed in the network, beginning with the initial node whose address is 1. The current value of `addressCounter` does not necessarily coincide with the number of nodes that are currently active in the network. In fact, the address of each newly created node is given by the updated value of `addressCounter`, whereas the value of `size` gives the number of nodes that are currently active in the network. Note that if any node is removed from the network, its address is not recyclable. Finally, we initialize the values of `newNode.into.bit0` through `newNode.info.bit5` to zero because these bit values give the address of the destination node for a message. These values will change when a message is to be sent from this node to a destination node.

The code for the method `removeNode` demonstrates how a node with the given address as the value of the parameter is removed from the current network, if that network currently contains a node with that address.

```
public void removeNode(int address)
// Removes node with the given address, if it exists
// in network.
// Precondition: Current network contains at least one node.
// Postcondition: Node referenced by parameter is removed from
// current network, decreasing network size by 1.
{
```

```
// Create iterator reference to find node with given
// address and initialize.
ListIterator iter = this.iterator;
// Advance forward, looking for node with given address.
while(iter.hasNext() && (iter.next().address != address))
  ;
// At this point, node with the given address is located.
// Suspend activity of network at node to be removed.
NetworkNode n = (NetworkNode)iter.next();
n.mode =  "BYPASS";
isActive = false;
// Decrease network size.
 --size;
// Remove node.  This uses remove method from Collection interface,
// with Object parameter given by the List object whose value is n.
remove(n);
// Resume normal network activity.
isActive = true;
} // terminates text of removeNode.
```

The next method returns the number of nodes currently active in the network.

```
public int networkSize()
// Returns the current size of network.
{
 return size;
}
```

The method `listNetwork` returns a list of the currently active network nodes and their respective `info` components.

```
public void listNetwork()
// Outputs a list of the network nodes and their info components.
{
 if(networkSize() == 0)
  System.out.println("List is empty");
 else
 {
  System.out.println("node address        message");
  for(ListIterator iter = this.iterator();iter.hasNext();)
  {
   NetworkNode n = (NetworkNode)iter.next();
   System.out.println(n.address + "          " + n.info.msg);
  } // terminates text of for-loop.
```

```
} // terminates text of else-clause.
} // terminates text of listNetwork.
```

The last method appearing in `NetworkInterface` is `processMessage`, simulating the process of sending a message to the destination node in the network. Its code is given by

```
public void processMessage
// Simulates the sending of a message from a source node.
// Precondition: The first 6 bits of message contains the address
// of the destination node.
// Postcondition: The destination node receives the message if
// the sender and the message contain valid node addresses.
{
 BufferedReader intIS = new BufferedReader(
                        new InputStreamReader(System.in));
stringType message;
System.out.println("Please enter the address of the source node:");
int source = Integer.parseInt(intIS.readLine());
System.out.println("Please enter the address of the destination
                    node:");
int destination = Integer.parseInt(intIS.readLine());
System.out.println("Please enter the message to be sent:");
message.msg = intIS.readLine();  // message.msg is an array of
                                 // characters.
// Locate the source node.
ListIterator iter = findNode(source);
NetworkNode n = iter.next();
// Send message if the source node is a valid network node.
if(n.address == source)
{
 message = toBitString(destination);
 n.info = message;
 sendMessage(source);
 n.info.msg[0] = '\0';
 } // terminates text of if-clause.
else // NetworkException class defined later
 throw new NetworkException("Error: message not sent");
} // terminates text of processMessage.
```

A driver for this implementation is given by

```
public static void main(String [] args) throws IOException
{
 // Construct new network object with no nodes.
```

```
                 Network lan = new Network();
                 char chVal = displayMenu();  // displayMenu coded below.
                 while(chVal != 'e' && chVal != 'E')
                 {
                  processChoice(chVal);  // processChoice coded below.
                  chVal = displayMenu();
                 }
              } // terminates main menu
```

The `static` method `displayMenu` was not defined as an instance method of `NetworkInterface` in our design. When invoked, it prompts the user for the choice of a network operation to be applied to the current network object or to exit from the simulator. Its code is described as

```
public static char displayMenu()
{
 BufferedReader intIS = new BufferedReader(
                        new InputStreamReader(System.in));
 System.out.println("Welcome to the LAN system admininstration");
 System.out.println();
 System.out.println("Please choose from the following options:");
 System.out.println("A - add a new node to the network");
 System.out.println("R - remove a node from the network");
 System.out.println("S - send a message");
 System.out.println("L - list addresses of nodes in network");
 System.out.println("E - exit");
 int choice = intIS.read();
 return (char)choice;
} // terminates text of displayMenu.
```

The `int`-valued variable `choice` stores the ASCII equivalent of the `char` value input interactively by the user. This is why the value returned by `displayMenu` is cast as a `char`.

The final method is `processChoice`. Its functionality is to select the proper method listed in `NetworkInterface` to apply, based on the user's choice at the prompt in `displayMenu`.

```
public static char processChoice(char chValue)
// Method used to perform selection made by user from displayMenu.
{
 switch(chValue)
 {
  case 'a':
  case 'A': // add node
   lan.insertNode();
   break;
```

```
  case 'r':
  case 'R': // remove node
   if(lan.networkSize() == 0)
     throw new NetworkException("Error: Remove node - network is
                                  empty");
   else
   {
     System.out.println("Please enter the address of the node to
                           remove";
     int rAddress = Integer parseInt(intIS.readLine());
     lan.removeNode(rAddress);
   }
   break;
  case 's':
  case 'S':  // send message.
   lan.processMessage();
   break;
  case 'l':
  case 'L':  // list nodes.
   if(lan.networkSize() == 0)
     throw new NetworkException("Error - network is empty");
   else
   {
     lan.listNetwork();
     break;
   }
  case 'e':
  case 'E': // exit program
   return(chValue);
  default:
   System.out.println("Error - incorrect choice entered");
   return 'x';
 } // terminates text of switch statement
 return 'x';
} // terminates text of processChoice.
```

We have made several references to the NetworkException class in some of the methods just coded. Its formal code is given here:

```
// Class NetworkException.
class NetworkException extends RuntimeException
{
 // Constructor.
 public NetworkException(String str)
```

```
        {
         super(str);
        } // terminates text of constructor
       } // terminates text of NetworkException class.
```

10.8 **Description of a Typical Execution**

A typical execution of this code begins with a call to displayMenu, which displays

Welcome to the LAN system administration

Please choose from the following options:
A - add a new node to the network
R - remove a node from the network
S - send a message
L - list addresses of nodes in network
E - exit

Initially, the user will respond with several successive choices to add new nodes to the network by pressing **'A'** or **'a'**. In each such case, processChoice calls insertNode. Each call to insertNode increments the static variable addressCounter. The first call inserts a node with address 1, the next has address 2, and so on. In addition, each such call increments the value of size by 1, which keeps track of the number of nodes that are currently active in the network.

If a subsequent prompt results in the user's choice to remove a node, and if the current network is not empty, the user will be prompted to supply the address of the node to remove:

Please enter the address of the node to remove

The user responds to this prompt by supplying that address, and removeNode is called. Assuming that the address supplied is that of a currently active node, that node is removed and the value of size decreases by 1. On the other hand, if the current network is empty, a NetworkException exception is thrown.

Now suppose the user wishes to send a message from one node to another by responding to the choice generated by displayMenu with **'S'** or **'s'**. Then processChoice calls processMessage, and the user must then respond to each of the following prompts:

Please enter the address of the source node:
Please enter the address of the destination node:
Please enter the message to be sent:

If we assume that the two nodes are currently active in the network, the message is sent using the code segment from `processMessage` given by

```
if(n.address == source)
{
 message = toBitString(destination);
 n.info = message;
 sendMessage(source);
 n.info.msg[0] = '\0';
}
```

Under all other conditions, a `NetworkException` exception is thrown.

If the user responds to the prompt in `displayMenu` to list the addresses of the nodes that are currently active in the network by pressing **'L'** or **'l',** the size of the current network is examined. If the value returned by `networkSize()` is zero, the response is

List is empty

But if `networkSize() > 0`, a list of the addresses and messages at each active node is displayed.

Finally, if the user responds to the prompt in `displayMenu` to exit by pressing **'E'** or **'e',** the `while`-loop in the main method causes execution to terminate.

We end this section by issuing a disclaimer. In describing the action of the network simulator, we have chosen to remain within the context of designing a Java application rather than using Java applets. The code for such methods as `displayMenu` might perhaps be rendered more user friendly if we had made some use of the facilities present in predefined Java graphics such as `java.swing`, and constructed several GUI's (graphical user interfaces) involving forms, buttons, and the like. We certainly invite the user to consider this option for the network simulation package just completed.

10.9 **Chapter Summary**

This chapter discussed two major topics. The first was an introduction to graphs and the construction of a hierarchy of classes implementing various graph ADTs. Specifically, two major categories of graphs were presented: (undirected) graphs and directed graphs. Each of these produced its own ADT and then implemented using a class. For technical reasons, we showed that it is useful to implement directed graphs as a parent class and then implement undirected graphs as a subclass of this parent class. The implementation details used in each of these uses a two-dimensional `boolean`-valued array called an *adjacency matrix*.

The second major topic discussed was that of a network. Here we defined the concept of a local area network using the ring topology and emphasized its value in important commercial applications. We presented a detailed sketch of the `Network` class and gave its implementation using such `java.util` facilities as the `List` interface and the `ArrayList` implementation.

EXERCISES

1. Perform depth-first and breadth-first searches for the graph described in Figure 10.8 from A_0 to A_3 and from A_1 to A_4.

2. Perform depth-first and breadth-first searches for the undirected graphs described in Figures 10.1 and 10.2 from A_0 to A_2.

Assertions and the `assert` Statement

APPENDIX OBJECTIVES

- To introduce the syntax and semantics of Java's `assert` statement.
- To discuss the significance of the `assert` statement in software design.
- To provide elementary examples of the use of the `assert` statement.

A.1 Introduction

We define an *assertion* as a `boolean`-valued expression that appears at a specific location in a sequence of Java statements and that should be `true` whenever execution arrives at that location. Thus, an assertion is a well-defined Java statement whose purpose is to check the truth of the current state of any computation at various stages during the running of a program.

Assertions were introduced as formal statements in Java in implementations using Java Development Kit (JDK) 1.4 or later. The general syntax of an `assert` statement is

```
assert <Assertion>;
```

where `<Assertion>` is a `boolean`-valued expression and `assert` is a new keyword. Semantically, when the flow of execution reaches an `assert` statement, first `<Assertion>` is evaluated. If the value is `true`, control passes to the processing of the first statement following the `assert` statement; if that value is `false`, an `AssertionError` exception is thrown.

A.2 Illustration of the Use of `assert` in Processing Stacks

Let us consider an example. In Section 1.3 we introduced `intArrayStack`, which implements the `intStack` interface. This interface describes the `pop` method, removing the `int` value at the top of the current stack object, and the top method, retrieving that same int value provided that the stack is not currently empty. If the current stack is empty, and either pop or top is attempted, a run-time error results. We can deal with this using assert by recoding each of pop and top as follows:

```
// Pop operator.  Implements pop method
// as described in intStack interface.
// Precondition:  Current stack is not empty.
public void pop() throws AssertionError
{
 assert !isEmpty();
 --topValue;
}
```

When this version of pop() is invoked, the assert statement is evaluated first. If the current stack is not empty, execution proceeds to the next line, which decrements the current value stored in topValue. If the current stack is empty, however, the pop method cannot be applied legitimately to that stack. In this case, the value of the assert statement is false—consequently, an AssertionError exception is thrown. This interrupts the usual flow of execution and instead causes the AssertionError to be handled by some appropriate use of the catch statement.

A similar situation exists in the top() method, which can be recoded as

```
// Top method.  Implements top method as
// described in intStack interface.  Retrieves
// value at top of the current stack.
// Precondition: Current stack is not empty.
public int top() throws AssertionError
{
 assert !isEmpty();
 return Info[topValue];
}
```

The behavior of assert is similar but not identical to its counterpart in C++, except that in C++ assert is predefined in the <assert.h> library. Thus, to use assert in any C++ program, we must include the preprocessor directive

```
#include <assert.h>
```

and then use the assert statement[1] using the syntax

```
assert(<Assertion>);
```

A more vivid difference between the two versions is that in C++, instead of throwing an exception in case <Assertion> is false, control of execution leaves the text of the program and is transferred to the system.

---

[1]This is discussed, for example, in Section 1.5 of De Lillo, Nicholas J. 2002. *Object-Oriented Design in C++ Using the Standard Template Library.* Pacific Grove, CA: Brooks/Cole.

GLOSSARY

abstract class—a class without objects that forms the basis of other classes derived from it.

abstract data type (ADT)—an aggregate consisting of two components: (a) an *application domain,* consisting of a collection of objects (instances); and (b) a finite and nonempty collection of *admissible operations* applicable to any object in the application domain.

abstraction—the ability of a language to implement a theoretical concept in simple and precise terms.

abstract method—a method that must be overridden in some subclass of the class where it is defined.

access modifier—a Java keyword that describes the mode of access available for a class or a field of a class. See also `private` member, `public` member, or `protected` member.

accessor—a method that does not change the state of an object to which it is applied.

Ackermann function—a recursive function ACK of two nonnegative integer arguments m, n defined by the equations (i) ACK(0,n) = n + 1; (ii) ACK(m,0) = ACK(m-1,n) if m > 0; (iii) ACK(m,n) = ACK(m-1,ACK(m,n-1)) if m > 0 and n > 0.

actual parameter—a variable or expression appearing in a call to a method and that passes information to that method for computation. See also *formal parameter.*

acyclic digraph—a digraph containing no cycles.

address calculator—a function whose argument is a key and whose value is an address in a data structure containing actual data. See also *hash function.*

adjacency matrix of a graph (or digraph)—a two-dimensional representation of `boolean` values whose rows and columns are indexed by the vertices of the underlying graph (or digraph).

adjacency set (of the initial vertex of a graph)—the set of all vertices to which the initial vertex is connected by an edge.

admissible operation—a method applicable to any entity on the application domain of some fixed abstract data type.

algorithm—a finite sequence of instructions that, when executed in order of appearance, produces a solution to a specific programming problem.

441

application domain—the collection of all entities satisfying the definition of some fixed abstract data type.

array—a data structure whose components are accessed in a random manner through the use of subscripts (indices).

assertion—a statement about some condition or relationship pertinent to some computation that can be either true or false at the time it is tested.

autodecrement operator—the operator defined as - -, applicable to integer variables and iterators.

autoincrement operator—the operator defined as ++, applicable to integer variables and iterators.

average-case analysis—an estimate of the average amount of processing steps required for an algorithm to complete its execution, given an input data stream of a specific size. See also *worst-case analysis*.

balanced binary tree—a binary teee in which the left and right subtrees have heights that differ by no more than 1. See also *binary tree*.

base class—see *parent class* or *superclass*.

batch processing—data and programs submitted together to form a processing unit.

big-O analysis—an analysis of the efficiency of an algorithm by counting the number of processing steps required for the algorithm to complete execution.

binary function—a function with two arguments.

binary predicate—a `boolean`-valued function of two arguments. See also *predicate*.

binary search—the process of searching that begins by examining the middle value of a sorted array and then moves to the half that is likely to contain the value sought, and so on, until either the value sought is located in the array or the search ends unsuccessfully.

binary search tree—a binary tree in which the value stored at each node is greater than the value stored at any node in its left subtree and less than the value stored at any node in its right subtree.

binary tree—a tree in which each node has a maximum of two children.

bit—a single binary digit described as either 0 or 1.

bitstring—a finite string of consecutive bits.

breadth-first traversal of a graph—a traversal of a graph that visits each node of the graph at a given level before visiting a node at the next highest level. See also *depth-first traversal of a graph, level (of a node in a graph)*.

bucket—an array of records maintained at each position in the hash table.

bucket hashing—a technique of hashing using open addressing in which several positions are available for storing values at each location in the hash table.

buffer—a storage unit maintained at any network node. See also *network node*.

bulk operation—an operation performed on a collection in a single execution, without causing the programmer to iterate operations on individual members of the collection.

bytecode—the output from a Java compiler resulting from the translation of a Java program. This bytecode is then executed by a Java Virtual Machine to obtain the final result of executing the source code. See also *compiler, Java Virtual Machine*.

capacity (of a vector or list)—the number of storage components allocated to the current vector or list.

catch block—a statement sequence whose execution handles an exception.

child—an immediate successor of a node in a tree.

circuit—a communications path between two network nodes through which data moves. See also *network node*.

circular hashing—a method of hashing in which the course of placing entries permits "wrapping around" to the initial locations of the hash table.

class—the central construct of an object-oriented design; it is a specific description of the characteristics and behavior of a collection of objects.

compile time—the time segment during which a compiler translates a program from high-level code (source code) into executable language.

compiler—a program used to convert high-level code (such as code written in Java) into a language that is more closely related to the underlying machine hardware (such as bytecode written for the Java Virtual Machine).

complete binary tree—a binary tree whose levels, beginning with that of the root node, are full except for the last, where the nodes are situated in succession from left to right.

complete graph—a graph with edges connecting each pair of its distinct vertices.

complexity—the formula that expresses the number of processing steps required for an algorithm to complete its execution, given a specific sequence of input data.

complex number—any number of the form `<realPart> + <imaginaryPart>i`, where `i` denotes the square root of `-1`.

concurrent—two or more tasks, processes, or events whose execution might overlap over the course of time.

connected graph—a graph for which a path exists between any pair of distinct vertices.

constant-time operation—an operation whose complexity is the same, regardless of the size of the collection to which the operation is applied. See also *complexity*.

constructor—a method used to create new objects of a given class.

container—the data structure used to store finite collections of values of some type.

correctness—a quality of software design that guarantees the production of the expected solution of a software problem for all possible admissible inputs.

central processing unit (CPU)—that segment of a computer's hardware in which the actual computations are performed.

cycle (of a directed graph)—a path (X_1,X_2), (X_2,X_3), . . . ,(X_{k-1},X_k) in which $X_1 = X_k$.

data field—a component of a class describing the data stored by any object constructed from that class.

depth-first traversal of a graph—a traversal of a graph that visits the successors of each of its nodes before moving to other nodes at the same level. See also *breadth-first traversal of a graph, level (of a node in a graph)*.

deque—a linear container of varying length, providing random access to any of its values, with constant-time insertions and deletions at each extremity of the container. See also *constant-time operation*.

dequeue—a synonym for the removal of a value from a queue.

derived class—the designated subclass in an inheritance relationship between two classes. See also *subclass*.

descendant of a node A—any node on a path rooted at A to a leaf.

deterministic—the property inherent in algorithms that states that each of its steps, with the exception of the first step, has exactly one predecessor.

directed edge of a graph—an edge in which the order of appearance of the vertices it connects is significant.

directed graph (or digraph)—a graph such that the order of appearance of the vertices it connects is significant. See also *graph, undirected graph*.

directed path (of a directed graph)—a finite sequence of directed edges beginning at an initial vertex of the graph and terminating at another vertex of that graph.

dispatcher—a program in a timesharing operating system devoted to changing the state of the process at the front of the ready queue from ready to running and removing that process from the front of the queue.

dispatching—the act of placing the process at the front of the ready queue in the running state and removing it from the front of the queue.

divide and conquer—a problem-solving paradigm that repeatedly subdivides the solution into smaller and simpler subproblems.

double hashing—a technique of hashing that uses open addressing in which two hash functions are used: the primary function provides the initial probe into the hash table, and the second yields the interval length in the probe sequence.

doubly linked list—a linked list such that each node contains two references: one to the next node, and the other to the previous node. See also *linked list*.

driver—a program used to test implementations of algorithms.

dynamic allocation—the assignment of storage to a variable while the program in which it appears is executing (at run time), as distinguished from *static allocation* (during program compilation).

dynamic binding—see *run-time polymorphism*.

edge—the link between two consecutive nodes on a tree or digraph.

efficiency—a principle of design in which the solution is executed in a relatively fast manner, using only the resources that are absolutely necessary for the completion of the solution.

empty stack—a stack with no values.

empty string—a string of length zero with no characters.

empty tree—a tree with no nodes.

encapsulation—the process of hiding and restricting access to the implementation details of a class definition.

enqueue—a synonym for the insertion operation of a queue.

equivalence relation—a binary relation existing among members of a collection of data values satisfying three conditions: (a) every value "is equivalent to" itself; (b) for any two values value1 and value2, if value1 "is equivalent to" value2, then value2 "is equivalent to" value1; and (c) for any value1, value2, value3, if value1 "is equivalent to" value2, and if value2 "is equivalent to" value3, then value1 "is equivalent to" value3.

Euclidean algorithm—an algorithm that uses recursive methods to find the greatest common divisor of any two positive integers.

exception—an abnormal state or event interrupting normal program execution; a class that signals a condition preventing normal program execution.

exception handler—a code sequence whose execution deals with an exception when that exception is thrown during the course of a computation. See *catch, finally,* and *try blocks.*

extensible object—an object that changes size dynamically and automatically.

Fibonacci function—a function generating the values of the Fibonacci sequence recursively by finding the sum of the two previous members of the sequence, beginning with 1, 1.

FIFO property—a property of a queue in which the retrieval and removal operations access the value inserted earliest. Also known as the *first-in, first-out property.*

final class—a class that is prevented from having any subclasses.

final method—a method of a class that cannot be overridden in any subclass.

final segment—in quicksort, those members of the array whose values are larger than the pivot. See also *pivot, quicksort.*

finally block—an optional part of a try-catch sequence that executes, regardless of whether an exception is thrown when the try block executes.

finite induction—a technique of mathematical proof that involves verifying some initial step and then verifying that each successive step follows from the assumed truth of its immediate predecessor.

folding—a technique of hashing in which the digits of the numeric key are involved in some computation, with the result lying within the scope of the subscripts of the associated hash table. See also *middle square technique.*

formal parameter—an identifier appearing in a method declaration that is replaced by an actual parameter when that method is involved. See also *actual parameter.*

4-node—a node in a tree containing exactly three data values and four children.

full binary tree—a binary tree whose leaves are all at the same level k and for which each possible position at level k is occupied by a node.

garbage collection—the return to the operating system of storage that was previously allocated to a program but is no longer being used.

generic class—a class that makes specific references to the `Object` class; a class whose objects can be constructed from any well-defined class that makes sensible use of the associated instance methods defined for that class.

generic method—a form of abstraction, used when the same algorithm is applicable to parameters, some of which are applicable to values of different specific data types.

graph—a collection of points or vertices and a collection of edges connecting some of those vertices.

graph traversal—an operation that starts at some specific vertex v and visits all vertices w for which there is a path joining v and w.

hash collision—the situation in which several different keys hash to the same value. See also *hash function, hashing.*

hash function—a function whose single argument is a key returning a value referring to a location in the hash table. See also *address calculator, hash table.*

hash table—a data structure, usually in the form of an array, whose entries provide an efficient form of searching for a value.

hashing—a search strategy that allows the user to specify a key value and that employs a fast and efficient lookup.

heap—a complete binary tree in which every node satisfies the property that its value is greater than the value assigned to each of its children. See also *complete binary tree.*

heapsort—a sorting algorithm on an array that first converts the array into a heap, then removes the heap's largest element, and then transforms the resulting semi-heap back into a heap.

hierarchical organization—the ability of newly created classes and/or interfaces to be derived from existing classes and/or interfaces by inheriting certain characteristics of these already-existing classes and/or interfaces. See also *hierarchy.*

hierarchy—a collection of classes and/or interfaces whose members form a hierarchical organization. See also *hierarchical organization.*

hub—the class or interface serving as the highest superclass in some hierarchy. See also *root (of a hierarchy).*

implement—to create a program executing the steps of an algorithm, or using a specific data structure to provide a concrete representation of some abstract data type.

infix—a notation for writing arithmetical expressions in which the binary operator lies between the operands (arguments). See also *postfix, prefix.*

import—to locate a program module in a library and apply it to the current user program.

index—an integer value used to provide a reference to some specific array component. See also *subscript.*

induction—see *finite induction.*

inductive proof—a proof applying the Principle of Finite Induction.

inductive step—the step in an inductive proof that assumes the statement P(k) is true for some value of k $\geq$ 0 and that shows that the result P(k+1) is true.

information hiding—a discipline that hides certain implementation details appearing in a module from the user and makes them inaccessible to computations performed outside the module.

inheritance—the process by which objects in a subclass can reuse characteristics and behavior defined for objects in a superclass.

initial segment—in quicksort, the sequence of values in the array whose values are no greater than the pivot. See also *pivot*.

inorder successor (of a node N of a binary tree)—the inorder successor of N's `info` component. The inorder successor is the leftmost node of N's right subtree.

inorder traversal—a traversal of a binary tree that visits a node only after it traverses the node's left subtree, but before it traverses the node's right subtree.

in-place algorithm—a version of an algorithm that places its result into the same container on which it operates.

insertion sort—a sorting algorithm that inserts the `ith` item into its proper position among the first `i` members of an array, for each `i`.

instance variable—a variable attached to some object constructed from a class.

instantiation—the process of constructing an object and (possibly) initializing its data members.

interactive user—a user communicating directly with the computer via terminals.

interface—a component listing and describing the methods of a class implementing some abstract data type.

interior node—any node on a tree containing at least one nontrivial child; any nonleaf node. See also *leaf*.

invariant—see *loop invariant*.

is-a—a relationship between classes stating that a subclass is a special form of a superclass using inheritance.

iteration—a single cycle of execution of a loop.

iterative algorithm—an algorithm using loops.

iterator—a class interacting with another class that represents a collection of objects whose purpose is to provide access to the next object or the previous object in that collection.

Java Collections Framework—a unified set of collection interfaces combined with efficient implementations of these interfaces.

Java Virtual Machine (JVM)—a program written for a particular platform that executes bytecode, which is the result of compiling a Java program. See also *bytecode, compiler*.

leaf—a node on a tree containing no children.

left child (of a node in a binary tree)—the root node of that node's left subtree. See also *left subtree, right child, right subtree*.

left subtree (of a node in a binary tree)—the subtree whose root is the left child of the given node.

legacy class—a small number of collection classes supported by Java before the Java 2 Platform was released in 1998.

level (of a node in a graph)—the smallest path length from the designated initial node in a traversal to that node.

level (of a node in a tree)—the level of the root node is zero; the level of any other node is 1 higher than the level of its parent.

lexical elements—strings identifying variables, keywords, operators, or punctuations.

lexicographic ordering—an order relation that imitates the ordering of character strings in a dictionary or the ordering of terms in a glossary.

LIFO property—a property of a stack in which retrievals and removals access the most recently inserted value. Also known as the *last-in, first-out property.*

linear container—a container in which all of its values are arranged in linear sequential fashion. See also *sequence container.*

linear probing—an open addressing strategy for resolving hash collisions in which a linear search is conducted (modulo the size of the hash table) for an unoccupied location in the hash table.

linear search—see *sequential search.*

linear-time operation—an operation on a data structure whose complexity is directly proportional to the current size of that structure.

linked list—a structure consisting of nodes connected to one another by linked storage. See also *linked storage.*

linked storage—a finite list of nodes, connected to one another in such a way that each member references the next node or `null`. See also *linked list.*

list—a linear container of varying size that provides linear-time access to any of its values and with constant-time insertions and removals. See also *constant-time operation, linear-time operation.*

load factor—a value between 0 and 1, indicating the percentage to which the hash table must fill before it grows automatically to its next size.

local identifier—the name of a storage location whose current value is visible within the block in which it is defined.

local variable—a local identifier that is a variable.

logarithmic-time operation—an operation on a data structure whose complexity is directly proportional to the number of times the size of the structure is divisible by 2.

loop invariant—an assertion that in some sense captures the essence of the computation performed in the loop body; it is true upon initial entry into the loop and each time control of execution reenters the loop.

map—a container that stores associations between key objects and value objects.

merge—a method applicable to array sections permitting the merging of two sorted array sections into a single sorted array section.

mergesort—a relatively fast sorting algorithm that first subdivides a finite sequence of unsorted values and then merges the two resulting subsequences into a single sorted sequence.

message—a single item of communication in a network.

method—a finite sequence of statements that has a name, (possibly) some formal parameters, and that might return a value. A method can be invoked any number of times with (possibly) different values assigned to each of its formal parameters.

method modifier—a keyword used to restrict the scope of access of members of some class, such as `public`, `private`, or `protected`.

middle square technique—a form of hashing that involves squaring the value of a numeric key and then extracting a number of consecutive digits (usually three) from that result.

modularity—a design property in which the problem decomposes into smaller and autonomous units, each of which contributes to the solution of the original problem and cooperates in producing that solution.

multiple inheritance—a form of inheritance in which a single subclass is inherited from two or more superclasses.

multiprogramming—a multiuser technique in which several processing jobs are kept in main memory at the same time. See also *timesharing*.

mutating sequence algorithm—an algorithm processing data in some container and modifying the contents of that container.

mutator method—a method that changes the state of some object.

network—a finite collection of communication links represented by hardware units used for processing and transmitting data.

network node—any point in a network where data are either received or collected.

network topology—a specific geometrical configuration of network nodes. See also *network node*.

node—a member of a list, graph, or tree that contains data and references to the succeeding and/or preceding member of the same data structure.

object—an instance of a class used to model a specific abstract data type; an aggregate of data and methods applicable to those data as specified by the class interface.

Object class—the predefined class that is the base or root of all class hierarchies.

object-oriented design (OOD)—a principle of software design in which objects are used to model the solution of some software problem. See *object*.

object-oriented programming (OOP)—a software engineering paradigm that views a program as a collection of objects that interact.

O(f(n))—order of magnitude of `f(n)`. See also *big-O analysis*.

open addressing—a technique of hashing in which the actual value(s) sought lie in the hash table.

overflow—a condition applicable to array implementations of stacks, indicating that there is no longer any space available for a specific push operation.

overloading—the ability of a single operator symbol or identifier to assume a number of different forms.

override—the ability to redefine a member of a class in a hierarchy in a subclass.

package—a collection of related Java classes. Access to one or more classes in a package is obtained using the `import` statement.

packet—a collection of bitstrings of some predetermined size. See also *bitstring*.

palindrome—a character string that reads the same from right to left as it does from left to right, as in "level".

parent (of a node A in a tree)—assuming A is not the root node, the immediate predecessor of A in the tree.

parent class—the superclass in an inheritance relation between two classes. See also *superclass*.

path—a finite sequence of edges connecting nodes of a tree or graph.

pivot—a value in an array segment around which the remaining values of the segment are subdivided during execution of quicksort.

polymorphism—the ability of an entity to assume several different forms; the ability of an operator to behave differently depending on the class to which it refers.

pop—the act of removing a value from the top of a stack.

portability—the ability of software to be transferred from one computer platform to another.

postcondition—a description of the state of a computation at the point of exiting a method and returning to the caller.

postfix—a notation for writing arithmetic expressions in which the binary operator follows both of its operands.

precondition—a description of the state of a computation when control of execution enters the text of some method.

predicate—a method returning a `boolean` value.

prefix—a notation for writing arithmetic expressions in which the binary operator precedes both of its operands.

primary clustering—a by-product of linear probing that results in a large number of keys hashing to a relatively small group of locations close to one another in the hash table.

prime number—any integer greater than 1 whose only divisors are 1 and itself.

primitive data type—either a numeric type or the `boolean` type.

priority queue—a queue that is either empty or is a finite sequence of values of a single data type, in which there is a well-defined comparison operation (ordinarily "less than"). Each newly inserted value is placed in its proper position according to that comparison operation.

`private` member—a member of a class that is accessible only to methods defined in its own class. See also `protected` member and `public` member.

projection—a form of folding in which certain digits of a numeric key are removed before the key is mapped to a subscript of the hash table. See also *folding, hash table*.

`protected` member—a member of a class that can be accessed only by members of that class, or by any methods of any descendant of that class. See also `private` member and `public` member.

pseudocode—a stylized, somewhat grammatical semicode language that imitates formal Java code.

pseudorandom numbers—an apparently random sequence of numbers that follows a specific recurring pattern.

`public` **inheritance**—a form of inheritance between superclasses and subclasses that permits `public` and `protected` members of a class to be inherited as `public` and `protected` members, respectively, of a subclass of that class.

`public` **member**—a member of a class that is accessible throughout its scope and to all user methods. See also `protected` member and `private` member.

push—the act of inserting a value onto a stack.

quadratic probing—an open addressing strategy for resolving hash collisions involving probing the hash table at locations k, $k + 1^2$, $k + 2^2$, $k + 3^2$, and so on, for an unoccupied location.

quantum—a preset time interval during which a process is permitted to execute in the CPU.

quaternion—an expression of the form $a_0 + a_1 i + a_2 j + a_3 k$, where a_0, a_1, a_2, a_3 are real numbers, and $i^2 = j^2 = k^2 = -1$, and $i*j = -j*i = k$, $j*k = -k*j = i$, and $i*k = -k*i = j$.

queue—a data structure that is either empty or contains a finite sequence of values of a single data type, permitting insertion of new values of that type from one end (called the *rear* or *back*) and removal of values from the opposite end (the *front*).

quicksort—a relatively efficient sorting algorithm that rearranges the values in an array around a pivot value and that uses recursion. See also *pivot, recursion.*

random-access data structure—a data structure in which the time required to access any value in the structure is independent of the location of that value in the structure.

random number generator—a possible choice of a hash function that involves generating a sequence of random numbers lying within the scope of the subscripts of the associated hash table.

rational number—any number taking the form a/b, where a is any integer, and where b is any positive integer.

ready queue—the queue containing all processes currently in the ready state, waiting to execute. See also *ready state.*

ready state—a state of a process waiting to execute in the CPU and currently appearing in the ready queue. See also *ready queue.*

rear of a queue—the back of a queue.

recurrence relation—a relation that computes the value of some member of a sequence using previously computed values in that same sequence.

recursion—a process solving a particular problem by solving combinations of earlier and smaller instances of that same problem.

recursive programming—a problem-solving paradigm that uses methods that invoke themselves for previously computed values, from their own scope.

red-black trees—a special adaptation of a 2-3-4 tree into a binary tree with red nodes or black nodes.

rehashing—a technique for resolving hash collisions involving more than one hash function.

reusability—the principle that states that a module design to solve a specific software problem can also apply to the solution of other software problems.

right child (of a node in a binary tree)—the root node of the node's right subtree. See also *left child, left subtree, right subtree.*

right subtree (of a node in a binary tree)—the subtree whose root is the right child of the given node.

ring topology—a network topology in which consecutive nodes are connected by links to form a ring-shaped configuration. See also *network node, network topology.*

root (of a hierarchy)—the class or interface from which all other components are derived. See also *hub.*

root node—the only node in a tree not having a parent; also, the only point of entry into a tree.

run time—the time segment during which the program's instructions (in successfully compiled form) execute. See also *compile time, compiler.*

running state—a state that describes the event that the given process is currently executing in the CPU.

run-time polymorphism—a version of polymorphism that permits the choice of an appropriate instance method from among those appearing in a superclass of some hierarchy with the same name in a subclass during program execution (also known as *dynamic binding*).

search tree—a tree whose nodes are organized in such a way that the retrieval of its values is efficient.

secondary clustering—a by-product of open addressing using quadratic probing in which only a small number of locations appear in the hash sequence, consequently limiting the effectiveness of quadratic probing.

selection sort—a sorting algorithm that sorts the components of an array in either ascending or descending order; the algorithm places the smallest (or largest) value in the initial position and then continues the process on the remaining array components.

semiheap—a complete binary tree in which the root's left and right subtrees are heaps. See also *heapsort.*

separate chaining—a technique of hashing in which hash collisions are resolved by maintaining linearly linked lists at each location in the hash table.

sequence container—a container that stores a finite collection of values of a single data type in a linear arrangement, in which each of the values occupies a specific position. See also *container, linear container.*

sequential search—the process of searching a finite sequence that begins by examining the first member and then examining successive members in their order of appearance.

Set—an interface in the Java Collections framework, having `HashSet` and `TreeSet` implementations. A set is a special kind of collection that does not allow for duplicate values.

set difference—a method returning the sorted difference of two sorted `Set` objects, in that order. If `S`, `T` are `Set` objects, then the difference of `S` and `T` is defined as the set of elements of `S` with all of those that are also elements of `T` removed, denoted as `S - T`.

set inclusion—a method implemented in the `Set` interface by the bulk method `containsAll`, returning `true` just when the `Collection` object whose value is given by the parameter is included in the current `Set` object.

set intersection—a method whose result displays the common values of two `Set` objects.

set membership—a boolean-valued instance method of the `Set` interface called `contains` that returns `true` if the `Set` object has a member whose value matches that of the parameter; that is, if the value is a member of the `Set` object. Otherwise, the method returns `false`.

set symmetric difference—if `S`, `T` are `Set` objects, then the symmetric difference of `S` and `T` is defined as the `Set` object that is the union of the differences `S - T` and `T - S`. See also *set difference, set union*.

set union—if `S`, `T` are `Set` objects, then the union of `S` and `T` is the `Set` object whose elements appear in at least one of `S`, `T`.

Shell sort—a sorting technique that produces a sorting of increasingly large array segments until the final sort produces a sorting of the entire array.

shift folding—a form of folding that takes groups of digits of some numeric key and then adds these groups to obtain a hash value. See also *folding*.

Sieve of Eratosthenes—an algorithm for solving the following problem: given any two distinct integers greater than or equal to 2, find and count the primes lying between these two integers, inclusive.

sifting—a process used to distinguish even and odd integers.

signature—a description of a method yielding its name, return data type (if it exists), and the parameters involved (if they exist).

simple cycle (in a directed graph)—a cycle (X_1, X_2), (X_2, X_3), . . . , (X_{k-1}, X_k) where X_1 and X_k represent the only pair of common vertices.

simple inheritance—a form of inheritance in which a subclass is derived from a single superclass. See also *multiple inheritance*.

simple path (in a graph)—a path that never passes through any vertex more than once.

simulator—a program that models the behavior of an actual physical system.

size (of a vector)—the number of elements present in the current vector. See also *capacity*.

sorted collection—a finite nonempty collection whose values are arranged in some specific order.

space efficiency—a measure of an algorithm's efficiency based on the amount of storage required for its implementation.

spanning tree—a subcollection of vertices and edges in a graph containing all of the vertices of the graph and a smallest number of edges to form a tree.

stable sort—a sorting algorithm that guarantees that equal values in the original unsorted sequence retain their relative ordering in the final sorted result.

stack—either the empty set or a finite sequence of values of a single data type into which values can be inserted (pushed) and from which values can be removed (popped); the values are pushed and popped from the same end (called the *top*).

Standard Template Library (STL)—a C++ library that provides basic components for I/O, string processing, containers (such as vectors, deques, lists, stacks, queues, and others), algorithms (such as sort, search, merge, and others), and support for a wide variety of numeric computations.

state—the collection of all of the data values of a container or the collection of all of the current variables at any point during the execution of a program where those containers or variables are defined.

static allocation—the assignment of storage to a variable while the code in which it appears is compiling (at compile time). See also *dynamic allocation*.

static data member—a value shared by all objects constructed from that class.

static method—a method whose reference appears outside the storage of any specific object constructed from that class; a method with no implicit object parameter.

static variable—any variable that is independent of any of the objects constructed from that class.

subclass—a class that inherits characteristics and behavior from another class, called the *superclass*.

subscript—an integer value used to provide a reference to some specific array component. See also *index*.

subtree—a tree whose root is any node of the current tree, together with all of the descendants of that node.

super—a keyword used to invoke the constructor of the associated superclass.

superclass—the class from which a subclass inherits characteristics and behavior (also known as *base class, parent class*).

switch—see *network node*.

3-node—a tree node containing exactly two data values and three children.

throwing an exception—the act of identifying an exception.

time efficiency—the effort to find the least number of processing steps for an algorithm.

timesharing—a device permitting several processes to share space in the CPU, with one process currently executing and the rest in the ready state waiting to execute. See also *multiprogramming*.

token—a fixed bitstring that circulates in a network when no message is being sent. See also *bitstring, network*.

token ring network—a network whose nodes are configured using a ring topology in which a token circulates among the links between consecutive nodes. See also *network, network node, ring topology, token*.

top (of a stack)—the end of a stack where values are inserted, removed, and retrieved.

top method—a method defined in the stack interface retrieving the value currently on the top of the stack.

traversal of a tree or graph—the act of moving from one node (vertex) to another in any tree (or graph).

trickle down—a downward movement of values of the nodes described in a heap.

trickle up—an upward movement of values of the nodes described in a heap.

2-node—a tree node containing exactly one data value.

2-3 tree—a search tree such that each node is either a 2-node or a 3-node and all leaves are at the same level.

2-3-4 tree—a search tree with nodes that are either 2-nodes, 3-nodes, or 4-nodes.

try block—a statement sequence preceded by the `try` keyword in which the occurrence of an exception might exist.

this—a Java keyword referring to the object just constructed.

thread—a program unit that executes independently of other parts of a program.

throughput—the amount of data generated by the computer for a fixed and given unit of time.

unary function—a function defined for a single argument.

underflow—a condition applicable to containers in which the container is currently empty and a removal or retrieval operation is attempted.

undirected graph—a graph in which the appearance of the vertices of any of its edges is insignificant.

user interface—that part of a class definition displaying the facilities available in the class to the user. See also *interface*.

vector—an object of the `Vector` class, assigned a contiguous block of storage similar to the allocation of storage for a one-dimensional array, and having a size and capacity that changes dynamically. See also *capacity* and *size* of a vector.

vertex—any node in a graph.

visiting a node—the act of performing some computation at any node of a tree or graph.

void method—a method that returns no value to the caller.

worst-case analysis—a determination of the maximum number of processing steps required for a given algorithm to complete execution, given the size of a specific input stream of data. See also *average-case analysis*.

INDEX